C0-AUY-749

Religion in Calabar
The Religious Life and History of a Nigerian Town

Religion and Society 27

GENERAL EDITORS
Leo Laeyendecker, *University of Leiden*
Jacques Waardenburg, *University of Lausanne*

MOUTON DE GRUYTER · BERLIN · NEW YORK 1989

Religion in Calabar

The Religious Life and History of a Nigerian Town

by

Rosalind I. J. Hackett

MOUTON DE GRUYTER · BERLIN · NEW YORK 1989

Mouton de Gruyter (formerly Mouton, The Hague)
is a Division of Walter de Gruyter & Co., Berlin.

BL
2470
.N5
H33
1989

The vignet on the cover of this book represents the symbol of the *Agathos Daimon,* the snake of the Good Spirit, known from Greek astrological and magical texts. As its Town God, the *Agathos Daimon* was believed to protect Alexandria, which was famous world-wide for its library with precious manuscripts and books.

Library of Congress Cataloging- in -Publication Data

Hackett, Rosalind I. J.
  Religion in Calabar.
  (Religion and society ; 27)
  Bibliography: p.
  Includes index.
  1. Calabar (Nigeria)--Religion.   I. Title.
  II. Series: Religion and society (Hague, Netherlands); 27.
  BL2470.N5H33   1988   291'.09669'4   88-8377
  ISBN 0-89925-394-6 (alk. paper)

Deutsche Bibliothek Cataloging-in-Publication Data

Hackett, Rosalind I. J.:
Religion in Calabar : the religious life and history of a
Nigerian town / by Rosalind I. J. Hackett. - Berlin ;
New York ; Amsterdam : Mouton de Gruyter, 1988
  (Religion and society ; 27)
  ISBN 3-11-011481-X
NE: GT

♾ Printed on acid free paper.

© Copyright 1988 by Walter de Gruyter & Co., Berlin. All rights reserved, including those of translation into foreign languages. No part of this book may be reproduced in any form – by photoprint, microfilm or any other means – nor transmitted nor translated into a machine language without written permission from the publisher.
Printing: Gerike GmbH, Berlin. - Binding: Dieter Mikolai, Berlin. - Printed in Germany.

This book is dedicated to my nuclear family and to all my friends and informants in the town of Calabar (Come And Live And Be At Rest) or "Canaan City", as it is affectionately known. It is also dedicated to the memory of Mary Slessor, that intrepid Scottish missionary, who has never been forgotten by the people of Calabar.

Witches ... are extra-prevalent on the Gold Coast and Calabar.

Mary Kingsley, *West African Studies* (1901)

When we heard about Calabar River how they have all English *Laws* in their towns and how they have put away all their *superstitions*, oh we shall be very glad to be like Calabar now.

Letter from the Akwa Family to Queen Victoria,
August 7, 1879
Musée de Douala, Cameroun

The Cross River State has become a state where the main industry is churches...

Dr. Nse Ekpo, M.H.A. (Ikpa Ikono)
January 1981

Preface

In 1975, just before I was about to set out for Ibadan, Nigeria, as a postgraduate student from the University of London, Professor Geoffrey Parrinder was kind enough to give me a copy of his *Religion in an African City* (1953). The book, which was a descriptive survey of the various forms of religious expression in the city of Ibadan, was to prove highly significant in two respects. Firstly, it enabled me to find my long-lost personal effects in the disorganized Nigeria Airways cargo shed in Lagos. The book was perched at eye-level on the top of one of my half-opened boxes amidst the mountains of cargo and the lava flow of contents. Someone had obviously gone through the box, examined the book and then thought better of stealing the rest of the contents. Secondly, the book turned out to be a most useful background to my work in Ibadan on the Aladura churches and later for my work in Calabar, as I wanted to meet Professor Parrinder's parting challenge to update his book.

This initial inspiration was delayed until I reached Calabar in 1979 to take up an appointment as Lecturer in Religious Studies at the University of Calabar. Not only was I in a far more favourable position to conduct a research project of this nature (the days of the full-time researcher in Nigeria being fast numbered), but Calabar seemed a far more manageable unit of study than the vast metropolis of Ibadan.

I was fortunate enough to meet Dr. Harold Turner in Aberdeen before returning to Nigeria in 1978. First and foremost he was a personal source of inspiration, instilling in me a fascination for the many facets of African religious creativity, and nurturing in me a penchant for the type of "detective" work which was to prove so fruitful in unearthing a mass of religious data in Calabar over the next few years. Secondly, his growing collection of materials on new religious movements on a global scale was a data bank of infinite value and a motivation to any researcher in this field. Some years later, one of Calabar's spiritual church leaders (who had met Harold Turner in the 1960s) was to remark significantly in the course of a service that I had been sent from England to study his church by my "spiritual father" - Dr. Turner!

During my time at the University of Aberdeen as Research Fellow (1979-83), I enjoyed many useful exchanges with friends and colleagues such as Dr. Adrian Hastings, Professor John Hargreaves,

Dr. Roy Bridges and Dr. Marion Charles Jedrej. I am particularly grateful to Dr. Jeffrey Stone of the Geography Department for his advice regarding my "religious mapping" and for putting me in contact with Laurie Maclean, whose expert cartographical recommendations I needed. In this regard, a special thanks goes to Lynn Urqhart, also of the Geography Department, for her skills and care in preparing the maps of Calabar. I also benefitted from the excellent support of the Aberdeen University Library staff, particularly those in the Africa and Inter-Library loan sections.

I have been able to discuss my work with several scholars in many different countries - Professors Ben Ray, Wyatt MacGaffey, Barry Floyd, J. G. Platvoet, Hans-Jürgen Greschat, Bengt Sundkler and Dr. Kim Knott. Professor Michael Pye was an important source of encouragement in the early stages.

I was privileged to spend a semester at Amherst College during the spring of 1984 as Copeland Fellow. I managed to complete several chapters there thanks to the conducive working environment and the most helpful and efficient staff of the Reference Section of the Amherst College Library. I am more than grateful to Professor John Pemberton 3rd for his invaluable academic support both then and now. Dr. Thomas Magnell, a fellow Copeland Fellow, helped me sort out philosophically many a concept and definition.

In Nigeria my thanks go to the Cross River State Government for permission to conduct research on the religious institutions in the Calabar Municipality. I should also like to thank the University of Calabar Senate Research Grant Committee for an award which enabled me to pursue my field work. The staff of the Surveys Division of the Ministry of Lands, Surveys and Town Planning assisted in updating my town plan of Calabar. I owe so much to my students at the University of Calabar, who not only were a constant source of information and enjoyment, but also constituted such an effective research team for the religious mapping of the town. I am especially indebted to my field assistant, Essien A. Offiong, an Efik student in Religious Studies at the University of Calabar, whose enthusiasm for, and knowledge of the field, opened so many doors to an outsider like myself.

Several individual Nigerians deserve a note of gratitude for their time and patience in answering my questions over a period of time: Etubom Ewa E. Henshaw, Dr. E. Nsan, Olive MacArthur Slessor, N.E. Asuquo, Eric Esin, Mr. and Mrs N.O. Akpan; Bishop Roland Obu, E.O. Bassey, E.U. Aye, and Dr. Ekpo Eyo.

Professor Andrew Walls extended an academic lifeline in 1979 by making me an Honorary Research Fellow in the Department of Religious Studies in Aberdeen. This enabled me to have an "academic home" to return to from Nigeria and to make use of much-needed library facilities and seminar discussions. He was ever generous in lending me books and pamphlets from his personal library and has provided the informed interest and stimulation which every postgraduate student needs from a supervisor.

I have to thank Dr. Simon Battestini for being my chief sounding-board and critic for many years. He was a constant source of advice and moral support both during our time in the field and later, as I sought to make sense of my abundant data.

The production of this book would not have been possible without the technical and collegial support of my department at the University of Tennessee, Knoxville. I am especially grateful to Professor Charles H. Reynolds, as well as my other colleagues, for their advice, help and forbearance in so many respects. Joan Riedl and a former colleague, Dr. Michael W. Harris, assisted with the editing. The insightful, thorough and constructive criticisms of the latter deserve a special mention. Needless to say, any faults or shortcomings remaining are my responsibility alone.

In conclusion, my greatest thanks go to the many church founders, prophets, priests and worshippers in Calabar (too numerous to mention) who gave substance to the project and allowed me the privilege of entering, quite literally, into their fascinating religious worlds.

Above all, this book is a regional study of religious pluralism, viewed from an historical and contemporary perspective. Different aspects of the book may appeal to different readers. The first section treats the historical development of the various religious groups and the ways in which they have (with varying degrees of success) adapted to the Calabar milieu. Those readers for whom extensive historical detail is less important than theoretical observations may limit themselves to the concluding reflections at the end of each section or chapter. I felt it necessary, however, to include such historical data, even though it lengthened the book. For while many readers may be familiar with the development of the Presbyterian and Roman Catholic churches in Africa, there is little documentation available on the Christian Scientists or the Rosicrucians, for example. Despite the specificity of some facts in relation to the Calabar context, most observations are probably relevant to the understanding of the same or similar movements in different contexts.

The second section is primarily concerned with contemporary forms of religion in Calabar. Initially it follows the model of the previous section on historical ethnography, by examining religion in terms of its institutional expressions and divisions. Then a more thematic approach is adopted, with the identification of patterns and developments in Calabar religion as a whole, as well as areas of interaction and interdependency. Throughout the study, I have worked with operational distinctions between indigenous and exogenous (or imported) religion, as well as between institutional and non-institutional (or popular) forms of religion. This, again, will permit readers to be selective on the basis of their particular interests.

Unreferenced claims and sources derive from my observations in the field over a period of four years. In these cases, the conversations and interviews would be too numerous or insignificant to cite. I use a referencing system with shortened titles if there is more than one work by an author. Following a European citation tradition, I do not give page numbers for newspaper references and only italicize foreign words and terms when used for the first time.

Rosalind I. J. Hackett
University of Tennessee, Knoxville
June 1988

Note on Orthography

The conventions of orthography employed in this work result from a combination of factors. Firstly, there is no consensus among linguists over one standard orthography in Efik-Ibibio; secondly, the literature in Efik-Ibibio and other languages of this language cluster shows the diversity of graphic systems in use. Therefore, I opted for a realistic, non-linguistic and simplified orthography, easy to produce and to read, based on the most commonly used conventions in the Cross River State. For example, obon (or ɔbɔn or obong) is reduced to **obong** <king>. Proper names are transcribed according to current usage, for example, Ison (or Isɔn or Isong) is reduced to **Isong.**

Abbreviations

CRS   Cross River State
RCH   Revised Church Hymnary
NTA   Nigerian Television Authority
HWTI   Hope Waddell Training Institution
UNICAL University of Calabar

Abbreviations of names of religious institutions are listed in Appendix 3.

Table of Contents

Introduction

There is much to be said for concentration on one particular town in order to obtain a detailed and factual study.

(E.G. Parrinder, *Religion in an African City*, 1953)[1]

There is need for more studies that treat, not of particular churches, but of the whole range of religious expression within a community or area.

(J.D.Y. Peel, "The Christianization of African Society", 1978)[2]

Preamble

Nigeria's major towns and cities have each developed a unique character. The town of Calabar's claim to fame, according to its inhabitants and the local press, is that it has become a "city of church industry". The meaning of that statement becomes clear as one wends one's way around the streets of both "old" and "new" Calabar: an array of religious buildings and signboards meets the eye, ranging from cathedrals to neighbourhood churches, to compound churches and prayer houses and healing homes. On Sundays especially this visual diversity comes alive with music and with people as they move around town in family groups or with friends to attend their respective places of worship. Around festival time (Christmas and Easter), church processions encounter traditional masqueraders, whose impressive colour and splendour are evidence of the richness and vitality of the Cross River cultural heritage.

The fascination with such religious diversity and a desire to understand its dynamics and lay bare its foundations proved to be the primary motivators of the present study. Calabar seemed to present itself as a highly suitable candidate for such a survey: in general terms it is a mid-sized town which, due to its relative isolation in the south-eastern corner of Nigeria, has not been marked by over-rapid urbanization and development. The traditional core of the town is intact but is now surrounded by modern office blocks and government buildings; the rural periphery is still very much in evidence. This heterogeneity is an important consideration in terms of religious diversity.

The decision to study the religious life of Calabar was not taken lightly given the vast amount of data collection and participant observation involved. Such an ambitious project was undertaken in the knowledge that residency and employment were assured over a four-year period in Calabar (1979-83) and research assistance was available from students in religion at the University of Calabar.[3]

Comparative studies

Before embarking on the present project, comparative studies on the range of religious expressions in a particular area were consulted. A number of studies on Japanese religion have appeared within the last twenty years which aim to provide a general understanding of the panorama of religion in Japan.[4] While their scope is much broader than the present study's, the methodology is important: instead of treating the various religious traditions in isolation from one another, there is a quest for a unified interpretation of Japanese religious history.[5] In this way the unity and diversity and the continuity of Japanese religion are represented.[6] Michael Pye also advocates the importance of studying

> the recurrent themes, images, values, assumptions and practices which together add up to a common base of Japanese religion upon which specific religious movements or institutions are reared.[7]

This common ground, according to Pye, is discernible not only in situations of an overtly religious nature but also by general observation of individual and social life and through the mass media.[8]

A similar approach has been adopted by some scholars for the study of Chinese religion.[9]   A variety of academic perspectives (anthropology, sociology, history of religions and traditional Sinological expertise in language, literature and culture) are utilized in an attempt to convey the character of religious expression in China as above all a manifestation of the Chinese culture so closely "woven into the broad fabric of family and social life".[10]

A collection of writings on the religious dimension of New Zealand's history, *Religion in New Zealand Society*, was published in 1980; the authors examine the contribution to New Zealand by the different religious traditions as well as trends in religious affiliation over the last fifty years.[11]

In Britain it is the sociologists who have made the greatest contribution to the study of religious life and activity in selected areas.[12]   The work by these British sociologists has been oriented towards demographic and statistical surveys with particular interest in church attendance and membership composition.   A major study of conventional and common religion in Leeds was begun in 1981.[13]   Over 1600 people (plus 200 university students) were interviewed on a variety of topics dealing with religious beliefs, practices and experiences.   The Leeds Survey has provided some valuable insights into contemporary religious beliefs and attitudes in Britain today although it does not focus on the religious institutions themselves nor on the religious diversity of the city of Leeds.

Clifford Geertz's ethnographic account of the religion of an East Central Javanese town (*The Religion of Java*, 1960) constitutes a seminal work in the field of area studies in religion.   Geertz distinguishes a "basic Javanese syncretism" which is a "balanced integration" of animistic, Hinduistic and Islamic elements or sub-traditions.[14]   Despite a certain parallelism of association between social strata and religious sub-traditions, Geertz is able to identify those overarching common cultural themes which unify this complex religious situation.   He portrays in detail the rich diversity of Javanese beliefs, rituals and values, demonstrating the processes of variation and conflict in addition to those of similarity and harmony.

In India a number of anthropologists have conducted research on the "sacred complex" or "sacred geography" of a particular town or centre. Since the pioneering work of L.P. Vidyarthi on the *Sacred Complex in Hindu Gaya*,[15] there have been important studies by Marie-Louise Reiniche on the spectrum of cults and festivals of a south Indian village[16] and by Akos Ostör on the religious life of a Bengali town.[17]

Moving to the African continent there have been a number of attempts to document the religion of a particular area. B.A. Pauw's *Religion in a Tswana Chiefdom* (1960) is a study of the religion of a rural Bantu community in the 1950s.[18]   While Pauw's main interest was in the "Separatist Churches" (he had a missionary background), he also conducted research into the "non-Separatist Churches" and traditional religion of the area. What is significant about Pauw's study is that he collected his data on the religion of the Tlhaping as an anthropologist, by living and working in the community over a period of time, which not only enabled him to situate his data against the background of Tswana culture and social structure but also to see the "interconnexions", as he calls them, between the various religious expressions and traditions in the community. He was also able to examine such trends and patterns as "moralism", "ritualism", "emotionalism", "separatism" and attitudes to the different church-types; this provides the reader with a more comprehensive, in-depth understanding of the role of religion in the lives of the people of this Tswana chiefdom.[19] The advantage of this type of approach is that it does not ignore the dynamics of religious change and interaction which are particularly interesting and complex in a society which, as the author himself describes it, is "in an advanced stage of transition from paganism to Christianity".[20]

Murphree's landmark study of the four main religions (Methodism, Roman Catholicism, Vapostori or Apostles and traditional) in a Shona chiefdom in Rhodesia (1969) focuses on the different levels of interaction and interdependence between them as they meet the complementary religious needs of different categories of the population.[21]

In 1970 Wyatt MacGaffey conducted a four-month study into the diversity of churches in Matadi, Zaïre.[22]   His aim was to examine the "contrasting personalities" of the churches in a town with a homogeneously Kongo population and show "the importance of certain sociological factors and the relationship between ideological factors and the organizational form of the churches".[23] The value of this type of study (which as MacGaffey himself claims is by no means exhaustive) emerges with regard to ideological factors of differentiation; through a synchronic and diachronic analysis, the author is able to categorize the churches according to means of salvation, attitudes toward healing and patterns of religious behaviour.[24]

Robert Wyllie's study of independent "Spiritist" or prophet-healing churches amongst the Effutu of Winneba in southern Ghana, while focusing on a particular stratum (arguably the most varied and complex), offers us a religious history of the town and a profile of its religious institutions in 1968.[25]

John Middleton's article entitled "One Hundred and Fifty Years of Christianity in a Ghanaian Town", is primarily concerned with the development of the Presbyterian congregation in the town of Akuropon in southern Ghana, but includes an interesting discussion on the role of the Presbyterian Church as one element in a total local religious system which includes other faiths. The town is small and not characterized by great religious complexity and diversity, yet Middleton observes that the majority of people do not treat their religious affiliations exclusively and turn to "other faiths" in different situations, which has the effect of generating a "single religious complex".[26]

A number of studies have been conducted on religious affiliation and practices in Freetown, Sierra Leone.[27]   All are fairly conventional in their treatment of the subject, with documentation on the main religious traditions, statistics of church attendance and some observations regarding the areas of decline and continuity of traditional religion.[28]   There is little attempt by any of the authors to examine in depth the different types of membership and participation or the interaction at either the individual or institutional levels.

John Peel calls Deniel's book on religion in Ouagadougou,[29] capital of Upper Volta (now Burkina Faso), "a rare example of a social survey of attitudes".[30]   Through a systematic series of interviews, a wealth of information is provided on the beliefs of Muslims and Christians (adults and youth), their attitudes to their religion and its effect on their lives, and to the religion of others.   There is also an analysis of a variety of cross-cultural themes such as morality, wealth, marriage and the future.[31]   The survey is very much oriented towards personal religion with conclusions drawn from the findings on the overall impact of religion (Christian or Muslim) on the lives of the inhabitants of Ouagadougou.

Moving to Nigeria itself, a number of towns and cities have been subject to various surveys in terms of their religious life and character.   In 1949, a Belgian, Jean Comhaire, wrote a short article on "La Vie Religieuse à Lagos" which was the first attempt at a comprehensive study of all religions in a particular area of Nigeria.[32]   Despite his overall characterization of the religious life of Lagos as "une confusion extraordinaire"[!] he saw Islam as the dominant and potentially unifying force. He identified a number of "sectes prophétiques" with observations on the location and clientèle and accounts for the varying successes of the Catholic Church and the different branches of Protestantism.   He provides no detailed information on the various movements, such as date of arrival or creation, number of branches etc., although he does include membership estimates for selected institutions at that time.

Ibadan is probably the most researched of all African cities in terms of its religion.   Parrinder's well-known survey of the different types of religious life in Ibadan from 1949-51 proved to be an important model for the study of "modern religion" in Africa. Parrinder rightly argues that Ibadan was an appropriate choice for this type of survey given its experience of "culture-contact" and "the mingling of religions".   The major part of the survey is devoted to a description of the various religious traditions: "pagan religion", Islam, Christianity (mission churches and "separatist sects").   Towards the end of the book, a number of common themes (worship, music, morality, symbolism, festivals and language) are treated together with sections on "Personal Religion" and "Currents of Religion".[33]

Parrinder's first-hand survey succeeds in providing us with a useful profile of the religious life of an African city as well as basic data on the various religious organizations at the time. However, the structure of the book is not conducive to an awareness of the religious history and developments of the city, nor are we able to obtain an idea of the interaction and interdependence between the various institutions and traditions or the way in which individual worshippers function within a religiously pluralistic environment.

The religious life of Ibadan is also featured in a later work entitled *The City of Ibadan*.[34] In a chapter on "Traditional Religion and Christianity", E. B. Idowu provides a descriptive account of various cults and churches in Ibadan. It is far from being an exhaustive survey with little factual data and background on the religious institutions mentioned, although he does make some attempt to account for varying religious orientations. He includes subsections on "religion and life" and more importantly, "the interaction of religions" where he refers to a "syncretism" of forms through processes of borrowing and acculturation.[35]

A recent survey conducted by the Statistics Division of the Ministry of Finance and Economic Development in Ibadan (1977) constitutes an important source of data on the various religious organizations (Christian and Muslim only) not just in Ibadan but also Oyo State as a whole.[36] There is detailed information on membership (by sex, denomination and location) as well as economic data relating to the number of church or mosque workers and general and charity expenditure.

A recent dissertation (1983) by Jacob Kehinde Olupọna describes and analyzes the religion of the Ondo people.[37] He examines the religious systems and world-views of the four principal religious groups in the town of Ondo - traditional religion, the Anglican Church, the Celestial Church of Christ and Islam.

In the 1960s an Uyo survey team investigated thirty-three independent and 17 mission-connected churches within a five-mile radius of Abak (in the Cross River State not far from Calabar).[38] Their work also included a brief history and description of 81 congregations.[39]

These various surveys of religion in particular African contexts reveal a number of shortcomings - lack of comprehensivenesss and depth, tendency to select certain types of religious organization, disregard for informal, "unofficial" forms of religious expression and failure to examine the interactive influences and dynamics of the religious "whole". As far as the Nigerian studies are concerned, the majority were conducted in the 1960s and therefore do not convey the complexity and heterogeneity of the contemporary religious scene.   An exception is the work of Olupọna which is more recent and which is written from both an historical and social-scientific perspective.

Objectives and methodology

Given the above considerations, the first aim of the present study, therefore, is to produce a comprehensive inventory of religious institutions (i.e. all formalized and institutionalized religious collectivities) in Calabar today.[40]   This is not only of interest in itself in that it provides a working database but also because it serves as a partial indicator of the range of religious expressions in the area.

The second objective is to trace the religious history of Calabar.   This involves the identification of the various forces and influences (social, economic, political or religious), and their interaction, which have stimulated the processes of religious change and pluralization.   The historical perspective provides an important background to our analysis of contemporary religion as well as giving greater depth to our understanding of particular religious institutions or types of religious expression.

The third objective of the study is to document and describe the religious life of Calabar today.   This involves not just a discussion of the place of the various religious organizations in the overall religious system and the life of the town, but also their interaction and interdependence.   An important emphasis of the study is on the non-institutional beliefs and practices which may be collectively termed "popular religion" and which form the basis of and complement the more institutionalized forms of religious expression. Data on these less overt and more latent forms of religion were collected from a variety of sources: popular literature, music, the mass media and numerous interviews. The introduction of this interpretive framework, based on the institutional/popular religion dichotomy, is intended to provide a more comprehensive and well-rounded picture of the religious spectrum in Calabar.

Finally, in keeping with the overall aim of the study to provide a unified interpretation, a number of common themes and trends are discussed, such as secularization, spiritualization, power, homogenization, conceptions of evil, as well as religious attitudes and behaviour. Particular interest is paid to the conversion process, as well as religious affiliation and mobility, since these are vital elements in the general dynamics of the religious whole.

The chief concern of the present work is with religious pluralism in a specific cultural context, in this case the town of Calabar in south-eastern Nigeria. The description and interpretation of the phenomenon is based on extensive fieldwork and participant observation. For the most part, this was conducted by myself, in the company of my research assistant, or by student assistants, thus lending a more empirical rather than theoretical orientation to the study. As a topic, religious pluralism is conducive to superficiality if the inventory stage is not transcended. We seek to do this by looking between and beyond the religious institutions themselves to more popular types of religious activities. However, it may be argued that the "holistic approach" or "macro-analysis", i.e. one which seeks to examine both the unity and diversity of religious expression within a particular community or area, has its own special value: it offers in effect a more realistic portrayal of the situation in terms of borrowing, overlapping and interaction at the institutional level and the way it is experienced and used by the participants or "consumers" in terms of experimentation, mobility and multi-membership.

A variety of methodological perspectives is required to treat such a heterogeneous and complex phenomenon as religious pluralism, particularly within a context of rapid social and cultural change. Our primary perspective is that of the history of religions, for we are concerned with the nature and manifestations of religious experience and phenomena. Every attempt is made to describe and analyze the data on the basis of the participants' own interpretation and understanding of their religious situation.

In the African context especially, religion, by virtue of its this-worldly orientation and integration in daily life, must be studied in context; it may not be divorced from social and natural realities. Hence the historical and phenomenological perspectives must be supplemented by those of the social sciences, namely the study of the effects of religion on society and vice versa and the institutionalization and socialization of the religious message. Calabar is an urban context which makes sociological concepts such as secularization, privatization, homogenization and conversion useful tools of analysis. By virtue of our holistic approach - the study of the ensemble of beliefs, practices and institutions in a chosen community and their cultural expression - and our use of fieldwork and participant observation, we draw upon the methods of the anthropologist. We avoid the use of questionnaire techniques in the survey for these tend to provide limited, if not misleading, information. We have similarly avoided reliance on statistical information for this is often unreliable and advances little our understanding of religion in the African context.

Faced with a large amount of data on the religion of a particular area, it is evident that there exist a number of possibilities as to how to divide up and present the information to the reader so as to do justice to both. We have tried to achieve a balance between the historical and the contemporary and the institutional and the thematic. We feel that this reflects to a large extent the experience of the participants as they manipulate traditional institutions and social concerns and individual needs. By the same token, data on individual or types of religious institutions and their development is more readily available to those who are interested, while our discussion of popular religion and cross-cultural themes is more helpful in gaining an insight into personal religion and the religious life and character of the town of Calabar today. Our paramount concern is to convey both the diversity and the unity of the religious life of a growing Nigerian town.

A working definition

A few words should be said about our working definition of religion. For the purposes of the present study, a substantive definition is more useful than a too comprehensive functional one. Roland Robertson's definition, for example, rests upon the substantive, cultural content of religious phenomena.[41] He defines religious culture as that set of beliefs and symbols (and values directly deriving therefrom) pertaining to a distinction between an empirical and a super-empirical transcendent reality; the affairs of the empirical being subordinated in significance to the non-empirical. He defines religious action as being shaped by an acknowledgement of the empirical/super-empirical distinction.

Our preference for this type of definition is influenced by the cultural connotations of religion in the Calabar context, where there is a virtual absence of non-theistic, non-supernatural meaning systems. There is a general cultural consensus that the referents of religion are the supernatural, the spiritual, the divine,[42] and a general awareness of a distinction between the sacred and the profane.[43]

Our definition therefore is exclusive in orientation since this is for the most part in line with popular understanding and interpretation. There are some grey areas, however, such as traditional healers, witchcraft and secret societies. Several of those interviewed refused to classify the aforementioned as religion, partly because of their negative connotations and, in the case of magic, its critical and occasional orientation. There is also some disagreement over whether spiritual science groups, such as the Rosicrucians and Eckankar (who indeed emphasize that they are not religious but rather "philosophical" and "mystical" organizations), should be labelled as religious. Many people have obviously been influenced by Christian- and church-oriented conceptions of religion. We have chosen to consider these marginal activities and associations as forms of religious activity since they have their own institutions, specialists and world-views, of which the supernatural is a referent.

Notes

1. (London: Oxford University Press), p. 4.

2. "The Christianization of African Society: Some Possible Models" in *Christianity in Independent Africa*, ed. E. Fasholé-Luke, et al. (London: Rex Collings, 1978), pp. 443-454.

3. The University of Calabar campus was itself a microcosm of religious activity: situated relatively close to the town centre, it had (in 1983) one of the highest proportions of junior staff of all Nigerian universities. This meant that the university represented a good cross-section of the wider society. Many religious organizations had a campus branch or representative and many religious gatherings were either staged on the campus (because of its facilities) or well publicized on campus notice-boards.

4. See, for example, H. Byron Earhart, *Japanese Religion: Unity and Diversity*, 2nd. ed. (Encino, CA.: Dickenson, 1974); idem, *Religions of Japan: Many Traditions Within One Sacred Way* (San Francisco: Harper and Row, 1984); Ichiro Hori, *Japanese Religion*, trans. Y. Abe and D. Reid (Tokyo: Kodansha International, 1972).

5. See the preface to Earhart, *Japanese Religion*, pp. vii-viii.

6. Ibid., pp. 2-3.

7. "Twelve Months of Japanese Religion", *Bulletin of the British Association for the History of Religions* 32(November 1980):6-7.

8. Ibid., p. 7.

9. See D.L. Overmyer, *Religions of China* (San Francisco: Harper and Row, 1986); and L.G. Thompson, *Chinese Religion: An Introduction*, The Religious Life of Man Series (Belmont,

CA: Wadsworth, 1979).

10. Thompson, pp. xi, 1-2.

11. B. Colless and P. Donovan, eds. (Edinburgh: T. and T. Clark, 1980).

12. See, for example, D.B. Clark, "Local and Cosmopolitan Aspects of Religious Activity in a Northern Suburb" in *A Sociological Yearbook of Religion in Britain 3*, eds. D. Martin and M. Hill (London: SCM Press, 1970), pp. 45-63; P.D. Varney, "Religion in Rural Norfolk", ibid., pp. 65-77; D. Martin, *A Sociology of English Religion* (London: SCM Press, 1967).

13. The research project is known as "Conventional Religion and Common Religion in Leeds" and was conducted by the Department of Sociology, University of Leeds from 1981-84.

14. (Chicago: University of Chicago Press, 1960), pp. 5-7.

15. (Bombay: Asia Publishing House, 1961). See also L. P. Vidyarthi, *The Sacred Complex of Kashi: a Microcosm of Indian Civilization* (Delhi: Concept, 1979).

16. Les Dieux et les Hommes: Etude des cultes d'un village du Tirunelveli, Inde du Sud, Cahiers de l'Homme, N.S. 18 (Paris: Mouton, 1979).

17. *The Play of the Gods: Locality, Ideology, Structure and Time in the Festivals of a Bengali Town* (Chicago: University of Chicago Press, 1980).

18. (London: Oxford University Press for the International African Institute).

19. Ibid., chapter 7.

20. Ibid., p. 237.

21. M.W. Murphree, *Christianity and the Shona* (London: The Athlone Press, 1969). See also his "Religious Interdependence among the Budjga Vapostori", in *African Initiatives in Religion*, ed. D.B. Barrett (Nairobi: East African Publishing House, 1971), pp. 171-80.

22. "The Diversity of Churches in Matadi, Zaïre", *Cahiers des Religions Africaines* 10,19 (janvier 1976):31-49. See also his "A Survey of Churches in Matadi" in *Modern Kongo Prophets: Religion in a Plural Society* (Bloomington: Indiana University Press, 1982), pp. 53-80.

23. MacGaffey, "The Diversity of Churches in Matadi", p. 31n.

24. Ibid., pp. 42-46, 48-49.

25. R.W. Wyllie, *Spiritism in Ghana: a Study of New Religious Movements*, American Academy of Religion Studies in Religion, 21 (Chico, CA: Scholars Press, 1980).

26. J. Middleton, "One Hundred and Fifty Years of Christianity in a Ghanaian Town", *Africa* 53,3 (1983):15.

27. See, for example, E. Fasholé-Luke, "Christianity and Islam in Freetown", *Sierra Leone Bulletin of Religion* 9,1 (June 1964): 1-16; idem, "Religion in Freetown" in *Freetown: A Symposium* (Freetown: Sierra Leone University Press, 1968), pp. 127-42; A.T. Porter, "Religious Affiliation in Freetown, Sierra Leone", *Africa* 23 (1953).

28. Fasholé-Luke, in "Religion in Freetown", states that according to the 1963 census there were 65 churches (15 different Christian denominations) and 17 mosques for a population of 127,917.

29. R. Deniel, *Croyances Religieuses et Vie Quotidienne: Islam et Christianisme à Ougadougou*, Recherches Voltaïques 14 (Paris/ Ougadougou: CNRS/CVRS, 1970).

30. Peel, "The Christianization of African Society", p. 453.

31. Deniel, pp. 297-309, 334-55.

32. *Zaïre* (Louvain) 3,5 (May 1949):549-56.

33. Parrinder, *Religion in an African City*, p. 4., chaps. 8 and 11.

34. Eds. P.C. Lloyd, A.L. Mabogunje and B. Awe (Cambridge: Cambridge University Press with the Institute of African Studies, University of Ibadan, 1967).

35. Pp. 235-47.

36. *Report on the Survey of Religious Organizations in the Oyo State* (Ibadan: Ministry of Finance and Economic Development, 1977). A total of 429 churches and 686 mosques were identified in Ibadan alone.

37. *A Phenomenological/Anthropological Analysis of the Religion of the Ondo-Yoruba of Nigeria*, Ph.D. dissertation, Boston University, 1983.

38. This was a team put together by the Mennonite missionary, Edwin Weaver. According to information from Dr. H.W. Turner, there was also an Uyo Inter-Church Study Group (inter-denominational) which met for monthly discussions in the early 1960s.

39. See Uyo Survey Team, *The Abak Story* (Uyo, E. Nigeria: the Team, 1967). Mimeo. Also E. Weaver and I. Weaver, *The Uyo Story* (Elkhart, Indiana: Mennonite Board of Missions, 1970).

40. This was originally planned as the first stage of the overall survey, but due to a delay (1980-81) in obtaining research clearance, the data was collected on a more gradual, haphazard basis until a more systematic religious mapping could be conducted (in April 1983). The results of the latter are

outlined in chapter 6. See also Appendix 1.

41. R. Robertson, *The Sociological Interpretation of Religion* (Oxford: Basil Blackwell, 1970), p. 47.

42. Not necessarily in personified forms, for there exist also abstract notions of "spiritual power".

43. This is in spite of beliefs concerning divine intervention in human affairs. In many ways Christianization and modernization have contributed to the differentiation and "reification" of religion.

Part One: Historical Ethnography

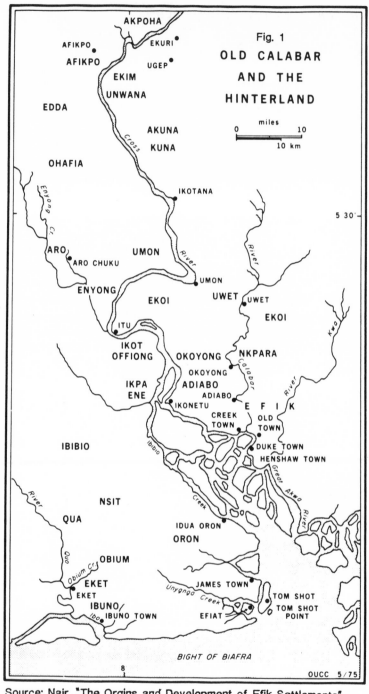

Source: Nair, "The Orgins and Development of Efik Settlements"

Figure 1: Old Calabar and the hinterland

Chapter One

Old Calabar

1.1 Background to Calabar

1.1.1 Geography

Calabar is situated in the south-eastern corner of Nigeria on a latitude of 04 57' north and a longitude of 08 20' east. To the north are the upper regions of the Cross River, Oban and Ogoja, while to the west are the lands inhabited by the Ibibio and Igbo peoples. Calabar is bordered on the east by Cameroon and to the south by the estuary of the Cross River which flows into the Bight of Biafra.[1]

The landscape of Calabar is dominated by its surrounding rivers; it is situated within the deltaic zone of the Cross, Calabar and Great Kwa Rivers. The town of Calabar stands on a narrow ridge of land (some 60 metres above the Bight of Biafra sea level) and is bounded by brackish and salt-laden water, mangrove swamps and degraded rain forest.[2]

Calabar's growth and development has been greatly influenced by its proximity to the sea, a distance of approximately fifty kilometres or thirty miles. The hinterland is characterized by plantations established in the seventeenth and eighteenth centuries by the local nobility.[3] Much of Calabar's food supply still comes from these outlying farms and the connections between the families and estates have been maintained. These rural areas are now being developed as a result of the penetration of roads, schools and local government institutions.

Calabar experiences a full humid equatorial climate, mitigated by strong land and sea breezes. There is rain all the year round, although December, January and February are comparatively dry. More than three quarters of the 3050 mm. rainfall occurs between May and October. The mean annual temperature is 26.1 Celsius with a high relative humidity ranging from 76.8 - 92%.[4] Many would argue that the climate, with its heavy rain and subsequent erosion, has not facilitated Calabar's physical and economic development.

1.1.2   Historical background

The town of Calabar has achieved renown for a variety of reasons. First, during the eighteenth and nineteenth centuries, Calabar developed into an important trading centre, chiefly because of its strategic location at the conjunction of the waterways. It was one of the first ports on the Nigerian coast to make the transition from slave to palm oil trade.[5]   While it is likely that the Dutch and/or the Portuguese penetrated the Cross River estuary in the fifteenth or sixteenth centuries, the first recorded contact of European trade with Old Calabar was in 1668.[6]   It eventually became the first headquarters of the British consul on the Bights of Benin and Biafra in 1849 and the first capital of the Oil Rivers Protectorate in 1891.[7]   In addition Calabar became known as the first centre of missionary expansion on the Bight of Biafra.

The origin of the name "Calabar" is uncertain although it is thought to have derived from the Portuguese "Calabarra" or "Calaboros" meaning "the bar is silent" and referring to the calm waters of the estuary.[8]   The Dutch, who were perhaps the earliest frequenters of the river, called the area "Olde Calburg".[9]   The dates of settlement of the various ethnic groups in Calabar have been much debated, likewise the origins of the main indigenous group - the Efik.

The history and development of Calabar is intimately linked to the history of the Efik people. The actual origins of the Efik are unknown, although oral traditions provide accounts of their migrations from Igbo and Ibibio territory (to the north-west of Calabar) to the present location.[10]

There would seem to be three successive stages in the history of Efik migration and settlement: (a) an Igbo phase (b) an Ibibio

phase and (c) the drift to the coast.[11]   There are some Efik who
advocate the "oriental" origins of their people, claiming that they
were living in Palestine or Egypt and had crossed the Sahara to
Sudan from where they wandered into Nigeria.[12]   This is believed
to be reflected in some of their elaborate burial rites and ceremonies.[13]

Evidence to support the "orientalist" theory is lacking and must
be considered highly improbable.   The period of Efik settlement
amongst the Igbo at Ibom in the vicinity of Arochuku is far more
tenable and has led to theories concerning the Igbo origin of the
Efik.[14]   During this period, the Efik reportedly clashed with the
Aro people for refusing to worship *Ibritam*, the Aro oracle,
sometimes referred to as "Long Juju".   The Efik claimed that they
were worshippers of *Abasi Ibom* (God of the Universe) alone, whose
ark in the form of *Usan Abasi* was carried along with them on
their journey.[15]   Whether it was solely a religious conflict,
therefore, which drove the Efik out of Igboland is unclear, but the
refusal of the immigrants to show respect for the Arochuku oracle
undoubtedly offended the Aro and may have been the catalyst
which led to the final expulsion.[16]

On leaving Ibom, the Efik dispersed into several directions.[17]
Several family groups settled at Uruan in Ibibioland.   This phase of
Efik settlement is well preserved in Efik tradition and has given
rise to the theory that the Efik are a sub-group of the Ibibio.[18]
The Efik refused to acknowledge the Uruan deity - *Atakpo-Uruan*,
and according to some reports even tried to impose their own way
of worship on the Uruan.[19]   This, together with fear of Efik
witchcraft,   generated   inter-ethnic   tensions   which   eventually
resulted in the rejection of the Efik. The people of Uruan were
said to have given them the name "Efik" deriving from a verb
meaning to press or oppress, since they were alleged to be
aggressive.   According to tradition, the Efik also captured the
sacred paraphernalia of the Uruan.[20]

Even if one disputes that the Efik were of Ibibio stock, it is
not surprising that some degree of cultural assimilation occurred
during their stay there.   In particular, linguistic similarities led one
observer to contend that Efik was a dialect of the parent language
Ibibio, having been corrupted at a later stage by contact with other

languages.[21]   Another notes the similarity of socio-political structures at this time, at least up until the period of Efik settlement at Creek Town.[22]   A village was composed of several *ekpuk* (extended family or lineage). Each ekpuk consisted of several *ufok* or compounds which in turn were made up of *idip* - a man with wives and children. The ekpuk, while virtually autonomous, were united by the secret society, village council and common religion.

The Efik and Ibibio peoples both shared a belief in Abasi, the Supreme Deity and a host of smaller deities and spirits known as *ndem* or *nnem*.[23]   Witchcraft, ancestors and the soul were also common features of their belief systems.[24]

The Efik moved on from Uruan to Ikpa Ene along the banks of the Cross River. Ikpa Ene was later known as "Akani Obio Efik" (Old Efik Town).[25] Some Efik groups left to go to Mbiabo, from where they expanded south to form the settlements of Ikot Offiong and Ikonetu.[26] The largest group of Efik moved on to Ndodoghi, whose swampy conditions forced them to move further to what eventually became known as Creek Town. Efik historians, date this as early as the fourteenth century,[27] while it has been situated later, sometime before the middle of the seventeenth century, before trade with Europe began.[28]

From now on Efik migrations were motivated by internal factors, namely lineage tensions, rather than by external aggressors.[29]   They crossed the river to form a settlement at Obutong or Old Town.[30]   The town prospered as European trade increased, often intercepting the trade destined for Creek Town.[31] Atakpa (or "Duke's Town" as it became known in the late eighteenth century, and later, Duke Town) was the next settlement to be founded, just below Obutong.[32]   This was followed by the establishment of Cobham Town and Henshaw Town.[33]

There is evidence that the Efik encountered both the Qua (the southernmost sector of the Ejagham people also known as the Akin) and the Efut (from what is now south-west Cameroon) on the land which eventually became the site of Old Calabar.[34]   Both peoples had fled to the banks of the Calabar River to escape war in their former territories. There has since been a great deal of cultural and linguistic interaction and intermarriage between these three groups, so that the Efut in particular are today virtually regarded as Efik.[35]

1.1.3   Efik social and political structures

Efik social and political organization is a good example of a segmentary lineage structure.[36]   The component lineages are derived from the two great lineages of the founding ancestors - Ema and Efiom Ekpo. The Efik have always placed great emphasis on kinship and this produced a division into nobles, commoners and slaves. Only those who could trace their descent through male or female links to one or other of the founders of the Efik community were eligible for ritual or political office. This did not prevent wealthy slaves and commoners from being politically and commercially active and influential. By the nineteenth century the structure of Efik society had become relatively stabilized, after fairly uneven patterns of expansion.

The community was divided into a federation of separate, self-governing segments, which were essentially corporate groups of patrilineal kin. Jones refers to these divisions as "wards" in a territorial sense, and "maximal lineages" in a kinship context. They have also been referred to as "towns", "families" or "houses" (*ufok*). Sub-divisions of the wards or houses corresponded to major lineages, while these ward sections were in turn subdivided into minor lineages or directly into a number of expanded families or enlarged households which corresponded to minimal lineages.

Genealogical segmentation and the development of the ward or house system is attributed by some to the growth of the slave trade. The head of a ward was selected usually on the basis of age, but latterly wealth and the capacity for leadership have become important criteria. There was no central governing body or council in the larger community and this perhaps accounted for the relative absence of warring political factions. Cultural integration and central political authority were provided by the tutelary cult of *Ndem Efik* and the *Ekpe* secret society.

There are no references to any single chief or overall political leader in Old Calabar. In the nineteenth century the honorific title

"king" was given to those ward heads who engaged in trade with
the Europeans. The Efik themselves did not credit the office with
sovereign powers. Eventually the number of kings in Old Calabar
was stabilized at two, one for Duke Town and one for Creek Town,
and at the beginning of the twentieth century to one, largely as a
result of internal strife and external interference from the colonial
and missionary powers. This also marked a departure from the
former trade-based political structure.

1.1.4   Demography and development

As a result of trade rivalries, Old Town was destroyed in 1767 and
Creek Town and Duke Town prospered.[37]   Under "Great Duke
Ephraim", Duke Town emerged as the principal trading settlement
at   the   beginning   of   the   nineteenth   century.   The   great
contemporary rulers Eyo Honesty II of Creek Town and Eyamba V
of Duke Town consolidated Old Calabar as one of the most
important trading centres on the West African coast. Both rulers
successfully negotiated the transfer from the slave to the palm-oil
trade   in   the   mid-nineteenth   century   and   resisted   European
domination.   They were instrumental in bringing Christianity to
Calabar in 1846 (see 2.2).

Old   Calabar   was   the   headquarters   of   the   Niger   Coast
Protectorate until 1900 and then of the Protectorate of Southern
Nigeria.   It was renamed Calabar in 1904 but suffered a major
setback when Lagos became the new seat of government in 1906.[38]
The economic superiority of the Efik as middlemen was gradually
undermined as the Cross River was opened up.   The decision to
develop Port Harcourt as a rail terminal and port instead of
Calabar in 1916 contributed to the latter's economic decline.[39]   The
fall of primary-produce prices in the late 1920s and 1930s created
unemployment and   social   tension (which   manifested itself in a
witchcraft revival).   Many Efik who had been trained as teachers
and civil servants migrated to administrative centres in other parts
of Nigeria.[40]   Calabar's decision to back the Action Group (a
political party) instead of the National Council of Nigeria and the
Cameroons   had   detrimental   economic   consequences.[41]   In   1961,

Southern Cameroon chose to leave Nigeria for political reasons. This compounded Calabar's depression, as trade was diverted to Victoria and many commercial enterprises were forced to close.[42]

The fate of Calabar changed when it became the capital of the South Eastern State in 1967.[43] Within a decade, the town became transformed into a successful administrative, commercial and political nucleus.[44]

Urbanization led to population growth, which is not easy to measure since there are no census figures available other than those of 1963.[45] According to one estimate, the population of about 70,000 before the civil war (1967-70) increased to 100,000 afterwards.[46] Using an estimated growth rate of 8.3% one arrives at a figure of about 250,000 for urban Calabar by 1977.[47] This would mean a higher figure for the 1980s, while the commonly accepted figures for the present-day population of Calabar range between 200,000 and 250,000. Despite the increase in the influx of migrants, particularly Ibibio, since the civil war ended, Calabar is still not considered to be over-populated compared with other Nigerian cities.[48] From a survey conducted in 1976, the year Calabar became capital of the newly formed Cross River State, it was discovered that 80% of the town's population are migrants.[49] The two main ethnic groups in Calabar are the Ibibio (45%) and the Efik (38%).[50] The Igbo are returning to Calabar, but there are no figures available.[51] There is also a small Edo community.[52] The two other indigenous groups, the Qua and the Efut, are minority groups, and have intermarried with the Efik.

So despite its relative isolation, having only been linked to the rest of Nigeria by road (rather than by inadequate ferry services) in the late 1970s, Calabar has taken on all the aspects of a growing Nigerian town experiencing the throes of urbanization and modernization. As memories of the Nigerian civil war of 1967-70 recede and the Igbo move back to Calabar (they were as numerous as the Efik before the war) and more and more people from other parts of the Cross River State migrate to the capital, Calabar is becoming a multi-ethnic urban community. Political power under the recent civilian government (1979-83) was in the hands of the Ibibio, while the Igbo and Hausa remain active in the commercial sector. Several Efik are to be found in the middle and upper ranks of the civil service, as well as in the medical teaching and legal professions. They remain the principal land-owners and custodians of traditional authority and culture. They reputedly have a high level of urbanization (41.5%) in marked contrast to the two related ethnic groups - the Ibibio (5.3%) and the Anang (3.6%).[53]

Despite the increasing dominance of the Ibibio in the political, cultural, economic and religious life of the town, Calabar is still considered as an Efik town. This is in large measure due to the presence and influence of the Obong of Calabar; he is both the Patriarch of the Efik and the Paramount Ruler of Calabar. Many would also point to the importance of the Ekpe Society in protecting the interests of the Efik. The clear majority of people are Efik-Ibibio speakers.[54] The Efik are proud of their centuries of trade and interaction with Europe and now resent the numerical superiority of the Ibibio and their growing influence. They claim the Ibibio have copied many of their customs and been responsible for the "mushroom churches" which have sprung up around the town in recent years. Many Ibibio in fact rather look to Uyo as their cultural and political capital.[55] An annual Ibibio Day is held (irregularly) in Calabar and Ibibio masquerades may be seen together with those of the Efik and the Qua at Christmas and Easter. However the majority of their ceremonial occasions, burials, marriages and chieftaincy installations are conducted in Ibibioland itself. Most Ibibio migrate to Calabar in search of education and employment and maintain ties with their home towns and villages as much as possible. The wealthier Ibibio construct homes in their villages for retirement. It is not uncommon for the Ibibio to return to the "mainland" to consult local diviners and herbalists in the case of sickness and misfortune.

Civilian rule in the early 1980s and the creation of politicized cultural associations (Nka Ekpenyong Nnuk [Efik]; Akwa Esop Imaisong Ibibio [Ibibio]; Afe Anang [Anang: a sub-group of the Ibibio]) heightened inter-ethnic tensions.[56] The media tended to de-emphasize the shared cultural, social and linguistic features felt by many Efik and Ibibio.[57]

The traditional urban structures and more recent development and growth of the town combined with Calabar's relative isolation (for the political, economic and geographical reasons outlined above) have resulted in a variety of social conditions and groupings existing within a limited geographical area. Bennetta Jules-Rosette notes the interest and the importance of this phenomenon in urbanizing Africa - "This proximity [between rural and urban] creates a direct link between custom, the remnants of colonial change, and the newer effects of urbanism."[58] The effects of this interaction have played a part in shaping the various religious expressions in the town, as we shall witness in the course of this study.

1.2   Traditional religion

In this section it is proposed to treat the earliest known forms of religion in Calabar. As explained earlier, the focus is predominantly on Efik religion at this stage. Such a task naturally poses methodological problems. Oral accounts are limited and not always reliable. Written records are often distorted by the hand of the writer. References to the cults are often incidental, rather than providing us with a direct account of particular beliefs and ritual activities.

While there are quite a variety of sources at our disposal, none pre-date the period of European contact. Efik folktales are considered to be a relatively unreliable source of ethnographic information.[59] Later accounts may be more comprehensive and helpful in some respects, but misleading in other ways, since it is not always easy to discern whether the writer is describing past or present forms of the religion, or both.

Additional problems stem from the tendency of some writers to make no distinction between the Efik and the Ibibio peoples, usually subsuming the Efik within the Ibibio group. These difficulties must be borne in mind as we attempt to reconstruct this early phase of Calabar's religious history. This section is based chiefly on the works of modern historians, both European and Nigerian, as well as on contemporary sources (mainly mission-ary and colonial). The viewpoints of the Efik historians, such as Aye and Akak, are particularly important here, since they contribute to our understanding of the Efik world-view and self-perception. Our examination of the traditional cults and institutions in present-day Calabar is reserved for section 5.2.

1.2.1   Ndem cults

Most writers on the history of Calabar agree that *Ndem Efik* is one of the earliest, if not the earliest, forms of Efik religion. Hence they designate Ndem Efik as the tutelary deity or deities of the Efik people, as opposed to the *ndem* or *nnem* of the Ibibio or Anang. The worship of the ndem (primarily river gods and goddesses) has had great religious and political significance for the Efik. Ndem Efik proved to be an important integrating force during the period of early settlement at Creek Town and Duke Town.[60]

Ndem can be conceived of and worshipped in either singular or plural terms - as an individual, named deity or as a collectivity of all the deities and spirits (mainly associated with water). "Ndem Efik" may therefore mean "the gods of the Efik", but it may also represent an abstraction of the former and be referred to in singular terms. This is reflected in the case of the king or *obong*, who, even today, is believed to represent, by virtue of his sacred office, the unity of the various ndem cults of the Efik people.

The early nineteenth century was the high point for Ndem Efik as a religious institution. Processes of centralization and institutionalization seemed to generate concepts of supremacy and this is reflected in references to Ndem Efik as the "Great God". The religious situation in Old Calabar, prior to the arrival of Christianity, is described as "polytheistic" since the Efik people:

> worshipped several gods and goddesses to whom they offered periodic animal and human sacrifices. For instance, Creek Town had worshipped Akpa Uyok; Old Town, Anansa Ikot Obutong; Cobham Town, Iboku Anwan; Henshaw Town, Esiet Ebom Nsidung or Sungku Mongko: but these were by no means all, and individual families and Houses had their patron gods and goddesses.[61]

Above this pantheon there existed a college of priests, headed by the chief priest, generally known as the Obong Efik or King Calabar.[62]   He was in charge of Ndem Efik which at that time afforded him political power and status, making him "virtually the most powerful man in the Calabar country".[63]   He combined the offices of both chief priest and paramount ruler, providing the all important link between the people, the college of priests and the deity.   This dual position and overall authority were conveyed through the title of "Edidem".   As the physical representation of the deity, he was honoured with the expression "Enye edi idem" - "He is the cult" or "He is the masquerade".[64] This Efik expression "edi idem", gradually evolved into "edidem" meaning "majesty".[65]

Ndem are primarily associated with water and are more commonly conceived and manifested in female terms.[66]   The association with water is appropriate to the traditional Efik occupation of fishing.[67]   Missionary accounts speak of albino girls being offered as sacrifices at Parrot Island just down river from Calabar.   Ndem are always prayed to for blessings, fertility and forgiveness and for the special protection which they are believed to extend to the people of Calabar.   Indeed the first reference to ndem - by Antera Duke, a local trader, in his diary of May 25, 1785 - is as "Old Calabar Doctor" - "wee go make doctor to Old Calabar Doctor".[68]

Spirit possession seems to have been a feature of the cults from the earliest times.   People with light skins are particularly subject to possession by ndem, and the use of white, as well as emotional dancing and music, are favoured by cult devotees.

By the middle of the nineteenth century the institutional aspects of Ndem Efik, which Akak likens to the Neptune and Minerva cults in ancient Rome, had begun to decline.   The Reverend Hope Masterton Waddell observed that by 1847 the office of the chief priest had fallen into disrepute and only a "decayed gentleman" could be found to accept the honour.[69]   There are various explanations put forward by both contemporary and recent writers, to account for the partial eclipse of Ndem Efik and its religio-political significance.   Aye describes the power of Obong Efik:

> his superior knowledge,... his exclusive right of
> possessing all the secrets of religion and sacrifices
> which were thought to place him far above the rest
> and ...the dependence on him of all classes for the
> instruction he chose to impart.[70]

But despite this status and the tributes he received, such as
refugee slaves and the skins of all leopards, Goldie suggests that
his power, which entailed certain taboos and restrictions, eventually
led to the decline of the institution.[71]   These included the
necessity of eating alone and more importantly the prohibition on
his engaging in trade.[72]   This was an insignificant factor when the
Efik were only fishermen, but decisive as they became slave
traders:

> While other Efik freemen could trade, grow wealthy,
> and build up retinues of slaves, the Ndem priest
> could not, until he was left with nothing but ritual
> importance in a ritual which itself had ceased to be
> very important.[73]

The priesthood had lost much of its influence by 1805 even though
it still retained a certain judicial role as late as the 1850s.[74]   The
various cults have in fact survived right up until the present day
and still perform a key role in the traditional coronation of the
Efik king or Obong of Calabar.

The fortunes of Ndem Efik were closely linked to the
fluctuating periods of trade. He concludes that since they were
primarily earth cults, their worship was neglected as there was a
move away from the land to the booming palm oil trade in the
1850s.[75]   As trade declined in the 1860s, there was a revival of
ndem worship.

Some observers have identified more political reasons to explain
the decline of the ndem cults.[76]   Edidem Eyo Ema of Creek Town
was the last paramount ruler to have the dual political and
religious authority. He exercised his political and judicial authority
through Ekpe, the new secret society. Because of the growing
importance of these two functions, the king delegated that of Ekpe

to his cousin Oku Atai Atai Ema Atai Iboku and the Atai as a whole. The power descended to his cousin Essien Ekpe Oku, the grandson of his cousin, when he eventually became the twenty-first ruler at Creek Town. It was the enlargement of the functions of the Ekpe institution which generated this transfer and redistribution of power.[77] As a result, the political, judiciary and legislative jurisdiction of the Ekpe Society naturally increased while that of Ndem Efik, which now existed as a separate institution, was considerably weakened.

As mentioned above, people refer to ndem in a variety of ways - as individual, localized deities, such as the popular "Anansa Ikang Obutong", worshipped by the people of Obutong (Old Town). These various, named deities, either male or female and associated with a defined locality, are collectively known as the gods of the Efik people and hence are described as Ndem Efik. It is a fluid, changing pantheon with deities attaining or losing prominence due to socio-historical circumstances (such as changes in habitation patterns) or the priesthood in charge, or due to a declining interest in the attributes of a particular deity.

It has not been possible to document in detail the changes referred to above, although the current pantheon is described in chapter five. There is, however, evidence of henotheistic trends with certain deities such as Ekpenyong or Anansa, gaining importance and popularity amongst the Efik as a whole. This is apparent in such phrases as "Anansa Ikang Obutong, Ndem Efik Iboku" meaning "Anansa Ikang Obutong is the deity of Efik Iboku" (the Efik people).[78] Whether Ndem is seen as an intermediary power or an end in itself depends ultimately on the beliefs and attitudes of individual devotees.

On some occasions Ndem is described as an abstract divine reality, or life-force, while "ndem" may also refer to the hosts of smaller, unnamed spirits believed to inhabit the earth and the water. In short, the concept of Ndem seems to represent both the unity and diversity of the Efik, serving as both an accessible personal deity for the individual or ward, and an identity-giving "supreme" tutelary cult, or "family of cults" for the Efik as a whole. It could be argued that the flexibility and sexual duality of the cults have aided their success and persistence, although the

markedly female emphasis and associations with nature have provided an important complement to the more male-oriented and
town-centred Ekpe Society.

1.2.2   Supreme deity

Before the rise of the Ekpe Society, the Efik pantheon was
dominated by Ndem Efik. References to Ndem on occasion reflect
concepts of supremacy.[79] This would seem to conflict with the
basic belief in *Abasi*, the supreme being who dwells in the sky and
is the source of life and death, as well as the ultimate source of
justice. Abasi is part of the Efik cosmology since the time of
their migrations:

> These activities did not in any way turn the Efiks
> from worshipping the true God of the Universe, who
> to them was regarded, known and called "Abasi Ibom"
> - the God of Ibom, where they sojourned among the
> Ibos.[80]

They even carried with them *Usan Abasi* - a symbolic relic of the
"Ark of God".[81] A distinction was also made between *Usan Ndem*,
the "Deity's plate", which contained white chalk (*ndom*) and yellow
chalk (*uto*) and *Usan Abasi* - "God's plate".[82] King Archibong
remarked to the Reverend William Anderson in 1862 that the
worship of Ndem Efik had been taught to the fathers of the
Calabar people, just as he had taught "the fathers of the white
people to worship in Bible fashion."[83]

Rev. Hugh Goldie wrote that Calabar people acknowledged a
creator and supreme being by the name of Abasi.[84] He further
described how a small circular mound was built in the entrance
yard of every house, on which were placed a few small dishes of
earthenware and some old bones, comprising often a human skull,
and this was known as *Isu Abasi* - the "face" or "presence" of
Abasi. Worship took place on a particular day of the traditional
eight-day week and a little water was poured into the dishes (*usan*)

as various prayers and supplications were made.[85]

According to one observation, the basins were placed at the foot of a particular type of tree which grew in most yards and that a land-turtle often hung from the tree.[86] The water in "God's dish" was never emptied out, only replenished, and prayers and wishes made over the dish expressed the desire for safety, success and length of life. The ancestors were also called upon during these occasions, and the prayers could be made over goats and fowls killed for friends arriving or leaving.[87]

In addition, young children, white chickens and kids were sometimes brought before the sacred basin with prayer in order to be consecrated to God and receive his name.[88] The ritual act was done as a thanksoffering, usually with a view to securing special blessings on the object of consecration. Goldie observes that the practices seemed to have fallen into disuse before the advent of the mission.

While there seems never to have been a highly systematized cult of Abasi - no formal priesthood or public worship, those cultic and symbolic aspects which were performed, mainly at the individual or family level, gradually gave way to other practices. That is not to say that the concept of Abasi disappeared from the Efik cosmology; there is every reason to suppose, as evidenced by the language and folklore, for example, that the Efik have always considered Abasi as the ultimate life-giver, judge and provider.[89] But it was precisely that power and transcendence that generated beliefs that God was too great to be worshipped directly. Exactly why or when this trend occurred is not clear. The rise of Ndem Efik in popularity and importance must offer a partial explanation in this respect. One commentator remarked that the various ndem or "idem" as he termed them:

> are inferior to God in power, but in some respects, deemed better off, as having more connection with earth and enjoyable things.[90]

P.A. Talbot, describing an earlier cycle of divinities among the Ibibio (among whom he classed the Efik), claims that Ete Abasi (Father God) and Eka Abasi (Mother God) were once principal

deities concerned with the creation of the universe.[91]   He then
refers specifically to the Efik, maintaining that they sacrificed to
both at the same time - a cock would be offered by the husband
and a hen by his wife.   The sacrifice was supervised by an old
priestess who gave up one yam, two plantains and some palm-wine
in a pit, from which clay had been dug for the building of
houses.[92]   He emphasizes that Ete Abasi and Eka Abasi had become
"shadowy divinities" for the Ibibio and had been largely replaced by
the sky god and creator - Abasi, and the earth goddess - Isong.[93]
In the case of the Efik, because of their occupations as traders and
fishermen, Ndem Efik seems to have taken on the role that Isong
played in the neighbouring Ibibio communities.   Belief in Eka Abasi,
on the other hand, has persisted vaguely among the Efik, although
her status is inferior to that of Abasi, being confined to childbirth
and the destiny of individuals.

    In the second chapter we shall see how the concept of Abasi
received a new lease of life from contact with the concept of God
as promulgated by the Christian missionaries.

1.2.3   Ekpe Society

The secret society or fraternity known as Ekpe (or Egbo in its
anglicized form) has somewhat obscure origins.[94]   At the time of
their migrations, the Efik possessed a secret cult known as *Nyana
Yaku* or *Mkpe*.[95]   When they moved from Uruan to their present
settlements, they encountered a similar society among the Efut and
eventually purchased the secret of the five small Ekpe grades from
one Archibong Ekondo who in turn had acquired it from the Ekoi
(Ejagham) at Usak Edet, now on the Cameroon side of the Cross
River.[96]   The authority of the newly evolving Ekpe Society passed
into the hands of Oku Atai and his descendants, as Eyo Ema and
his descendants were responsible for Ndem Efik.[97]   So while the
Efik were involved in the later development and elaboration of
Ekpe, it is not possible to argue that they were the originators.[98]
Some maintain that the roots of the present-day Ekpe Society lie
in the original Nyana Yaku society.[99]

    There is some evidence to show that Ekpe was originally a

women's society, probably imported to Calabar from the Ekoi (in present-day Cameroon).[100]   As the society developed, the men wrested the power away from the women. This view would appear to have little support amongst the Efik themselves, who claim that the only secret society where there was an enforced transfer of power is the *Obon* society. There is reportedly nothing in Ekpe mythology to suggest its female origins, whereas there are several songs in the Obon society which refer to the leadership of women in the early stages.[101]

As regards the dating of the emergence of Ekpe, Latham demonstrates that the society could not have been founded before 1720, but adds that a more reasonable estimate would place the date of the foundation of Ekpe closer to the middle of the eighteenth century.[102]   The first office holder was Esien Ekpe Oku, grandson of Oku Atai, who became Eyamba I, the president of Ekpe.[103]

The majority of sources seem to agree that the Ekpe Society was originally an essentially religious cult. "Ekpe" in Efik means "leopard" and is said to have been a mysterious and invisible being inhabiting the forest, and which could not be seen by the uninitiated. The *ekpe* was occasionally "captured" and brought to town for traditional ceremonies, on which occasions its fearful roar could be heard by everyone, while only the initiates knew the exact source of the sound. Likewise the esoteric ritual ceremonies associated with the cult could only be performed by members of the fraternity. Ekpe was represented by a messenger, *Idem Ikwo*, a masquerade in a multi-coloured costume (*esik*) and a black hooded and knitted garment, with a bunch of leaves in his left hand to denote his forest origin.[104]   He wore a bell tied to his waist to announce his arrival, for he would terrorize with the whip or stick he carried those who were not initiates.[105]

Members of the society used the fearful aspect of the cult to enforce law and order while at the same time claimed to be interpreting the desires of Ekpe who had to be propitiated for the well-being of the community.[106]   In this way, the ancestors occupied an important place in the society's belief and ritual systems.

Trading patterns began to change in Calabar towards the

mid-eighteenth century as Efik traders began to receive credit from the European traders, and the slave market developed. The Ekpe Society quickly adapted itself to the changing conditions. It not only became the supreme authority and law enforcement agency, but also made laws and controlled commercial activities through its power to collect debts and punish offenders - "its authority was sacrosanct and was above challenge".[107] Even the king and other secular rulers were subject to its edicts and laws.

The successful expansion of the Ekpe Society was certainly linked to the fact that it was a common organization which transcended lineage ties. Its membership was also opened eventually to free men, slaves, women, young or old, and even foreigners - all those who could afford the initiation fees - although the higher grades (Nyamkpe, Okpoho, Okuahama and Nakanda) were in reality restricted to the wealthy and the privileged. The lower grades were, in descending order, Mboko, Mboko Mboko, Mkpe, Mbakara and Edibo.

Thus, with its religious legitimation, Ekpe provided an important integrating force, particularly in a period of social and economic upheaval in Efik society. It was able to become the central organ of government because of its orientation toward the problems of commerce in contrast to Ndem Efik which had weakened as fishing ceased to be the basis of the economy.[108]

1.2.4   Witchcraft

The Efik belief in witchcraft (*ifot*) is generally considered to be both ancient and persistent, manifesting itself at times of social, political and economic instability. From the earliest times, there were believed to be two types of witchcraft - *afia ifot* (white witchcraft) and *obubit* (black witchcraft). White witchcraft was employed for protective and positive purposes, while black witchcraft, the most common type, was used to cause harm and destruction to others.

Witches were traditionally believed to have the ability to transform themselves into a variety of animate and inanimate objects, and to:

> travel to any distant country the same night and
> back with incredible speed, either by possessing
> wings and flying in the air or sailing on the
> seas in groundnut shells or on cocoyam
> leaves.[109]

They were believed to achieve maximum operation by night and
hence were associated with nocturnal creatures such as owls, bats,
cockroaches and moths.[110]   Dogs barking and cocks crowing at
night were believed to signify the nefarious activities of witches.
Tall trees, notably the silk cotton tree (*ukim*) were said to be the
particular abode of the witches where they would congregate for
their nightly feast and sacrifices, devouring the hearts of their
victims.   They would only appear there in their raw red flesh,
having abandoned their skins in their homes,

The destructive powers of witches encompassed mysterious
deaths, nightmares, sickness, barrenness, impotence, persistent sores
and the mysterious appropriation of people's money.   A rainbow
signified to the Efik that a witch was drinking money from the
house at the end of the rainbow.[111]   The mode of communicating
witchcraft to another person was believed to be through food,
notably oily dishes such as coconut rice, plantain or yam cooked in
oil.   The actual nature of the *ifot* substance is unclear, but
Jeffreys noted that the gall-bladder of a leopard was called "ifot"
and so the human gall-bladder could be similarly credited.[112]
Within Efik society, witchcraft has traditionally been associated
with both sexes.   Some writers describe ifot as an esoteric art,
others refer to it as a "secret society".[113]   It may also have a
wider meaning, pertaining not only to those suspected to be in the
professional practice of wizardry, but to any person found to be
wicked, heartless, fearless, and, in the case of youths, insulting,
with no respect for the elders and the aged.[114]   In other words,
anyone displaying behaviour considered to be abnormal or
threatening to the social order was potentially a witch.

Those who suspected that they were subject to bewitchment
usually consulted an *abia-idiong* or diviner.   These so-called

"witch-doctors" would try to detect the offending evil-doers and offer preparations (at a price) to free and protect the afflicted from such malevolent influences. In this connection, we come to the Efik belief in the absolute power of the "esere bean" (*Physostigma venemosum*) over witches.[115] This dark-coloured, oval-shaped bean, which contains a powerful narcotic, was used so extensively in the killing of witches that it became known world-wide as the "Calabar bean". The seed was administered in the form of a potion to witchcraft suspects. If death resulted, this was proof of guilt and believed to be a natural consequence of the encounter between "esere" and the "ifot" substance in the abdomen of the guilty person.[116]

In the early literature, the ordeal is referred to as "drink doctor" or "chop nut", such as in the diary of Antera Duke for June 15, 1787 - "... so wee hear King Aqua was mak all his wife to Drink doctor so 11 wife Dead by the Drink Doctor ..."[117] There were variants of the ordeal involving boiling oil and "alligator pepper".[118]   Many human lives were lost as a result of these ordeals.   Accusations and ordeals were a means of expressing the social and political tensions of the community.[119]   The death of a king was a source of great instability and revealed lineage rivalries, which were resolved by accusations and counter-accusations of witchcraft, and demonstrations of innocence.

In addition, the esere bean was believed to have protective powers against witches. It was put with money, or tied to a sore limb, and often kept in houses to drive away witches at night. The use of the esere bean was eventually banned by the Nigerian government.

Accused witches were subject to special burials, to prevent their returning to the land of the living. They could be blinded and had a clay pot (*eso ntibe* - used for drying shrimps over the fire) placed over their heads. The corpse was either buried facing the ground or burnt, and the ashes distributed so as to neutralize the *ekpo ifot* (witch ghost).[120]

The *mbiam* oath involved swearing on a liquid which was believed to have the power to punish liars. The form of the oath was usually "If I do such-and-such, *mbiam*, you kill me."[121] Mbiam was believed never to harm an innocent person and to show signs before causing a guilty person to swell up, sicken and die.[122]   Such signs could be a forest bird building a nest in a house, a white vulture, or a rare kind of millipede.[123]   Rev. Hope Masterton Waddell records in his diary how the death of Archibong I in 1852 occasioned severe tension in the town, which was only allayed by all parties swearing mbiam.[124]

Mbiam was used in trading agreements to ensure fulfilment of contract, on wives to ensure faithfulness in the absence of the husband, and on newly purchased slaves who had to swear that they would not try to escape.[125]

Ibok were employed as powerful medicines, serving as protective or destructive agents.[126]   The *abia-ibok* or "medicine-man" was consulted on such issues.   Waddell describes the objects used as: "human skulls, heads of deer, goats, or alligators, the land tortoise hung up to a sacred bush in the yard, or a young chicken."[127]   In addition, a plantain, an egg and a chicken were frequently found at crossroads to ward off evil or to break some feared spell.[128]

1.2.5   The soul and death

The concept of the soul or *ukpong* was one of the earliest beliefs of the Efik and indeed other Cross River peoples.   It was thought that every individual had a soul in an animal - *ukpong unam*. There was a hierarchy of animals, the leopard being the highest, followed by wild dogs, crocodiles, boa constrictors and other snakes, wall geckos and so on.[129]   Children were taught never to kill a wall gecko (*ukpong eyen*) as it could be someone's soul.[130] It was held that "whatever happened to the animal affinity also happened at the same time and in the same way to the human being whose affinity it was."[131]   The choice of animal was made before birth and was influenced by Eka Abasi (mother god). Personality and behavioural characteristics were considered to be determined by the animal soul - if a child crawled on his/her belly, he/she would be associated with a snake, sleeping with eyes half-open designated a fish affinity.[132]   Types and manifestations of sickness were also influenced by the particular affinity.   It was common for a child to be taken to the diviner (*abia-idiong*) to determine his/her animal soul and to know how to approach it and what to offer in terms of sacrifice.

The animal or "bush-soul" as it was sometimes called, could even determine the choice of a marriage partner, for there had to be compatibility at this level - the man with a leopard bush-soul choosing a woman with a similar bush-soul in another animal for example.[133]   Children might introduce alien souls (as reincarnations) into the family community; these were either tolerated or eradicated by a diviner.[134]

Beliefs seem to vary about whether the soul remained continuously in animal form or was subject to periodic metamorphosis, usually during sleep.[135]   The Chief of Old Town, Willy Tom Robins, was upset when the missionaries cleared the ground at the foot of the hill. He claimed that he kept his shadow (ukpong) in the thicket around the spring-head where Anansa, the goddess of Old Town, dwelt, and he accused the missionaries of showing disrespect to his soul.[136]

In the case of severe sickness, with the patient failing to respond to the treatment of the "native doctor" (abia-ibok), the diviner (abia-idiong) would place a bowl in the open yard, ask people to move back and then watch the playing of the sun's rays on the open surface.[137] He would attempt to charm the "shadow" of the sick man to him, but if it flitted away to the sun and would not enter the bowl of water, then this signified that the soul of the man had already departed and that his death was imminent.[138] The separation of the soul from the body and its inability to return, usually due to the activity of witches, were a great source of fear.

From the earliest period of Efik settlement in Calabar and up to the nineteenth century, the Efik were renowned for their elaborate funeral ceremonies. Nobles and kings were buried along with their personal objects as well as their wives and slaves. It was believed that *obio ekpo* or "ghost land" was an extension of this earthly life. In Efik tradition, it is popularly recounted how the iron palace of the great Efik ruler, Eyamba V, which he had ordered from England, was demolished in the reign of Archibong II. The latter claimed that he dreamt he saw Eyamba V in the "ghost land" without a shelter and that he requested that his palace be sent to him there.[139]

Hope Waddell gives an account of the burial of King Eyamba V in May 1847:

> For the King's interment a great pit was dug, wide and deep, inside a house, and at one side of it a chamber was excavated, in which were placed two sofas. On these the body was laid, dressed in its ornaments, and a crown on its head. Then his umbrella, sword and snuff-box bearers, and other personal attendants were suddenly killed, and thrown in with the insignia of their offices, and living virgins also, it was said, according to old custom. Great quantities of food, and trade goods, and coppers were added; after which the pit was filled, and the ground trampled and beaten hard, that no trace of the grave might remain.[140]

On the death of a king or noble a mourning house (*ufok ikpo*) was erected in the compound of the deceased and friends and relatives would sleep on mats. The women would wail each morning at dawn, before dispersing to reassemble in the evening.[141] *Ufok ikpo* could last between one week and several years. The widows then observed *mbukpisi*, a special mourning period during which they kept their hair uncombed, their clothes unchanged, ate with wooden spoons off a piece of calabash and rubbed cow-dung on their face and bodies each morning as a sign of sorrow.[142] The culmination of the period of mourning was marked by public wailing in the streets, led by the senior wife as chief mourner. Other ceremonies included *utim udi* or "pounding the grave" and *eyet anwa* or "tears outside" which was a public demonstration of mourning conducted at *efe ekpe* or the "palaver shed".[143]

The burial of an eminent Efik man was subject to special conditions. He was buried secretly within the house or in the bush and the death was often kept secret for several months. People dying from particular diseases were also ritually treated so as to neutralize the evil forces which could threaten the remaining community.

The *ndok* ceremony which was held biennially in November or December seems to have had some connection with the spirits of the dead. It was essentially a ritual which involved the purging of the town of the spirits of people who had died in the two preceding years. Effigies known as *nabikim* were made and eventually thrown into the river amidst much noise-making and uproar.[144] The fact that the effigies had animal forms suggested some link between these representations and the animal souls of the departed relatives.[145] Later accounts describe the effigies as resembling human beings - "Judases" - and that the whole ceremony had been suppressed by 1913.[146]

Reincarnation also featured in the Efik belief system. Some believed that seven reincarnations were necessary before final judgement by Abasi.[147] It was possible to choose reincarnation and either return to the same family or further afield. Spirits about to reincarnate were thought to dwell around Tom Shott Island just down river from Calabar. People believed that if a child died, marked in some special way, having lost a leg or an arm for example, and another child was born with similar defects, then this was proof of reincarnation and the child was named accordingly.[148] If several children died in succession of the same mother, she would be advised by the diviner to burn the corpse of one of the children.[149]

Notes

1. E.U. Aye, *Old Calabar through the Centuries* (Calabar: Hope Waddell Press, 1967), p. 1.

2. Personal communication from Professor B. Floyd, Department of Geography, University of Calabar, April 1982.

3. Aye, pp. 1-2.

4. P.E.B. Inyang, "Pollution: A Factor in the Climate of Calabar and Environs" in *Calabar and Environs: Geographic Studies*, ed. P.E.B. Inyang, et al. (Calabar: Department of Geography, University of Calabar for the 23rd Nigerian Geographical Association Conference, Calabar, 16-21 March 1980), p. 20.

5. K.K. Nair, *Politics and Society in South Eastern Nigeria: 1841-1906* (London: Frank Cass, 1972), p. xiii.

6. See A.J.H. Latham, *Old Calabar 1600-1891: the Impact of the International Economy upon a Traditional Society* (Oxford: Clarendon Press, 1973), p. 17.

7. Ibid.

8. Nair, *Politics and Society*, p. 2; Aye, p. 4.

9. W.F. Daniell, "On the Natives of Old Callebar, West Coast of Africa", *Journal of the Ethnographical Society of London* 1 (1848):210.

10. The best source for information and debate over Efik origins and migrations is A.K. Hart, *Report of the Enquiry into the Dispute over the Obongship of Calabar*, Official Document 17, Enugu, 1964. (Hereafter referred to as the Hart Report). K.K. Nair's *The Origins and Development of Efik Settlements in*

Southeastern Nigeria, Papers in International Studies: Africa Series, no. 26 (Athens, Ohio: Ohio Center for International Studies, Africa Program, 1975) is the most helpful and objective account so far. The topic is also treated by the Efik historian E.U. Akak in his *Efiks of Old Calabar*. Volume 1, *Origin and History* (Calabar: Akak and Sons, 1981) who sets himself "the arduous task of demolishing the illogicality of the Ibibio origin of the Efik". (Foreword by Chief Magnus Oku).

11. Nair, *Efik Settlements*, p. 8.

12. See Akak, *Origin and History*, pp. 27-29 and his *Efiks of Old Calabar*. Vol. 2, *Language Origin and Grammar* (Calabar: Akak and Sons, 1982) where he attempts to demonstrate the linguistic affinities between Efik and Hebrew and Egyptian (p. 131f.).

13. Aye, p. 27.

14. See A.E. Afigbo, "Efik Origin and Migrations Reconsidered", *Nigeria Magazine* 87 (Dec. 1965):272. M.D.W. Jeffreys, in an article entitled "Efik Origin", *Nigeria Magazine* 91 (Dec. 1966):297, rejects Afigbo's argument and claims that Arochuku was originally Ibibio territory.

15. E.O. Akak, *A Critique of Old Calabar History* (Calabar: Ikot Offiong Welfare Association, 1981), p. 287. Nair, *Efik Settlements*, pp. 10-11. Akak maintains that "Ibom", meaning "mighty" or "almighty", was already part of the Efik language and used to name the area where they settled amongst the Igbo (*Origin and History*, p. 38).

16. Nair, *Efik Settlements*, pp. 11-12.

17. Hart Report, para. 65, p. 25.

18. See M.D.W. Jeffreys, *Old Calabar and Notes on the Ibibio Language* (Calabar: Hope Waddell Press, 1935), p. 1f and M.E. Noah, *Old Calabar: the City States and the Europeans,*

1800-1885 (Uyo: Scholar's Press [Nig] Ltd., 1980). For critiques of Noah's book see E.O. Akak, *A Critique of Old Calabar History* and a review by Ewa E. Henshaw, "Old Calabar: the City States and [the] Europeans, 1800-1835 [*sic*] by Sunday [*sic*] Efiong Noah" [1981?]. Typescript.

19. Nair, *Efik Settlements*, p. 13.

20. Ibid., p. 16.

21. Jeffreys, *Old Calabar*, p. 23f. Today linguists consider Efik and Ibibio as belonging to the same language cluster. Both languages belong to the Niger-Congo family and more precisely to the Benue-Congo division (Cross River: Delta Cross: Lower Cross group) according to J.H. Greenberg's *Languages of Africa* (Bloomington, Ind.: Indiana University Press, 1963).

22. Latham, *Old Calabar*, pp. 12-13.

23. See for example, P.A. Talbot, "Some Ibibio Customs and Beliefs", *Journal of the African Society* 13,51 (April 1914):241-58 and J.S. Ukpong, "Sacrificial Worship in Ibibio Traditional Religion", *Journal of Religion in Africa* 13,3 (1982):162. See also Monday B. Akpan, "Ibibio Traditional Religion and Cosmology", paper presented at the Pan-Ibibio Language and Culture Symposium, University of Calabar, April 1984 (part of his forthcoming work on the history of the Ibibio).

24. J.C. Messenger, "Ancestor Worship among the Anang: Belief System and Cult Institution" in *African Religious Groups and Beliefs*, ed. S. Ottenberg (Meernt, India: Archana Publications for Folklore Institute, 1982), pp. 63-75, and J.W. Lieber, *Efik and Ibibio Villages*, Human Ecology and Education Series, Vol. 2: South East State, Occasional Publication No. 13 (Ibadan: Institute of Education, University of Ibadan, 1971) - a study which reveals the similarities that existed in the rural areas during the 1960s.

25. Akak, *Origin and History*, p. 42.

26. Ibid. pp. 42-43; Aye, p.32.

27. Aye, p. 31 and Akak, *Origin and History*, p. 45.

28. Latham, *Old Calabar*, p. 10.

29. Nair, *Efik Settlements*, p. 20.

30. Ibid., p. 22 and Aye, pp. 32-33.

31. Aye, p. 33.

32. Aye ascribes its foundation to a deliberate attempt on the part of some Creek Town families to gain easier access to European ships (pp. 35-36). Nair suggests that it was rather due to normal population drift, *Efik Settlements*, pp. 24-26.

33. Ibid., p.27f. and Latham, *Old Calabar*, pp. 33-34.

34. As Calabar was known in the pre-colonial period. Ibid. p. 10 and Aye, p. 40.

35. Aye, p. 41.

36. The following account relies on G.I. Jones, "The Political Organization of Old Calabar" in *Efik Traders of Old Calabar*, ed. D. Forde (London: Oxford University Press for the International African Institute, 1956), p. 120f.

37. Nair, *Efik Settlements*, pp. 30-32.

38. Latham, *Old Calabar*, p. 149.

39. Ibid., p. 150.

40. Aye, p. 162.

41. Ibid., p. 165.

42. Ibid., p. 164 and Ekanem, "The Demography of Calabar", p. 24.

43. A. O'Connor, *The African City* (London: Hutchinson, 1983), p. 50, who points out that Calabar was one of the slowest growing urban centres in Africa before 1967.

44. Ibid.

45. According to the 1963 population census of the Eastern Region, Calabar Urban County Council had 74,410 inhabitants. See *Population of Nigeria: 1963*, vol. 1: *Eastern Region* (Lagos: Federal Census Office, 1964), p. 2.

46. Latham, *Old Calabar*, p. 150.

47. Ekanem, "The Demography of Calabar", p. 26.

48. E.M. Abasiekong, "Rural-Urban Migration in the Cross River State: a Case Study of Daily-Paid Migrant Workers in Calabar" in Inyang et al. p. 51.

49. Ibid. pp. 50-62.

50. The relatively low figures for the Efik are accounted for by the large numbers (some would say as high as 50% of all Efik [total c.200,000]) who live and work in other parts of Nigeria and abroad.

51. Many of them are students and teachers, as well as petty traders.

52. Consisting of several hundred members, judging from the numbers who turned out to greet the Oba of Benin when he attended the coronation of the Obong of Calabar in November 1982.

53. U.I. Ukwu, "Urbanization and Its Implications for the Development of Nigeria", in *Readings in Social Sciences: Issues in National Development*, ed. E.C. Amucheazi (Enugu: Fourth Dimension, 1980), p. 127. The author defines urbanized communities in terms of the population in settlements of 20,000 or more persons (in 1963).

54. Many people, such as from the upper regions of the state, speak Efik as a second language since Efik was the main literary language (the Bible was translated into Efik in 1868) and the language of commerce (in addition to English).

55. It is now the capital of the newly created (September 1987) Akwa Ibom State. The Cross River State University was established there in 1983.

56. These associations were banned by the new military government in 1984.

57. There has been a tradition of intermarriage between certain Efik and Oron families.

58. B. Jules-Rosette, ed., *The New Religions of Africa* (Norwood, N.J.: Ablex Publishing Corporation, 1979), p. 224.

59. See D.C. Simmons, "Analysis of Cultural Reflection in Efik Folktales," *Journal of American Folklore* 74,292 (1961):140. See also his thesis, *An Analysis of the Reflection of Culture in Efik Folktales* (Ph.D. dissertation, Yale University, 1960) which is a rich source of many aspects of Efik culture.

60. Latham, *Old Calabar*, p. 35.

61. Aye, p. 28

62. Ibid.

63. Ibid.; Rev. H. Goldie, *Calabar and Its Mission* (Edinburgh: Oliphant, Anderson and Ferrier, 1890; rev. ed. with additional chapters by Rev. J.T. Dean, 1901), p. 43.

64. E.O. Akak, *Efiks of Old Calabar*, vol. 3, *Culture and Superstitions* (Calabar: Akak and Sons, 1982), p. 297.

65. Ibid. The use of this title "edidem" or "majesty" was banned by the British colonial authorities as it was felt to compromise British sovereignity. Recent Efik kings have started to make use of the title once again.

66. Interview with Dr. Emmanuel Nsan, Calabar, June 26, 1983.

67. Latham, *Old Calabar*, p. 35.

68. Chief Ukorebi U. Asuquo, "The Diary of Antera Duke of Old Calabar (1785-1788)", *The Calabar Historical Journal* 2,1 (June 1978): 32-54.

69. Rev. Hope Masterton Waddell, *Twenty-Nine Years in the West Indies and Central Africa: a Review of Missionary Work and Adventure, 1829-1858* (London: Nelson, 1863; new ed. London: Frank Cass, 1970), p. 315.

70. Aye, pp. 28-29.

71. Goldie, p. 43.

72. Ibid.

73. Latham, *Old Calabar*, p. 35.

74. Ibid.

75. Nair, *Politics and Society*, p. 56.

76. Akak, *Culture and Superstitions*, p. 296.

77. Ibid.

78. Akak, *Culture and Superstitions*, pp. 298-99.

79. Aye, p. 28; Akak, *Culture and Superstitions*, p. 293.

80. Akak, *Culture and Superstitions*, p. 300.

81. Ibid.

82. Ibid.

83. Nair, *Politics and Society*, p. 57.

84. Goldie, p. 42.

85. Ibid.

86. Waddell, p. 381.

87. Ibid.

88. Ibid., p. 640.

89. See for example D.C. Simmons, "Specimens of Efik Folklore", *Folklore* (London) 66 (December 1955):423; Waddell, p. 380; Goldie, p. 306f.

90. Waddell, p. 640.

91. P.A. Talbot, *The Peoples of Southern Nigeria*, vol. 2: *Ethnology* (London: Oxford University Press, 1926; reprint ed., London: Frank Cass, 1969), p. 61.

92. Ibid.

93. Ibid., p. 62.

94. The Ekpe Society among the Efik should not be confused with the Ekpo Society among the Ibibio, which is also a male secret society, but is not centred on a leopard-spirit cult. See S. Preston Blier, *Africa's Cross River: Art of the Nigerian Cameroon Border Redefined* (New York: L. Kahan Gallery, 1980) p. 9. The main function of Ekpo is the purging of the society of malingering *ekpo* (ghosts or spirits), hence ensuring fertility and societal well-being. In the past it was also the chief source of law and order in the community. Masqueraders of the Ekpo society wear wooden face masks, unlike Ekpe masqueraders whose main source of symbolism is the body mask.

95. Hart Report, para. 81.

96. Akak, *Culture and Superstitions*, p. 288; Latham, *Old Calabar*, p. 36.

97. Akak, *Culture and Superstitions*, p. 288.

98. Hart Report, para. 186.

99. Akak, *Culture and Superstitions*, p. 290.

100. P.A. Talbot, *Life in Southern Nigeria* (London: Macmillan, 1923), p. 162; see also Information Division, Calabar, *Ekpe Systems in South Eastern State*, vol. 1, July 1975, p. 5.

101. Interview with Dr. Ekpo Eyo, Director of Antiquities and the Nigerian National Museums, Washington, D.C., August 14, 1984. In contrast, the Ngbe (or Mgbe) Society among the Ejagham (a secret society structured on leopard-spirits and pre-dating Ekpe) accords a greater place to the theme of femininity and female sybolism and apparently credits women with knowing the secrets of Ngbe (rites and writings), before men did. See R.F. Thompson, *Flash of the Spirit: African and Afro-American Art and Philosophy* (New York: Random House, 1983), p. 236.

102. Latham, *Old Calabar*, p. 36.

103.Ibid.

104.Aye, p. 70.

105.For an account of Ekpe (Ngbe) ritual among the Ejagham, see E. Leib and R. Romano, "Reign of the Leopard: Ngbe Ritual", *African Arts* 18,1 (November 1984):48-57. See also S. Ottenberg and L. Knudsen, "Leopard Society Masquerades: Symbolism and Diffusion", *African Arts* 18,2 (February 1985):37-44.

106.Latham, *Old Calabar*, p. 37. See also Information Division, *Ekpe Systems*, which describes the leopard as the most feared animal in the region and therefore the appropriate symbol of authority, p. 4; Thompson, *Flash of the Spirit*, chapter 5, especially pp. 239-41 and his *African Art in Motion: Icon and Act* (Los Angeles: University of California Press, 1974), pp. 173-91, for an excellent account of the Ngbe Society (close similarities with the Ekpe Society) - its rituals, masquerades, writings, symbols and its function of balancing the power of spirit/nature with the authority of town/elders.

107.Aye, p. 70.

108.Latham, *Old Calabar*, p. 40

109.Aye, p. 70.

110.Ibid.

111.D. Simmons, "An Ethnographic Sketch of the Efik People", p. 21.

112.M.D.W. Jeffreys, "Witchcraft in the Calabar Province", *African Studies* 25,2 (1966):97.

113.Noah, *Old Calabar*, p. 32; Waddell (*Twenty-Nine Years*, p. 279) notes that when addressing Europeans, the Efik referred to witchcraft as "free-mason".

114.Akak, *Culture and Superstitions*, p. 340.

115.Aye, p. 80.

116.Ibid.; see also Jeffreys, "Witchcraft in the Calabar Province", p. 96.

117."The Diary of Antera Duke" in *Efik Traders*, ed. Forde, p. 107.

118.D.C. Simmons, "Efik Divination, Ordeals and Omens", *Southwestern Journal of Anthropology* 12 (1956):223-28, observes that unlike some West African peoples who rely on one or two divinatory methods, the Efik possess several forms of divination (*afia* or "trap").

119.Nair, *Politics and Society*, p. 54.

120.Aye, p. 82.

121.D. Simmons, "Notes on the Diary of Antera Duke", in *Efik Traders*, p. 72.

122.Simmons, "An Ethnographic Sketch", p. 21.

123.Ibid.

124.Waddell, p. 499.

125.Simmons, "Efik Divination", p. 226.

126.Simmons, "An Ethnographic Sketch", p. 20.

127.Waddell, p. 277.

128.Ibid.

129.Interview with Etubom Ewa Henshaw, Calabar, August 5, 1982.

130.Ibid.; Akak, *Culture and Superstitions*, pp. 278-79.

131.Simmons, "An Ethnographic Sketch", p. 20; Goldie, p. 51.

132.Interview with Etubom Henshaw.

133.J. Parkinson, "Notes on the Efik Belief in 'Bush Soul'", *Man* 6 (1906):121.

134.Ibid., p. 122.

135.Talbot, *Life in Southern Nigeria*, p. 88.

136.Waddell, pp. 550-51.

137.Ibid., p. 548.

138.Ibid.

139.Aye, p. 48.

140.Waddell, pp. 336-37.

141.Aye, p. 26; Simmons, "An Ethnographic Sketch", pp. 22-23.

142.Simmons, "An Ethnographic Sketch", p. 23.

143.Ibid. For an additional account of Efik funerary rites, see Talbot, *Peoples of Southern Nigeria*, vol. 3, pp. 513-15. See also Simmons, *Cultural Reflection in Efik Folktales* (1959), p.334f.

144.Waddell, p. 366.

145.Ibid., p. 367.

146.See D.C. Simmons, "An Efik Judas Play", *The Nigerian Field* 26,3 (1961):100-110; Talbot, *Life in Southern Nigeria*, p. 246.

147.Interview with Etubom Henshaw.

148.Waddell, p. 381.

149.Ibid.

Chapter Two

Missionary Beginnings

2.1   Introduction

In this chapter we shall trace the planting of Christianity in
Calabar and the subsequent diversification of missionary activity in
the area.   This is in itself a major topic, but our particular
interest will be to highlight those people, events and conditions
which generated religious growth and change in our place of
study.   We are particularly interested in the processes which led to
the establishing of the early Christian denominations in Calabar.
Greater emphasis has been given to the case of the Presbyterians,
who, as missionary pioneers in the area, have had the greatest
influence on the religious life of Calabar.[1]   Our descriptive analysis
of the roots of Calabar religion in this and the earlier chapter will
serve to illuminate our understanding of later religious developments.   Special attention will be paid to those areas of interaction
between Efik traditional beliefs and customs and Christian religion
and culture, as well as to the effects of these early religious
changes for Calabar society.

2.2   Early Christian contacts

The earliest contacts with Christianity for the Efik seem to have
been in the late seventeenth century.   Father Francesco da
Monteleone, a Portuguese priest, received requests for missionaries
from certain Calabar chiefs.[2]   The proposed Calabar mission never
came to fruition as Father da Monteleone was unable to obtain the
necessary support from the Vice-Prefect of Angola.[3]   Later Efik
also encountered Christian ideas and beliefs, prior to any sustained
missionary activity, through their trading relationships with
Europeans.[4]   These trade contacts had generated an early literacy
among the Efik,[5] as well as a desire for selected aspects of
European civilization, notably its education.[6]   James Holman, who
visited Old Calabar in 1828, remarked in his diary for March 12:

> If the Christian Missionaries were to establish
> schools in the towns on the banks of these rivers,
> they would be very likely to prove eminently
> beneficial to the people, who are very desirous of
> receiving every kind of instruction, more particularly
> a knowledge of writing....[7]

The impetus towards achieving such ends came from wider economic and political changes occurring early in the nineteenth century. With the abolition of the slave trade, pressure was brought to bear on the Calabar chiefs by the British officials to sign slave-trade treaties in 1843. They were asked to renounce their slave traffic in return for compensation and British trade and friendship, or face the constant threat of British naval power.[8] Because of their cordial relationships with the British traders over the years and admiration for their superiority in many fields - "every good thing we have comes from the white people because they know more than we"[9] - the chiefs were willing to sign the treaty. However they were concerned about the commercial vacuum created by the suppression of their former means of livelihood. They sought new forms of agriculture and economic development:

> Now we can't sell slave again, we must have too
> much man for country, and want something to make
> work and trade; and if we can get seed for cotton
> and coffee, we could make trade. Plenty sugar cane
> live here, and if some man can teach we way for do
> it, we get plenty sugar too... Mr Blyth tell me
> England glad for send man to teach book and teach
> for understand God all same as whiteman. If Queen
> do so, I glad too much.[10]

King Eyamba V wrote a similar letter to Commander Raymond a few days later.[11] The Efik had had some experience with Europeans, for more than two centuries, but not with missionaries. They appear to have requested the latter for two reasons: firstly, the missionaries were the agents of the transfer of knowledge and not the transient traders.[12] Secondly, as seen in the above letter, there was a tendency to view power in religious terms. In other words many believed that the Bible held the key to European technical (and for some, cultural) superiority and that the missionaries possessed the knowledge to unlock its secrets for the Africans.

There were also significant developments occurring around this time at the Presbyterian Mission in the West Indies. The hope was growing that "among the emancipated Christians of the West Indies, valuable agents would be found for propagating the gospel in the land of their progenitors."[13]   Inspiration was received from the work of Sir T.F. Buxton, *The African Slave Trade and its Remedy*. The Scottish Missionary Society, which was responsible for the Jamaican Presbytery, considered the founding of a mission to Central Africa to be premature. However, plans were made for the "conversion of Ethiopia" and Blyth and Anderson, members of the Mission, while visiting Scotland in 1842, were able to gain support and direct information concerning Old Calabar from ship captains, and eventually were able to submit a formal proposal to the Calabar chiefs to settle the Mission there.[14]   The response was long in coming, but it contained an invitation, with an assurance of land for the use of the Mission.

2.2.1   Presbyterian inroads

The Mission to Calabar was eventually adopted by the United Secession Church (USC).[15]   So it was under these auspices that the pioneer missionaries - Mr. and Mrs. Samuel Edgerley, Andrew Chisolm, Edward Miller, a boy George - led by Rev. Hope Masterton Waddell from Dublin, set out for Calabar on January 6, 1846, on board the Waree from Liverpool.[16]

Before leaving England, Hope Waddell had received a deputation from the Baptist Missionary Society (BMS), remonstrating against the plans of the USC to move to Calabar.[17]   There was a longstanding rivalry in Jamaica between the Scottish Presbyterians and the English Baptists. An exploratory visit to Calabar had been made by Clark and Prince of the BMS in 1841; Dr. Prince was well received two years later in Calabar and in 1845 a station was claimed in Duke Town but no permanent worker was appointed.[18] Eventually an agreement was reached in London and in Calabar between the rival missions and the Baptist minister, Mr. Sturgeon, recently arrived in Calabar, agreed to abandon his project and return to Fernando Po.

The missionary party was received by King Eyamba V of Duke Town and King Eyo Honesty II of Creek Town. Large Bibles were presented amidst ceremonies of welcoming speeches and responses. King Eyo is said to have replied: "Now I am sure God will love and bless me, for I am very glad you come with this book."[19] King Eyo, like many others, had decided that the transfer of power was to be effected via the sacred text.

The missionaries approved the land which had been allocated to them on an elevated landscape (still known as "Mission Hill"), between Henshaw Town and Cobham Town, overlooking the Calabar River. King Eyo made it clear to Hope Waddell and his team that many of his chiefs were reluctant to encourage "white people to live in the country" for fear of eventual European domination.[20] They also made a visit to Obutong or Old Town, to arrange with the ruler, Chief Willy Tom Robins, for the establishment of a school there. It was notably on this score, in terms of the education they would provide, that the missionaries were welcomed into Calabar society.

Political and economic motivations were not absent however, as evidenced by the initial tension between the kings over where the Mission station would be situated. With the intervention of Governor Beecroft, it was agreed that Duke Town and Creek Town should each have a station.

At Duke Town, Sunday and other meetings were held in rotation in either the King's yard or those of the influential "gentlemen" of the town, notably those who were signatories of the letter of invitation in 1843. In Creek Town, the focus of the nascent church was the compound of King Eyo, and King Eyo himself was very often the interpreter for church meetings and services.[21]

2.2.2   Conversations with King Eyo

Hope Waddell used to engage in lengthy discourse on religious
matters with King Eyo. Their doctrinal and ethical bargaining
brought about several changes and reforms in Calabar society; their
exchanges also provide an important insight into missionary
attitudes towards traditional customs and beliefs as well as insight
into the reaction of people like King Eyo to the encroaching
Mission.

Rev. Hope Waddell and King Eyo soon discovered that they
shared "the primary truth of all religion" - in the words of Eyo,
"Every man knows that God lives, and that he made all things." As
they elaborated their discussion of the Ten Commandments, Eyo
showed his full acceptance of the second commandment, being
somewhat exceptional in the way he had rejected the *abia-idiong*
and their "juju". With regard to the keeping of the Sabbath, he
showed himself willing to give up "Calabar Sunday" (the Ekpe day
in the traditional eight-day week) and keep God's Sunday instead.
He was careful to add that such changes would meet with
opposition and would have to be introduced gradually. He was
impressed with the seventh commandment concerning marriage, and,
despite his own polygamous situation, remarked - "that be very
good law".[22]

Waddell records that great attention was paid to the miracles
of Jesus, particularly the resurrection.[23]   On another occasion,
while debating the issue of "juju" or *ibok*, Eyo declared yet again
his contempt for such objects and means, while he did add that
some Calabar customs, such as libations and sacrifices, were meant
to honour God.[24]   In their discussions they found affinity between
certain Hebrew rites and customs, for example circumcision and the
sprinkling of blood on doors, and local practices.[25]   Hope Waddell
claimed that his listeners did not understand the concept of sin
only "bad thing".[26]   However, they were able to relate to the fact
that Christ came to destroy the works of the devil, and that
witchcraft was one of the works of the devil.

2.2.3   Secular education or religious instruction?

Earlier plans by the Mission to develop agricultural projects had to
be shelved in the face of a flourishing oil palm trade and the
already well-established Efik commercial heritage. As the schools
in the Mission stations became operative, it became evident that
the "three R's" were being taught, but that the "fourth R"
(Religion), was receiving the greatest emphasis. Some pupils began
to withdraw claiming that their conversion to Christianity was the
primary aim of the missionaries.
     One of the school boys, a son of old Egbo Jack, refused
Christian instruction saying that his father sent him to school to
"saby trade book" and that he "no want to saby God".[27] This type
of reaction would seem to reflect the "secular" views of European
technology that some of the Efik (albeit a minority) must have
acquired from interaction with European traders, many of whom
cared very little about the "Book". Large crowds were attracted to
the Sunday schools in Calabar enjoying:

> the music and the drama as well as the
> opportunity to reinforce their reading skills,
> casting some doubt on the view that Africans
> wanted European education without European
> religion.[28]

In order to boost school attendances, children were lured with gifts
of books and clothes.[29]
     For Hope Waddell especially, the Bible was at the heart of all
other forms of "book" and of civilization and prosperity. In this
respect, the Calabar Mission represented a rather old-fashioned,
Scottish concept of the "organism of truth".[30] The school was
likewise the "nursery of the infant church".[31] It was the young,
unhardened minds which would prove more fruitful to the aims of
the bearers of the new religion. This is why the Presbyterians
tended to establish schools before churches, and brought in
emigrant Christians to swell the teaching ranks. It should be
noted, that the funds of the USC, which became the United
Presbyterian Church of Scotland (UPCS) in 1847, were limited, and

inadequate for the needs of a more sophisticated technical education.[32]   Energy was directed, however, to the printing press, as biblical and educational texts were translated into Efik and produced for use in the schools and church meetings.[33]

2.2.4   Humanitarian warfare and reluctant reforms

Missionizing zeal went hand in hand with the quest for civilization - a natural consequence of "the bounding self-confidence of mid-Victorian England".[34]   This was reflected to some extent in missionary attitudes to traditional customs:

> These your fashions are all contrary to the law of God and to your common sense, and must be changed, if you wish to have God's blessing of many children.[35]

Some individuals manifested extreme reactions. Samuel Edgerley, stationed at Old Town had no sympathy for the religion and culture of the "degraded and heathen people".[36]   In 1849 Edgerley entered the "palaver house" or Ekpe shed and kicked the Ekpe drum. He further offended the people and the authorities in 1854 by breaking the sacred egg and some images in the Anansa shrine at Obutong. The incidents provoked a furore in all quarters and the European traders (not the misssionaries) exerted pressure on the Acting Consul, Lynslager, in 1855 to destroy the town and put an end to the "horrid" practices and crimes for which Old Town was renowned.[37]

The act of destruction was carried out by H.M.S. Antelope on February 18, 1855. Terms were then laid down for the rebuilding of the town, missionaries were to be protected, human sacrifice abolished, twins and orphans handed over to the Mission and the esere bean ordeal to be supervised through Duke Town.[38]   Consul Hutchinson remarked at the time that "Queen Victoria and her gentlemen wish commerce and Christianity to flourish wherever the English flag waves".[39]

The Efik rulers, aware that their authority was being

increasingly eroded by the combined efforts of the Europeans, reacted by "blowing Ekpe" on the Mission House, which was tantamount to a traditional proclamation of martial law.[40]   The town authorities objected to the way in which the Mission House constituted a sanctuary for refugees from Efik law.   However their action and objections were shortlived in the face of another European show of force.

We need to retrace our steps slightly, in order to appreciate how successive reforms generated the type of religio-political clashes described above.   In 1849, at the behest of the missionaries, "Ekpenyong" - "the universal household idol" was officially denounced by King Eyo and his chiefs.[41]   On the occasion of *ndok*, the biennial purgation of the town, all the objects associated with Ekpenyong were cast into the river.   Ironically, the event took place on a Sabbath, much to the grievance of Hope Waddell.[42]

Human sacrifice, which accompanied the deaths of kings and chiefs, was undoubtedly the greatest source of concern for both missionaries and traders.   Before the government took steps in this direction, the missionaries and traders had formed a society in 1850 and brought pressure to bear on King Archibong of Duke Town and King Eyo of Creek Town for an Ekpe law (*mbet Ekpe*) to be passed suppressing human sacrifice.   Once this was achieved, Hope Waddell recommended that the mandate of the society be broadened and the name be changed to the Society for the Abolition of Inhuman and Superstitious Customs and for promoting Civilization in Calabar (SAISC).[43]   The main purpose of the society was to watch over the operation of the Ekpe law and promote the abolition of other inhuman customs such as the poison ordeal, the killing of twins and substitution   ary punishments.[44]

In the same year, the Mission at Creek Town rejoiced over the Ekpe law banning Sunday markets.   "Calabar Sunday" would no more interfere with God's day and to this effect the king had an ensign hoisted over his house every Sunday morning.[45]   Ajayi remarks that the external involvement of the British (Governor Beecroft had joined the SAISC in November 1850 and promised naval support) in matters of internal reform instigated by the missionaries was extremely questionable as a method of reform.   He argues that the civilizing zeal of the Presbyterians was exploited by the traders and the Consul as a means of weakening the African states.[46]

The missionaries were troubled by constant breaches of the laws, but it was significant that it was an internal revolt which was to ensure a break with tradition. As King Archibong I of Duke Town neared death in 1851, the slaves, who lived and worked in the outlying plantations, banded themselves together to prevent any further inhumation of their members.[47] They had heard of the new Ekpe law against human sacrifices and took a solemn covenant of blood (*eta iyip*) for their mutual protection. They were known as the "Nka Iyip" or the Blood Companions and they eventually marched into Duke Town to terrorize the urban nobility. The Blood Companions outnumbered the Ekpe fraternity and, together with the support of those unprivileged members of the nobility who had moved out to the plantations in the nineteenth century, they constituted a serious threat to the power of the urban élite. While their covenant was proscribed, their influence had the desired effect of curbing the number of human sacrifices and in 1861 they surrendered their authority back to the Ekpe Society.[48]

2.2.5   "Women no fit saby book"

From the outset, the missionaries and notably their wives had devoted much of their energy to improving the status of women and alleviating their particular sufferings. They battled against human sacrifice which affected not only the female slave population, but also the wives of deceased kings and chiefs, as they were expected to accompany them to the life beyond (*obio ekpo*).

They sought to end the persecution of twin mothers, by harbouring them and their children in the sanctum of the Mission House. The greatest opposition to the work of the SAISC on this issue came, in an unexpected way, from the women themselves. It was the elderly women, the matrons or dowagers of great families, who had gained freedom and independence by widowhood, and influence through their children, who fiercely repudiated Hope Waddell's teaching on the subject.[49] In 1871 a twin-mother was received into the church fellowship at Creek Town and despite the initial uproar, King Eyo VI and his chiefs finally acquiesced, and twin-mothers and their children were permitted to enter the town unmolested.[50]

The education of the female population met with strong cultural opposition in the early stages - "They no can saby book.... It no fit they pass boy."[51] Hope Waddell drew on his various powers of persuasion to show that educated Christian women made the best wives and mothers. He also argued on the basis that girls had to serve God and seek salvation as well as the boys, and should "know the word of God for themselves".[52] Convinced by his arguments, the king and his chiefs consented to their daughters attending school.

These prevailing attitudes naturally affected the attendance of women at church. At the time of the arrival of the Mission, Henry Cobham, a shrewd and active businessman, expressing the views of many of his fellow men, insisted that "Book [Bible] no good for women, and women no fit saby book."[53] It was only in 1850 that women attended church for the first time. Subsequent attendance was sporadic until 1868, when a land dispute between Ikoneto and Okoyong drew the Efik men away for a period of three weeks. During their absence the women took the opportunity to start attending church in far greater numbers, a trend which was not to be reversed.[54]

The question of dress for women was another point of controversy. In 1862 an Ekpe law was passed prohibiting women from putting on a gown if their husbands had not purchased the full rights of Ekpe honours. The missionaries encouraged the women to defy the law and "put on a covering as required by decency and God's word".[55] The rebellious action of the women received public support and led to the eventual repeal of the Ekpe law.

Polygamy was condemned by the missionaries as being contrary to God's law. They considered the status of the woman in a polygamous household as barely above that of a slave. Greater emphasis was placed on this issue than for example on domestic slavery.[56] Slaveholders were to be admitted into the church but not polygamists. Their inflexibility on this score revealed a lack of understanding of the political and social importance of this traditional institution.[57]   The confinement of widows also came under attack; the missionaries wanted the period of confinement reduced from six or eight years to two or three weeks.[58] Resistance to the reforms delayed the processes of change, much to the impatience of the missionaries.

2.2.6   Consolidation and subversion

The Presbyterian Mission did not record its first baptism until 1853.   This seven-year delay reflected a policy of extreme caution on both sides.[59]   Rigorous ethical demands had to be met which many found too much at variance with prevailing cultural norms. In addition, the missionaries promoted conversion as an affair of the individual, stressing personal commitment and development, while the Efik were used to taking decisions on a collective basis.[60]   Goldie was aware of this when he wrote about King Eyo Honesty's reluctance to present himself for baptism: "I fear the king may be making it too much a town matter".[61]   There were, of course, inevitable misunderstandings, such as when King Eyo revealed (in 1853) that he thought only missionaries could get baptized.[62]

In order to eliminate problems of communication, by 1862 the Presbyterians had published the New Testament in Efik and the complete Efik Bible in 1868.   It was a significant step towards eventual indigenization.   Several of the missionaries made a point of teaching in Efik and used Efik folklore as a medium for biblical instruction.[63]

The Presbyterians had an important advantage in their task of evangelization.   The recipients were already convinced of the superiority of, and the need for, "God-man's fashion".   Hutchinson relates that sacrifices were made to the "God of the white man" at Parrot Island, strategically located because it faced the sea "over which the God of the nations that sent them articles of European manufacture is supposed to preside".[64]   The missionaries capitalized upon these yearnings for Western civilization by emphasizing the establishment and development of schools as a priority over actual churches.[65]

By the time Hope Waddell left in 1858, he had been able to record a slow, but steady increase in church membership.[66] The formation of the Presbytery of Biafra in that same year gave an important impetus to the work of the Mission.[67] It meant more local (and eventually indigenous) control of the affairs of the Calabar Mission. But the relatively limited expansion into the interior, partly due to restrictions on missionary travel imposed by the Calabar rulers, the high mortality rate among missionaries and the general policy of consolidating gains, met with disapproval in Scotland. It was the arrival of the eccentric and charismatic female missionary - Mary Slessor, in 1876, which was to provide a much needed expansion and revitalization of the Mission.[68] She made new inroads into the hinterland and pressed for grass-roots education and vocational training.[69] Known as Eka Kpukpro Owo (the Mother of All Peoples), she battled for civil rights and championed the cause of women and orphaned children until her death at Use in 1915.

At first, the missionaries had effected change by appealing to the rulers and the Ekpe authorities, but they were to appeal increasingly to the British authorities for support in the speedier implementation of their objectives. They found the Ekpe Society to be a repressive form of government and sought to destroy its power. To some extent this was achieved with the Hopkins Treaty of 1878 which was drawn up by the pro-missionary Consul, David Hopkins, and signed by the king and chiefs of Duke Town "to put an end to the murderous customs of the people".[70] The treaty, which represents something of a landmark in the interaction between the missionary and traditional world-views, outlawed human sacrifice, the use of the esere bean, the killing of twins, as well as the harassment of women by Ekpe masqueraders. It also reduced the period of mourning and confinement of widows to one month and guaranteed the freedom of the town to twin-mothers.[71]

Another major development in 1879 was the agreement by King Archibong III to be publicly crowned in Duke Town Presbyterian Church and swear a Christian Oath which was in effect a solemn ratification of the 1878 treaty.[72] While the traditional coronation (*uyara ntinya*) was retained, this nonetheless constituted another institutional landmark, for it was tantamount to the establishment of Christianity as a "state religion".

The suppression of some customs and practices did not always spell total elimination, but sometimes led to religious and cultural regeneration. For example in the case of *ndok* - the biennial purgation of the town from all evil spirits - the ceremony, according to contemporary accounts, appears to have gone into decline for reasons which are not clear, but only to reappear in a changed form.[73] The "driving the year" ceremony (*ubin usua*) has become institutionalized as a New Year's Eve celebration, while the *nabikim* effigies have been reinterpreted as "Judas" figures in a boys' ceremony which takes place on Good Friday.[74] It is possible that the Judas play (*mbre Judas*) dates back to the end of the nineteenth century, even though the metamorphosis was most likely generated by non-Efik influences.[75]

The ceremony of "throwing water" or *uduokmong* consisted of a form of baptism for a slave entering his new master's house.[76] He was required to stand under the eaves and water was thrown onto the roof so as to run down onto his head, signifying his introduction to a Calabar family and separation from his old country and customs.[77] With the decline of slavery, the meaning of this ceremony, as well as the actual term, were transferred to the Christian rite of baptism.[78]

The declaration of the Oil Rivers Protectorate in 1885 brought important changes for the town of Calabar, which in turn served to consolidate the Presbyterian cause. There was an increase in the European population, as well as an influx of rural migrants and English-speaking West Africans to work in the colonial government as clerks, artisans and messengers.[79] While some of the latter were a useful addition to the Mission, others chose to increase the facilities for public drinking in Calabar.[80]

Before turning to a brief assessment of the image and impact of the Presbyterian Mission, we should examine two significant developments in the religious history of Calabar.

2.2.7   Internal and external competition

Calabar's first recorded schism, at least within the Christian tradition, was not an indigenous reaction to colonial domination. It occurred in 1881 as the result of an ongoing tussle between the missionaries Anderson and Ross. It was essentially a clash of personalities and generations. Ross, tempestuous and impatient, criticized Anderson for his collusion with local rulers, and was eventually recalled by the home mission.[81]   Ross refused and started his own church on land given by Eyamba House.[82]   The whole issue was complicated by local politics, which was why Ross was able to draw off five teachers and a substantial part of the congregation. Ross had established a reputation for himself as the "terror of all oppressors" and many thousands of people reportedly wrote to Scotland in his favour.[83]

When Ross died in 1884, it was expected that the congregation would return, but they did not and Mrs. Ross managed to find a successor from the Grattan Guiness Institute in London to perpetuate the work of the schism.[84]   The breakaway group therefore survived, but never acquired the recognition that Ross had sought. Goldie naturally saw the whole affair as detrimental to the "cause of the Gospel" in Duke Town, as people started to enquire if there were two Gods.[85]   Details are scarce on the eventual fate of the church, but it seems that it was taken over by the Apostolic Church, after some association with the Primitive Methodists and the Qua Iboe Mission.

The second important development in the religious life of Calabar was engendered by the arrival of a small Hausa batallion as part of the establishment of the Protectorate in 1891. The Hausa soldiers brought with them their Islamic religion and before long Muslim traders from the north came to Calabar and a mosque was built.   Rev. John Taylor Dean describes how the Efik were impressed by the strange dress and habits of the newcomers and their regular devotions, and he predicted that this vague fear might lead to eventual imitation.[86] This was not to be the case.

2.2.8   "God-man's fashion" reviewed

It has been argued that the most significant social changes in Calabar society were not brought about by the work of the Mission but by an internal restructuring of economic, social and political relationships.[87] The Efik, epitomized by King Eyo Honesty, showed the capacity to adapt internally, to "modernize" without becoming "westernized" or "Christianized".[88] The failure of the missionaries to effect a more radical evangelization was due, in the view of one observer, to their lack of understanding of the traditional system and their predominantly ethnocentric approach.

Others consider that the Mission had an influence out of proportion to its size, but that the actual impact of Christianity on the structure of Efik society was nil.[89] The abolition of particular customs was only of significance to those concerned, although Latham recognizes the importance of the Mission households in protecting and emancipating refugee slaves.[90] For some the main influence of the Mission as stemming from its teachings on equality, which had the strongest appeal among the slaves.[91] The threat which this posed to the Efik social system was one of the reasons why many of the Efik rulers, while supporters of the Mission in many respects, held back on baptism and full church membership.

Efik historians by and large write positively about the Calabar Mission, although they are generally (as in the case of Aye and Akak) products of the missionary system. Aye states "Jamaica and Scotland have combined to influence Calabar history, not for evil but for good, and have seasoned it more abundantly."[92] Akak writes in similar vein, reserving his appreciation for the humanitarian efforts of the early Europeans.[93]

Ayandele writes enthusiastically about the way in which, and the pace at which, the Presbyterian missionaries devolved power on their converts.[94] Not only were Africans given posts of responsibility on the Mission Committee, but they were also put in charge of Mission stations.[95] Ayandele considers this trust of the Africans by the Presbyterians as quite exceptional for the time, and believes it to have been the main reason behind the absence of sectarianism in the Mission.[96] Ayandele's observation is indeed valid for the early period of Presbyterianism in Calabar (although he appears to discount the Ross schism): Presbyterian polity, particularly in terms of translating the Bible into Efik, was to have sometimes unintended consequences for later religious development.

In terms of the Nigerianization of the Mission's Education Authority, there was a commitment to Nigerian control from 1945. Despite a certain paternalism in practice, Nigerian Presbyterians were in charge of the Presbyterian school system at the time of the country's independence in 1960.[97]

Many would argue that it was in the field of education that the Presbyterians made their greatest contribution and impact. (This was perhaps all the more remarkable given the essentially evangelical constitution of the Mission in the early days and the fact that few of the missionaries had received any educational training.) Their educational objectives were firmly grounded in the Presbyterian ideals of democracy and equality. Education was to be available to all, children and adults. Mass education was considered to be essential to both active mass participation in church government and personal salvation. Full membership in the Mission community was dependent on attaining acceptable minimal literacy levels, as well as the profession of faith. Presbyterian schools were characterized by their well-rounded education - "school success was measured morally, physically and personally, as well as intellectually".[98]

The leper colony at Itu was a microcosm of social, educational and medical development. The Presbyterian policy of interdenominational cooperation reflected the Mission's adaptation to changing conditions and had beneficial consequences in the educational sector.[99]

In our examination of the establishment of the Presbyterian Mission in Calabar we have been primarily interested in religious interrelationships, but have also tried to be aware of the interplay of the religious domain with social, economic, political and cultural factors. The encounter was fundamentally between two cultures and world-views, although in reality it was far more complex.[100] Neither side represented a homogeneous entity: there were the viewpoints of the British authorities, the traders and the missionaries, as well as the differing views within each category.

Among the Efik themselves, there were divergent opinions over whether the Europeans should be encouraged and emulated, or mistrusted and rejected. We should not ignore the possible role played by certain of the ship captains (such as Captain Turner who was the intermediary between the Efik rulers and the Presbyterian missionaries in the initial stages) in shaping Efik decisions. Nor should we disregard the influence of those Efik who had travelled to Britain to learn English and commerce.[101]

The Efik soon realized that the religious component was not only central but subversive. In order to receive the benefits of European knowledge, they found themselves increasingly obliged to make compromises and bargains, which ultimately entailed changes and reforms within their own society. Several Efik leaders had anticipated this disruption from the outset, when the missionaries had chosen to install themselves on *akai ekpo* (evil forest or "bad bush") where the corpses of slaves and twin-babies were placed. This symbolic superimposition was seen by many as a foretaste of future developments. Initial caution later gave way to cultural defence: "It be Calabar fashion" was a popular response. There was never the type of resistance which might have generated nationalistic religious or political movements. Efik conservatism and their trading heritage facilitated the growing assimilation of European beliefs and customs. Although, as has been shown earlier and will be apparent in the course of the study, the degree of synthesis varied considerably. The fact that cricket took on divine significance and that English etiquette became a behavioural model for the Efik élite should not be taken as evidence of a unilinear process of Europeanization.

Conceptions of power were an essential feature of this early period of religious interaction. The missionaries appeared to fear resistance and failure rather than the traditional religious powers per se. The Efik feared colonial might, but they also demonstrated a fear of the perceived and latent power behind "God-man's fashion", such as when Hope Waddell exploited people's fear of a total eclipse of the sun (in 1848), explaining it as a show of God's power and wrath because the Efik were not respecting his teachings and His "Holy day".[102] Both sides drew on collective support (Ekpe Society, colonial authorities) to further their cause and protect their interests. Both shared a belief in the Supreme Being (although this was not recognized by many of the early missionaries), but the missionaries were believed to have more access to and manipulation of God's power through their greater ritual knowledge.

The following account recorded by Rev. Hugh Goldie in the late 1880s merits inclusion here since it sheds light on Efik attitudes to the Europeans:

> Got an account of a man who died last week and returned to life, bringing a message from Abasi to the effect that white men were quite right in saying that it was wrong to kill people for the dead, or to keep human skulls as charms, but their objects of devotion and rites of worship were quite proper....The white people were charging too much for their goods. Unless they returned to their former charges, Abasi would prevent the growth of the oil-nuts, and would teach the Calabar people to make cloth and all kinds of goods for themselves.[103]

The "message" reflects a tendency to treat white people as a single category; there is an obvious respect for the religious ways of Europeans, but resentment concerning economic exploitation. The speaker refers to a type of millennial solution which would entail a divinely enforced transfer of knowledge and eventually, power.

By the end of the nineteenth century, the facts spoke for themselves: the Presbyterians had succeeded in laying the foundations of Christianity in Calabar. For almost half a century they enjoyed a virtual monopoly of the Mission field around Calabar. By the turn of the century, the religious landscape was changing and they were starting to operate amidst a situation of denominational pluralism.

2.3   Early religious pluralization

Before the 1880s, the only other neighbour of the Presbyterians engaged in the evangelization of south-eastern Nigeria was the Church Missionary Society (CMS) Niger Mission.[104]   However the mission fields of the latter and the United Presbyterian Church of Scotland were sufficiently well apart to prevent conflict.   The Baptists had settled in Victoria in the Cameroons, and a spirit of fellowship and cooperation existed between all the various missionaries scattered along the Guinea Coast.[105]   The latter part of the nineteenth century marked the end of the peaceful coexistence of previous years.   This was chiefly due to Calabar's increased status as capital of the new Oil Rivers Protectorate. Other missions wanted to move into the town, if only to cater for their members who had migrated to the region.

2.3.1   The "foreigners'" church and the Niger Delta
Pastorate

Before the start of the twentieth century, civil servants and commercial people from Sierra Leone, the Gold Coast, the Gambia, Liberia and Yorubaland had begun to settle in Calabar, and, since they were mostly Anglicans and Methodists, they initially worshipped in the only Protestant church in the town - Duke Town Church of the United Free Church of Scotland (UFCS - as it became known from 1900).[106]

As a result of strained relations, the group eventually severed their Presbyterian connection and started to convene their own meetings and services at a local residence.[107]   The congregation was at that stage known as the Foreign and Native Pastorate Church or the "foreigners' church".   The first church building, known as Holy Trinity Church, was dedicated in May 1911 by Venerable Archdeacon D.C. Crowther.[108]

The Foreign and Native Pastorate Association was persuaded by Bishop James Johnson to affiliate with the Niger Delta Pastorate (NDP) which then proceeded to enter into negotiations with the UFCS over the establishment of the new church.[109]   As Calabar was felt to be the privileged domain of the Presbyterian Mission, for the NDP to open a church it was agreed, firstly, that they should surrender Arochukwu to the UFCS, and, secondly, that Efik who were already Christians should not be admitted into membership of the new church.[110]   The agreement was revoked finally in 1919,[111] and Efik were to be admitted to the church, but services were not to be held in the Efik language.   It was hoped by the NDP that this lifting of the ban would help stem the exodus of members into some of the other newly created churches.[112]

The first two converts, an Efik and an Igbo, were baptized in Holy Trinity Church in March 1915.   The church began with a Yoruba and an English section and soon added an Igbo section, a structure which it has retained up until the present day.   The Igbo aspired after greater autonomy and in 1939 a rift was narrowly averted.[113]   By 1952 the congregation stood at 2000 (English 300, Yoruba 500, Igbo 1500).[114]

For a time, during the Second World War and some years after, Holy Trinity Church hosted "state services" perhaps because of its links with Britain and its wide-ranging congregation.   Work began on a new church building in 1964, which was to be destroyed only a few years later by federal troops during the Nigerian civil war.[115]

2.3.2   Missionary colonization and boundary disputes

At the beginning of the twentieth century, Rev. Wilkie established a reputation for himself as a fervent defender of Presbyterian supremacy in Calabar, battling (in vain) against the encroachment of the Catholics, the NDP, the Wesleyans and the African Church from Lagos.

There was friction generated also by the establishment of the Primitive Methodist Mission at Jamestown, a few miles down river from Calabar, in 1894.[116]   Several years later in 1905, the Primitive Methodists asked to place a man in the port to handle their transport and freight.[117]   The Presbyterian Foreign Mission Board was dismayed by what they saw as an attempt to begin work in Calabar, particularly in view of the fact that there were extensive unevangelized territories around the present Methodist posts.[118]

Wilkie sought government support to try to stem the flood of missions. This resulted in a government declaration of May 2, 1907, in which it was stated that "no Branch establishment of any mission is allowed to be instituted without first obtaining the necessary permission from the Government."[119]

Had the decree become operative, it would have marked the beginning of government control over evangelism, with curtailment of the freedom of expansion.[120] The CMS took steps to have the policy revoked and Wilkie was ridiculed by the Wesleyans for having involved the government unnecessarily in missionary matters.[121]

A conference was called at Calabar in April 1909 to map out the member missions' fields (UFCS, PMM, and the Qua Iboe Mission [QIM], led by Rev. Samuel Bill).[122] The conference was reconvened in June after a survey of the territories had been conducted, although the NDP were still not included. Members agreed to respect the territorial rights of the others and recognized their "common enemy" - Roman Catholicism.[123]

Following the boundary settlements and inspired by the Edinburgh Missionary Conference in 1910 with its recommendations for missionary cooperation, the Presbyterians organized a conference in Calabar one year later to discuss practical issues such as discipline, marriage, training of ministers, education and attitudes to African music and dance.[124] Wilkie made a plea for an end to denominational competition in order to establish the "one Church of Christ".[125] In the face of the galloping success of the "native churches", he recommended a free-for-all in the mission field.[126] While his proposals were not adopted, the conference provided an important impetus to territorial and membership expansion.[127] A Continuation Committee was appointed to carry on the work.[128]

2.4   Roman Catholic Mission

In the last decade of the nineteenth century, Chief Essien Etim
Offiong III, while on business tours of West Africa, came in
contact with the work of the Roman Catholic Mission (RCM).[129]
He was particularly impressed with the progress that the RCM had
made in Matadi, Zaïre, over a period of fifteen years, compared
with the achievements of the Presbyterians after almost half a
century in Calabar. As a result he wrote to the Pope requesting
for the RCM to be extended to Calabar. The letter was referred
to the Asaba Vicariate and in 1894 two French priests, Rev. Drs.
Léon and Lejeune and another priest, visited Calabar from Onitsha,
returning finally in 1903 to begin the work of the Mission.[130]

When Father Shanahan, a Holy Ghost priest, arrived in 1908, he
was quick to realize that education was the most powerful means of
evangelization and "faith could not exist without knowledge". The
development of schools henceforth preoccupied the Catholics,[131]
becoming not only the major source of conversion, but also a place
for worship, such as is still the case today.[132]

Sister Mary Charles Walker, an Irish Sister of Charity, arrived
in Nigeria in 1923, in response to a call by Bishop Shanahan, after
the French sisters (Sisters of St. Joseph of Cluny) in charge of the
only girls' school in the Vicariate, had been withdrawn.[133] Sister
Mary Charles proved to be an outstanding educator and was
instrumental, not only in the reorganization and the setting up of
numerous schools, but also in the creation of an indigenous
religious congregation - the Congregation of the Handmaids of the
Holy Child Jesus (HHCJ) - in 1931.[134]

The Holy Child Sisters, an international order involved in girls'
education, arrived in 1930 to supplement the work of the HHCJ.
The first Efik priest, Rev. Father Michael Offiong, was ordained in
1972, some sixty-nine years after the establishment of the RCM in
Calabar.[135]

Calabar remained part of the Vicariate of Southern Nigeria
until 1934 when Calabar and Ogoja provinces were made into the
Prefecture of Calabar with Mgr. James Moynagh as first prefect.
Calabar achieved the status of vicariate in 1947, and diocese in
1950.[136] Members of St. Patrick's Missionary Society (Kittegan

Fathers) have also been active in the diocese.[137]

Some Efik Presbyterians showed their support by contributing to the building of the Sacred Heart Cathedral in Calabar.[138] The RCM attracted more Ibibio, Qua and Efut than Efik adherents.[139]

2.5   Wesleyan Methodists

In 1775 two runaway slaves were brought to England, where they gained their freedom and were given Christian instruction in Methodist circles in Bristol.[140] After one of them had accepted baptism, the "two young princes from Calabar in Guinea" returned to Calabar and asked for missionaries to be sent.[141] Two German brothers, by the name of Syndrum, who were members of the Methodist Society in Bristol, went out in response to the call, but soon died and were not to be replaced.[142]

Owing to tension between the NDP and the Wesleyan Methodist Mission (WMM), the latter eventually broke away from the "foreigners' church" in Calabar to form their own congregation around 1914, under the leadership of Rev. W.G. Nicol, the Sierra Leone schoolmaster.[143] The development of the Wesleyan congregation occurred chiefly in response to the situation of the Methodist "diaspora". There was the use of Efik by the Presbyterians, which "strangers" and "travellers" could not understand.[144] There was also the fear that members of the Methodist "diaspora" if not strengthened in the field "on their returning home are completely lost to Methodism".[145] They either converted to another denomination or gave up church life completely. These types of problems were not limited to the Methodists alone, as we shall see in our discussion below on the growth of the spiritual churches.

In 1926 the Primitive Methodists took over the running of the Wesleyan Methodist Church in Calabar, since the Wesleyan authorities claimed that they could not keep up the administration of the Calabar branch because of the distance from the Lagos headquarters.[146] In 1932 there was the union of the Methodist

Church, resulting in the creation of the Methodist Church of
Nigeria. Calabar became part of the Eastern Nigeria district.

2.6   Lutheran Church

The villages of Ibesikpo near Uyo were under the sphere of
influence of the Qua Iboe Mission (QIM), and by 1925 there were
at least fourteen churches in the area.[147] However discontentment
grew at the inability of the QIM to provide educational institutions
in the immediate vicinity for their children, and so they made their
own plans to train a pastor.[148] Jonathan Udo Ekong left for the
United States in 1928. It seems that the Jamaican Presbyterian
missionaries at Creek Town influenced the decision of the Ibesikpo
people, saying that black-led American churches were a better
proposition than white-led European ones.[149]

After disciplinary action by the QIM, sixteen Ibesikpo
congregations seceded in December 1930 to form the Ibesikpo
United Church.[150] This was seen as an interim measure, for their
main ambition was to affiliate with a major missionary body which
would furnish the necessary educational support.[151]

While in the United States, Ekong made contact with a group
of American blacks in the Lutheran Church - Missouri Synod, who
were interested in planning missionary work in Africa.[152] After
many deliberations and setbacks caused by the economic depression
of the thirties, the Lutheran team finally arrived in Nigeria in
1936. Black American clergy began to arrive just a few years ago
in Port Harcourt.[153]

The establishing of the Lutheran Church in Calabar itself
followed the pattern of the other churches, in that Lutheran
members who travelled to Calabar for work set up house groups for
worship, rather than join any of the other existing Protestant
churches.[154] These house groups grew into larger congregations to
form eventually the various churches of the Calabar district. The
growth of the Lutheran Church in Calabar differed from other
districts in that the early members were established Lutherans and
not from other Christian demominations.[155] Until the onset of

the civil war, the Christian Radio Station in Uyo, which was run by the Lutheran Church, beamed religious radio programmes to Calabar.

2.7   Qua Iboe Mission

The Presbyterians were unable to keep up with the demand for missionaries, notably in outlying areas such as Ibeno, on the mainland coast to the south-west of Calabar.   When the people there expressed their wish for the Presbyterian Mission to be extended to their own area, they received a negative reply. The letter was referred to Grattan Guiness at Harley College (an evangelical, non-denominational college which supported many missions).[156]   One of the students, Samuel Bill, chose to undertake the mission.   He arrived at Ibeno in 1887 and before long the newly established mission, by the name of the Qua Iboe Mission (QIM), had its headquarters at Belfast and a steady stream of converts and communicants.[157]   The move to Calabar was delayed by the boundary agreements and it was not until 1965 that the QIM established itself in the township.[158]

2.8   Presbyterian developments

In 1895 the Hope Waddell Training Institution was opened.[159]   It was a comprehensive school, modelled on the Scottish omnibus school concept, intended to meet the urgent need for industrial and technical training.[160] The school reportedly had the honour of introducing soccer to Nigeria, and of producing *The Calabar Observer*, the first regular eight-page journal in southern Nigeria at that time.[161]   The school went on to become one of the leading boys' secondary schools in Nigeria, drawing pupils from all over the country, many of whom went on to become national figures.   The school therefore played a key role in expanding the sphere of influence and reputation of the Presbyterian Church in Nigeria.[162]

The present Duke Town Church was officially opened in 1904 to cope with the larger congregations. There was a growth of interest in the writing and publication of Efik church hymns around this time.[163] In 1921 the Synod of Biafra was constituted, followed in 1930 by the formation of the Christian Council of Nigeria. In 1929 the United Free Church of Scotland merged with the established Church of Scotland. The Presbyterian Church of Biafra was instituted in 1946, but it later became the Presbyterian Church of Eastern Nigeria in 1952, to be renamed the Presbyterian Church of Nigeria in 1960.

Centenary celebrations began in 1946, together with a period of self-examination, since it was recognized that the growth of the church and its spiritual life had been slow in comparison with the work of the Mission in the educational and medical fields.[164]

Notes

1. No attempt is being made in the present study to write a definitive study of the Presbyterian Mission in Calabar since the information is available elsewhere (see below).

2. See P. Streit and J. Dindinger, eds., *Bibliotheca Missionum*, Afrikanische Missions-Literatur, vol. 16 (1600-1699) (Freiburg, 1969), p. 724.

3. Ibid.

4. See Daniell, "On the Natives of Old Callebar", p. 223.

5. See A. Shepherd, *The Origins and Development of Literacy in Old Calabar to c.1860*, M.Litt. thesis, University of Aberdeen, 1980.

6. See E.A. Ayandele, *The Missionary Impact on Modern Nigeria: 1842-1914* (London: Longman, 1966), p. 3.

7. Cited by Aye, p. 110.

8. See J.F.A. Ajayi, *Christian Missions in Nigeria, 1841-1891: The Making of a New Elite* (London: Longman, 1965), p. 54.

9. Eyo Honesty II (1846) cited by Ayandele, p. 17.

10. Letter from Eyo Honesty II to Commander Raymond, Man-of-War Ship "Spy", Creek Town, December 1, 1842 cited in Waddell, Appendix II, p. 664.

11. Ibid., pp. 663-64.

12. The traders sometimes remained in the area for at least a year, but they lived on board ship and conducted most of their transactions from there.

13. Waddell, p. 206.

14. Ibid., p. 208.

15. The United Secession Church was formed in 1820 from dissenting groups which broke away from the Church of Scotland early in the eighteenth century because of disagreements concerning patronage (the practice that allowed wealthy landowners to appoint ministers to local parishes). It united with the Relief Church to form the United Presbyterian Church in 1847. The Free Church of Scotland was organized by dissenting members of the Church of Scotland in 1843. They were known as the Evangelicals, and, as stricter Calvinists, they disagreed with the other main group in the church - the Moderates - chiefly over the question of patronage. The Free Church grew rapidly within a few years and in 1900 merged with the United Presbyterian Church to form the United Free Church of Scotland, which reunited with the Church of Scotland in 1929.

16. Waddell, p. 228.

17. Waddell, p. 229.

18. C.P. Groves, *The Planting of Christianity in Africa*, vol. 2 (London: Lutterworth Press, 1954), p. 37.

19. Aye, p. 116.

20. Ibid.

21. Ibid., pp. 119-20.

22. Ibid., pp. 275-6.

23. Ibid.

24. Ibid., pp. 277-78.

25. Ibid., p. 291.

26. Ibid., p. 278.

27. Ibid., p. 289.

28. W.H. Taylor, "Missionary Education in Africa Reconsidered: the Presbyterian Educational Impact in Eastern Nigeria", *African Affairs* 83,331 (April 1984):195. See also his thesis, *Calabar - An Educational Experiment*, Ph.D. dissertation, Exeter University, 1980.

29. The same methods were employed in the administering of vaccinations against the dreaded *isoti* or smallpox. Only those who promised to attend Sabbath worship received the vaccine. See A.A. Okon, *The Church of Scotland and the Development of British Influence in Southern Nigeria*, Ph.D. thesis, University of London, 1973, p. 207.

30. Personal communication from Prof. A.F. Walls, December 1984.

31. Ajayi, p. 134.

32. Ibid., p. 57.

33. See A.N. Ekpiken, *A Bibliography of the Efik-IbibioSpeaking Peoples of the Old Calabar Province of Nigeria: 1668-1964* (Ibadan: Ibadan University Press, 1970), p. 81f. for a list of such works.

34. Ayandele, p. 9.

35. Waddell, p. 383.

36. Ayandele, p. 23.

37. Ayandele, pp. 23-24; Ajayi, pp. 54-55.

38. Ayandele, p. 24.

39. Ibid.

40. Ibid., p. 25.

41. Waddell, p. 397.

42. Ibid.

43. Ibid., p. 65.

44. Waddell, p. 423.

45. Ibid., p. 438.

46. Ajayi, p. 65.

47. Aye, p. 96f.

48. Ibid., p. 100.

49. Waddell, p. 484.

50. Goldie, pp. 230-31.

51. Waddell, p. 346.

52. Ibid.

53. Aye, p. 119.

54. Ibid., p. 124.

55. Goldie, p. 216.

56. Ajayi, p. 103.

57. See Nair, *Politics and Society*, pp. 62-63.

58. Aye, p. 130.

59. Referring to a letter from Young Eyo Honesty in 1849, Hope Waddell wrote: "he ... inquired the way of salvation and desired it but was not prepared to give up all for it. We ... would not hurry him to make a profession by baptism before his heart was so confirmed in the love of truth that he could be defended for consistent obedience to it." (p. 396)

60. Taylor, "Missionary Education", p. 197.

61. Goldie, p. 169.

62. Ibid., p. 168.

63. Ibid., chapter 15; Waddell, pp. 379-80.

64. Cited by Simmons, "Notes on the Diary of Antera Duke", p. 69.

65. The first chapel was not opened until 1855.

66. There were 21 native communicants, 24 catechumens and more than 150 at church services. See Waddell, p. 630. Goldie was to remark some years later that many of the early converts were non-Efik, see Ajayi, p. 121n. Some were of slave origin, such as the first convert and his sister.

67. See D.M. McFarlan, *Calabar: the Church of Scotland Mission, 1846-1946* (London: Thomas Nelson, 1946), p. 52.

68. There are several works on Mary Slessor; the most recent is by J. Buchan, *The Expendable Mary Slessor*, (Edinburgh: St. Andrew's Press, 1980).

69. Taylor, "Missionary Education", pp. 197, 200.

70. Akak, *Culture and Superstitions*, p. 346.

71. Ibid., p. 347.

72. See the *Souvenir Programme of the Coronation Service of His Royal Highness Edidem Bassey Ephraim Adam III* (Calabar: Coronation Planning Committee, 1982), p. 23.

73. See Simmons, "An Efik Judas Play", p. 105.

74. Ibid.

75. Ibid., pp. 107,109.   See also P.E.H. Hair, "Beating Judas in Freetown", *The Sierra Leone Bulletin of Religion* 9,1 (June 1967):16-18 who suggests that the custom passed to Calabar from Freetown.   He also examines the evidence that this was originally a Roman Catholic practice which was a feature of the former Portuguese settlements in West and Central Africa. He further points out that "Judas-burners" were common in Liverpool, having copied the idea from Spanish and Portuguese sailors or Irish Catholics.   It is not improbable, therefore, that the Efik who travelled to Liverpool in the seventeenth and eighteenth centuries to learn commerce and English, may have observed the custom there.

76. Waddell, p. 539.

77. Ibid.

78. Aye, p. 96.

79. Goldie, p. 353.

80. Ibid., p. 354.

81. Ajayi, pp. 264-65; Goldie, p. 247; for a full account of the affair, see A.J.H. Latham, "Scottish Missionaries and Imperialism at Calabar", *Nigeria Magazine*, nos. 132-133 (1980):47-55.

82. Ajayi, p. 265.

83. Umi Ndi Africanus to Editor, *The African Times*, February 1, 1882, p. 20.

84. Goldie, p. 248.

85. Ibid., p. 247.

86. Ibid., p. 354.

87. Nair, *Politics and Society*, p. 69.

88. Ibid.

89. Latham, *Old Calabar*, pp. 102-3.

90. Ibid., p. 105.

91. Noah, *The City States*, p. 111.

92. Aye, p. 134.

93. Akak, *Culture and Superstitions*, p. 348.

94. Ayandele, p. 192.

95. The Reverend Esien Esien Ukpabio, the first local convert and first local minister, was put in charge of Adiabo, and Reverend Asuquo Ekanem was given the responsibility of Ikonetu (ibid).

96. Ayandele, pp. 194-95.

97. Ibid.

98. Ibid., pp. 196-97

99. Ibid. pp. 201-3.

100.Cf. R.W. Wyllie, "Some Contradictions in Missionizing", *Africa* 46 (1976):198.

101.See Shepherd.

102.Okon, p. 197.

103.Goldie, p. 155.

104.G. Tasie, *Christian Missionary Enterprise in the Niger Delta: 1864-1918* (Leiden: E.J. Brill, 1978), p. 205.

105.O. Kalu, *Divided People of God: Church Union Movement in Nigeria, 1875-1966* (New York and Lagos: Nok Publishers, 1978), p. 2.

106.Orok O. Asuquo, *Patronal Festival Sermon*, Holy Trinity (Anglican) Church, Calabar, June 10, 1979, p. 4.

107.*History of the Holy Trinity Anglican Church 1911-1961* (Calabar: Jubilee Committee, July 1-9, 1961), p. 3. Asuquo, *Patronal Festival Sermon*, p. 4.

108.Asuquo, p. 4.

109.Tasie, pp. 220-21.

110.*History of Holy Trinity*, p. 5.

111.Ibid.

112.Ibid., p. 6.

113.Ibid., pp. 7-8.

114.Asuquo, p. 7.

115.In a survey conducted in 1964 the Anglican Church in Calabar recorded an adult membership of 871 (much reduced compared to the figures of 1952) and two ordained clergy, but no church workers for its one branch. See Kalu, *Divided People*, appendix IV, p. 116.

116.See F.W. Dodds, Memorandum on Boundaries, February 9, 1939, p. 1. Typescript.

117.Kalu, *Divided People*, p. 2.

118.Ibid.

119.Tasie, p. 222.

120.Ibid.

121.Ibid., pp. 222-23.

122.Ibid., p. 223.

123.Kalu, *Divided People*, p. 3.

124.Kalu, *Divided People*, p. 4.

125.Ibid., p. 5.

126.Tasie, p. 227.

127.Ibid., p. 228.

128.Groves, vol. 3, p. 292.

129.The information regarding the establishment of the RCM is taken from the private notes of Rev. Fr. Aloysius N. Ebong, Calabar. The latter consulted the archives of Frank U.A. Offiong (one of the sons of Chief E.E. Offiong III) Essien Town, Calabar and interviewed Etubom T.A. Effiom (a contemporary of Chief Offiong), and also consulted his undated diary at No. 6 Ewa Nsa Street.

130.Sister R. Edet, "History of the Catholic Church in Calabar: 1903-1950", Calabar, [1979]. Mimeo.

131.See C.M. Cooke, "Church, State and Education: the Eastern Nigeria Experience, 1950-67", in *Christianity in Independent Africa*, ed. E. Fasholé-Luke et al., p. 193. See also P.B. Clarke, "The Methods and Ideology of the Holy Ghost Fathers in Eastern Nigeria, 1885-1905," *Journal of Religion in Africa* 6,2 (1974), who notes that at the beginning of the twentieth century the school in Old Calabar run by the Holy Ghost Fathers with its 300 pupils was the most prosperous of all their schools in eastern Nigeria, p. 97.

132.Edet, "History of the Roman Catholic Church in Calabar", p. 21.

133."The Handmaids of the Holy Child Jesus: Origin and Development" in *Golden Jubilee Magazine of the Holy Child Federated Alumnae - Cross River State Zone* (Calabar, 1980), p. 12.

134.See O. Isong, "Handmaids of Holy Child Jesus: Body of Exemplary Clergies", *The Sunday Chronicle*, September 19, 1981.

135.P. Kwendi, "Father Offiong's 10th Year of Priesthood", *The Nigerian Call*, August 4-7, 1982.

136.Cooke, "Church, State and Education", p. 193n.

137.Ibid.

138.See W.T. Morrill, *Two Urban Cultures of Calabar, Nigeria*,
Ph.D. dissertation, University of Chicago, 1961, p. 255.

139.C.M. Cooke, *The Roman Catholic Mission in Calabar:
1903-1960*, Ph.D. dissertation, University of London, 1977, pp. 2,
284.

140.Groves, vol. 2, p. 36.

141.Ibid., pp. 36-37.

142.John Wesley himself discouraged the promotion of mission in
Africa at that time, ibid., p. 37.

143.Tasie, pp. 211,220.

144.Ibid.

145.Ibid.

146.Information from Rev. E. Ayankop, Aberdeen, December 19, 1983.

147.See P.M. Volz, *The Evangelical Lutheran Church of
Nigeria: 1936-1961* (Calabar: Hope Waddell Press, 1961), p. 2.

148.Ibid., p. 3.

149.Information from Rev. K. Grankie, Lutheran missionary,
Calabar, April 29, 1983.

150.Volz, p. 4.

151.See Groves, vol. 4, p. 189.

152.Volz, pp. 4-7.

153.Information from Rev. K. Grankie.

154.Volz, pp. 40-41.

155.The following account is drawn from Volz, pp. 40-42.

156.Groves, vol. 3, p. 187.

157.Ibid.

158.Interview with Pastor I.F. Umoren, Qua Iboe Church, Calabar, May 11, 1981.

159.It is impossible to give a comprehensive account here of the growth of the Calabar Mission. A few significant events and dates are mentioned, but for a fuller treatment see McFarlan, *Calabar: the Church of Scotland Mission.*

160.Taylor, "Missionary Education", pp. 199, 201.

161.Aye, p. 146.

162.Mr. E.U. Aye, former headmaster of HWTI, has written a comprehensive history of the school which was in press in 1983. Details of publication were not available.

163.Ibid., p. 154.

164.McFarlan, p. 173.

Chapter Three

Religious Pluralization

3.1   Introduction

This chapter is very much a continuation of the previous one as it is concerned with the religious history of Calabar; while dealing also with the historic, mainline churches, the focus is more on the emergence of indigenous religious groups and the arrival of overseas or exogenous, pentecostal and evangelical organizations and spiritual science groups.

Chronological development will be followed so that a composite picture of religious growth in Calabar can be built up. Wherever necessary, religious phenomena and changes will be related to wider social and political events. There will be some discussion of general trends during this period, which falls approximately between the second decade of the twentieth century and the end of the 1970s.

3.2   The heyday of Calabar: 1910-1929

The early part of the twentieth century in Calabar's religious history was largely dominated by the major missionary bodies and their territorial disputes. In general, Calabar experienced a period of development at this time, as the Protectorate and the missions worked towards the establishment of bureaucratic, medical and educational facilities. The First World War served to dampen missionary activities, by acting as a drain on financial aid and technical personnel. Knight, in his study of evangelical Christianity in Nigeria, claims that the effects of World War I were far more detrimental to the missions than World War II.[1] This was undoubtedly due to the fact that indigenization was barely under way in most of the churches and so their dependency on the parent institutions left them vulnerable to shortages of funds and personnel. In some ways, though, this served to stimulate indigenous activity in the mission churches.

A member of the United Native African Church, A.A. Obadina, while stationed in Calabar, started to preach to the local people and soon opened an "opposition church" to the Presbyterian

Mission.[2] His own church was a schism from the Anglican Church led by J.K. Coker in 1891. It was one of the separatist churches which were formed in Lagos from the 1880s onwards after breaking away from the Anglican, Methodist and Baptist churches over issues such as white domination and polygamy. The present Bishop of the Calabar branch of the African Church (which is known as the Christ African Church), Rt. Rev. E.E. Ironbar,[3] claims that the church reached Calabar in 1918 and that it was a branch of the Bethel African Church founded in Lagos by Coker in 1901.[4]

The Christ African Church in Calabar has retained its Anglican structures and liturgy if not its links. It quickly established itself as an Efik church, attracting people who were at odds with the mission churches over questions of polygamy and secret society membership. It also demonstrated a more accommodating attitude to burial - non-members could (and still do) receive burial rites (at a fee).

Islam gradually filtered into Calabar after the First World War via incoming traders, mostly from the north of Nigeria. The first mosque was built in 1918 on Calabar Road, but its role as the Central Mosque for the entire Muslim community gradually declined as the result of a dispute between the Yoruba and Hausa communities; the Hausa people eventually broke away to build the Bogobiri mosque in what has become the Hausa sector of the town.[5] The former Central Mosque was later acquired by the Ahmadiyya movement.[6]

While the Christ African Church represents the first African independent church to be established in Calabar, the Salvation Army (SA) represents the first of the imported or exogenous groups to evangelize in the area. Although the SA did not finally take root in the township until 1928, Commissioner George Scott Railton, William Booth's lieutenant, had visited Calabar and Lagos as early as 1903.[7]

As a result of the latter's open-air meetings, people wrote enthusiastic letters to the headquarters in London, pleading for missionaries, while others decided to set up groups in the name of the Salvation Army. One such group seems to have been created in Creek Town in 1905 or thereabouts, with strict rules against intoxicating drinks, and orders to take care of oneself and preach the Gospel.[8] Their Efik name was "Nka Erinyana no Christ", which literally translated meant "The Society who help [sic] others in the name of Christ".[9]

This small group, about which unfortunately we know very little, seems to have constituted the first institutionalized indigenous response to mission Christianity. The founder members apparently belonged to the Presbyterian Church, but were impressed by their fleeting contact with the Salvation Army and decided to form a semi-autonomous, revitalization group along SA lines.[10] However, by the time the official SA began work in Calabar in 1929, the group had been reabsorbed into its original mother church, the UFCS.

There was a group known as "Nka Edinyana" (presumably the same group as above) in Creek Town, and their leader, Tom Okon Nyamse, was the author of "Ikwo Nka Edinyana" (Hymns of the Companions in Service) which won great popularity in Creek Town and Duke Town.[11] The Presbyterians failed to utilize this indigenous religious creativity and potential, as they were "merely interested in fitting the Africans to be subordinates to Europeans..." and trained them "in only minor theological and educational careers."[12]

The initial work of the Salvation Army in Calabar was pioneered by a Nigerian couple, Brigadier and Mrs. Labinjo.[13] People were attracted to the SA on account of the uniform, aggressive evangelism and Lantern Services, which featured the use of acetylene-powered lantern projectors with slides depicting the Gospel story.[14] (Hope Waddell had actually made use of one previously in the 1850s). As one Territorial Commander vividly reported - "Thousands have flocked to these services, and have received the gospel through the eye gate as well as the ear gate and great good has been accomplished".[15]

The issue of polygamy proved to be as significant for the SA as for other churches, in one way or another. The SA decided to allow polygamists not only to be ordinary members, but also to join the ranks of the semi-official Corps Council and Men's Meeting.[16] This gave polygamists, disciplined by other churches, an opportunity for further Christian involvement and in turn speeded the development and growth of the SA, since many of these converts were leading men in their community and were already familiar with the Christian faith.

In 1925 the SA was already making inroads into the Cross River area from Port Harcourt. They attempted to take over a "prayer house" which had seceded from the Wesleyan Church. Despite unfavourable court rulings, they eventually won the right to hold public meetings and the "new faith", renowned for having a "high spiritual quality", began to expand rapidly through the lower Cross River region.[17]   SA leaders recognized that this expansion was attributable only partly to the work of the church itself. The other major factor was the Spirit Movement of 1927 which spread like wildfire among the Efik and Ibibio peoples of Uyo division. While the phenomenon of the Spirit Movement was not directly centred on the town of Calabar but rather on Uyo, approximately 40 miles to the north-west, its repercussions were significant for the area as a whole.

Three non-pentecostal missions (UFCS, Primitive Methodist Mission [MM], QIM) had been at work in the area since the end of the nineteenth century. Without warning and for no apparent reason, although some tension had been generated by new taxes, a census and the establishment of forest reserves, people began holding spontaneous meetings, confessing their sins and displaying many of the ecstatic phenomena associated with a pentecostal revival.[18]   This has been acknowledged as the beginning of the Spirit Movement. Rev. J.W. Westgarth, a strongly evangelical and revivalist member of the QIM, was working in the area at the time. He treated the behaviour of his church members as a revival from the Holy Spirit and attempted to guide and control the phenomenon. The government response was less favourable, labelling it as a type of "African witch-hunt" for there were reports of the movement getting out of hand, with people extorting confessions, torturing those who refused, as well as destroying traditional shrines and defying the chiefs and elders.[19] Government reports suggest that the movement was fuelled by indiscriminate use of revivalist and occultist literature.[20]   Some missionaries, less sympathetic than Westgarth, saw the "spirit people" as "juju people or they have read some books from America"(!)[21]

This was a pentecostalist-type revival, which pre-dated the arrival of the first Western pentecostal church by about six years. However little or no evidence came to light of healings or prophesyings, two features considered basic to most African movements of this kind.[22]

The momentum of the Spirit Movement only lasted about three years (1927-30), but the consequences were far-reaching. Firstly there were high dividends in terms of general Christian conversion and renunciation of traditional religious beliefs and practices. The pastoral capacities of the missions in the area were exceeded, which contributed to a dissatisfaction with Western forms of Christianity.[23] Several offshoot movements resulted, some of which later grew into independent churches in their own right. An interesting example is the Obere Okaime Christian Mission which began in 1927 and still uses its own divinely revealed language and script.[24]

Repercussions of the Spirit Movement were felt in Calabar, and within a few years both independent and mission churches, which had been generated by and benefitted from the revival, were moving into the urban areas. One such case was the British pentecostal organization - the Apostolic Church.

3.3   The witchcraft scare: 1930-39

Missionaries from the Apostolic Church (AC) from Britain arrived in Lagos in 1931 in response to a Macedonian call, prompted by the Revival then taking place in Ibadan, Ilesha and Lagos. In November 1932, the visit of Pastors G. Perfect and I.J. Vaughan to Calabar marked the birth of the AC in eastern Nigeria, when three pre-existing assemblies of some ninety members were accepted into the Apostolic fold.[25] However the date of 1933 is more readily cited as the year when the AC began its mission in earnest in the Calabar area.[26] It was in the course of 1933 that the church staged its first open-air service which was to prove highly significant for the growth of the organization in the light of events at the time.

The contemporary situation is perhaps best described in the words of Rev. I.B.I. Ita:

> ... a very critical moment, when the land was blacked out with the rampant power of witchcraft, superstition and death. When Old Calabar was mourning and wailing her departed noble sons, Heaven was shut up against our land.[27]

In the early 1930s Calabar had been struck by a period of depression, caused by the collapse of primary produce prices and subsequent unemployment, and spurred on by a revival of witch-craft.[28] In addition, a spate of deaths of eminent citizens, notably four leading lawyers, provoked fear and panic and fuelled dormant witchcraft beliefs.[29] In response to the crisis, a campaign led by Rev. J.K. MacGregor of Duke Town Church sought to disprove the existence of witchcraft (ifot) by arranging a series of meetings in the various churches under banners and posters declaring: CHRIST OR IFOT. WHICH?[30] That these attempts proved largely abortive was confirmed by the great success of the first Apostolic meetings which, in contrast, distributed posters claiming: THERE IS WITCHCRAFT. The Duke Town open-air service and a Creek Town evangelistic campaign attended by the well-known evangelist, Joseph Babalola (who had by then joined the AC), ensured a healthy start for the AC. By the end of 1933, several Nigerians were ordained apostles, prophets and pastors at the first Convention.[31]

The Jehovah's Witnesses (JW) began their work in Nigeria in the 1920s. It was some years later, in 1928, that Watch Tower representatives began visiting Calabar and attracting people with their literature and evangelism techniques.[32] An evangelistic team set out almost immediately and before long a few local pioneers, namely E.O. Nwanyo, E.E. Kadana and P.A. Ita were baptized and began organizing the preaching activities of the group. Their early nucleus was known as "Nwanyo's church" since they met in the latter's home. People were impressed by the teachings on the millennium and felt that such Biblical truths had been hidden from them by the missionaries of their (former) churches.[33]

The JW distinguished themselves as being the first religious organization in Calabar to conduct house-to-house preaching. Some people were attracted by this new form of evangelism, although there appears to have been some confusion over earthly and heavenly wages.[34] There was also a positive response to the strongly biblical orientation of the JW, unaided by any attempt to use cultural superiority as a tool of conversion.[35]

The Hill of Salvation Mission is most probably the oldest of Calabar's indigenous churches. According to Elder Jackson Ukpong, the church was founded in Calabar in 1938 as the result of an early schism from the Apostolic Church.[36]

3.4   World War II and its effect on Calabar: 1940-1949

While Nigerian territory was not directly involved, the Second World War seems to have at least had the effect of limiting missionary and indigenous religious activities in the area, both financially and in terms of personnel. In addition, since the witchcraft scare of the 1930s, there had been an exodus of educated Efik to other administrative centres in Nigeria. The reputation of the Efik by this time as skilled government administrators facilitated this process. Ironically this exodus was to be instrumental in stimulating religious growth and diversification in Calabar. Many Efik found no Presbyterian churches in the places where they were stationed and resorted to other Protestant churches or experimented with new forms of religion. In some cases these new forms were transplanted to Calabar.

The Church of Christ, the Good Shepherd is an example of this process of religious transplantation. Mrs. Lucy Harriet Harrison, born in 1900 in Creek Town, followed her husband to Lagos in the 1930s. After his death, she tried unsuccessfully several spiritual churches until receiving a spiritual injunction in 1940 to form her own prayer group. By 1946 she returned to Calabar to found a third branch which became the headquarters of the expanding independent church.

This was the same year that a group of five Apostolic Church (AC) members broke away from the parent body to form the Mount Zion Church. They had disagreed whether members could seek medical treatment. These founders, led by Pastor John Ubok Udom, urged members to practise faith-healing. Tension mounted further over church government. A group of Nigerian apostles accused the white missionaries of selfish domination and lack of interest in establishing schools.[37] It was this series of incidents that led to the establishment of Mount Zion in 1946. The leadership consisted of John Eshiet Etefia, John Ubok Udom, J.B. Ettefiah and Robert Prince Akpabio.[38]

John Eshiet Etefia is the sole spiritual head of the Mount Zion Church; the others have since died. Bishop Etefia originated from Ikot Akpadem in Ikot Abasi Local Government Area, but has spent most of his life in Calabar. He had some early contact, through his parents, with the Faith Tabernacle, an American pentecostal group active in Africa since the 1920s. Before long the new spiritual church had affiliated with a religious organization in Oakland, California - the Mount Zion Light House Full Gospel Church, and amended its name accordingly to reflect the affiliation. It was not possible to ascertain how this affiliation came about, partly because the relationship is no longer active.

The Church of Christ, a branch of the conservative and fundamentalist Protestant organization from the United States known as the Churches of Christ,[39] began in Calabar shortly after World War II largely due to the efforts of one individual, Mr. C.A.O. Essien.[40] He obtained information from an international correspondence club in the United States concerning a Bible correspondence course offered by Lawrence Avenue Church of Christ, Nashville, Tennessee.[41] Mr. Essien took the course and then began a class of his own, teaching the same material to about twelve others. Before long they started to develop congregations in the neighbouring Efik, Ibibio and Igbo areas. After three years they claimed to have 10,000 converts from the Presbyterian, Methodist and spiritual churches, but mainly from among non-Christians.

In 1950 two white missionaries from South Africa visited Calabar to inspect Essien's work and make plans for the future. As a result, two missionaries were sent out from Tennessee in 1952, with others following to make up a regular team of foreign staff of six to ten members. Between 1950 and 1962 the church reported a trebling of its membership figures which represents a rapid increase compared to the growth rates of the Presbyterian and Qua Iboe churches at this time. The church itself accounts for this success in terms of the emphasis laid on evangelism training and indigenous church government.

3.5   Political independence approaches: 1950-1959

There seems to be little correlation between the political changes that were in the air at this time and religious growth and change. Perhaps the migrations and/or aspirations of some of the founders mentioned below might have been affected by the final phase of colonial rule, but we were unable to document this.

In September 1952, while serving as a cook/steward on the oil palm plantation at Ikot Omin, on the outskirts of Calabar, Etim Akpan Otong received a call in a dream to "Go and preach to other churches".[42] He was told that God had selected him for a mission and he was given a series of instructions to carry out. This involved going to various mission churches in the area and exhorting them to make prayer a central feature of their liturgies because of the danger of witchcraft. He was also asked to instruct the A.M.E. Zion Church to change its name to the "National Church of Nigeria" as part of a plan to unite all the churches in Nigeria. He was given three Biblical passages as a protection against challenges to his authority.

As predicted, he was rejected by the aforementioned churches and, after being baptized into the Apostolic Church, he seems to have started to gather round him a group of sick people, mainly estate labourers. This independent group eventually became known as the "National Assembly Church of Nigeria" and spread on a limited scale to other parts of Nigeria, as well as Britain and Spain. Bishop Otong's overriding concern for Christian unity was manifested in the important role he played in the formation of a local Christian council in the late 1950s (see chapter 7).

At approximately the same time as Otong's dream was materializing in the form of the National Assembly Church in Calabar, the Apostolic Faith Mission was moving into the township, having already established its headquarters at Ikot Enwang, a few miles out of Ikot Ekpene. According to Pastor A.F. Ufford, some members of the Hill of Salvation Mission, a small spiritual church founded a few years earlier, became dissatisfied with the teachings of the latter and, "because of their thirst for righteousness", wrote to the headquarters of the Apostolic Faith Mission, a pentecostal and holiness church in Portland, Oregon. A missionary arrived and preached at the Hill of Salvation Mission. A schism followed, as a small group broke away and rented a house at 34 Abua Street to form the Calabar branch of the Apostolic Faith Mission in 1953. Land was acquired for a temporary building before the present location at Ekpo Abasi Street became the main site in 1975.[43]

In 1954 another prayer band was formed by a pharmacy superintendent, Ekpenyong Ekeng, and his partner Effanga Odiong Effanga.[44] It was officially registered with the government in 1964 under the name of God the Hosts Prayer Temple.

The year 1956 was to prove extremely fruitful in terms of new religious groups. The Baha'i Faith began its first spiritual assembly in the area at this time.[45] The group was largely made up of Igbo who were to leave some years later on account of the civil war. The seeds of the Baha'i Faith were actually sown one year earlier in 1955 by a Ugandan writer, Enoch Olinga, who visited Calabar briefly from his station in the Cameroons to explore the possibilities of missionary work there.[46]

The pattern of creation and transplantation of a small spiritual church, the Holy Chapel of Miracles, are reminiscent of the Church of Christ, the Good Shepherd, founded some ten years earlier. Mrs. Theresa T.A. Effiong, a Calabar indigene, had migrated to western Nigeria on account of her work as a midwife. Born and bred a Catholic, she seems to have had some association with the

Celestial Church of Christ (an Aladura or spiritual church in western Nigeria) at a later stage.

She recounts the founding of her own spiritual church as having occurred in Oshogbo. At first she resisted her calling, revealed through the visions of a woman friend, preferring to maintain her Catholic connections. Eventually she heeded the call, realizing that she was not getting the necessary spiritual insight and knowledge of God within the Roman Catholic Church. The Holy Chapel of Miracles was subsequently born.

The Blessed Spiritual Mother, as she later became known, explains that two of the earliest revelations from God clarified and predicted the future role of the church - that it was to be a church of the "East", and that its members were the chosen people of the East (i.e. eastern Nigeria). They were also told that the church "would not explode into many branches" - a prophecy which has remained valid up until the present day.[47]

After the church moved to Calabar in 1956, to settle there finally as it were, it adopted a Sabbatarian orientation. Details on how and when this occurred are not available, but it seems likely that the founder was influenced by literature from the Seventh-Day Adventists.

Arriving from the east but originating in the west of Nigeria, the Eternal Sacred Order of the Cherubim and Seraphim (ESOCS) represented one of the larger and more established of the Nigerian independent or Aladura churches. The church claims direct descent from the founder, Moses Orimolade Tunolashe, of the now much fragmented Cherubim and Seraphim movement.[48] However, its beginnings were humble enough in Calabar after being brought by members of the Enugu branch in 1956. The church almost collapsed when the founding Igbo members were forced to return home during the civil war. The few remaining members met for worship at the mosque on Calabar Road, which had been temporarily abandoned by the fleeing northerners. Towards the end of the war, the church was reactivated by the return of indigenes and their families.[49]

In 1956, Olumba Olumba Obu, who had moved to Calabar from Biakpan,[50] for the purposes of trading, became the leader of a prayer meeting that was held twice a week (Friday and Sunday) in his Eton Street residence.[51]   Obu became popular because of his healing and prophetic powers.   He also gained renown for his familiar blessing - "Go, I have solved all your problems."[52]

In 1958 the growing prayer group of around sixty members moved to new premises along Mbukpa Road.   The organization was officially registered in 1964 as the Brotherhood of the Cross and Star (BCS) with the following aims and objectives:

1.   To advance Christian Religion by spreading the Gospel of our Lord Jesus Christ to all parts of the world.

2.   To carry out Practical Christianity of healing the sick, helping the poor, and relieving the distressed.

3.   To establish Christian schools and colleges from time to time which shall be non-profit making, and shall be conducted in accordance with the Education policies of the Government concerned.[53]

Within a few years, larger premises were acquired not far away at 34 Ambo Street, to accommodate the international headquarters of this successful and rapidly expanding organization.

3.6   Independence and civil war: 1960-1969

Independence did not provoke any immediate or remarkable religious responses within Calabar itself.   In fact, the preceding and subsequent decades were periods of far greater activity in terms of the arrival and installation of new religious groups.   The civil war, in contrast, from 1966-70, was to have a marked effect on religious trends.   During the war period, many regular types of religious activity were suppressed, stimulating new forms of religious expression.   This new religiosity found a ready audience both during and after the war, as people, traumatized and insecure, sought an outlet for new social and religious needs.   The war, of course, was a disruptive factor, notably in relocating people and peoples; such effects had interesting consequences for religious growth and innovation. People returning to their places of origin, brought with them new religious ideas and practices.

The origins of the Pentecostal Assemblies of the World, Inc. (PAW), an American interracial pentecostal holiness church, in the Cross River area can be traced to a former member of the A.M.E. Zion Church in Ikot Abasi, Ephraim Ironbar.[54] Following a vision in 1941, Ironbar pressed for a more "spiritual" way of worship in his church, with greater reliance on the Holy Spirit. This was rejected by the church authorities and Ironbar left the church with a small group of followers, with no intention to start anything more than an informal prayer group. After being taken to court by his former church and acquitted, he came into contact with PAW literature and, finding an affinity with his own beliefs, he wrote to the headquarters in Indianapolis. Today the church claims to have more than two hundred branches all over Nigeria, although many are concentrated in the mainland part of the state. The PAW was introduced to Calabar in 1962 and has maintained a single branch at 28 Idang Street. The branch is run by Pastor E.E. Ephraim, son of the late founder and currently the proprietor of the Glad Tiding Printing Press. He studied accountancy in the U.S. as well as some Bible courses with the PAW.

The Spiritual Christ Army Church (SCAC) is a breakaway movement from the church known as the Christ Army Church in Bakana, Port Harcourt; the latter is a product of the Garrick Braid revival of 1916. The SCAC moved to the Cross River area in 1927 and a branch was founded at Abak. The civil war and the creation of new states destroyed the common identity (i.e. as minority ethnic groups and disprivileged political areas), as well as the financial links, between Port Harcourt and Abak. The Cross River branches went independent after 1970. Before that, in 1964, a branch of the SCAC had begun in a rented room at 18 Atakpa Street. It later moved to a permanent site at 21 Atakpa Street.

There have been two schisms of this church in Calabar, namely the St. John Christ Army Spiritual Church and the St. Paul Christ Army Spiritual Church (in Big Qua Town and Essien Street). Relations remain cordial as joint services are held annually.

Healing is practised through fasting and prayer, and members wear red and white prayer gowns.

The Christ Apostolic Freedom Church (CAFC) came to Calabar in 1964 from Ukpon in Eket Local Government Area, the home town of the founder, Bishop N.N. Nkoro, who died in 1975.[55] This church is interesting in that it represents an eastern Nigerian version, in the form of a direct schism, from a western Nigerian Aladura church - the Christ Apostolic Church. Mr. Nkoro, who worked in Ibadan in the 1940s, appears to have separated from the parent body in 1950 on grounds of oppression and exploitation of the members. A branch of the Christ Apostolic Church was already in operation in Calabar by 1961; it was established by an Ibibio, Rev. E.G. Essien, with help from the parent body in Lagos.

The CAFC began its life in Calabar in 1964, like many aspiring new religious movements, with an open-air service on what is now the district headquarters, 19 Atuambom Street. It has retained many of the features of its Aladura parent - faith-healing, witch-craft protection and fervent prayer.

Almost the same pattern of creation can be observed with regard to the Divine Order of the Cherubim and Seraphim (DOCS) as with the previous church (CAFC). A group of members of the Eternal Sacred Order of the Cherubim and Seraphim in eastern Nigeria were unhappy about the "undesirable practices" of the ESOCS, including the purported disappearance of sick people taken to Bar Beach for healing.[56] They broke away and applied for registration of the DOCS in 1965 with the headquarters at Port Harcourt. The Calabar branch owes its origin to a Yoruba man, Isaac Owedeyia, who established the ESOCS at 9 Clifford Street in 1953.[57] The church was taken over by Bishop J.E. Udok in 1954; it changed hands in 1965 becoming the Calabar headquarters of the DOCS.[58] Bishop Udok has remained the overall leader of the DOCS and is a well-known figure in the town on account of his frequent prophecies which are always reported in the local press. There are currently three branches in the town, the headquarters at 50 Ebito Street and two smaller branches at Efut Abua and Okom Ita.

The Christian Methodist Episcopal Church (CME) established itself in Calabar in 1966.[59] It originated in the United States where it was created by black members of the Methodist Episcopal, South in 1870 and was known as the Colored Methodist Episcopal Church before changing to its present name in 1954.[60]

In 1967 Effiong Etim, known as "Itu", led a breakaway group from the Brotherhood of the Cross and Star. Although the church or "bethel" (as Brotherhood branches are known) at Ikot Ishie was retrieved from him, he went on to set up his own spiritual church - Christ Salvation Church.

Shortly before the civil war, a well-known American pentecostal church - the Assemblies of God - was brought to Calabar from Aba by the Christ's Ambassadors (the evangelism wing of the church).[61] The church had grown rapidly in Igboland since the 1940s and was therefore identified in the early stages in Calabar as an Igbo church. Church membership was seriously affected, therefore, by the civil war. A few indigenes managed to keep the church going until it was revived again after the war by an evangelization campaign. Only this time converts were drawn from the local population.[62]

The war had begun, although its impact was yet to be fully experienced in Calabar, when, in 1967, "The Church, the Body of Christ" (CBC) was founded by the late Mr. Eyo O. Ita. Mr. Ita was a fairly well educated man and a member of the Society of Radiographers. He began healing people in his home but this led to tension with the church he was attending at the time - the Apostolic Church. After expulsion from the AC in 1967, he continued the spiritual healing on an informal basis, within the context of a house prayer group. A prophecy from a blind man led to the institutionalization of the group whose name "The Church, the Body of Christ" was taken from 1 Corinthians 12:20-27. The first converts were those who came to Mr. Ita's house for healing, until the group moved to 31 Hart Street, now the headquarters of the movement, and started attracting a wider following. The first evangelists ordained were Pastor Asuquo Ita and Pastor Bassey Edem in 1968.[63] At the death of the founder in 1972, a leadership crisis ensued and a schism called the United Body of Christ established its own base on the mainland at Etinan. Another breakaway group organized by relatives of the late founder, exists at 6 Nkwa Street.

Only one religious group seems to have started in Calabar during the war and that was the God's Kingdom Society (GKS). Mr. I. Isang was transferred from Lagos to Calabar at this time and together with Mr. E. Ekpo and their families they introduced the GKS to Calabar. GKS was founded in Nigeria in 1934 and has been described as a Hebraistic or Judaistic religious movement, with unitarian tendencies and a strong predilection for the Old Testament.[64]

3.7   The post-civil war revival: 1970-1974

The 1970s proved to be a period of almost frenetic religious revival and growth. The general sense of relief and desire to rebuild after the civil war were quickly followed by the oil boom of the mid-seventies, the repercussions of which were felt in the religious sector. The general mood of optimism was accompanied by increased economic and political opportunities, particularly in the late seventies.

The first new religious organization to establish itself in Calabar after the liberation of the town by federal troops was the Spiritual Kingdom Church of Christ (SKCC). This was a spiritual church centred on the town of Ikot Ekpene and founded by John Akpan Bassey (later known as Edidem "Spiritual King" Bassey) between 1946-48.

Bassey had been a member of the Apostolic Church for some ten years but had been affected by the ongoing leadership disputes in the church. After a series of visions, he was directed to found a church known as the "Kingdom" over which he would rule as "King". This Anang spiritual church eventually took root in Calabar when one of the ordained members, Apostle Joshua, came to town in 1970 after the war in search of tailoring work to support his family. He subsequently decided to open a branch of the church and erected a signboard, although in the early stages worship was held under a tree.[65]

The Holy Face Church (HFC) off Atakpa Street began its

existence in Calabar in 1971 as a prayer group within the Roman Catholic Church. The Holy Face Society had in fact begun as far back as 1920 in Uyo as a devotional association introduced by the missionaries.[66]   It derived ultimately from the Confraternity of the Holy Face founded at Tours in France in the latter part of the nineteenth century.[67]   Approval for the society was withdrawn in 1944 following a change of missionaries, and the leader at that time, Benedict Julius, sought unsuccessfully to rehabilitate the society and a secession resulted, known as the Holy Face Catholic Church.[68]   This independent church came under the influence of the Mennonite missionaries working around Uyo from 1959 onwards and became a member of the United Independent Churches Fellowship.[69]   It differed little from the surrounding independent churches with a Protestant background apart from retaining a few Catholic ritual objects such as the crucifix and the rosary.[70]

It is interesting that the Holy Face in Calabar seems to have begun as a prayer group within the Catholic Church, but by 1982, under pressure from members of the group, took steps to become more autonomous. Most of these same members retain communicant status in the Catholic Church.

A small, but highly intriguing, group known today as Jesus the Superet Church (JSC) or the Superet Light Mission, was started in 1971 by a group of five men at 26 Chamley Street in Calabar. They had acquired Superet literature from the headquarters of the organization - the Superet Light Center in Los Angeles. Perhaps best described as a psychic church, Superet Light Center was founded in California in 1925 by Dr. Josephine de Croix Trust, called Mother Trust by her followers.[71]   Considered to be a light and aura scientist, Mother Trust developed a Superet Science based on the manifestation of God's light through our light atom aura. This type of "scientific Christianity" appealed to Francis Akpan, then a member of the Apostolic Faith, and now an ordained minister and leader of the Superet Church in Calabar.[72]

In 1972 the Lagos-based Crystal Cathedral (CC) moved to Calabar. The founder, a Cross River man, Leader Brother Archibong Edem Inyang, was born and raised in the Presbyterian tradition at Oku-Iboku, Itu Division.[73]   He showed great interest in music and in 1956 began having visionary experiences.   He

experimented with several spiritual churches before moving to Lagos
to work for the Nigerian Ports Authority in 1960. Four years later
he began a prayer group in his own home at Ebute-Metta, a
district of Lagos, which became the Crystal Healing Home in 1967.
In 1972 the healing home was registered as the Crystal Cathedral
Church, the same year as the church moved to Calabar, although
the headquarters remained at Lagos until very recently. A large
cathedral is currently under construction at the other main branch
at Oku-Iboku.[74]

3.8   The "oil boom" churches: 1975-1979

While 1975-79 is remembered as the oil boom period and the run up
to civilian rule, an event of considerable religious significance was
the visit in 1976 of the evangelical and pentecostalist crusader from
Tulsa, Oklahoma - T.L. Osborn. Many were impressed by his
powerful style of preaching and impressive organization, but most
particularly by his teachings and emphasis on the Holy Spirit. As a
result of his visit, many sought a more spiritual type of worship,
either through founding a new religious movement or by joining an
existent spiritual church, or through devotional associations or
informal prayer groups.

American connections led to the founding of the Institute of
Religious Science in 1975. Rev. M. Obionwa, an automobile
engineer with some secondary education, gradually started to build
up a small branch of the United Church of Religious Science
(headquarters in Los Angeles).[75] He himself belongs to the
International New Thought Alliance and followed correspondence
courses as well as a period of overseas training in order to improve
himself as a metaphysical teacher.[76]

The American experiences of two Efik men led to the founding
of two, somewhat different, spiritual churches in Calabar in 1976.
Efiota Efiom was a native of Ikot Ishie, Calabar, although he spent
most of his youth in Lagos before travelling to the U.S. in 1953 to
study electrical engineering. An unhappy marriage led him to

reject his Presbyterian and later Catholic affiliations and experiment with a variety of churches and religious groups, before settling with the Church of Christ Unity in Los Angeles in 1972. After being ordained in the church, he resolved to return to Nigeria to establish his own Unity Church of Africa, which would have similar principles and structures to the mother church.

Back in Calabar he rented the Conference Room at the Metropolitan Hotel,[77] and conducted a prayer group there on a regular basis and embarked on the distribution of tracts. This publicity drive paid off and with the support of the foundation members he was able to transfer the nascent church to his house at 8A Odukpani Road, which was redecorated and refurnished for its new function. The church seems to have accommodated itself increasingly to local needs (for instance, polygamy and healing) and before long the name was changed to Friends of Jesus or "F.O.J." as it is more commonly known. American influences are still apparent in the teachings of the founder, on "positive thought" for example.[78]

Paul Louis Eyo, the Efik founder of the Christ the Shepherd's New Kingdom Flock: The Temple of the Eternal Blessings of God (CSNKF), began life as a staunch Catholic, progressing to junior seminary level, before becoming a leading member of the Brotherhood of the Cross and Star. In 1975 he was sent by Leader Obu to develop the movement in the U.S. After a lengthy leadership dispute, he took steps in 1976 towards forming his own group, which was to materialize in Calabar some months later (c.1977) as CSNKF.[79]

Theresa Sunday U. Inyang, an illiterate trader, was one of the many indigenes who returned home after the civil war. She had previously been a member of the Roman Catholic and Lutheran churches before trying a spiritual church when she first arrived in Calabar. The reasons for her eventually deciding to form her own church are not clear, but it undoubtedly stemmed from the dreams and visions she was reportedly experiencing at the time. The first converts were, as in the case of other churches of this type, sick people, and within three years they had managed to erect a small concrete building for worship. As a result of a vision, the church became known as the Church of God Lamentation of Jehovah

(CGLJ).

In October 1977 a small prayer group came into existence led by seven members of the Apostolic Church in Calabar. The initiative seems to have come from Mr. A.O. Akwaowo, who, in 1976, had sent a prayer request to the Faith Pool Prayer Group in Ghana. His "special need of deliverance" was fulfilled and this not only served as a catalyst, but also marked the beginning of a relationship between Faith Pool, whose headquarters are in Tampa, Florida, and Akwaowo's nascent movement.

In late 1978, five of the original group broke away from the AC after a spiritual call and in January 1979 the Truth and Life Church (TLC) was formally inaugurated. The church acknowledges that its early spiritual impetus was rooted in the Osborn campaign of 1976. The remarkable evangelistic efforts on an international scale of this small, yet rapidly expanding, spiritual church will be discussed in chapter five.

The Church of God of Prophecy (CGP) is a direct descendant of its American parent of the same name in Cleveland, Tennessee.[80] The church arrived in Calabar from Etinan on the mainland in 1978.[81]

The most recent church founded by a woman in Calabar emerged in 1978. Mrs. Maddie Raymond had been receiving spiritual calls for several years, until she was finally unable to resist the divine command that she should begin a church - the Mount Olive Church of Christ - in Calabar itself, rather than at her home town of Ikot Ndung on the mainland.

She began her ministry at her residence at 27 Enebong Street, before moving to larger premises at Ekpenyong Ekpe Street in March 1981. This young government clerk, with some secondary education, was eventually joined in her enterprise by her husband, a young mathematics lecturer at the University of Calabar. He has taken on an increasingly managerial and executive role, while his wife is responsible for pastoral and spiritual matters. In 1983 he left for Britain to study for a higher degree; both he and his wife see this as an opportunity to establish links with overseas churches.

The Celestial Church of Christ (CCC), one of Nigeria's largest spiritual or Aladura churches, did not reach Calabar for almost twenty years after it first became active in Nigeria.[82] The church was brought into the area by an army officer, Mr. E.A.A. Averehi, in 1966.[83] He held prayer sessions in his room at the 13th Infantry Brigade of the Nigerian Army.[84] The first converts were Averehi's army colleagues who were cured of different sicknesses through prayer.

In 1978, the CCC was officially instated in Calabar. It was the year when many miracles were reportedly performed, including a "raising from the dead".[85] The army authorities threatened to dismiss Averehi for turning the barracks into a church. He eventually sought early retirement in 1980 to work full-time on the church, which by then had obtained a plot of land next to St. Patrick's School at Ikot Ansa. There are now three branches of the church in Calabar municipality, and it continues to attract Yoruba migrants and people from the armed forces.

An Igbo woman by the name of Prophetess Odozi-Obodo brought her small church - Christ Holy Church of Nigeria (CHCN) to Calabar from Onitsha in 1979. The church has remained an Igbo church because of its use of the Igbo language. It suffered a recent setback after being asked to leave the original site on the university campus, where the prophetess had a large clientèle of Igbo students.

The case of A. Peter Akpan and his recently created Spiritual Fellowship (SF) provide an excellent example of how the trauma of the civil war led certain individuals to experiment and innovate in the religious domain. Mr. Akpan was shocked and disillusioned by the ethnic rivalries in his own church (Methodist) during the war. He felt that "there should be more to religion than what we find in the churches".[86]

After two major crises, his father being burnt alive by the Biafran troops, and the sudden death of his former secondary school teacher, who had just returned from overseas study, Akpan began a spiritual quest, reading avidly all types of religious literature, notably mystical and metaphysical works. In 1977 he published his own book, *The Path of Holiness*, a synthesis of mystical and metaphysical ideas. At that time he was a lay preacher in the Methodist Church and the Scripture Union campaigned to have him banned.

The generally positive response to the book led to the formation in 1979 of a group of around twenty-five people who met to improve their spiritual development through meditation and discussion of metaphysical and mystical texts. The fellowship became dormant when Akpan left for the Netherlands to assume a post of Commercial Counsellor to the Nigerian Ambassador. Since he returned in 1982, he has set about reviving the group and he plans to retire soon from his post as head of the Federal Ministry of Commerce (Calabar branch) to devote himself fully to the work of the group and his own spiritual development. He has acquired a plot of land off Ekpo Abasi Street at Effiong Nwan Street and intends to construct a building there for meetings and private meditation.[87]

The last religious group that we shall document within this decade (1960-70) is the Unification Church (UC), founded by the Korean, Rev. Sun Myung Moon.[88]   Unification missionaries had been in Nigeria since the late sixties and the church was in fact registered in Lagos in 1970, with the aid of trustees from the Cross River State as well as a church (Concordant Teaching Mission) and land donated to the UC by Rev. Obong at Eket.

The UC began to hold meetings and an occasional conference in the house of a member in Calabar in the late 1970s, but without much success, so that in 1981, the Japanese missionaries, Mr. and Mrs. Kijima, were recalled to Lagos.   While there was an obvious interest in the attractive literature and audio-visual materials of this international religious organization, as well as the possibilities it offered for travel and study abroad, the failure of the church to take root in Calabar seemed to stem from the missionaries' emphasis on theology and total commitment to the Unification Family.   The fact that the representatives of the UC in Calabar were Japanese should not be underestimated as a possible barrier to the successful communication of the movement's message.

3.9   Concluding remarks

Over the several decades of religious growth that this chapter has covered, it is apparent that once the foundations had been laid by the various mainline missionary bodies at the beginning of the twentieth century, the time was ripe for the efflorescence of a wide range of religious orientations, whether indigenous, exogenous or both. It has been suggested, for example, that the dominance of the Church of Scotland in Calabar, and its emergence as the civic or "state" church had the "unexpected result of making the Efik less fastidious in their choice of and support of other sects".[89]

From available information, the majority of the religious groups, in the first half of the century at least, recorded a steady (although not uniform) increase in membership figures, branch expansion, church buildings and medical and educational projects. The Population Census of the Eastern Region of Nigeria, (1953) records that 73.9% of the population of Calabar municipality were Christians.[90] In the 1963 Eastern Region population census, the figures for the religious distribution of Calabar urban show 97.7% of the population to be Christians, 0.8% Muslims and 1.5% others. Whatever the accuracy of such figures, they may be considered as indicators of the broader trend of Christianization in Calabar.[91] The land was still fertile for first-time converts and it is not until the later period (post-civil war) that changing and more complex patterns of religious affiliation and behaviour become common.

It is tempting to see the correlation between education and mass conversion; many of the schools were church-run and education was a major objective. But in some cases conversion constituted an alternative means of mobility, power and satisfaction for the deprived, the powerless and the uneducated. We shall, however, reserve our discussion of the issues of conversion or religious affiliation and association until a later stage. (See chapter 10.) There is no doubt, however, that the increased mobility, literacy and communication fostered by the colonial period contributed to the patterns of religious change and innovation that were to follow. We have only to look at the biographies of individual founders in this respect, notably the men, who had more access to educational and employment opportunities and hence were more subject to external influences than women.

It is interesting to speculate why certain periods in Calabar's history, which could have been significant for religious growth, did not prove to be so. For instance, the 1918 influenza epidemic, followed by the economic recession, produced in some parts of Nigeria, notably the Delta region and the West, major revival movements with subsequent waves of religious independency. In Calabar, despite the proximity of the 1927 Spirit Movement in Uyo division which could have had major repercussions, this did not prove to be the case. Between 1910 and 1940, apart from the establishment of the Anglican, Methodist and Lutheran missions, only four new religious groups are known to have entered the area - three from overseas and one from Lagos; and only one indigenous spiritual church was founded. It seems likely that, given the contemporary references to a period of "witchcraft and superstition", that people resorted to traditional means of redress rather than seeking solace through new religious outlets.

In the decade prior to independence, we start to see several examples of local religious innovation - four out of seven new religious groups which emerged during the 1950s were due to local religious initiative. Similar figures apply to the post-independence period. In other areas of Africa, Ghana for example, religious independency was most definitely stimulated by political independence. It should be remembered that Calabar was geographically, economically and politically isolated from the centre of political activity at the time and, as noted earlier, had suffered from a significant exodus of its qualified indigenes, rendering it both a stagnant and depressed corner of the country.[92] This may offer a partial explanation for the relative absence of new forms of indigenous religious expression during the early decades of the twentieth century.

Another possible factor was the major Igbo presence in Calabar from the 1940s up to the civil war. Igbo migration to Calabar began with the expansion of Calabar as a port following the Protectorate. Morrill, citing the 1953 census, shows how the Igbo population increased from 303 to 15,613 between 1931 and 1953.[93] He also describes Igbo religion as characterized by the belief that religion was a personal matter, together with a strong support and loyalty for the two "traditional" Igbo churches - Anglican and Catholic. In addition the needs of individuals and the migrant Igbo community as a whole were taken care of by the various Igbo voluntary associations.[94]   This rather conservative approach to religion and apparent dislike of religious deviance may have had some influence on the overall religious situation at the time.[95]   The reverse effect is also possible in that the Igbo presence and domination of some churches (Roman Catholic, Anglican and Assemblies of God, for example) generated resentment and even caused some people to disassociate themselves from such organizations (particularly at the time of the civil war) and seek new affiliations.

The real momentum for religious change came with the civil war. The initial curtailment and then reshaping and revitalization of religious experience and activities altered the face of religious life in Calabar.[96]   There was a process of "destructuring" and "restructuring"; normal patterns of religious behaviour were disrupted as people sought refuge in the churches, after abandoning their homes and villages.[97] Prayers for protection and deliverance became the central religious activity as well as a yearning for more spiritual power. In some cases people found themselves thrown together in desperate situations, hiding in the bush, or in one another's homes. Informal prayer groups were generated by these circumstances, some of which survived and went on to become spiritual churches after the war. Many clergy confirmed that the general experience of deliverance, as people rushed to the churches to offer thanksgiving when the war was over, benefitted religious organizations in general. However, a certain amount of restructuring was to occur as many people questioned the validity and relevance of their previous religious affiliations and sought new forms of expression and fellowship.[98]

That such new paths were sought, and materialized, is evidenced by the twenty-two new religious organizations known to have originated in or been brought to Calabar during the seventies. Of these, twelve were local. Economic considerations should not be overlooked in this respect. For some people, their livelihoods destroyed by the war, the alternative of establishing a small ecclesiastical enterprise was an attractive, and usually fruitful, course of action.

There are some interesting observations with regard to religious growth during this period under investigation. While there is an evident input of exogenous religious institutions particularly in the early decades of this century, it would be inaccurate to describe the inhabitants of Calabar as passive recipients of new and unsolicited religious groups. In the majority of cases, it was through the initiative of a particular individual or group that religious growth and diversification occurred. In some cases, "branches" of the overseas bodies were established in Calabar before the missionaries actually arrived to launch the mission officially themselves.[99]

We have seen the importance of randomly acquired religious literature in stimulating religious choice and change, also the role of increased mobility, notably overseas travel or study. Fifteen (excluding the mainline mission churches) out of the forty-six religious organizations known to have taken root in Calabar before 1980 are of overseas origin. The early imported movements were British in origin, but these have been superseded by the more popular American groups. In the next chapter we shall see whether this predilection for "religious internationalization" is sustained.

In terms of the emergence and development of the various religious institutions, there are identifiable patterns. In the early stages the first converts or sympathizers would meet informally at the home of the founder or initiator (often generating a "healing home" type of arrangement) or, in the case of some of the less healing-oriented prayer groups, a room or small building would be rented. On the whole, though, it was a domestic location which provided the initial starting point. All groups aspired to acquiring a plot of land where a small shelter could be erected (to protect worshippers against the inclemencies of the rainy season) and eventually to building a more permanent concrete building, to opening new branches. A fairly good indication of the success rate of a religious group is the time lapse between the four stages. There are of course some groups which never develop beyond the first or second stages. These will be among our considerations in the next section, as we focus on the religious situation in the town of Calabar today.

Notes

1. See C.W. Knight, *A History of the Expansion of Evangelical Christianity*, D.Th. dissertation, Southern Baptist Theological Seminary, Louisville, Kentucky, 1951.

2. J.B. Webster, *The African Churches among the Yoruba: 1888-1922* (Oxford: Clarendon Press, 1964), p. 111. The dates of this are uncertain, but he probably began his preaching activities sometime after 1910. Webster maintains that there was dislike of the dictatorial methods of the Presbyterian mission in Calabar more than anywhere else in Nigeria. It was an ideal opportunity for the African churches, who, protected in a sense by the mission comity agreements, had the field to themselves and exploited the unrest with good results (p. 96).

3. Interview with Rt. Rev. E.E. Ironbar, Bishop of Christ African Church Cathedral, Calabar, January 25, 1981.

4. The history and schismatic developments of the African Churches are extremely complex and it is therefore difficult to trace the exact origins of the church in Calabar.

5. It was not possible to determine the dates of the dispute nor of the founding of the Bogobiri mosque.

6. Date unknown.

7. Major W. Allott, *Pioneering in Nigeria* (Lagos: Salvation Army Territorial Headquarters, December 1970), p. 3. Mimeo.

8. Ibid.

9. F.W. Dodds makes reference to this religious group in his Memorandum on Boundaries, p. 1.

10. There were similar reactions to, and misconceptions of, the Salvation Army in the Congo at approximately the same time, notably in the form of the movement known as the Eglise des Noirs by Simon-Pierre Mpadi. Cf. W. MacGaffey, *Modern Kongo Prophets*, (Bloomington, IN: Indiana University Press, 1983), pp. 41, 195-6

11. Aye, p. 154.

12. Ibid., p. 155.

13. Allott, p. 28.

14. Ibid., p. 33.

15. Ibid., p. 34.

16. Ibid., p. 39.

17. Ibid., pp. 42-45.

18. H.W. Turner, "Pentecostal Movements in Nigeria" in his *Religious Innovation in Africa: Collected Essays on New Religious Movements* (Boston: G.K. Hall, 1979), p. 123.

19. Ibid.

20. Ibid., p. 124.

21. Uyo Inter-Church Study Group, "The Spirit Movement in Ibibio Land", n.d. Mimeo.

22. Ibid., p. 123.

23. Allott, pp. 45-46.

24. I visited the church on two occasions in June/July 1983. The headquarters are situated at Obot Akai, Aka Ididep in Ibiono Local Government Area with about 10 small branches in surrounding villages. The founder of the group, Bishop Akpan-Akpan Udofia, is alive and active.

25. T.N. Turnbull, *What God Hath Wrought* (Bradford: The Pilgrim Press, 1959), p. 81.

26. See Pastor E.E. Okon, "Brief Outline of the Inception of the Apostolic Church in the Cross River State Field" in *The Apostolic Church Nigeria Golden Jubilee Souvenir Brochure* ([Lagos]: The Church, 1981) p. 10.

27. See Rev. I.B.I. Ita, "Early History of the Apostolic Church in Great Britain and Calabar Province", Uyo Inter-Church Study Group Paper, n.d. Mimeo.

28. Latham, *Old Calabar*, p. 150.

29. Aye, p. 157.

30. See Ita, p. 3.

31. Elder M. Thompson Uko, "Heralding the Golden Jubilee of the Apostolic Church Organisation", *The Sunday Chronicle*, October 18, 1981.

32. Information received from a personal communication from the late Elder E.O. Kadana, Calabar, November 11, 1982. See also B.P. Edet, "Christianity in Calabar: A Case Study of Jehovah's Witnesses", University of Calabar term paper, January 1983, p. 8, who names the representative as Mr. Nduaquibe and that he visited Calabar in January 1934, which is later than Mr. Kadana's version.

33. Ibid.

34. Ibid., p. 10.

35. Ibid., p. 11.

36. Information obtained by Essien A. Offiong, Calabar, August, 1984.

37. Uko.

38. T.O. Abia, "The Mount Zion Light House Full Gospel Church of Nigeria", University of Calabar research report, July 1981, p. 1.

39. The church is not linked to churches of the same name in other parts of Africa (such as in Uganda and Zaïre - see A. Hastings, *A History of African Christianity 1950-1975*, African Studies Series 26 [Cambridge: Cambridge University Press, 1979], pp. 127-8, 231). Nor is it a member of the Fellowship of the Churches of Christ in Nigeria also known as TEKAN or the Church of Christ in Nigeria (see D.R. Barrett, *World Christian Encyclopaedia* [Nairobi: Oxford University Press, 1982] p. 532). For the origins of the church in the U.S. see S.Y. Ahlstrom, *A Religious History of the American People* (1972; reprint, N.Y.: Doubleday, 1975), vol. 2, pp. 295-96.

40. The Churches of Christ commenced missionary activity in Nigeria in 1947 just after World War II (see Barrett, *World Christian Encyclopaedia*, pp. 528, 531).

41. See J.B. Grimley and G.E. Robinson, *Church Growth in Central and Southern Nigeria* (Grand Rapids, Mich.: William B. Eerdmans Publ. Co., 1966) p. 344f. The following account is based on this source.

42. Information on the National Assembly Church was collected by Essien A. Offiong in May 1982.

43. Interview with Pastor A.F. Ufford, Calabar, April 6, 1981. The Apostolic Faith (AF) was founded by a Methodist laywoman, Mrs. Florence L. Crawford who had received the Baptism of the

Holy Spirit at Azusa Street, Los Angeles. She began preaching up the West Coast of the U.S. before establishing a base at Portland, Oregon. Drawing on her Methodist heritage, Rev. Crawford preached a holiness doctrine like that of the Church of God (Cleveland, Tenn.). The AF has developed large scale home and foreign missions. See J. Gordon Melton, *The Encyclopedia of American Religions* (Wilmington, NC: McGrath, 1978), vol. 1, pp. 264-65.

44. See E.A. Offiong, "Schism and Religious Independency in Nigeria: A Case Study of Calabar", University of Calabar long essay, June 1983, p. 17.

45. The Baha'i Faith stems from Sufi and messianic movments in Persia in the mid-nineteenth century. The teachings focus on the essential oneness of all revealed faiths with the Baha'i Faith as the crown and summation of all faiths. See Melton, vol. 2, p. 352.

46. Interview with Mr. F. Ekpe, leader of the Calabar local spiritual assembly, Calabar, April 9, 1981; Local Spiritual Assembly of the Baha'is of Calabar, *The Baha'i Faith: An Introduction* (Calabar, n.d.), p. 3. Mimeo.

47. Interview with the Blessed Spiritual Mother, Holy Chapel of Miracles, Calabar, May 8, 1983.

48. See J.A. Omoyajowo, *Cherubim and Seraphim: the History of an African Independent Church* (New York and Lagos: Nok Publishers, 1982).

49. Interview with Senior Apostle Ekpo and church elders, Calabar, November 10, 1981.

50. Biakpan is situated between the Cross River and Igboland.

51. See Offiong, p. 17.

52. See Pastor Umoh James Umoh and Pastor Asuquo Ekanem, *Brotherhood of the Cross and Star* (Calabar: Brotherhood of the Cross and Star, 1979), vol. 1, p. 11.

53. Umoh and Ekanem, p. [iv].

54. For information on the Pentecostal Assemblies of the World, Inc. (PAW), see W.J. Hollenweger, "Black Pentecostal Concept" *Concept* no.30, special issue (June 1970):59-67; see also A.M. Shulman, *The Religious Heritage of America* (San Diego: A.S. Barnes, 1981) p. 283. Information on the PAW in the Cross River State was collected by Essien A. Offiong in September 1982 and July 1984.

55. See B. Akinyanju, "Christ Apostolic Freedom Church", University of Calabar term paper, 1982, p. 8.

56. G.U. Akpabio, "The Religious and Social Impact of Three Independent Religious Movements in Calabar Municipality", University of Calabar long essay, 1983, p. 14.

57. This information regarding the origins of the ESOCS does not agree with the account given by ESOCS leaders, see 3.5.

58. Ibid., p. 15.

59. See H.V. Richardson, *Dark Salvation: the Story of Methodism as It Developed Among Blacks in America* (Garden City, NY: Anchor-Press/Doubleday, 1976), pp. 224-239. A useful summary of the church's mission work in Africa appeared in the *Nigerian Chronicle*, March 21, 1981.

60. Melton, vol. 1, p. 194.

61. The Assemblies of God was founded in Arkansas in 1914 as a loose organization of independent pentecostals. It soon developed organizational structures, including major publishing and educational enterprises. The church's statement of

fundamental truths includes belief in the Bible as Word of God and in the fall of man, salvation in Christ, baptism by immersion, divine healing and the resurrection, as well as an absence of Holiness theology. See Melton, vol.1, pp. 271-72.

62. Interview with Pastor Isangidigh of the Assemblies of God, Calabar, March 9, 1981. According to Knight, p. 204, Mr. and Mrs. W.L. Shirer of the AG in the U.S. were called to Port Harcourt in 1939 by a group of Nigerians who had been influenced by the widely distributed Faith Tabernacle literature. As a result of their visit, the first AG missionaries (Everett Phillips and his wife) arrived in 1940.

63. See G.U. Akpabio, "Report on The Church, the Body of Christ", University of Calabar term paper, 1981, p.1.

64. H.W. Turner, "A Typology for African Religious Movements" in his *Religious Innovation in Africa*, pp. 85-86. See also D.I. Ilega, *Gideon M. Urhobo and the God's Kingdom Society in Nigeria*, Ph.D. dissertation, University of Aberdeen, 1982.

65. See E.I. Isege, "Report on the Spiritual Kingdom Church of Christ", University of Calabar term paper, 1982, pp. 3-4.

66. See D.B. Barrett, *Schism and Renewal in Africa* (Nairobi: Oxford University Press, 1968), p. 181.

67. See H.W. Turner, "African Religious Movements and Roman Catholicism" in his *Religious Innovation in Africa*, pp. 150-51.

68. Ibid.

69. Ibid., p. 151.

70. Ibid.

71. Melton, vol. 2, p. 105.

72. Interview with Francis Akpan, Calabar, April 4, 1981.

73. *Short History of the Crystal Cathedral Church* (Lagos: Crystal Cathedral Church, 1976), pp. 6-13.

74. Interview with Leader Brother Inyang, Calabar, November 2, 1981.

75. See Melton, vol. 2, pp. 60-61; the Institute (later to become the "United Church") of Religious Science was founded by Ernest Holmes in 1927, together with the *Science of Mind Magazine*. Melton classifies the organization with the Metaphysical family and underlines the confluence of ideas between the International New Thought Alliance and Religious Science.

76. Interview with Rev. M. Obionwa, Calabar, March 2, 1982.

77. The largest and most expensive of all the hotels in Calabar.

78. See N.V. Umeobi, "Report on the Friends of Jesus", University of Calabar term paper, July 1982, p. 3.

79. The bitter clashes which marked this particular schism will be discussed in 7.7.

80. See Melton, vol. 1, p. 257. The Church of God of Prophecy, under A.J. Tomlinson, withdrew from the original Church of God (Cleveland, Tenn.) in 1922. The church is pentecostal and evangelical, stressing justification by faith, sanctification by faith, sanctification as second work of grace, speaking in tongues as the initial evidence of being filled with the Holy Spirit, divine healing and the second coming of Christ. The government is central and theocratic. See *Yearbook of American and Canadian Churches 1984*, ed. C. H. Jacquet (Nashville: Abingdon Press for the National Council of the Churches of Christ, 1984), p. 44.

81. In 1983 during our survey it was discovered that services were no longer being held at the church.

82. The church was founded in 1947 by Samuel B.J. Oschoffa in Dahomey, now the Republic of Benin. It has achieved its greatest concentration in western Nigeria. See R.I.J. Hackett, *Oschoffa and the Celestial Church of Christ* (Ibadan: Spectrum Books, forthcoming).

83. Akamkpa was actually the original station of the CCC in Cross River State in 1968, but it was abandoned when those who founded the church there were disbanded at the end of the civil war. Report of a sermon given by Superior Senior Leader E.A.A. Averehi at the opening of the new Akamkpa branch of the Celestial Church in the *Nigerian Chronicle*, July 5, 1983.

84. Military personnel are often the vehicles of this church's expansion.

85. A characteristic feature of this church's success.

86. Interview with Mr. A. Peter Akpan, Calabar, April 20, 1983.

87. Interview with Mr. A. Peter Akpan, Calabar, June 1, 1982.

88. See Melton, vol. 2, pp. 225-27.

89. Morrill, *Two Urban Cultures*, p. 222.

90. *The Population Census of the Eastern Region of Nigeria*, 1953, vol. 1, pp. 4-5.

91. See Table 5A.3 in *Population Census Nigeria: 1963*, Eastern Region (Lagos: Federal Census Office, 1964).

92. See Morrill, *Two Urban Cultures*, pp. 106, 198; Latham, *Old Calabar*, p. 150.

93. Morrill, *Two Urban Cultures*, p. 108. In comparison, the number of Efik and Ibibio in Calabar in 1953 was 16,000 and 12,191 respectively.

94. See R.N Henderson, "Generalized Cultures and Evolutionary Adaptablility: a Comparison of Urban Efik and Ibo in Nigeria", *Ethnology* 5,4 (October 1966):365-91.

95. Morrill, *Two Urban Cultures*, p. 154. The first Igbo independent spiritual church to become established in Calabar was the Christ Holy Church in 1979.

96. Cf. Hastings, *History of African Christianity*, p. 237, who notes that ordination in the Catholic Church in Africa began to slow down in the seventies, except in Nigeria "which had been low in the past, now mounted impressively, particularly after the Civil War".

97. Interview with Mrs. A. Ekwere, Chief Catering Officer of the University of Calabar and choirmistress of the Crystal Cathedral Church, Calabar, February 14, 1982. She recounted how she and her family fled to a small church just outside of Calabar. The pastor persuaded his flock to remain in the church during an air raid and all were saved except for one man who jumped out of the window. She also emphasized that it was a time when people prayed fervently and made vows to renew religious obligations if their lives were spared.

98. See K. Enang, *Salvation in a Nigerian Background* (Berlin: Dietrich Reimer, 1979), p. 331.

99. See for example the Salvation Army (3.2), the Apostolic Church (3.3), the Church of Christ (3.4) and the Calvary Baptist Church (3.7).

Part Two: Contemporary Religion

Chapter Four

Non-Indigenous and Institutional Religion

4.1   Introduction

Leaving behind Calabar's religious past, we now move to the contemporary religious situation. The next two chapters will examine the modern religious scene in a more conventional way, that is by looking at the institutional forms of religion, their nature and characteristics, and their impact and place in the present-day religious and social life of Calabar. The material in these two chapters will be sub-divided by category or type of institution, with reference to individual organizations as the need arises.

This chapter and the next will contain data on groups already discussed in the previous section, as well as on new groups and movements which have only become part of Calabar's religious scene since the beginning of the 1980s. We are interested in the new relationships that are developing between many of Calabar's religious groups and their overseas parent (or former parent) bodies, and the way these relationships are expressed in terms of symbolism, religious texts, financial aid, missionary presence, music, language, etc.

In both of these chapters we are concerned to give some idea of the world-views constructed by the various religious groups. An understanding of these "microcosmogonies" as Fernandez calls them, will not only enable us to see how they relate to the "macrocosmogonies" or wider social realities, but also to understand the religious choice of individuals, which is in turn shaped by their world-views and life-circumstances.[1]

4.2   From mission to mainline churches - and after

For several decades the Presbyterian and Roman Catholic churches enjoyed a position of civic and ecclesiastical prestige. This image was based on the strength and composition of the membership; social and civic dignitaries belonged to these churches, lending to the latter both authority and status in the community. Together with the remaining Protestant groups - Methodist, Anglican, Baptist and Qua Iboe, they constituted, at least up until the civil war, a powerful ecclesiastical front, unchallenged by Islam (a situation unlike that in some other areas of Nigeria) or by any major "sectarian" forces.

This position of authority was generated not just by the longstanding presence of the missions in the area, but also by their educational activity. Before the 1970s and the government takeover of all schools run by voluntary agencies, most people had received all or some of their education in a church school, usually either Presbyterian or Roman Catholic. The most highly regarded secondary schools in the town today are the still the Hope Waddell Training Institution (Presbyterian, boys), the Holy Child Secondary School (Catholic, girls) and the Edgerley Memorial Secondary School (Presbyterian, girls).

Since the 1970s the mainline churches have suffered a considerable erosion of their prestige. They have experienced an exodus of dissatisfied worshippers to the spiritual churches, or at best a reduction in commitment and allegiance of many of their members, who seek fulfilment of (more critical) religious needs on a temporary basis elsewhere, or who cease attending church regularly, appearing only for festivals or *rites de passage*. People have accused the mainline churches of ignoring issues such as healing and witchcraft, and de-emphasizing the role of prayer and evangelism. But in spite of these setbacks and criticisms the former mission churches, notably the Presbyterian and Roman Catholic churches, are still generally regarded as the mainline or "orthodox" churches in Calabar today.

For the most part the missionary relationship of dependence upon a parent body for financial and personnel support has ceased.[2] The various Protestant bodies are now autonomous with indigenized leadership structures. The Roman Catholic Church while it does not enjoy the same degree of autonomy, has, despite the continuing presence of expatriate clergy, taken steps to increase the number of Nigerians in positions of authority.[3] Despite the obvious desire for indigenization, this has not always been accompanied by a move to sever links with the overseas parent bodies. Instead new relationships based on sharing, rather than dependence, have come into being. The Presbyterian Church of Nigeria is a good case in point. Almost a year after the last Church of Scotland missionary departed,[4] a "Presbyteries' Partnership" was launched between the Calabar and Dundee Presbyteries.[5] The aim of the partnership, still very much regarded as an experiment, is to share different experiences and techniques of evangelism, as well as fund-raising and liturgical changes, and to operate a staff exchange programme. The Calabar Presbytery feels that it has much to contribute in terms of the nature of its worship - particularly the joyful vibrancy and spontaneity of the thanksoffering.[6]

The role of women in the churches is also another area of change, albeit slow compared to the religious authority exercised by women in the traditional sector and the spiritual churches. The Lutheran Church now ordains women pastors, so too does the Presbyterian Church, which ordained their first woman minister, in 1982.[7] This is felt to be a timely, yet cautious recognition of the contribution of women to the growth and development of the church, both in the past and today. However there is still a highly disproportionate relationship between female participation and female leadership in these churches. Women have found an outlet through the various devotional associations and women's societies, where they may have some degree of independence and authority, as well as the possibility of shaping their own religious expression and experience.

Modifications in liturgical structures have also occurred over the last few decades or so. While there has not been any radical attempt to tamper with the respective ecclesiastical traditions, there have been moves to "Africanize" the worship, usually through the elaboration of the post-sermon, thanksoffering section of the service. This normally involves the singing of "native airs" and gospel choruses and dancing round (inside and out) the church to make the necessary offerings. In many cases it is the youth group who may be responsible for directing the music and movement; they frequently shut down the organ and bring out the drums and other traditional instruments, if this is permitted. It is a time of great spontaneity and rejoicing and has become an observable pattern in all the mainline churches in the last decade. There is, however, little desire to integrate it with the more formal and conventional first part of the service and achieve a full synthesis of European and African forms; although some would argue that the first part of the service is now experienced as being fully African. Some churches, notably the Roman Catholic and the Methodist churches, have been active in composing their own hymns and liturgical responses, in the respective local languages. On the whole, however, the mainline churches (at least in the urban context) tend to resemble, and indeed perpetuate, their ecclesiastical heritage in terms of architectural design, dress, symbolism, liturgy and doctrines.

For some, the religious world-view and social image projected by the former mission churches is consonant with their individual world-view and life-style. The dignified burial, wedding and baptismal services appeal to the élite. The chapel at the Hope Waddell Training Institution is especially popular in this respect. The religious and moral values propounded by the mainline churches - duty, service, moral rectitude, honesty, responsibility, etc. - are meaningful to the Western-educated leaders and professionals within the community, as well as, of course, to those older members of the congregation who were born and raised by the missionaries.

It is the mainline churches which are looked to as the mouthpiece of moral opinion and social criticism, for example on issues such as abortion, corruption and education, although as we shall see later, some of the spiritual church leaders have gained a reputation for speaking out on political and economic matters as they affect the community or nation as a whole. In the local press it is the sermons of the mainline churches which are given the greatest publicity. These churches also operate the Boys' and Girls' Brigades.

It is worth examining the mainline churches in the light of the ethnic divisions within Calabar. While the Presbyterian Church, because of its earlier hinterland expansion, numbers the neighbouring Ibibio, Igbo and northern Cross River peoples in its Calabar congregations, it is primarily an Efik church.[8] This is evidenced by the role of the Presbyterian Church as the "state church", for it serves as the location for all kingship ceremonies (coronations and memorial services), as well as many state inter-denominational services.[9]

An interesting development in the last year or so, has been the attempt to revive the Igbo Presbyterian Church which occupied a building at Garden Street.[10]   This would allow the Igbo community in Calabar to worship in Igbo, thus constituting a departure from the use of Efik by all the other branches.

The Lutheran and Qua Iboe churches, because of their mainland provenance, are noticeably Ibibio churches, from which the Efik are virtually absent.   The Baptist Church, with its strong roots in western Nigeria, exists in Calabar essentially to serve the Yoruba community.   For a long time they worshipped in the Red Cross building, near Watt Market, before recently acquiring land and a building of their own.[11]

The Anglican Church, up to the time of the civil war, had built up a strong congregation, mainly composed of Igbo and Yoruba, as well as some Sierra Leoneans.   It was in fact the Anglican Church which hosted the first inter-denominational service in Calabar, during the Second World War.[12]   Because of the strong Igbo presence in the church, it was ransacked by the Federal troops in 1967.   For the next twelve years, the much reduced congregation worshipped in the church hall, until the church was rebuilt.   The new building, an imposing structure even though not quite complete, seems to have revitalized the Anglican community in Calabar, and the pews are filling up again.   The church faithfully retains its Igbo and Yoruba services, which precede the main service in English at 10:30 a.m.   The vicar-in-charge, Canon W.G. Ekprikpo, is an Igbo from Port Harcourt, the seat of the Niger Delta Diocese, of which Calabar is a part.

During the civil war, a group of Methodists in Calabar who were refugees from Ikot Ekpene, became dissatisfied with the way of worship at the Wesleyan Church at Beecroft Street and began worship at Mayne Avenue Primary School.   In 1976 they were able to open a branch church at Atamanu.   The church has retained a strongly evangelical orientation **and** now attracts a purely Ibibio and younger, lower class congregation, in contrast to the mainly Efik élite who attend the older Wesleyan Cathedral at Beecroft Street (in the centre of old Calabar), with its English services and traditions.[13]

The Roman Catholic Church, by virtue of its outreach and expansion within Nigeria, perhaps attracts the widest spectrum in terms of ethnicity.[14]   The Sacred Heart Cathedral is the largest and most impressive of all the religious edifices in Calabar. While some of the changes ushered in by Vatican II, particularly those relating to "contextualization" and "indigenization", were welcomed, others, concerned with "demystification", were unpopular. The development of the various devotional associations, such as Our Lady of Fatima, Block Rosary, Blue Army Crusade, and St. Jude's Apostolate, has catered to such religious needs as prayer, healing and ritualism.[15]

Some important structural changes introduced by the Bishop, Dr. Brian Usanga, resulted in the creation of a number of new parishes in order to reduce the size of the churches.[16] This was obviously also a move to combat the popularity of the "neighbourhood church" as established by the spiritual churches and the Apostolic Church, for example. The Pope's visit to Nigeria in 1982 was an important moment in the church's history, even though Cross Riverians were disappointed that their state was not included on the Pope's itinerary.[17]

The new phase of independence, which the former mission churches have entered into, has exposed them to a stark commercial realism. Several of the churches have embarked on projects intended to generate funds for maintenance of the clergy, branch expansion and building programmes. For example, the foundation stone for the Mary Slessor Hostel on Mission Hill was laid in July 1980 by the Presbyterian Church. The church envisages the hostel as a small training centre for young women as well as providing accommodation facilities on a commercial basis. In July 1983 the first limited liability company in the history of the Nigerian church was formed, with the intention of reactivating the Hope Waddell Press and Bookshop.

Welfare activities have long been part of the tradition of the mainline churches, and it is largely in terms of their humanitarian contributions that they are remembered. In modern times this aspect of the churches' work has declined somewhat due to lack of funds and personnel, and the government take-over of such institutions. Apart from regular donations made to needy causes, some of the churches still operate rural training centres, leprosy hospitals and workshops for the handicapped (all situated outside of Calabar), but these are now peripheral areas of concern compared to the tasks of evangelism and survival in the face of mounting competition from an ever-widening range of religious options.

4.3   Islam

Islam has remained a minority religion in Calabar, being restricted for the most part to Yoruba and Hausa migrants who come to Calabar either for trading or as members of the armed forces. The number of Muslim students at the University of Calabar is almost negligible, but has grown sufficiently in recent years to generate a small Muslim community and the building of a small mosque.[18]

A Cross River State Pilgrim's Board was in operation from to 1976 to 1982 until it was dissolved by the State Governor because of political and ethnic rivalries. Nearly 3000 Muslims from the area performed the *Hajj* between 1976 and 1982.

Muslim festivals are celebrated with regularity by the Muslim community in Calabar and are covered by the local media. At such times Muslim leaders express their support for the government and in turn make appeals regarding their needs, such as for a Muslim cemetery and an extension to the Muslim primary school.

While the number of Efik and Ibibio converts to Islam is understandably very low, one of the most active Muslim leaders in Calabar is Efik - Alhaji Sulaiman A.O. Offiong. He has served as Chairman of the Pilgrims' Board and Secretary of the Central Mosque. More recently he has established a group known as "The Voice of Islam" to propagate the faith in and around Calabar. His van, equipped with a public address system, is now a familiar sight on the streets of Calabar. Alhaji Sulaiman Offiong has also written a series of articles on the tenets of Islam for the *Nigerian Chronicle*.[19] Articles by Muslims have been appearing with increasing frequency in the local press, which may suggest an attempt by certain Muslims to publicize their faith in the face of mounting and often aggressive proselytizing by evangelistic Christian groups. It may also be a reflection of the current waves of Islamic revivalism and fundamentalism being felt in Nigeria, as well as in other parts of the Islamic world. (See chapter 9.)

4.4   Exogenous religious institutions

In order to work through this extremely varied set of religious institutions, classified together for the purposes of the present study because of their common non-Nigerian origins, the following sub-divisions will be used.[20]   Evangelical, pentecostal and holiness groups will be treated together in the first category. The Jehovah's Witnesses will constitute the second category as they are a sufficiently large and distinctive group. The third category will consist of the Seventh-day Adventists, the Salvation Army and the Christian Science Society - which are not united in any ritual or doctrinal way, but within the context of this study, they share a similar sectarian response to the world, as well as roughly similar growth patterns in Calabar. The fourth group is characterized by the Black American churches (AME and CME), while the fifth category will consist of the spiritual science movements.

4.4.1   Pentecostal and evangelical organizations

While it could be argued that the pentecostal, evangelical and holiness churches and movements would be more correctly treated separately, on account of their doctrinal and historical differences, for practical reasons they have here been treated as a single category. In addition, it will be shown that, in the modern context, internal and external factors have worked to reduce the heterogeneous aspects and generate a homogeneity between the groups. It is very common for groups to combine (albeit in varying degrees) an interest in the gifts of the Holy Spirit, personal salvation and sanctification. (This is even more so the case with the indigenous movements which will be discussed in the next chapter.)

4.4.1.1   Apostolic Church

The Apostolic Church has recorded successful growth and expansion in the area. According to the 1980 field statistics, Calabar Field

Assembly recorded a total of 9 districts and 82 assemblies or branches with 8,898 communicant members and 2,070 adherents. It certainly has more branches than any other church in Calabar, although many are small, with the exception of the headquarters at Edgerley Road.[21]

The Apostolic Church in Nigeria is still regarded by the mission headquarters of the church in Bradford as a mission field, despite the church's long existence in Nigeria (since 1931).[22] Only a few missionaries remain, however, and the Golden Jubilee celebrations in 1981 provided the occasion for the drawing up of a constitution for the eventual autonomy of the Nigerian church.[23]

The church seems to attract people for a variety of reasons: firstly, it combines the structures and activities, and to some extent, the status of a mainline church, yet with a content and ideology more akin to a spiritual church. The very lively and emotionalist services, always in the local language, with the use of drums and clapping to excite the members, incorporate faith-healing and visionary experiences, as well as personal testimonies.[24] Apostles and prophets form part of the church hierarchy and fears of bewitchment are taken seriously, with regular early morning prayers for healing and deliverance. Women and youths are excluded from leadership responsibilities, but are allowed to form their own groups and hold monthly rallies, at which they may preach.[25]

The Apostolic Church, popularly known as "Obosi", has carved out a place for itself in Calabar Municipality, not only by virtue of its longstanding presence, but also because of its willingness to take part in inter-denominational services and welfare activities. Its more sectarian tendencies are apparent in the way it disciplines its members.[26] This, along with leadership struggles, its length of time in Calabar and tendency to encourage individual spiritual talents, is one of the factors which acccounts for the number of schisms from the church. There have been six known schisms from the Apostolic Church in Calabar to date: Mount Zion Light House Full Gospel Church (1946); Spiritual Kingdom Church of Christ (1946); The Church, the Body of Christ (1967); Christ the Shepherd New Kingdom's Flock (1976); the Truth and Life Church (1978) and the Jesus Christ Healing and Evangelical Movement (1981 - not a complete schism as yet).

4.4.1.2   Apostolic Faith Mission

The AF is more obviously dominated by the holiness doctrines and practices of the parent body in Oregon. Its bi-monthly newspaper, "The Light of Hope," comes directly from the U.S.A., although the Lagos headquarters is planning to start its own publication soon.[27] Missionary visits are scarce and there is no financial aid, except through the supply of papers and tracts and Sunday School books.[28] The architectural design of the church and the use of space follow the American model. Music is regarded as central to worship, and it is classical and gospel in style.

Women are allowed to become pastors and ministers (the American founder was a woman), but there are none in the Calabar church. In addition there is no segregation or symbolic differentiation between the sexes. The service is characterized by a combination of intense fervour (notably the extemporary prayers) and military-like discipline and order. There is also a strong emphasis on morality and avoidance of worldliness and unbelievers. Members of the church were attacked in August 1981 by an excommunicated member. See the *Nigerian Chronicle*, September 1, 1981. Since that day the gates of the church compound have remained locked except at service times.

Despite the fact that an Efik hymn book has been in use since 1955 and the service is conducted in both Efik and English, there is little concession shown by the AF to the African context in terms of external features. In addition, the strict moral code has served as a deterrent for many. Nonetheless, those who attend like the simple, orderly worship, devoid of ceremonialism and formalism and yet "Spirit-filled", as well as the clearly defined community characterized by a strong fundamentalism and sense of commitment. The church attracts over a thousand people to its Sunday morning service.   The AF maintains an exclusivist approach to other churches and does not engage in external relations, although for the first time in 1983, the church used the media to invite members of the public to attend its annual Christmas concert.

4.4.1.3   Assemblies of God

The AG is one of the faster growing churches in Calabar today. A visit to the headquarters at Fosbery Road on a Sunday morning reveals a congregation of over 500 people, engaged in lively worship. The key themes of the sessions are problems and blessings, while the sermons and exhortations emphasize personal experience, repentance, salvation, the power of the Holy Spirit and the Second Coming of Christ.

The evangelical, pentecostal and revivalist orientation of the AG attracts a fairly wide, although generally younger, cross-section of people, which may be partly linked to its use of English as the language of communication in all services. The egalitarian ideology of the AG is reflected in the number of people who are involved in the different stages of the service. The youth are extremely active in daily open-air evangelism, notably through the highly trained Christ's Ambassadors. For example, at an Evangelistic Crusade organized by the church in November 1981 at the Calabar Sports Stadium, the youth staged a motorbike cavalcade each evening through the town.

The AG in Calabar resembles an ecclesiastical body rather more than the original conception of a loose, non-hierarchical association of independent ministers and local groups. There is some evidence of the latter in the form of a campus revivalist group and Sunday School run by Dr. and Dr. (Mrs.) E. Eko. Although the church in Nigeria is autonomous, close contact is maintained with the American parent body through resident missionaries in the country (not in Calabar). The church uses literature published in English by the church in Accra, as well as a local newspaper - *The Nigerian Evangel* - produced in Aba.

4.4.1.4   Miscellaneous groups

A series of smaller churches, with varying blends of pentecostalism and evangelicalism, also operate within the Calabar township - the Calvary Baptist Church, the Christ Faith Evangelical Church, Christ for the World Mission and the Church of Christ. The Church of God of Prophecy ceased its activities in 1983 due to lack of support. These churches have not had the success of organizations such as the AG and AC. Some face institutional extinction perhaps because of poor leadership, exclusivity or inflexibility imposed by their parent bodies.

4.4.1.5   The Holy Spirit and cultural reinterpretation

Reflecting on the continuing expansion and success of the pentecostal and evangelical churches, there are some general observations which can be made. Firstly, a puritanical code of behaviour and distinctive group structures have an evident appeal in an environment of increasing social and moral dislocation and normative confusion. So too does the "cultural reinterpretation" of which Jules-Rosette speaks in *The New Religions of Africa*:

> the parallel expressive forms in music, dance and oratory represent creative combinations of indigenous cultural patterns with external media for representing them.[29]

The indigenous cultural patterns are spirit possession, prophecy, ecstatic phenomena, emotionalist worship and faith-healing. With the pneumatological emphasis of the churches, and their encouragement of a direct experience of the Holy Spirit made manifest through charismatic gifts and visible signs and results, the theme of "cultural reinterpretation" is the most illuminating perspective. The fighting of spirits with the Holy Spirit and the quest for spiritual power are an integral part of their world-view.

The "class" interpretation, that evangelical and pentecostal movements appeal to the oppressed, lower classes, seems to be less appropriate in the Calabar context, where political oppression at least, is relatively absent. While the former may be the case in the Americas, in Calabar a good section of the middle class as well as the lower classes are represented. This is notably the case with the evangelistic associations which are able to attract university professors, teachers, doctors, civil servants and other professionals into their ranks; they constitute a growing and influential minority. People are also drawn from a variety of ethnic backgrounds, particularly once the church or organization is well established.

It is also possible to identify ideological elements conducive to modernization within pentecostalism and evangelicalism. For example, psychological traits and patterns of behaviour are encouraged which are conducive to success in a capitalist economy, such as self-denial, self-discipline, individualism and leadership qualities.[30] The system even provides support in the case of failure or frustration.[31] The basis for regional integration through common forms of religious experience provided by these groups is especially important when there is a sizeable migrant population, as in Calabar today.

Just as pentecostalism and evangelicalism may be considered as "modernizing" forms of religion, in that they facilitate the socialization of individuals in an urban, developing context, and create new communities which transcend former traditional or ethnic ties, we need also to take account of the way in which they may create new barriers, this time between the "saved" and the "unsaved". This is manifested in the anti-ecumenism and exclusivism of many of the churches. For example members of the Assemblies of God are not allowed to become lawyers, nor to belong to village associations or social clubs. For some this orientation may constitute the major source of attraction as they are welcomed into a closely-knit, yet international, network with promise of a new life and new opportunities in this world and the next.

The suggestion that this type of religious expression, originating as it does mainly in the U.S., is a form of "religious multinationalism",[32] has some validity, although the diversity of the groups and emergence of indigenous forms of pentecostalism and evangelicalism would seem to weaken the idea of any cultural or religious imperialism.

If this type of religion is flourishing in modern-day Calabar, it may also be due to the fact that they offer the same "goods" as the spiritual churches, minus the stigma which some people still attach to the latter, namely "superstition", "ritualism" and "cultism" (i.e. the restrictions of an esoteric cult).

4.4.2   Jehovah's Witnesses

The number of JW's in Calabar has now reportedly climbed to over 10,000 with 7 Kingdom Halls and 21 congregations. There are several congregations per hall, some English (7) and some Efik-speaking, as well as Yoruba and Igbo.[33] Bands of smartly dressed JW evangelists, brandishing their briefcases and copies of The Watchtower and Awake, are now a familiar sight on the streets of Calabar and JW literature has a wide circulation as it is inexpensive, provocative and easy to understand. The practice of house-to-house evangelism is particularly suited to the African context, where visitors are readily welcomed into every household and discussion on religious matters is a popular pastime. This is in contrast to the Western context where the privacy of the home is considered of great importance.[34]

The JW world-view, symbolized in the concept of the Kingdom, is clearly defined and comprehensive, with a strong inclination towards moral issues (from personal to global). A strong morality and millennial ideas, whereby the corrupt shall be condemned and the elect shall be elevated to heaven as the witnesses of truth amongst humankind, are evidently popular and relevant in the midst of social and political upheavals and injustices. A carefully articulated theodicy which interprets this world as under the invisible authority of Satan is balanced by other-worldly teachings on the Kingdom of Jehovah.[35] For some adherents this type of explanation of the injustices of the world may serve as a symbolic, regulatory mechanism to compensate for an individual's suffering and misfortune.

While the organization does not adopt a reformist attitude

towards the problems and evils of the world, in terms of promoting social, medical, political or educational development, it does offer a blueprint for order, action and meaning for the individual as part of a national and international network. This is an important factor in explaining the appeal of this type of movement to the urban youth.

Many JW converts emphasize the value of the learning experience and knowledge accrued from membership of the organization. The centrality of Bible study and active evangelism within the organization is reflected in the time and effort given to training people in these skills, usually through the "Theocratic School". Young people are instructed on how to speak, dress, project themselves and communicate with unbelievers. Such skills are important with regard to social mobility.[36] In addition, the youth and the lower classes are attracted by the egalitarian spirit of the JW and the possibility of advancement and responsibility within the organization regardless of education or social status.[37]

While the various congregations organize themselves in a fairly autonomous way, their world-view is structured according to the American JW model.[38] The music is light classical, often performed by full orchestras and produced by JW groups in Britain, Germany or the U.S.; no African music is permitted. The majority of the literature is either of British or American origin, although an increasing number of texts are being translated into the local languages. In Calabar, the missionary presence is only really felt at the time of the Annual District Convention, when a visiting missionary will deliver a number of public addresses. It has been argued that the rapid indigenization of the JW in Kenya helped generate a popular, lay organization centred around local communities rather than a professional hierarchy.[39] The same is true for Calabar also.

The convention is a popular event and draws at least 2000 people from all over the state. It may be viewed as an attempt to create a microcosm of peace, order and fellowship, a reflection or foretaste of Jehovah's Kingdom within the macrocosm of disorder, disharmony, war and injustice. The creation of the microcosm has tended to isolate the JW from the surrounding society, although the history of the organization in Calabar is not one of persecution and alienation as in some other parts of Africa. Certain features of the JW are unpopular, at least with relatives of members, for instance the absence of memorial services and wake-keeping, as well as of infant baptism.

4.4.3   Salvation Army, Seventh-day Adventists and Christian Science

The Salvation Army (SA) distinguishes itself, externally at least, from other religious organizations in the area by its use of a military-style uniform and brass band. Indeed it is this aspect of the church, as a religious army, together with its "military" hierarchy and discipline, its simple, fundamentalist message, its popular tunes and informal and colloquial style of preaching, that seem to draw converts. Because of insufficient funds and members, the church in Calabar does not engage in the conventional social welfare activities which characterize the work of this organization in other contexts. There are currently two branches in the town: the headquarters at Goldie Street and another branch at Chamley Street, founded in 1972, which is led by a woman, Captain Williams. Membership, including recruits, in the five branches in the Calabar area (three are situated in outlying districts) does not exceed 400. At one time Calabar was the headquarters of the Eastern Region of the SA, but in 1952-54, the headquarters moved to the mainland where the church was proving more successful. This trend has been reflected up until the present day, perhaps because of the greater possibilities for open-air evangelism in the rural areas, such as march-pasts and "compound revivalism" usually conducted by the SA women.[40]

Despite its sectarian characteristics, with prohibitions on tobacco, alcohol, night clubs and "worldly societies", the SA has not opted for a radical evangelicalism, but has rather gained the status of a small, mainline church, and for this reason has encountered little opposition. It belongs to the Christian Council of Nigeria and takes part in civic ceremonies and inter-denominational services.[41]

The church uses Efik as its main language and the SA

Songbook is already in its fifth edition. The missionary connections are still felt, not just at convention time when they receive overseas visitors, but also in terms of the hierarchy and organization, as some of the staff at the Lagos Secretariat are from Britain. In addition, training programmes for commissioned officers are organized from the London headquarters.

The Seventh-day Adventists (SDA) have become known in Nigeria for their educational and health reforms.[42] The Calabar branch of the church is small, less than a hundred members.[43] Welfare activities are limited to fund-raising for the national projects which are seen as the "fruits of the heavenly kingdom".[44] The Sabbath School is an important and democratic feature of the life of the church, allowing all members, particularly the youth, to participate in, and lead, Bible study and discussion.[45]

The SDA are known in Calabar because of their belief in the seventh-day sabbath as well as their various dietetic taboos, such as abstention from shellfish, pork, coffee, tea, alcohol and tobacco.[46] The millennial teachings do not seem to predominate among the Calabar SDA, the emphasis being rather on personal faith and discipline, as well as collective evangelism. The latter is an important area of concern, since there are plans to speed up the development of the church in eastern Nigeria, as it has lagged behind the western branches.

In 1983 the SDA was the only church in Calabar with a full-time resident missionary - Pastor H. Lukko from Finland. Literature from the institution's headquarters in Washington, D.C. is used and occasionally translated into Efik.[47]

Despite its presence in Calabar for more than a decade, Christian Science (CS) has experienced little growth; the membership today numbers around thirty members. Given the primary focus of CS on healing, it is important to speculate why the group has not had more success in an environment such as Calabar where health is a predominant concern. There would appear to be three possible explanations. Firstly, physical and mental suffering are not seen as an existential reality in the CS world-view, but rather as an illusion, and realization of the "false claims" of matter leads one to the realization of one's true spiritual being - sinless, healthy and undying.[48] Such metaphysical conceptions of evil and suffering diverge from prevailing beliefs in Calabar, which tend towards the externalization and personification of evil, and ritual redress. In other words, CS offers a this-worldly salvation acquired through mental as opposed to ritual operation and manipulation. In addition, as a system of healing based on metaphysical ideas, reading is a primary activity for Christian Scientists and this presupposes a certain degree of literacy and education. A third observation relates to the overall organization of the movement, which revolves around the strong, central control of the Mother Church in Boston, excluding virtually any possibilities for innovation or at least adaptation to local cultural needs.

The healing and spiritual powers of women, reflected through the founder, Mary Baker Eddy, and the large number of female practitioners (healing specialists) and members in the movement in general, are not reflected in either the membership or hierarchy of the group in Calabar. CS teachings and healing techniques tend to have a far wider circulation, through individual subscribers to the literature of the movement, than is reflected by the current status of the branch in Calabar.

In 1978 a revelation led the Church of Jesus Christ of Latter-Day Saints (CJCLDS) to open its priesthood to blacks.[49] This revoked earlier church policy based upon an inspired "translation" by the founder, Joseph Smith, which declared that blacks were cursed with regard to the priesthood.[50] By 1981 the newly founded mission to Africa was organizing a conference in Calabar to try to gain a footing in an area hitherto unevangelized by the main Mormon church.[51]

Given its late arrival on the Calabar "mission scene", the CJCLDS is planning to engage in low-level evangelism, with an emphasis on development projects, notably agricultural.[52] Members of the public who attended the inaugural meeting in Calabar in 1981 were interested in the emphasis on family ties, both past and present, on Old Testament practices and the mythological and millennial teachings regarding the new Zion in the Book of Mormon. Many people were impressed by the presentation of a new, lavishly illustrated sacred text - the Book of Mormon. The message of the Americans regarding progress and development was also well received, as well as its unsectarian acceptance of worldly pursuits and comforts, and adoption of modern facilities.[53]

4.4.4   Black American churches

There are two black American (Methodist) churches operating in Calabar today: the African Methodist Episcopal Zion Church (AMEZ) and the Christian Methodist Episcopal Church (CME). Both have two branches, but have marked little growth or development considering that they have been in Calabar for more than twenty-five years. AMEZ has been more successful in the mainland part of the state, chiefly because of its schooling programmes, but is nonetheless a well known church in Calabar township; it has approximately 350 members. The AMEZ is popularly considered to be fairly "orthodox" in liturgy and structure.[54] While it would like to be seen as a mainline religious body (as in the U.S.) and indeed interacts with the mainline churches at inter-denominational services, it belongs to the Christian Community of Nigeria in Calabar, a rival organization to the Christian Council of Nigeria, which caters more to the independent churches (see chap. 7). As in the case of the Apostolic Church, AMEZ is an organization which serves as a training ground for many future independent and spiritual church founders and leaders.

4.4.5   Spiritual science movements

In this section we are dealing with an extremely heterogeneous collection of movements. They nonetheless share certain definable characteristics, namely a quest for spiritual knowledge and power, higher states of consciousness and a direct religious (ecstatic) experience, as well as the use of procedures, techniques and practices which draw on hidden or concealed forces in order to manipulate the empirical course of existence.

In a Western context, movements of this nature would be referred to as "cults". This terminology would be confusing in the African context, since the term is used to refer to a system of

beliefs and worship associated with a particular object of worship, a deity, for example. Instead we have chosen as an overall term "spiritual science movements", since the search for spiritual knowledge and power through the use of scientific, or at least pseudo-scientific means, characterizes most of these groups.[55]
Given the array of groups within this section, some form of sub-classification was deemed necessary. One alternative was to sub-divide in terms of predominant orientations, namely metaphysical, spiritualist, psychic, occult and mystical. There are important differences between the above: for instance, the metaphysician believes that he/she can have knowledge of the world and the cosmos through human reason (though not as a result of logical knowledge). The mystic, on the other hand, believes that direct knowledge of God, of spiritual truth, or of ultimate reality, is attainable through immediate intuition, insight or illumination, in other words in a way which differs from ordinary sense perception and which is not dependent on the medium of human reason. The psychic is considered to be subject to non-physical forces, while the occultist is concerned to discover the concealed, the unknown, the esoteric, that which lies beyond the realm of human understanding, but which is not necessarily supernatural - astrology or parapsychology for example.

However since many of the groups are highly eclectic, particularly in the Nigerian context, it will be useful only to use these distinctions to highlight tendencies within particular groups, rather than as classificatory labels. So the data is divided up in terms of origins, i.e. whether a group is of Western or Eastern origins, since this is to a large extent indicative of particular orientations. It is also consonant with our decision to classify broadly on the basis of origins, since this was considered the most appropriate and effective way to approach the material in the present study.

In the following accounts of the different spiritual science movements which have become part of Calabar's religious scene, there is an observable emphasis on individualism and interiorization, and an attitude of "self-sufficiency" with regard to spiritual experience. This has obvious consequences for group structure and identity, but does not automatically entail a thoroughgoing anti-institutionalism. Some forms of social expression occur but they are not binding or absolute.[56] There are also varying degrees of esotericism, modernism and instrumentalism, but these will be discussed after the historical description.

4.4.5.1   Western-related groups

Twentieth century Rosicrucianism claims historical continuity with an ancient Egyptian occult order, although its connections are more apparently with the Western magical tradition, Theosophy, Freemasonry and modern parapsychology in varying degrees.[57] There are various Rosicrucian bodies, but it is the Ancient and Mystical Order of the Rosae Crucis (AMORC), perhaps the largest and most well established, which has become part of Calabar's religious landscape. The AMORC headquarters for all of Nigeria stand proudly on the State Housing Estate in Calabar, with architecture and symbolism reminiscent of Ancient Egypt.[58]

This esoteric fraternal order, founded in 1915 by H. Spencer Lewis in New York City, has steadily increased its membership through a massive public relations campaign.[59] It began in Calabar in 1956, although some people were already receiving Rosicrucian materials from the headquarters in Lagos. In 1975 Calabar was granted "chapter" status. AMORC claims not to be a religion, but describes itself as a "mystical philosophy", a "worldwide cultural fraternity" or an "age-old brotherhood of learning". One of its main aims is to help people to discover their secret powers of inner vision and cosmic consciousness and to develop their psychic power of attraction. There is a strong orientation towards goal-attainment and problem-solving, as evidenced by one of their free booklets which is frequently advertized in Nigeria, as well as in other parts of the world: "The Mastery of Life".

AMORC regularly arranges public lectures, as well as television programmes in Calabar, and a good deal of the literature is available locally for purchase.[60] In this way, Rosicrucian teachings have a wide dissemination, although the inner philosophy and techniques are only available through correspondence courses from the headquarters at San José, California.[61] Initiates are also able to attend the weekly lodge-type ceremonies at the Apollonius Lodge in Calabar.[62]   The Rosicrucians in Calabar publicize their annual reenactments of the ancient ceremonies marking the Building of the Great Pyramid and the New Year.   The Lodge plans to build the first planetarium in Africa.[63]

One of the reasons that could be adduced for the success of the AMORC in Calabar and in Nigeria as a whole, is its similarity to the Masonic model.   While operating as a secret society, with initiation into different grades and esoteric knowledge, AMORC as an organization is not restricted to particular ethnic groups, as in the case of traditional secret societies.   The AMORC world-view has international, even cosmic dimensions, and a content which is seen as "scientific" and modern".   This has obvious attractions for migrant professional men who have become disillusioned with conventional church worship and yet still want to be part of a support network, which may equally satisfy their religious needs. By the same token, it is the secret society image which has engendered hostility towards the AMORC.   Their esoteric rites are popularly linked with "magic" and "witchcraft", particularly those that surround the burial of their members.

The Aetherius Society (AS) was publicized, on the occasion of its introduction to Calabar in February 1982, as "an international spiritual brotherhood".   It is perhaps more accurately described as a "flying saucer" or "UFO" (unidentified flying objects) cult, with an explicitly religious structure which combines the teachings of occultism and yoga.[64]   The society was founded by a medium, George King, in Britain in 1955, and has since spread to Los Angeles.[65]   Meetings have been held in Calabar since 1982 and attract mostly men, some of them highly placed; topics treated include   spiritualism,   spiritual   discipline,   "scientific   prayer", communication with extra-terrestrial beings for advanced spiritual and material powers, healing and karmic patterns.

The Church of the New Jerusalem (CNJ) is founded on the teachings   of   the   Swedish   mystic,   Emmanuel   Swedenborg (1668-1772).   A branch of the church is situated at Etinan on the mainland, but there are plans to extend the church to Calabar.[66] The secretary of the CNJ was an undergraduate student at the University of Calabar from 1978-82 and took the opportunity to circulate Swedenborgian literature, mostly amongst students.[67]

Works by Swedenborg where he describes the supernatural spheres and their activities, such as "Heaven and Hell", "The Last Judgement", as well as doctrinal studies such as "The True Christian Religion" are the most popular, as from his concrete visions he sought to give answers to the sort of questions ordinary Christians would ask, such as - What is heaven like? What really goes on in hell? How do spirits live?[68] His work was however tinged with spiritualism and Kabbalism.[69] In later years he claimed that he had received revelations directly from God about the hidden spiritual meanings in the Bible.[70]

The Institute of Religious Science (IRS) which has a very small following in Calabar, stands in the New Thought tradition and yet its worship and organization resemble any liberal Protestant church.[71] The metaphysical teachings which are most popular in the Calabar context are those concerning healing, as perpetrated through the church's publication - *The Science of Mind*, and other booklets such as "Spiritual Healing" and "Your Mind is Creative". The latter was found in use at the Friends of Jesus Church;[72] there are undoubtedly individual subscribers as well.

The JSC or Superet Light Mission is primarily concerned with psychic phenomena. The founder, Mother Trust from Los Angeles, was an aura scientist who claimed to have the mission of bringing to the world Jesus' light teaching. She also claimed to have discovered the secret of Mother God. In a revelation she was told, "This is the new name, Superet, which is the everlasting fire in God's sacred purple Heart."[73] She went on to discover that there are two purple hearts united in one, and that the Holy Ghost is the Mother God.[74]

As part of their prayers and liturgical responses, members repeat - "In the name of the Father and the Mother God and the Superet Heart of God". They still claim however, that Jesus Christ (who was borne by the Mother God through Mary) is the head of the church.[75] Their worship centres around meditation on the words of Mother Trust, whose disembodied voice (she died in 1958) is heard via a well-worn cassette, and the contemplation of the Superet Heart, the symbol of Light given to believers. There are also readings from the Bible and hymns from Moody and Sankey.

While the current leader of the small church, whose membership stands at 132 (in 1982), is a man, there is an egalitarian attitude to the roles of the sexes. Half of the Church Council is made up of women, and two women are undergoing ministerial training, which consists of a five-year correspondence course and exams administered by the U.S. headquarters. Many of the books that members may buy to study at home focus on healing. Illiterates are taught to read. It is mainly the lower classes who are attracted to this small, yet very disciplined church, which at least demonstrates that this type of religiosity appeals to not just the higher classes of educated men. Their Prince of Peace Movement holds meetings and rallies for healing and spiritual development and because of its "non-sectarian" approach and has succeeded in attracting a wider range of people that those who are actual church members.

4.4.5.2   Eastern-related groups

The Eastern-related spiritual science groups are a more recent phenomenon in Calabar. For example, Eckankar (ECK), or the Secret Science of Soul Travel, was originated by the ECK Master, Paul Twitchell, in California in 1965. His spiritual and visionary experiences in India and Tibet form the literary basis of ECK, which teaches the direct path to God, or the path of total awareness.[76]   The Eckankar Society of Nigeria, with headquarters in Lagos, began an extensive campaign to launch the movement in the country from 1981.[77]   In 1982 about 250 people attended a seminar in Calabar and heard the Area Mahdi, Benjamin Anyaeji, a well-known television personality because of his frequent broadcasts about ECK, talk about his earlier incarnations, and how, through ECK, everyone could learn "how to be a god". He emphasized that the path of ECK was a path to God and not just for the development of psychic powers and occult knowledge.[78]   He nonetheless delighted the crowd with descriptions of his "lower" and "higher" powers, notably his ability to stop rain on the road so as to facilitate his journey and how he had reached the higher spiritual levels, where one was free from polarities - good and evil

- and could instead become "causative".

The saffron-coloured robes of Hare Krishna devotees were first sighted in Calabar in October 1981. They were on a reconnaissance tour from Lagos. Several months later a "Hare Krishna Bookmobile" was observed selling books outside the main post office in Calabar. There is little doubt that free or reasonably priced literature, such as that offered by the International Society of Krishna Consciousness (ISKCON), is an attractive feature of any religious movement, especially on university and college campuses. The initial membership package for life members includes books, a diary, a calendar, records and cassettes, posters and devotional gifts and an "International Travel Passport" with opportunities for free meals and accommodation in ISKCON centres worldwide.

In Lagos, people have been drawn to the movement by its feasts and festivals, and emphasis on devotionalism.[79]   It seems likely that ISKCON will recruit with difficulty given its alien cultural mode and strict monastic rules of conduct for devotees.[80] In addition, marital relationships are decided by the group and their offspring are committed to Krishna rather than to the parents. However, the family structure of the Krishnaite group, with members submitting in obedience to the father figure of the Spiritual Master, provides an atmosphere of communality and conviviality, as well as a highly structured life with few individual decisions. The potential appeal of such a group is to marginal individuals in a disorienting urban context.

The Holy Spirit Association for the Unification of World Christianity, more commonly known as the Unification Church (UC), was founded by Sun Myung Moon in Korea in the 1950s. Moon claimed to have received visions directly from Christ instructing him to complete Christ's unfinished work.[81]

The Unification Church has been in Nigeria for some years but without much success. The church was registered in Lagos in 1980.[82]   There was difficulty over land and trustees; they eventually used the land (and church - the Concordant Teaching Mission) handed over to them by Reverend Obong at Eket in 1976. The missionaries had trouble obtaining visas for full-time missionary work and so they had to come in as electronics engineers (for one of the church companies) and engage in church work as a secondary activity.[83]

In Calabar the UC was able to meet at the home of Mrs. Asama who had joined the movement while doing further studies in Business Administration in the U.S. The small group in Calabar of not more than ten people met to study the "Divine Principle", the basic scripture revealed to Reverend Moon. Occasionally one-day conferences were organized to stimulate public interest. People were impressed initially by the group's elaborate organization, seen particularly through its literature, teaching aids and films. They were also drawn by the messianic aspirations of the UC with its aim to unite all religions and fight against the satanic forces of evil and communism (the latter of course a less meaningful threat in Calabar than in some other parts of the world). The concept of the Unified Family is also important, with the prominence given to family relationships and strict sexual mores, structured around the charismatic father figure of Reverend Moon. There is also the added attraction of being one of those chosen to travel to the New York Unification Seminary for training programmes.

The UC presents itself as Christian organization, but is in fact a combination of messianism, Christian fundamentalism, Oriental dualism, clairvoyance and healing.[84] The church is strict about discipline and instruction, and exerts a totalitarian hold over its full members, expecting them to lead an austere existence and renounce parents, family and career. Again, such demands seem out of place in the African context, to all but the most marginal and deprived.

In 1981 the Calabar group of the UC closed down and Mr. and Mrs. Kijima, the two Japanese missionaries, left for Lagos to try and strengthen the mission there. In speculating on the failure of the group to set down roots in Calabar, there would seem to be several factors involved. Firstly, non-Western missionaries, barely fluent in English, were in charge of the group; secondly, the building used by the group for meetings was located in an inaccessible part of town; thirdly, limited funds were available to the group because of the problems at the Lagos headquarters. The UC, while failing to make an impact in an institutional way, has nonetheless continued to proselytize in a more subtle and high-level way, through the invitations extended to Nigerian and other African academics to attend the international conferences held at regular intervals in different parts of the world. In 1983 plans were being drawn up between the UC and the Brotherhood of the Cross and Star for the former to provide the financing for a large fishing project organized by the Brotherhood of the Cross and Star in the Cross River area.[85]

The Subud Brotherhood (SB) is another organization with a precarious future in Calabar.[86]   The official launching of Subud Nigeria, in 1981, was postponed indefinitely, due to industrial action in the state capital.   Of Indonesian origin, the movement teaches that by means of spiritual exercises known as "latihan", one can gain access to God's power by complete surrender of the self and the senses.[87]   SB is not publicized as a religion.[88]   For that reason, people of all faiths are invited to participate in the direct religious experience characterized by surrender, ecstasy and even trance.   The movement has virtually no organization, leadership or direction, only "helpers" who are capable of transmitting the "spiritual chain reaction".[89]

The Calabar group, based at the "National Spiritual Centre" (the headquarters of SB in Nigeria), has a resident "Helper", as well as a few regular members and irregular enquirers.   They have produced their own constitution and have also had printed local editions (in English) of the founder's (Bapak) speeches and addresses.

Since 1981 the Calabar Reading Circle of the Grail Movement of Nigeria has been publicizing its presence in the area by inviting people to an annual public lecture on "The Grail Message: *In the Light of Truth*".   The advertisements addressed those who are concerned about "any issue concerning human existence in Creation" and spiritual knowledge in general.   People are informed that the solutions to all such existential questions are to be found in the three-volume work, *In the Light of Truth*, by the founder Abd-ru-shin.

The penultimate group in this section is Baha'ism or the Baha'i Faith (BF).[90]   In some respects it is difficult to include the BF along with the previously described spiritual science groups, since the Baha'i emphasis is rather on social, ethical and practical realities, rather than on mystical questions; but a survey of the type of new religious movements we have been discussing, in Calabar as elsewhere, would seem incomplete without Baha'ism.[91]

The local BF community in Calabar consists of thirty members, mainly Nigerians and a few Iranians. A Calabar Baha'i Centre was inaugurated on New Year's Day, March 20, 1983. Baha'i Centres have also been created in some outlying rural areas, but considering that the group has existed in Calabar since 1956, it has experienced minimal growth.[92] Perhaps the explanation lies in the nature of its message - world peace, one God, one Religion, harmony of science and religion, sexual and racial equality - which is too idealistic and universal, even maybe too progressive, for the needs of most people in Calabar.[93]

A translation programme is under way to publish Baha'i texts in Efik. Baha'i texts in English have already been produced by the National Assembly in Lagos.[94] The BF have been active in publicizing in the local Calabar press the persecution that they have suffered as a group in Iran, and have also used the media to put across their teachings.

In February 1979 a Japanese new religion by the name of Tensho-Kotai-Jingu-Kyo (TKJK) undertook a tour of Nigeria to publicize its organization.[95] Calabar was included on the movement's itinerary but it is unlikely that there were any lasting effects from the visit. TKJK announced itself to the Nigerian public as "the universal spiritual religion for World Peace and Redemption of evil spirits". The movement, which links Buddhist and Shinto elements, is otherwise known as the "Dancing Religion" because of the quiet swaying dance meant to lead its devotees into a state of *muga* (non-self - Buddhist-derived).[96]

Another of Japan's major new religions, Soka Gakkai, has branches in Lagos and Zaria, but no known activity in Calabar as yet.

4.4.5.3   An occult explosion?

A few words need to be said in concluding this section about the type of religiosity these spiritual science movements represent and the type of religious needs they seem to be fulfilling.

First and foremost, they offer the possibility of a direct contact with the sacred, allowing the development of a "religious self-sufficiency". Increased access to the sacred, while this may entail for some a more intensely emotional experience and a deeper and more satisfying spirituality, essentially encourages an instrumentalist and manipulationist type of religion, with the development of techniques and methods which lead to "higher", "deeper" or inner levels of existence and consciousness. This spiritual power and knowledge is believed to have direct empirical and beneficial consequences in the life of an individual.

Ways in which the spiritual science movements differ from the mainline and exogenous Christian groups is their denial of the personal attributes of the divine, which is balanced by the central role played by charismatic "guru" figures in several of the movements. There is a tendency to reject historical traditions and conventional ecclesiastical structures and hierarchies. Individualism predominates over group structures; the Rosicrucians (AMORC) advertize "Your Home is Your Temple" with photographs of affluent-looking white males pouring over metaphysical texts in the comfort of their armchairs. Once the devotee has acquired the teachings and techniques, he/she is responsible for his/her spiritual destiny; soteriological responsibility has shifted away from the divine or divine/human mediator to the individual. This type of religiosity has obvious attractions for those who are disillusioned and dissatisfied with more institutional and conventional forms.[97] Many of the spiritual science groups in fact renounce the status of "religion". Being involved with these groups is a source of supplementary religiosity in addition to church affiliation, for example. That is why it is common to find people experimenting and dabbling with the various groups and techniques - what could be described as "amateur occultism".[98]

Within the Western context, the spiritual sciences have been labelled as "counter-cultural" and as part of an "alternative reality tradition".[99] These terms are inappropriate in the Nigerian situation. As far as the churches are concerned, the spiritual sciences represent a deviant form of religiosity and constitute "modern and sophisticated forms of witchcraft and superstition".

The spiritual churches of indigenous origin have displayed mixed reactions; some, such as the Brotherhood of the Cross and Star, have openly incorporated occult teachings, others condemn such religious organizations under the rubric of "worldly societies". The greatest continuity and affinity would appear to be with the traditional world-view, with the emphasis on the integration of the spiritual and material worlds, the esoteric and initiatory aspects, as well as in terms of such concepts as "power". Many amateur occultists therefore see their attempts to attain higher levels of consciousness as a revitalization process and as consonant with the world-affirming and pragmatic orientation of traditional religious beliefs and practices.[100]

While no statistics are currently available, it is still possible to observe the types of recruits which are drawn to the spiritual science movements. They are usually middle-aged men, well-educated professionals, civil servants, bankers, technologists or businessmen. There are very few women, except in those movements which emphasize creativity, such as Eckankar, or emotional and ecstatic experience. There is virtually no evidence to suggest that these religious groups in Calabar have a greater appeal for alienated or marginal individuals, or those seeking a sophisticated form of escapism. Rather they are drawing into their ranks people who have become dissatisfied with conventional religious world-views and who are instead searching for new sources of meaning and spiritual power. They are enticed by the challenge of an "advanced path", "superior knowledge", as well as by the time-honoured values of discipline, love and service. Elements of the traditional ethos here merge comfortably with the message of modernity. The nature of the clientle must also be linked with the fairly high standard of literacy which is required for immersion into the spiritual sciences, as well as the economic means to have access to these sources.[101]

It is perhaps too early to predict an "occult explosion", but we have nonetheless been able to demonstrate the interest being shown in these new movements, as well as the influence they are having on religious attitudes and behaviour in general. Further light will be thrown on these points in subsequent chapters as we examine indigenous spiritual science movements and more general trends in personal and popular religion. Since we are concerned to describe the processes of adaptation as well as adoption, it is pertinent to highlight at least one area where the spiritual sciences are being modified by the Calabar context: that is in promoting a greater instrumentalism - the techniques and knowledge are seen as a means to an end, usually healing and an increase in personal power, rather than as an end in themselves, such as the "transformation of desire" or the "ultimate transformation of self".[102] In other words, amongst spiritual science devotees and amateur occultists in Calabar, an intensified, more "spiritual" religious experience is considered as a means to an end, rather than as religion for religion's sake.

Notes

1. See J.W. Fernandez, "Microcosmogony and Modernization in Modern African Religious Movements", Occasional Paper No. 3, Centre for Developing Area Studies, McGill University, 1969, p. 5.

2. The few remaining missionaries in the area (Cross River State) are employed in theological colleges, rural schools and training centres, as well as hospitals and leper colonies.

3. The sole Nigerian cardinal to date is Cardinal Dominic Ekandem from Ikot Ekpene in the Cross River State.

4. Mary Archibald, the headmistress of Union Secondary School, Ibiaku, Cross River State.

5. See the *Programme of Inaugural Service of Calabar/Dundee Presbyteries Partnership*, held at Duke Town Presbyterian Church, Calabar, July 11, 1982.

6. See *Tradition and Change - the Presbyterian Church of Nigeria, Calabar*, joint television production by the University of Calabar and the University of Aberdeen, 1980.

7. See Very Rev. Akanu A. Otu, *The Ordination of the Reverend Mgbeke G. Okore: First Woman Minister of the Presbyterian Church of Nigeria* (Aba: The Presbyterian Church of Nigeria, 1982). Mimeo.

8. Branches of the church situated in the Qua and Efut areas of the town - namely Akim Qua Presbyterian Church, Big Qua Presbyterian Church and Efut Ekondo Presbyterian Church tend to have a sizeable proportion of Qua and Efut people in their congregations.

9. It is actually Duke Town Church which enjoys this role, by virtue of its position in history and its prime location, at the heart of old Calabar, opposite the main Ekpe temple on Eyamba Square, the central ceremonial plaza.

10. Since the civil war, the premises have been used for archival storage. The proposal to revive the church was submitted to the 1983 Synod; the result is not known.

11. Personal communication from Rev. Dr. J.A. Laoye, Calabar, May 5, 1980.

12. See Asuquo, *Patronal Festival Sermon*, p. 7.

13. Tensions have been brewing for some years over the fate of the old wooden building at Beecroft. Some members have campaigned for its demolition in order to construct a modern and larger building on the same site. Others have argued in favour of preserving the building on account of its historical importance. The Patriarch moved in support of the latter group and issued instructions to seek an alternative piece of land for the construction of the new cathedral.

14. The statistics provided by Barrett (*World Christian Encyclopaedia*, p. 530) on the Calabar diocese (larger than the town itself and bordered by the Ikot Ekpene and Ogoja dioceses) are as follows: 28 congregations; 131,700 adult members; 239,480 affiliates; 50% Ibibio, 40% Efik and 10% Igbo.

15. Interview with Sister Maria Immaculata Offiong, Vicar-General of Handmaids of the Holy Child Jesus, Calabar, May 3, 1983.

16. Henshaw Town, Efut Abua, Marian Road, Ikot Ansa, Ikot Esu [Diamond Hill], College of Technology, St. Paul's Chaplaincy [University of Calabar]. See Mina U. Akan, "Changes in Some Christian Churches since 1960", University of Calabar undergraduate project, 1982.

17. See for example, S.N. Owan, "Why the Pope Won't Visit CRS", *The Nigerian Chronicle*, February 11, 1982.

18. This and other information concerning Islam in Calabar was obtained from S. Yekini Alabi, graduate assistant in the Department of Religious Studies and Philosophy, University of Calabar.

19. "The Teaching of Islam", June 20, 1982; "Prayer - the Pillar of Islam", July 22, 1982; "Zakat as the Third Pillar of Islam", September 14, 1982.

20. The mission-related institutions or mainline churches and Islam have been treated separately despite the fact that they also have exogenous origins. The exogenous religious institutions being treated in this section could have been labelled "sectarian" in contrast to the "mainline" institutions, but the explicit use of this term has been avoided.

21. The Apostolic Church: Cross River State Field, Field Statistics 1980. Mimeo. It should be noted that the Calabar Field Assembly covers an area more extensive than that of the municipality alone. There are 1,544 communicants and 1,052 adherents.

22. The church grew out of the great Welsh revivals of the first decade of the twentieth century. The headquarters are at Penygroes, Glamorgan.

23. See *Golden Jubilee Souvenir Magazine of the Holy Child Federated Alumnae - Cross River State Zone* (Calabar, 1980).

24. The church has used the *Revised Church Hymnary* in Efik up until now; they are currently translating their own Revival Hymnary. Interview with Pastor E. Okon, Field Superintendent, Calabar, April 1, 1981.

25. Ibid. In Calabar and the 13 other Field Assemblies in the Cross River State, the women's groups outnumber the Witness and Sunday School groups.

26. See for example the case which made the headlines of Calabar newspaper, *The Nigerian Gong* (October 11-17, 1982), concerning a young woman who was suspended for six months by the Apostolic Church for dancing at the Independence Day celebrations in October 1982.

27. Interview with Pastor A.F. Ufford, Calabar, April 6, 1981.

28. Turner notes that the church was also receiving healing cloths from across the Atlantic. "Pentecostal Movements in Nigeria", p. 126.

29. Jules-Rosette, in *The New Religions of Africa*, p. 222.

30. W. Wedenoja, "Modernization and the Pentecostal Movement in Jamaica" in Glazier, ed., pp.40-41.

31. Ibid.

32. See T.J. Chordas, "Catholic Pentecostalism: A New World in the New World" in Glazier, ed., p. 163.

33. See B.P. Edet, p. 10. The membership estimate is perhaps over-generous. Information received from Mr. E. Effanga, Calabar and Mr. Mkpa, Creek Town, November 21, 1982.

34. Cf. B.R. Wilson, "Jehovah's Witnesses in Kenya", *Journal of Religion in Africa* 5,2 (1973):135.

35. See S. Cross, "Independent Churches and Independent States: Jehovah's Witnesses in East and Central Africa" in Fashol -Luke et al, eds., *Christianity in Independent Africa*, p. 304.

36. See for example the *Theocratic Ministry School Guidebook.*

37. Interview with Abel Usoro, University of Calabar student and member of JW Atamunu congregation, July 15, 1982. The same point is made by Bryan Wilson with regard to the success of the JW in Kenya ("Jehovah's Witnesses in Kenya", p. 135).

38. See for example the Convention programme of 1982: "Arranged and directed by the Watch Tower Bible and Tract Society of Pennsylvania," p. 1.

39. Wilson, "Jehovah's Witnesses in Kenya", p. 147.

40. Interview with Captain M.U. Ekpo, Calabar, June 29, 1981.

41. The SA is very much a borderline case in that it could equally have been classified as a mainline church.

42. See "Operation Concern", a brochure produced by the Welfare Department of the Seventh-day Adventist Church, Ikeja, Lagos State, n.d.

43. Calabar was granted an Advising Committee in 1982 which is a step towards full mission status, although this is dependent on finance and number of baptisms. The date of the arrival of the SDA in Calabar is not known but it is believed to be sometime in the 1940s since SDA reached Aba in 1924 and Port Harcourt in 1930. See Knight, p. 202.

44. Sermon preached by Pastor H. Lukko at the Annual Harvest Ingathering, Seventh-day Adventist Church, Calabar, December 12, 1981.

45. I witnessed a group of junior staff of the university who were members of the SDA, meet on an almost daily basis after work for Bible study in preparation for Sabbath School.

46. B. Wilson, *Religious Sects* (London: World University Library), p. 101.

47. Early in 1983 a signboard entitled "Church of God (Seventh-Day)" appeared in front of a small and temporary structure, not far from the relatively longstanding building of the SDA church on Goldie Street. While some members of the latter were quick to dismiss its possible links with their own organization, it is most likely an independent adventist church which could have originated from the General Conference of the Church of God (see Melton, vol. 1, p. 469 or The Church of God (7th Day) (Salem, West Virginia) or The Church of God (Seventh Day), (Denver, Colorado) (see *Yearbook of American and Canadian Churches 1984*, pp. 44-5). It is not known how the church came to set up a branch in Calabar.

48. From a lecture delivered by Bruce Fitzwater C.S., a member of the Christian Science Board of Lectureship, entitled the "The Logical Certainty of Christian Science Healing", The West African People's Assembly Hall, Calabar, February 13, 1983. Wison, *Religious Sects*, p. 146.

49. See Shulman, p. 231.

50. See Wilson, *Religious Sects*, p. 203.

51. The Church of Jesus Christ in Nigeria, a small church operating on the mainland around Abak, used to have a branch in Calabar on the university campus near the government primary school. The church is associated with the Church of Jesus Christ [Bickertonites] (a reform or breakaway church of the Mormon family with headquarters in Monongahela, Pennsylvania and founded by William Bickerton in 1862) (see *Yearbook of American and Canadian Churches*, p. 45 and Shulman, p. 234). The small Abak church was originally an independent Christian group which was associated at one time with the Qua Iboe Mission, as well as the Salvation Army and the Mennonites. Information received from Professor A.F. Walls, December

1984. The land they used in Calabar was eventually acquired by the University for development purposes and the members now return home to the mainland for Sunday worship. Information from Dr. M. E. Akpan, Department of Political Science, University of Calabar and elder of the church, December 1982.

52. Interview with Elder Miles H. Jensen and Elder Rex C. Reeve, a member of the first quorum of seventy and Executive Administrator for the Church in Africa and the British Isles, and Africa West Mission President, Bryan A. Epsenschied, at a meeting organized by the CJCLDS in Nigeria at the Metropolitan Hotel, Calabar, February 16, 1981.

53. It was not possible to determine whether the CJCLDS made any inroads in Calabar itself, beyond a few individuals; the missionaries were expecting a more favourable response from the rural mainland areas. Ibid.

54. Cf. W. Johnson, "The Africanization of a Mission Church: The African Methodist Episcopal Church in Zambia" in *African Christianity: Patterns of Religious Continuity*, eds. G. Bond, W. Johnson and S. Walker (New York: Academic Press, 1979), pp. 89-108. See also R.W. Wyllie, *Spiritism in Ghana: a Study of New Religious Movements*, AAR Studies in Religion, 21 (Chico, CA: Scholars Press, 1980) who describes the doctrines and teachings of the AME Zion in Ghana as "patently Methodist" (pp. 8, 23, 90-94).

55. It is not possible here to enter into a philosophical discussion concerning the rationality or scientific status of these movements. But since they tend to be concerned with the super-sensible and non-experiential knowledge, we shall continue to use the terms "pseudo-scientific" and "pseudo-rational". Neither of these terms is however indicative of an empiricist aversion to, or criticism of, such knowledge.

56. R.S. Ellwood Jr., *Religious and Spiritual Groups in Modern America* (Englewood Cliffs, N.J.: Prentice-Hall Inc., 1973), p. 20.

57. See Melton, vol. 2, p. 178.

58. The building was dedicated in 1978.

59. Melton, vol. 2, p. 182.

60. Popular texts which circulate freely are the "Mystic Life of Jesus" and "The Secret Doctrines of Jesus" by H. Spencer Lewis.

61. One Rosicrucian member in Calabar showed me an impressive list of mail-order items available from the Californian headquarters. It included a range of ritual and meditational aids such as busts of Nefertiti and Akhnaton, scarab beetles, candelabra and incense, as well as a diverse range of reading matter.

62. Meetings for discourse take place on Saturdays, and for worship and meditation on Wednesday evenings.

63. Information obtained from a talk given by Professor U. Enyenehi, Professor of Biological Sciences at the University of Calabar, on "Mysticism and the World Order" at the University of Calabar on January 20, 1983 and a broadcast given by the Grand Master of AMORC (Calabar) on "Contemplation", NTA Channel 9, Calabar, February 27, 1983.

64. See Ellwood, p. 150.

65. Melton, vol. 2, p. 207.

66. Arthur Clapham was the first representative of the "New Church" (as the Swedenborgian Church was then called) to visit Nigeria (Port Harcourt, Aba, Ibadan and Lagos) in 1934. (Swedenborg himself was particularly interested in the Negro race.) Prior to that in 1930 a Ghanaian, Africanus Mensah, who was a correspondence student with New Church Theological College, opened a book room in Port Harcourt for the sale of Swedenborgian literature. See Knight, pp. 203-4. Mensah later moved to Owo but a series of New Church groups sprang up in the area occasioning the periodic visits of British representatives. In this way, New Church must have spread to Ibibioland and thence to Calabar.

67. For example, "This is Our God" and "A Great Revelation", both published in 1965 in Australia and written by Basil Lazer.

68. See Ellwood, p. 65.

69. Ibid.; Melton, vol. 2, p. 88.

70. Shulman, p. 462.

71. Ellwood, pp. 3-4.

72. See 3.8.

73. Melton, vol. 2, p. 105.

74. See J.C. Trust, *Key to Success* (Los Angeles: Superet Press, 1948), pp. 25-6.

75. Interview with Rev. Francis U. Akpan of the Superet Light Mission, Calabar, December 14, 1982.

76. Shulman, p. 379.

77. The movement actually started in Benin City where it is now the most active and produces a bi-annual newsletter. 64 groups have now been established all over Nigeria since 1973. In Lagos there exists an Eckankar House with a library and other facilities. The Calabar group began in 1981.

78. See Paul Twitchell, *Dangers of the Psychic World for Truth Seekers* (Menlo Park, CA: Eckankar, 1980). This was a leaflet made available to conference participants.

79. Melton, vol. 2, p. 372.

80. Ellwood, *Religious and Spiritual Groups*, p. 241.

81. Ellwood, *Religious and Spiritual Groups*, p. 291; Shulman, p. 476.

82. There are some doubts about the accuracy of this date.

83. Interview with Mr. Kijima, missionary for the International One World Crusade, the international youth brotherhood wing of the church, Calabar, April 10, 1981.

84. Shulman, p. 478.

85. The UC missionaries, as well as visiting officials of the organization, had always expressed interest in the BCS and had arranged an interview with Leader Obu shortly before their return to Lagos.

86. In the U.S. Subud is experiencing a decline in numbers. J. Needleman, *The New Religions* (New York: E.P. Dutton and Co, Inc., 1970), p. xii; also Ellwood, *Religious and Spiritual Groups*, pp. 287-88.

87. "Inaugural Address by the National Chairman of Subud Nigeria", a talk prepared for the formal launching of Subud World Association in Nigeria, December 11, 1981 (Calabar: Subud Nigeria, 1981), p. 3.

88. Bapak, "The Nature of Subud", *For Applicants to Membership of the Subud Brotherhood* (n.p.: Subud Publications International Ltd., n.d.), p. 10.

89. See "Inaugural Address", p. 8.

90. Ellwood, *Religious and Spiritual Groups*, p. 275.

91. Ibid., p. 276.

92. The BF claims to have 10,000 members in 150 local groups in Nigeria, with many more in Cameroon and Zaïre. Interview with Mr. Friday Ekpe, "leader" (there are no official leaders or clergy) of the Calabar Local Spiritual Assembly, Calabar, April 9, 1981. Mr. Ekpe belongs to the Continental Board of Counsellors for Africa based in Nairobi. He travels widely in Africa visiting the various Baha'i groups and is the only African member of the West African board.

93. See Uwen Umo, "My Encounter with the Baha'i Faith", *The Nigerian Chronicle*, January 21, 1981.

94. For example, *An Outline of Baha'i History, Laws and Administration* (Lagos: The National Spiritual Assembly of the Baha'is of Nigeria, 1978); *The Spiritual Destiny of Africa* (Lagos: The National Spiritual Assembly of the Baha'is of Nigeria, 1982).

95. See *Sunday Times*, February 11, 1979.

96. Information on this movement was supplied by Professor M. Pye, Philipps-Universität, Marburg.

97. See M. Eliade, "The Occult and the Modern World" in his *Occultism, Witchcraft and Modern Fashions* (Chicago: The University of Chicago Press, 1976), p. 63.

98. Occultism tends to predominate over mysticism and metaphysics.

99. Ellwood, *Religious and Spiritual Groups*, p. 42f.

100.There are even some concrete attempts to fuse traditional and occult ideas. In January 1983 I received an invitation to a "traditional religious ceremony" in Oron to mark the coming out from a three-year "Holy Confinement" of Mrs. Atim Otu Ita, a priestess of the chief Oron deity, *Ebin Obo*, (known as *Afiawan Ukim* among the Efik). Invitees were informed that this exercise was not an attempt to revive traditional religion per se, but "to establish the depth of discipline and holiness expected of the ancient deity worshippers". The ceremony was linked to the gradual transition from the Piscean to the Aquarian Age; the "New Age" is to be accompanied by disasters and destruction, the fulfilment of the cosmic laws of cause and effect and retributive justice.

101.The literature of the Grail Movement and AMORC are to be noted in this respect.

102.Needleman, p. 13; Ellwood, *Religious and Spiritual Groups*, p. 5f.

Chapter Five

Indigenous and Institutional Religion

5.1   Introduction

This chapter is concerned with indigenous and institutional forms of religion in modern Calabar, notably the diversification of indigenous religious movements and institutions that has occurred since the last decade. We shall begin first by examining how traditional religious institutions and phenomena have fared in the modern context.

5.2   Traditional religion

From an institutional perspective, traditional religion has declined in terms of the number of functionaries, adherents, and ritual or cultic activities. But the fact that priests are at a premium and that very few people would claim to be "traditionalists", in the sense of maintaining a wholly traditional world-view or being practitioners or devotees of a particular cult, should not be interpreted as the imminent demise of this dimension of the religious life of Calabar. Not only have certain traditional institutions persisted and been revitalized in the modern context, but there are interesting examples of modification of traditional forms and content to suit modern needs.

5.2.1   Ndem cults

The cults of the local deities and water spirits have suffered considerably in the face of both Christianization and modernization. They have been obvious targets for attack by both Christians and progressives, though perhaps have suffered most critically in terms of internal erosion - the unwillingness of descendants of the priestly lineages to take on such status and responsibilities.

Actual cultic locations, in the form of shrines, have virtually disappeared. Rites and sacrifices are rarely performed calendrically and communally. It is more common for individual supplicants to consult the various practitioners or diviners on a private and critical basis.

Certain deities, by virtue of their popularity, continue to maintain a place in Calabar's religious life. The acid test seems to be whether they are included on the "libation list", in other words those deities specifically named during libation rituals at major ceremonies. The list, which reflects the Efik pantheon at a particular moment in time, will vary as individual deities are added or subtracted, according to popularity and community recognition, historical significance and priestly influence. According to an Efik leader, the current list is:

Anansa Ikang (f)	Nkong Inuakpa (f)
Afia Anwan (f)	Anwakang (f)
Ekpenyong Ekpenyong (m)	Atakpo (m)
Isunku Monko (f)	Akpanim (?)

Atakpo and Akpanim are shared with the Ibibio, dating back to the period of Efik settlement in Uruan.[1]

Anansa, believed to dwell in the river around Old Town or Obutong, is still, some would claim, the most prominent of all the Efik deities. Obutong is now virtually uninhabited due to the construction of the Calabar Cement Company (CALCEMCO) and the naval base there, but because, historically, it was the first Efik settlement after Creek Town, Anansa is always given pre-eminence in the list of deities. Her continued popularity and presence are also manifested in the navy vessel named after her - the S.S. Anansa, which is permanently moored at the Eastern Naval Command Headquarters in Calabar. A series of accidents during the construction of the new port complex in Calabar in the late seventies, obliged the Nigerian Ports Authority to perform the necessary sacrifices to enable work to continue. Critical events of this nature, such as drowning or ferry accidents, are readily attributed to the ndem and their anger at having been neglected. The necessary sacrifices will hurriedly be performed in order to placate the deity in question and restore harmony.

The cult of Ekpenyong, one of the male ndem, has been revitalized through his role as patron deity of Nka Ekpenyong Nnuk

- a cultural and philosophical organization, created in 1979 by the Efik youth. In addition to its social and political aims, the group is attempting to stimulate Efik cultural awareness through the use of masquerades and other activities. Sacrifices to Ekpenyong are being revived on an annual basis, during the month of November. Ekpenyong is believed to protect Calabar and in particular his devotees. In popular mythology it is recounted how he temporarily halted the landing of the federal troops in Calabar during the civil war, until the necessary sacrifices were conducted to assure him of their positive intentions.

5.2.2   Kingship

The king or *obong* of Calabar represents an important and continuing focus of Efik cultural identity. Despite his virtual loss of political power, the Obong is still revered as the patriarch of the Efik people. He is considered to be the "living representative of all the spiritual and physical components of the Efik".[2]   By virtue of his investiture, it is believed that he becomes more than an ordinary human being, he represents both aspects of existence. He is accorded elaborate funerary rites as he continues to be a man of special eminence in the after-life. Some of the rites have been modified; for example human sacrifice has been replaced by the sacrifice of a cow, and the king's possessions are not buried with him as before.

The rituals and ceremonies surrounding the installation and enthronement of the Obong have, in contrast, been carefully preserved. The traditional coronation (*uyara ntinya*) is performed in the ancient shrine of one of the Efik tutelary deities - known collectively as Ndem Efik Iboku. The coronation of the present king in April 1982 was performed in the *Efe Asaba* (Shrine of the Cobra), which was first used as an Ndem shrine in 1660.[3]   The chief priest or priestess is involved in the actual crowning of the Obong and the final salutation by the Ekpe Society concludes the traditional kingmaking process. This demonstrates the complementarity of the two traditional religious institutions: Ndem, with its female and nature associations, and the Ekpe Society, identified with the land, the town and male power, are both necessary components of the making and maintaining of a king, as they are symbols of life itself.

The festivities surrounding the installation of a new Obong, which occur at a later stage over a period of a week, provide an important opportunity for the various traditional societies and masquerades to perform their ritual dances and plays, many of which grew out of the cults of Ndem and Ekpe.[4]   While the religious content may have been lost from many of these traditional forms, or is meaningless to many of the participants and spectators, some traditional religious norms and cultural conceptions are being communicated and perpetuated in this way. The whiteness and rich adornment of the ndem dancers symbolize the attributes of the "mermaids" who inhabit the river and are believed to protect the people of Calabar. The aggressive movements and dark, vivid colours of the Ekpe masqueraders symbolize the fearful *ekpe* forest spirit, which is "tamed" by the initiates in order to exert their authority over it, and maintain law and order in, the community.

5.2.3   Ekpe Society

The Ekpe Society is clearly another major vehicle of religious and cultural traditions. Like the kingship institution, it has suffered a considerable loss of political and judicial power, notably in the urban areas, where it has been unable to maintain its authority in the face of modern government and an increasingly pluralistic community. In response to these changes it has undergone something of a metamorphosis and now styles itself as an "esoteric philosophical society". Some would even describe it as a "gentleman's club", along masonic lines. Opinions differ as to whether the fraternity is flourishing or declining, but there is no doubt that the majority of leading figures in Efik society are members, for they see Ekpe as the most complete expression of their identity; many others are attracted by the cultural and social benefits afforded by membership.[5]   In modern times the Ekpe Society has come to represent a bulwark against political subordination by the Ibibio and Igbo peoples, largely through its ability to provide a common denominator and unifying force for the Efik, Qua and Efut peoples, and through its mystical, fearful and esoteric aspects which are a source of power and authority, and attraction.[6]

Ekpe temples are to be found in the various corners of Calabar township and Ekpe masquerades are a common sight on the streets whenever there is an important burial, or chieftaincy installation; they also appear on public holidays such as Christmas and Easter, or even at the opening of a new commercial enterprise. Despite the modification of some of its functions, Ekpe still retains its religious core. The actual deities worshipped by the initiates are a closely guarded secret, but respect is offered to Ndem Efik, Abasi and the ancestors. There are cases of Efik men refusing to associate themselves with Ekpe on account of their Christian faith, but committed Ekpe members argue that there is no contradiction between Ekpe and Christianity: no anti-Christian activities are performed in Ekpe, on the contrary it encourages a strong sense of brotherhood and communal welfare.

The absence in Calabar of a regular cycle of farming or fishing festivals as in some other parts of the Cross River State, has not facilitated the survival of the traditional religious domain. It is the resilience of the more urbanized and politicized Obongship and Ekpe institutions that have counteracted the downward trend. There is yet another area of traditional religious activity, namely healing and divination, which is sufficiently public and institutionalized to deserve our attention in this section.

5.2.4   Healers and diviners

The signboards of traditional healers are a familiar feature of Calabar's religious landscape. Many healers are situated on the rural periphery of the town, while others who have recently moved in from the mainland, have acquired plots of land in the reclaimed New Airport zone, to the south of the town centre. While the majority combine the functions of both herbalist (abia-ibok) and diviner (*abia-idiong*), it is still possible to find a rain expert or "doctor" (*abia-edim*) in operation.[7] The urban rain expert, whose main function is to stop rather than produce rain, finds himself hired by a variety of people and groups - churches, political parties and wealthy individuals.[8] His is nonetheless a dying breed.

Healing homes are a more profitable livelihood. Essentially structured around the skills of a particular individual as healer, diviner or prophet, a healing home may refer to the compound of the former or actually designate a building constructed for the purposes of healing in its widest sense. It usually depends on whether the practitioner treats his healing activities as a principal or secondary occupation. For example, there is a signboard which advertized "Healing Home", "Beer Parlour" and "Dry Cleaning" all at the same address!

While the model of the healing home is basically a traditional one, in order to attract clients in a modernizing and religiously competitive environment, many of the diviners and herbalists have become eclectic and multi-functional, so that the border between "traditional", "neo-traditional" and "syncretist" is often difficult, if not impossible, to determine. In fact several healing homes may go on to become spiritual churches, as we witnessed earlier in the case of the Brotherhood and the Crystal Cathedral. Christian symbols are common and so is the use of mysticism and the occult, although our survey revealed one Muslim healing home.

A good example is the Okopedi Healing Home and Okopedi Enterprises, which has developed into a commercial venture, selling all mannner of magical and occult charms and concoctions, many of Indian origin. Okon Okopedi travelled to India for a three-month training period in "astro-science". He attracts those seeking fortune in life, love, success in exams or business, as well as the usual quota of sick people.[9]

In 1983 the "Mother Jah Shrine" came to local attention, with its bizarre combination of violent healing and exorcism techniques, Rastafarianism and the occult. The shrine was eventually burnt down by an irate public and some neighbouring members of the Brotherhood of the Cross and Star.

An important observation is that the majority of the healing homes in Calabar, ranging from the purely traditional (now rare in town) to the overtly syncretic,[10] are founded and run by Ibibio and Anang men, many of whom come to settle in Calabar to cater for the increasing numbers of non-Efik migrants. Efik traditional religious specialists, apart from resident priests or priestesses, are instead situated just outside of Calabar, in the plantation areas. An Efik person will therefore travel out of town to consult a diviner or herbalist, usually associated with his or her particular family.

Modern times have spelt hard times for many institutional aspects of Calabar's traditional religious dimension, but through the dynamic processes of revitalization, modification and innovation, some form of continuity is assured. As we have seen, that continuity does not necessarily follow predicted patterns, i.e., calendrical and public forms ceding to critical and private manifestations. Survival is linked to expediency, whether it is economic, political, cultural or, of course, religious. The traditional religious domain has therefore become more variegated and fragmented and consequently more difficult to research; in the following chapter we shall consider the statistics on traditional religious institutions generated by our survey. In chapter seven we shall examine more closely the persistence and influence of traditional religious beliefs on Calabar religion as a whole.

5.3   Spiritual self-determination - the hallmark of the new churches

In chapter four, we sought to cover, in a fairly comprehensive way, the various imported religious bodies and assess their current role and status in the wider community. We tried to highlight briefly the dominant characteristics and dynamics of each group so as to build up an idea of their world-view in relation to other religious groups, and also to the wider socio-cultural whole. We shall return to this particular approach in the present section, but only with regard to selected groups. This will allow us to gain a deeper insight into the worlds of particular spiritual churches which are distinctive, yet illustrative of indigenous, Christian-related innovation and response.

5.3.1   Brotherhood of the Cross and Star

The Brotherhood (BCS) is the largest and most well known of all the spiritual churches and indigenous religious movements in Calabar today.   It is impossible to discuss an organization such as the BCS without referring to the central role of the founder and Sole Spiritual Leader - Olumba Olumba Obu.[11]   Not only is the whole church ostensibly structured around his leadership and authority, but his sermons and pronouncements form the basis of all beliefs and doctrines.

The two main thrusts of Obu's teachings are love (*ima*) and power (*odudu*), which is essentially the power of the Holy Spirit. Without the love of God and fellow human beings, the world as well as individuals become "spiritually deficient".[12]   The message of "Love One Another" is the key to the solution of all problems. The emphasis is on "Practical Christianity", which is the motto of the "New Age" or "Kingdom of God" as manifested on this earth through the BCS.   The concept of the "Kingdom" is an important one as it reflects both the millennial beliefs and the mission of the church.   It is realized through "Brotherhood" which signifies the unity of and love for all the creations of God.[13]

The meaning of "Cross" suggests a sharing in the sufferings of Christ and the problems of others, as part of a redemptive process.[14]   "Star" means simply the reign and glory of Christ, although Obu suggests "Star" is the hidden name for the light of the "New Age".[15]   However, at the end of a sermon on that theme he is more explicit: "Brotherhood of the Cross and Star... is going to be the STAR, the new name for all Churches in the world."[16]

"Sole Spiritual Head" is the most commonly used appellation for the leader of the BCS, but he is also regarded as the second reincarnation of Christ, the personification of the Holy Spirit, and even God himself.[17]   The divinizing of Obu is a process which has been occurring since the 1970s and constitutes a response by his followers to his charisma and miraculous healing powers.[18]   It is reflected in the literature, with earlier pamphlets entitled: "A man who could be a living God in disguise", progressing to the more explicit later publications: "His Deity is Revealed".   The editorial of the first issue of the BCS journal begins as follows:

Hail, All Bow
Behold Olumba Olumba Obu
King of Kings
The Conqueror and Vanisher
Sole Spiritual Head of the Universe[19]

Obu's own reaction to such eulogizing is highly ambivalent. When interviewed, or in public pronouncements, he refers his critics (for this has become a highly controversial issue in Calabar's religious circles) to his publication: "I AM NOT GOD but Olumba Olumba Obu".[20] While manifestly a denial of his divinity, the language in this, as elsewhere, is very ambiguous at times, for example, "I and the Father are one" or "I am the Way, the Truth and the Life". In addition, Obu personally signs and approves all circulars and even many of the published materials, which quite clearly contain references to his divinity. One of the more recent publications (May 1983?) being circulated by the organization is entitled: *The Supreme Being: Holy Father Olumba Olumba Obu*.

The beliefs surrounding Obu's unique status date back to his childhood and early youth when he gained a reputation as a teacher and healer. Today he is regarded by many as a man with exceptional, if not supernatural, powers and capabilities. For instance, he sleeps and eats very little, following a mainly fruitarian diet. He preaches every day, often for several hours at a stretch; he sees and prays for over one hundred people per day; he leads a very simple, if not frugal existence, dressing in either white or red soutanes or white singlet, shorts and wrapper; he never travels anywhere, except to go on foot to the nearby 26 Mbukpa Road bethel (the original bethel) where his wife resides. He claims not to have returned to his birthplace at Biakpan (in Akamkpa Division, on the edge of Igbo territory - an area of serious border disputes) since 1955, even though the rural town has become a place of pilgrimage for the church and is known as "Bethlehem", "New Jerusalem" and the "Promised Land" to members. The waters of the Biakpan stream are believed to have special healing powers; fruits and crops are believed to grow untended in "the Garden of Eden" (a plot of land set aside for agricultural development). The name "Biakpan" is also believed to be a derivative of "Obio Akpan Abasi" meaning "the city of the son of God" in Efik. He also maintains that he is uneducated and yet takes great pleasure in astounding people with his knowledge of the Bible and his ability to quote relevant texts at random.[21]

Worship in the BCS is plain and simple with no use of candles or incense or other ritualistic forms and objects. The architecture of the bethels is unimpressive and decoration is kept to a minimum, with little use of symbols. Each service (and there are several per day) follows a pre-determined order, with prayers, hymns (all composed "in spirit" by members of the church), thanksofferings and choruses, and the "Golden Text and Sermon".[22] The biblical texts and readings are always drawn from the New Testament alone, although the Leader may make passing references to the Old Testament where relevant. Everyone wears a white soutane and shoes are forbidden. There is no gender segregation in the church, but the ordained members sit near the front, and at the headquarters, no-one enters the altar area except Obu himself.

The high points of the church's ritual cycle are the three annual Pentecostal Conventions held at Christmas, Easter and Anniversary time (in August). These gatherings last for a month at a time and many thousands of people attend from the branches worldwide.[23] It is a time for business meetings to be held as well as an occasion for spiritual and evangelistic fervour. Street outings take place and members parade on the streets of Calabar, proclaiming the glory of Obu and the Brotherhood. Instead of Holy Communion which is seen as a memorial of Christ's death, "love-feasts" are held, which celebrate Christ's return to earth (in the form of Obu).

Moral injunctions are a prominent feature of Obu's teachings.[24] Tobacco, sexual immorality, abortion, murder and stealing are among those sins most frequently condemned by the church.[25] Members are also exhorted to refrain from polygamy, from any type of witchcraft or secret society, and from magic or traditional herbal remedies. Obu teaches that sin causes bewitchment and misfortune, and emphasizes the importance of confession and ascetic practices such as fasting, for as he commonly says "it is necessary to mortify the flesh to obtain spiritual power".

The experiential dimension of the BCS naturally focuses on the leader, O.O. Obu. While Obu preaches that BCS is a spiritual organization where the Holy Spirit is active and spiritual gifts and manifestations proliferate, most of the accounts by members of their spiritual experiences (which are either published or circulated as testimonies) describe their experience of Obu in dreams, visions and auditions. Sometimes his face or his name "OOO" appear to people either at a time of crisis or shortly before their eventual conversion to BCS.

An electrifying moment during the services at Ambo Street is when Obu "dispenses" spiritual power to the congregation. Ecstatic behaviour in the form of trance possession, glossolalia, as well as uncontrolled dancing and emotional outbursts occur. Spiritual manifestations in the course of the service are somewhat discouraged in Obu's presence. Strict guidelines and discipline are imposed on prophets because of the risk of commercialization of healing and prophetic gifts.

The BCS is hierarchically structured as follows:

> The Sole Spiritual Leader
> Students and Christ Servants
> Ordained members: Bishops, Pastors, Apostles, Senior
>   Prophets, Prophets
> Elders
> Spirited Children
> Choristers
> Congregation
> Children [26]

Students and Christ Servants serve the BCS on a full-time basis. The former are celibate (and hence tend to be younger). Both Students and Christ Servants lead an ascetic and monastic way of life at the headquarters before being posted to a bethel. All belong to the "Christ Universal School of Practical Christianity" which was inagurated in 1971.[27] Ordained members (apart from the Bishops) do not function on a full-time basis. Their selection is also dependent upon the choice of the Leader. Pastors have such spiritual gifts as healing, prophecy, visions and dreaming, and are responsible for the administration of bethels. Apostles may not assume the latter responsibility. The role of prophet or prophetess carries with it the usual spiritual gifts, which is why it is emphasized that all ordained members are in fact "prophets". Spirited children are non-ordained visioners.

Music plays an important part in terms of evangelism[28] and as a stimulant to the spiritual life of the community: "Spiritual works are known to be pronounced when spiritual songs are hot and stimulating".[29]   Choir festivals and competitions have become increasingly popular.   The music could be characterized as gospel songs and choruses, with Obu as the overriding theme (for example, the popular refrain "I am safe, safe, surely safe in Obu"); no instruments are employed, whether African or Western.

Each zone of the BCS is governed by an Education, Labour and Welfare Board and a Leader's Representative.   There are also Leader's Representatives (one male, one female) stationed at each bethel.   All are answerable directly to the Leader and must present reports at The Spiritual Council of Churches, a general business meeting held annually at the December convention.[30]

Women are ordained as prophetesses, senior prophetesses, deaconnesses and evangelists.   They may exercize their spiritual gifts of prophesying and healing.   Some attain important positions of responsibility in the running of the church.[31]   Women are also appointed as "mothers" of bethels, responsible for the preparation of feasts and welfare of visitors.   This seems to be the type of background role played by the Leader's wife, who is known by everyone as the "Holy Mother".

The church now claims to have over 1000 branches.[32]   There are rumours of "several million members".   There are believed to be 29 bethels in Calabar alone.[33]   The greatest concentration of BCS bethels is in the Uyo area, although many of these are certainly small village bethels, with no more than a few score members. Through the agency of migrants, as well as active evangelism and development, branches have been established in almost all the nineteen states of Nigeria, as well as other West African countries, such as Ghana, Liberia and Cameroon.[34]   There are now well established branches in Britain, West Germany and the U.S., and plans to consolidate groups in Trinidad, India and the U.S.S.R.[35] This rapid expansion is attributable not just to the evangelizing zeal and world-conquering aspirations of the organization, but also to a well co-ordinated evangelism programme, backed up by strategic publicity campaigns.[36] Brotherhood teams have gone on tours to the U.S. and Britain every year since 1980, meeting church leaders, and healing and preaching.[37]

Leader Obu has made every effort to demonstrate his concern for welfare activities, not just within the church by building a centre for the handicapped and giving shelter to the destitute and unemployed, but also by donating to charitable organizations on a much wider scale.[38] In this way he has earned government approval for his efforts and together with the visible signs of BCS success and expansion: printing press, guest house, canteen, bookstore and Globemaster Services (the commercial wing of the church which engages in catering, tailoring and international trading); this has helped attract some of the higher ranking members of Calabar society.[39] The integration of the latter into influential positions, combined with a committed full-time work force of generally lower class and younger people, have contributed to the successful growth of the organization. In addition, Obu courts the establishment and projects himself as the preserver of the status quo, morality and harmony. But he also seeks to maintain his distance by criticizing the government on certain issues.[40]

The BCS claims to be more than just another church: it is the New Kingdom, the New Age, it is Brotherhood. The focal point of the millennium is the headquarters at Ambo Street in Calabar. This "City of God" is like a spiritual and physical microcosm of the Brotherhood macrocosm; it is a holy place characterized by purity, blessings and protection.[41] In many ways it resembles a typical African compound, particularly the healing home model (which was its original format), structured around the "Father", to whom people come for help, cures and solace. It also represents a type of holy community, a self-contained and clearly defined, inner world to which one can escape or retire from the vagaries of the hostile, outer world. But these models do not sufficiently portray the dynamism of Brotherhood as a concept and an institution. It is a world which is ascending, moving towards an apocalyptic fulfilment in the year 2001, in contradistinction to the rest of the world

which is heading for downfall and destruction.[42]   It is like a vision
and a network which radiate outwards from the charismatic figure
of Olumba Olumba Obu, who nurtures the worldwide development
and expansion of the organization through his personal charisma,
teachings and symbolism.[43]   As a banner at the entrance to the
Brotherhood   compound   during   one   Pentecostal   Convention
appropriately declared: "O O O YOUR WORLD."

5.3.2   Holy Face (Spiritual) Church (HFSC)[44]

This small spiritual church has been included in this section as it
represents an example of the "healing home" or "prayer house"
model, in the initial stages of routinization and institutionalization.

Mr. S.A. Okpo, who is a builder and contractor from Ikono
Local Government Area on the mainland, was born and bred a
member of the AME Zion church.   He received very little
education, just enough to read the Bible in Efik.   He moved to
Calabar from Enugu as a result of the civil war, where he
encountered a woman (in 1971) who travelled from Ikot Ekpene to
inform him of her vision that he was destined to found a church.
He ignored this early "calling" and continued to rise in the
leadership of the AME Zion church, participating to the extent of
personally financing a new branch of the church.   In 1978 his son
fell sick and they took him to a "prayer room" at Palm Street in
Calabar, known as "Holy Face".[45]   After his son received a
successful cure there, Mr. Okpo continued to attend the latter for
evening prayers, while maintaining his AME Zion affiliation.   In his
own words he justified this dual membership because of the
differing functions of the two institutions: "Holy Face was a prayer
house with visions, and prayers and healing, and AME was just a
church".[46]   A vision by the pastor of the Holy Face prayer group,
that Okpo should be given a key to start his own church (not a
prayer house it was emphasized), led Okpo to decide, in 1981, to
use the land he had purchased for his own residence to build a
church instead.

By 1983, the growing congregation of around 100 was meeting
for worship in a small, corrugated iron construction on a plot of

land at the edge of the main highway leading out of Calabar. Catholic influences abound in the devotional imagery and ritual symbolism. It has lived up to its designation as a "spiritual church", with the normal pattern of worship frequently interrupted by the "workings of the Holy Spirit" through glossolalia, visions and ecstatic behaviour.[47]

Healing and protection are major concerns of the HFSC, shaping not only the pattern and content of the worship, but also the use of symbols and sacred space. On one occasion at the Sunday morning service, a young man, complaining of a "loss of power", sought the healing prayers of the congregation.[48] One of the church's spiritual team, which incidentally is composed entirely of women, a young prophetess and secondary school student, revealed in a trance that the young man's "power" had been taken by another, whose name she would not or could not reveal. She prescribed a series of ritual activities which he had to perform, there and then, but the chief message is that he should continue attending the church for cure and protection. This is an obvious channel of recruitment or conversion.

The compound as a whole reflects the designation of the founder that his church is a "church for the helpless".[49] A special praying ground is situated just beyond the church building, as well as a "pit" for the seriously sick (intended to recreate the resurrection of Christ from the tomb); chains, used for the restraining of the mentally insane, are also evident. At the back of the compound there are some temporary living quarters, occupied mainly by women who may be seeking help with fertility or childbirth problems, or a short-term respite from domestic difficulties. For special cures, swords, stones, salt, needles, keys, padlocks and crosses will be used. The music includes well-known hymns, the most popular being those which speak of "victory".[50] The predominant music, however, has a distinctly traditional flavour; it is accompanied by spontaneous dancing, clapping and ecstatic behaviour.[51]

The appeal of this type of small, neighbourhood or "compound church" lies in its direct approach to people's problems, its size and sense of community which recreate to some extent the traditional compound where people (notably the poor, illiterate and alienated) may come for support, entertainment and generally feel "at home". And yet, both leaders and members share an avid desire for expansion, institutionalization and recognition, with dreams of concrete cathedrals and fleets of evangelism buses. This is not illustrative of pure materialism, but is rather grounded in the belief that a successful church (that is, one that exhibits rapid growth and development) is only successful if spiritual power is the motivating force. While that power may stem from, or be mediated by the charisma of a particular person, usually the founder or leader, it is a power that can be, and must be, enjoyed collectively and democratically. In the following section we shall see that the concept and structure of the "compound church" are not necessarily lost in the processes of expansion and development.[52]

5.3.3   Truth and Life Ministries International

With the Truth and Life Church (or Truth and Life Ministries International [TLMI], as it is now called), we are moving in the direction of a new breed of spiritual and independent church. It is a religious organization which outwardly does not resemble the "typical" image of an African independent church, for it lacks the ritual symbolism, taboos and music normally associated with such churches. In many ways it seems to owe more to non-indigenous origins and influences than to its own indigenous roots. This is particularly evident in the language and doctrines which are distinctly pentecostal and evangelical. Preaching styles recall those of the American born-again evangelist than the African prophet.

The aims of the TLMI are enshrined on their new bus:

CHURCH PLANTING EVANGELISM DELIVERANCE
BIBLE STUDIES

The founder, Rev. Dr. A.O. Akwaowo, emphasizes the importance of the concept of "ministries" rather than the more restrictive notion of a "church".[53] The historical development of TLMI can be traced as follows:

Truth and Life Evangelistic Group	1977
Truth and Life Church	1979
Construction of church building	1980
Truth and Life Church International	1981
Truth and Life Ministries International	1982

More recently TLMI has sought a wider orientation with a radio, television and cassette ministry, as well as a monthly newsletter and magazine (*The Miracles*). The "Deliverance Hour Ministry" publishes the transcripts of the sermons of Akwaowo, which treat such topics as "The New Birth", "The Rapture and the Second Coming of Christ" and "Have Faith in God". There is also a Business Reply Service and mailing list, which allows non-members to benefit from the ministry.

The use of such techniques stems largely from the business acumen and dynamism of the founder, who was once a Personal Secretary in the State government. His organizational skills have also been influenced by his American training and experience; he has attended a three-month Bible conference in San Diego.[54] He recently received an Honorary Doctorate of Divinity from Covington Theological Seminary in Rossville, Georgia.

TLMI, which now has over 400 baptised members in three branches on the mainland in addition to the headquarters in Calabar, and scores of non-member "supporters", exhibits a remarkable degree of what may be termed "internationalization". By internationalization we understand the establishing of, or desire to establish, international contacts in the religious field. TLMI has built up a considerable network of international relationships: the Osborn Foundation International (Tulsa, Oklahoma); Christ for the Nations, Inc. (U.S.A.); Oral Roberts Evangelistic Association (Tulsa, Oklahoma); Covington Theological Seminary (Georgia); Church of God Mission International (Benin City); Scripture Gift Mission (London); Faith Pool Prayer Groups (Ghana and Florida). The relationship of TLMI with these groups is not one of dependency, it is rather one of spiritual counselling and "supplementation", through the provision of books, tracts, cassette tapes, and perhaps the occasional visit of a representative.[55] Some financial aid was received from the All Nations For Christ Program (Texas) to help establish a branch at Itu. Akwaowo believes firmly in the importance of "spiritual independence" for his organization and its followers. He has plans to establish a printing press and Bible school. He has taken the initiative to found an "international evangelistic team" whose members (from Nigeria, U.S., U.K. and India) will evangelize in one another's countries.[56]   To this end, Akwaowo undertook a missionary journey to India (Kotagiri, Coimbatore, Singanallur) in March 1983.[57]   Within Nigeria itself, Akwaowo has adopted a cooperative attitude towards other churches and evangelistic associations. He was chairman of the inter-denominational committee for the International Year of the Disabled, and encourages freelance preachers, including women, to use his pulpit. He is wary, however, of merger or affiliation attempts.

For any religious organization to succeed in Calabar, its world-view must correspond at some point with those of its potential adherents, and it must offer a blueprint for action in accordance with people's needs. In this respect the TLMI does not differ from any other religious group which is enjoying sustained growth and development. Healing, prayer and miracles are vital components of the world of TLM. For those unable to come to the "compound" for prayer and "laying-on of hands", "faith-prayer cloths" are sent out to them or they are visited at home. For those troubled by witchcraft, fasting and prayer are the prescriptions for "deliverance". In place of ritualistic techniques, the supplicant is treated to soteriological concepts and evangelical rhetoric mediated and interpreted by Akwaowo and his team for local needs. Akwaowo does not, therefore, represent the charismatic leader as characterized by Obu; he is rather the leader with rational-legal authority who uses his entrepreneurial skills to organize a small ecclesiastical "business".

5.4   New trends and developments

5.4.1   The revivalist movement: a new breed of spiritual
church

The type of organization created by Akwaowo is not an isolated example of this new type of spirituality.[58]   It is "new" in that these groups, which are founded by Nigerians for Nigerians in Nigeria, are drawing increasingly on a repertoire of language and techniques, forms and concepts, which stem largely from the American evangelical and pentecostal traditions.   The leaders of the Nigerian movements are engaged in a process of interpretation and adaptation of the former to local needs and conditions.   These movements are characterized by an internationalist and expansionist vision, and they also exhibit to some extent inclusivist or non-denominational tendencies, which has not been a predominant feature of the mission or later "sectarian" churches in the area.

These indigenous revivalist movements, as we shall term them, are motivated by a new identity (as "born again" and sanctifed Christians) and a redefined concept of salvation (more personally and theologically oriented), as well as being characterized by more flexible structures than the conventional "church" model.

An example of this new breed of spiritual church or revivalist movement is the Revival Valley Ministries (RVM).   The movement was begun in March 1981 by Rev. Idem Ikon.   By March 1983 more than three hundred people were worshipping on a regular basis in a rented school room at the West African People's Institute at Diamond Hill in Calabar.   In addition to street meetings and conventions, RVM produces a bi-monthly newsletter entitled the *Harvest Digest* with information and photographs of the movement's activities and "successes", an address by the director, or an outside contributor and testimonies of "saved members".[59]   RVM has established three "tabernacles" or churches in Calabar and other parts of the state.   The director, Rev. Ikon, describes his conception of the Victory Tabernacle:

> [It] is a church for all. As far as we know, this is
> the only non-denominational church in Calabar. It is
> a home church. The Victory Tabernacle has no
> membership but fellowship. No creed but Christ. No
> book but the Bible. No law but love.[60]

It is significant to note that the main time for worship is on
Sunday evening at 6 p.m. This allows people to attend other
churches in the morning. As in the case of the Truth and Life
Ministries, prayer and healing are important features of the
movement's world-view. RVM has undertaken evangelism campaigns
in Cameroon and Gabon and lists an address in New York for
American subscribers.

Another revivalist movement, although much smaller, is the
Christ Life Evangelistic Ministry (CLEM). They meet at St. Mary
Primary School, Howell Street on Sundays at 3 p.m. as well as mid-
week. Their main emphasis is Bible study; the leader, Brother
A.E. Oroh, spent one year at a Bible College in Lagos.

The Deeper Christian Life Ministry is an indigenous ministry
which operates out of Lagos. The founder, W.F. Kumuyi, reputedly
a secret society apostate and a lecturer at the University of Lagos,
is a prolific writer of tracts. These tracts are circulated freely by
the Calabar group, which organizes evangelical conferences on
themes such as "Key to a Successful Marriage" and "How to be a
Good Christian Wife".

Akrasi Evangelism exists within another indigenous spiritual
organization - the Mount Zion Light House Full Gospel Church -
and hence functions as a type of revitalization movement. Elder
A. Akrasi, a leading member of MZLH, imports devotional and
evangelical literature and distributes this as a source of
supplementary spirituality, reaching a wider audience than the
MZLH alone.

Apostle Samuel Adam Ephraim Bassey, who was a pastor
(Apostle) of the Apostolic Church in Lagos, began a healing and
prayer crusade there in the mid-1960s, preaching from church to
church. He eventually acquired his own "sanctuary" with the
encouragement of the AC. After contact with the World Healing
Crusade in Blackwood (New Jersey?), Apostle Adam changed the

name of his movement from "Christ Healing Crusade" to "Christ Healing and Evangelical Movement". He brought the movement to Calabar in 1981, making use of borrowed land and a small building to hold his daily (evening) meetings for prayers, healing and Bible study. Apostle Adam publicizes the movement (albeit in a limited way since he received very little schooling and is already into his seventies) as "inter-denominational" and "non-sectarian". He most obviously conceives of the movement as a supplementary source of spirituality for churchgoers, as is evidenced by the timing and nature of the meetings. He is currently looking to the AC for assistance in drawing up the constitution as well as in providing financial aid.

The Missionary Fellowship (MF) represents another type of indigenous religious organization to emerge in modern Calabar. It is concerned primarily with "Child Evangelism" and "Literature Evangelism", in other words Christian religious instruction for both children and adults (the former through Sunday School classes and the latter via correspondence courses and lectures [study kits]). Emphasis is laid on the training of adults as Sunday School teachers as one of the most significant "missionary" tasks. In this respect the MF, which has been operating in Calabar and other parts of the state since 1970, exists as a type of service organization for individuals who, while maintaining other religious affiliations, wish to improve certain religious skills. To this end, the MF operates a small bookshop and library, and organizes occasional seminars. Sunday School is held on a regular basis at the Hawkins Road Primary School; many parents send their children there while themselves attending other religious institutions. MF makes use of evangelical tracts and literature, but is against any form of pentecostalism. They produce an occasional publication entitled *The Messenger*, which includes reports by members of the MF, letters, testimonies, Bible studies and moral exhortations.[61] One of the unique features of the Missionary Fellowship has been to engage in "ferry evangelism" - the distribution of free tracts and sale of Christian literature on the board the Calabar-Oron ferry.

Newspaper readers in Calabar are bombarded with publicity from the many "evangelistic associations" and "ministries", inviting them to attend their revivals, seminars and camp meetings (with free food and accommodation) or simply to send in their prayer requests. Not all of these groups are Calabar-based, many are located on the mainland; for example, the New Testament Ministry of Evangelist John Anso at Oron advertizes regularly in the *Nigerian Chronicle*, inviting people to write in for advice on "how to be saved". As described earlier, these revivalist movements result from indigenous initiative, but are noticeably influenced by imported religious teachings and techniques. It is impossible to document fully here the growing multiplicity of these movements, although we shall have cause to refer at a later stage to the trends reflected in this fast-growing form of religiosity.

5.4.2   Indigenous spiritual science movements

An even newer breed of religious movement is the indigenous spiritual science movement. This represents an attempt to indigenize and institutionalize the spiritual science teachings and ideas, such as we described in 4.4.5. While cases of this type of movement are not numerous, they are likely to increase in the future.

The Spiritual Fellowship, founded by Mr. A. Peter Akpan in 1980, emerged as a response to the book he wrote in 1977 entitled: *The Path of Holiness*. The main theme of the book is "spiritual development", which the author understands as a graduated path of knowledge by which the student attains higher levels of consciousness and spirituality: "Spiritual development leads to a higher knowledge and, in all realms, knowledge is power."[62] The author's teachings regarding the acquisition of spiritual power stem from a variety of religious, mystical and occult sources.[63]

At his weekly meetings on a Sunday evening, Mr. Akpan delivers a lecture on a theme such as reincarnation, love, service, money, the human mind or the reappearance of Christ. There are no prayers or hymns; Mr. Akpan considers "churchly religion" to be inferior to the more mystical and metaphysical variety. And yet his renunciation of "esoteric individualism" and call for service as the fruit of study and meditation, reflect his Methodist upbringing as well as his African sense of community. He vets carefully incoming participants and demands a high level of literacy (in English), which has tended to restrict membership, particularly in terms of women. The group currently meets in a private house and includes people from a variety of religious backgrounds: Muslim, Presbyterians, Apostolic Church and Brotherhood members.

The Esom Fraternity Company (Nigeria) is another example of an indigenous spiritual science movement, which, although it is based on the mainland, is known in Calabar because of its relationship with the Brotherhood of the Cross and Star. The director Professor Assassu Inyang-Ibom F.E.O., L.E.C, B.Sc., claims to have been converted to the Brotherhood after having encountered Obu on his astral travels and through mystical and occult research.[64]

Despite Professor Inyang-Ibom's declaration that he is the "Harbinger of the Brotherhood of the Cross and Star", he seems to maintain a certain degree of autonomy. In 1980 he announced that he was in the process of establishing an inter-denominational institution in Ukanafun Local Government Area, for the training of "priests" and "nuns" in the "healing arts and sciences".[65] Plans have also been released for the building of a "cosmic hospital" at Ibiak-Keffe in Oruk local government area.[66] The project is a joint venture of the Society of Metaphysicians in Britain, the Grace Bible Church of Florida and the Esom Order. Drugs and personnel are to be supplied by Indian associates. The cosmic hospital will treat sicknesses which "defy medical cures" by "mystical impulses".

Strictly speaking TUB or The Universal Body exists more as a blueprint than in reality, but we shall describe this nascent religious organization, since it is a good example of the new trends in religious innovation that we have been discussing. Cyril Owan, who comes from Ikom in the north of the Cross River State, owns and runs the Green Revolution Bar and Restaurant opposite St. Margaret's Hospital in Calabar.[67] In his late thirties, he receives a steady stream of visitors who come to him for friendly and spiritual advice, particularly seeking his "mystical predictions". He resides in the police barracks just behind his restaurant, but seems to be on suspension from active duty in the police force. He was born and bred a Catholic, but left the church seven years ago because he considered it to be a "selfish church which hides secrets", likening it to a "mystical organization" since salvation is only available, in his opinion, to the reverend fathers and sisters.

After a spell of six months with the Brotherhood, appreciating the greater freedom and mobility there, he discovered the Psychology School of Thought through their literature. He started to receive their lectures and metaphysical tests, mainly concerning predictions. He attended a four-month course conducted by a European in Lagos.

For many years, Cyril Owan had kept up his membership in AMORC, following their training programmes and advancing to the rank of "Frater" in the Rosicrucian hierarchy. In the last few years he has become dissatisfied with their "slow, solid training" and has decided that he does not want their type of knowledge - that is, how to attain the link between human knowledge and the Universal Mind and how to tap the source of life. He is nonetheless still in possession of several items of Rosicrucian paraphernalia - an altar, candelabra, incense, bust of Nefertiti, etc., and has their "Supply Bureau" catalogue at hand should further ordering be required.

Now he feels the need to be more spiritually independent, although admitted to having planned his own religious organization since 1974. He intends to call it "The Universal Body" or "TUB" for short and has acquired a small plot of land, but has no helpers. He wants it to be a place where people from all social levels can "come and reason" and "know what they are worshipping".

The above comments relate to the importance that he attaches to knowledge, particularly of an esoteric kind. At times he calls this knowledge "Christ-consciousness" - having greater illumination and hence greater impregnability to dangers and evil forces. It is in the area of his mystical predictions and calculations that the influence of his associations with spiritual science movements is more apparent. It is interesting to note that despite the varied background and eclecticism of Owan and his nascent religious movement, he nonetheless talks of founding a new "church". As we saw in the previous chapter, the church model still predominates. Owan also wants his religious organization to be acceptable to the government, since he predicts a time when religious freedom will be at a premium.

5.5 Concluding remarks

Of all the religious groups that we have examined both in this and the previous chapter, it is the traditional religious dimension whose *raison d'être* is most threatened by modern social and cultural changes. Institutional decline and content modification and erosion have resulted from an ongoing, and at times, merciless attack by other religious groups, mostly Christian. In addition to external factors it is also possible to identify an inability of the traditional world-view to relate to the religious and social needs of a rapidly changing society; its internal dynamics have not responded to widening boundaries. We have, however, been careful not to speak of traditional religion in terms of a unilinear regression. We have attempted to identify areas or features of revitalization and modification such as healing, conceptions of evil, secret societies and kingship. In chapter eight, it will become apparent how certain elements of the traditional world-view form part of an underground reservoir of beliefs and fears which fall more readily under the rubric of "popular religion". Beliefs such as spirit possession and witchcraft may not form part of the official doctrinal corpus of many religious organizations in Calabar, but they may nonetheless be highly influential in determining individual religious choice and behaviour.

Our examination of indigenous religious groups and movements has revealed a wide range of diversity, reflecting a certain freedom from traditional or external restraint. It is nonetheless possible to discern four main types or orientations:

1. the healing home[68]
2. the independent church
   a. the African church
   b. the spiritual church
3. the revivalist movement
4. the spiritual science movement

All four (with the exception of the African Church) are concerned with this-worldly "blessings" and "solutions" to problems and suffering, and the means of empowerment or acquisition of spiritual power. The latter three types lay stress on direct religious experience, whereas the first type of movement is expressly concerned with healing (in its fullest sense). The healing home (or prayer house as it is sometimes called) is structured around the specialist (often a herbalist or someone with healing powers) and his/her compound. The clientèle attends on a critical rather than a calendrical basis, since regular worship is not a feature of the healing-home type. The use of magical means is common and there is a strong tendency towards eclecticism and syncretism. A good example of this type of movement is the Okopedi Healing Home (see 5.2.4). Healing homes that are more traditionally or magically oriented are less likely to develop into spiritual churches than those groups which draw more readily on Christian beliefs and symbols.

The second type (independent church) is sub-divided into spiritual and African churches. The spiritual-church type lays greater emphasis on ritualistic and visionary means as well as on prayer.[69] In this respect, the charismatic or prophetic leader plays a crucial role in shaping the world-view of the movement, which, on the whole, tends to be more accommodating to its traditional environment than types (3) and (4). The movements in this category vary in the emphasis they give to Christian doctrines and practices. The spiritual church is akin to the Aladura or Zionist church-types; the African Church, which in many respects is an African version of the mission church resembles the Ethiopian or separatist churches in other contexts. It is a minority type in the Calabar context.

The third type, the revivalist movement, is governed by Biblical norms and hence is more readily characterized as Christian-related. One of its major concerns is evangelism and to this end makes use of imported evangelistic techniques and literature. The degree of incorporation and acceptance of evangelical and pentecostal teachings and phenomena varies from group to group. These movements are also characterized for the most part by their strict moral codes (possible influence of holiness teachings) and simple, unceremonial ritual format. They also project an image of the integration of Christianity and modernization.

The indigenous spiritual science movement is concerned with issues of mystical power and knowledge, particularly as they affect an individual's spiritual development. Teachings and techniques such as meditation or astral projection, may derive from non-indigenous sources, but are reinterpreted for local needs.

All types of religious movement discussed above represent a quest for religious self-determination, motivated by the belief that the time has come for spiritual maturity and religious independency. Although, as we have seen the development of new and autonomous structures does not entail an automatic rejection of Western (or Eastern) religious ideas and forms. An underlying tension does seem to be discernible over the general question of institutionalization and development: the desire to be visible to the wider society, to demonstrate signs of success and progress. This is in conflict with the attempt to create small-scale religious communities or compound churches where experience and fellowship are primary features.

It goes without saying that none of the categories we have proposed above is exclusive; there is a good deal of borrowing and interaction (sometimes clandestine) between the various movements. Whether it is a borrowing of ideas or forms, such as revivalism, occultism, meditation or a particular type of healing, the net result is a blurring of distinctions: for example, the Mount Zion Light House Full Gospel Church which operates as a spiritual church and yet exhibits the characteristics of category (3), the revivalist movement; the Brotherhood of the Cross and Star, once a healing home and now a spiritual church which draws on mystical and occult teachings.

The indigenous religious movements are still fighting for public recognition.[70]   A basic distrust of local products (including religion) is combined with a recognition of the relevance of the movements to contemporary Nigerian needs and problems. The movements themselves raise money to purchase air-time on the broadcasting media and some leaders make public pronouncements and predictions in the local press concerning local, national and even international issues.[71]   On the whole, though, they steer away from political issues and involvement, emphasizing the need for individual, rather than social reform.

The kaleidoscopic array of indigenous religious movements described in this chapter is a testimony not just to the world-creating capacity of religion but also to the vitality and creativity of religion in Calabar today.

Notes

1. Interview with Dr. E. Nsan (leader of the Efik youth organization: Nka Ekpenyong Nnuk), Calabar, June 26, 1983.

2. Ibid.

3. See *Souvenir Programme of the Coronation Service*, p. 21.

4. See "Efik Dances", *Nigeria Magazine* 53(1957):164.

5. Dr. E. Nsan claims that Ekpe membership has increased in recent years, partly due to the cultural revival. Interview, June 26, 1983.

6. Interview with Dr. Ekpo Eyo, then director of the Nigerian National Museums, who also notes that the former Cross River State Governor, Dr. Clement Isong, (non-Efik, an Ibibio from Eket) sought initiation into Ekpe at Creek Town, as a means of furthering his political career, but the secret plot was foiled at the last minute by preventing the governor and his entourage from reaching the Ekpe shrine where the ceremony was to have taken place.

7. A film was made of a rain expert's ritual on the outskirts of Calabar at Ikot Ansa in July 1980. (See *An Ibibio Rain Expert - Abia-edim*, a joint production by the University of Calabar and the University of Aberdeen, 1981). He claimed to have moved to Calabar from Etinan because there was more business in the state capital. He cited a variety of clients, including the neighbouring St. Patrick's College. In addition to the occasional fees for his work as a rain expert (around 200 Naira or £150 a time), he supplemented his income with carpentry.

8. See "The Rain Makers", *The Nigerian Chronicle*, March 20, 1982.

9. The Okopedi Healing Society is undoubtedly the most institutionalized of the healing homes in Calabar. They have published a *Proclamation of the Okopedi Healing Society* (Calabar: Okopedi Enterprises [Mystic Division], n.d.); *Okopedi Healing Home Catalogue* (Calabar: Okopedi Enterprises, 1978/79 and an update, n.d.). Many of the items such as mystical rings (₦ 45.50), books such as the *Great Book of Magical Arts* (with seven seals and case) (₦ 150.20) and cures or protective charms such as "Grade I Life Time Protection" against poisoning, gunshot wounds, witchcraft, accidents, etc. (₦ 2500.50) can prove extremely costly. (N.B. At the time of writing, one pound sterling was equivalent to ₦1.20.)

10. E.g. "The Homeopathic and Botanic Medical Clinic: Occultist, Astrologer, Physician" (signboard seen at 59 Ebito Street).

11. See Umoh and Ekanem, "What makes the Brotherhood of the Cross and Star Unique?" in *Brotherhood of the Cross and Star*, pp. 8-9.

12. See Umoh James Umoh, "Love One Another - That is the Message from Leader Olumba Olumba Obu, the Sole Spiritual Head, Brotherhood of the Cross and Star" in *West Africa*, March 8, 1982, p. 674.

13. See "What is Brotherhood", a Spiritual Sermon delivered by O.O. Obu and published in *What is Brotherhood? What is Cross? What is Star?* (Calabar: Brotherhood Press, n.d.), p. 2.

14. See "What is Cross?", ibid., pp. 23-38.

15. "What the Star Denotes in the Brotherhood of the Cross and Star", ibid., p. 44.

16. Ibid., p. 49.

17. Pastor Offu Ebongo, "The Leaders [*sic*] Secretary's Desk" in *Brotherhood of the Cross and Star Journal* 1,1(January 1982):4.

18. See Umoh and Ekanem, pp. 10-13, "Why do His Members refer to Olumba Olumba Obu as God in Human Form?"

19. *Brotherhood of the Cross and Star Journal*, 1,1 (January 1982):3. See also a more recent publication: *The Supreme Being: Holy Father Olumba Olumba Obu* (Calabar: Brotherhood Press, [1983]).

20. (Calabar: the Brotherhood Press, n.d.).

21. I had personal experience of this when interviewing Obu on one occasion - he cited over 30 references which were relevant, in one way or another, to the points covered during our two-hour interview on January 11, 1981 at the headquarters, 34 Ambo Street, Calabar.

22. See Umoh and Ekanem, pp. 80-82; *The Handbook of the Brotherhood of the Cross and Star* (Calabar: Brotherhood Press, n.d.).

23. Simultaneous translation into at least six languages from Efik may occur - usually English, Igbo, Yoruba, Ijo, French, Ashanti, etc. At the Easter Pentecostal Convention in April 1981, 9668 people attended the Easter Sunday morning service (official church count).

24. See for example, "Abortion is Murder" in *Brotherhood of the Cross and Star Journal*, pp. 7-15; *Key to a Successful Marriage Life* (Calabar: Brotherhood Press, n.d.).

25. In fact, 56 sins are enumerated in the "Divine Instruction for the Followers of God in Brotherhood of the Cross and Star", in Umoh and Ekanem, p. 78.

26. See Umoh and Ekanem, p. 88f.

27. See *Christ Universal School of Practical Christianity* (Calabar: Brotherhood Press, 2nd. ed. 1979).

28. At least ten record volumes have been produced and marketed on a wide scale by the various Brotherhood choirs.

29. Umoh and Ekanem, p. 91.

30. The Minutes of these meetings have been published since 1979.

31. See the profile of Senior Deaconness Itam Asuquo Ibia in *Brotherhood of the Cross and Star Journal*, 1,1 (n.d.):53.

32. Umoh and Ekanem, p. [xv]. See also pp. 173-79 for names of registered bethels.

33. See E.A. Offiong, "Schism and Religious Independency", p. 25 and Figure 5.

34. The movement has been unpopular in Cameroon and the representative, Barrister Dinka (Nigerian, Ibibio), and some members were imprisoned by the Cameroonian government for several months in 1982.

35. I was told by members that there were at least four in London, one in Sunderland, one in Liverpool, and a nascent one in Birmingham (as at 1983). According to Rev. George Providence there are 300 baptized members of the BCS in Trinidad. The *Herald of the New Kingdom*, April 27 - May 3, 1984, p. 1.

36. See Umoh and Ekanem, "Press Comments", pp. 152-70; Pastor Umoh James Umoh, who was Labour Editor of the *Daily Times* in Lagos for some years, has played a crucial role in this respect, placing advertisements for the BCS in the *New York Times* and *West Africa*.

37. See "The Youth Fellowship's Visit to London" in *Brotherhood of the Cross and Star Journal*, 1,1 (January 1982):41-46. See also "Brotherhood Missionaries' Tips", *Herald of the New Kingdom*, April 27 - May 3, 1984, p. 8.

38. Obu was the Patron of the Red Cross Organization in Calabar in 1983.

39. In addition to the lawyers, government officials, teachers, and ex-politicians who are regular members, there are those who visit Obu secretly for prayers, such as the steady stream of incumbent and aspiring politicians during the last elections in 1983. Personal communication from Friday M. Mbon.

40. For example, see *Weekly Review*, April 6-12, 1981, vol. 1, no. 16 - the weekly BCS newspaper which is produced on an irregular basis.

41. See "A Testimony by a Nigerian Soldier" in *The Supreme Being*, pp. xiii-xviii, which describes the failure of the Federal troops to invade the BCS headquarters at 26 Mbukpa Road during the civil war, because of the "mysterious nature of the Sole Spiritual Head of the Brotherhood of the Cross and Star", p. xvi.

42. See "The Supreme Leader of the Universe in 2001 Years" in *The Everlasting Gospel*, vol. 2 (Calabar: Brotherhood Press, n.d.), pp. 43-47.

43. For instance, BCS members are distinguished not only by their use of white, but also by the way they dance and the way they greet one another: "Peace" "or "The Peace of the Father" and "Thank You Father" are common salutations.

44. The name of the church is not yet finalized: at times they use the Holy Face (Healing) Church or the Holy Face of Jesus Christ Church.

45. This group, as well as the Holy Face Church described in 3.7.4, are offshoots of the Holy Face Society, a devotional organization in the Catholic Church which seceded in 1944 to form the Holy Face Catholic Church.

46. Interview with Rev. S.A. Okpo, Calabar, March 2, 1983.

47. The church claims that one of their prophetesses (a secondary school pupil) prophesies in "Latin". A linguistic analysis of the recording revealed that the sounds had no meaning in any language.

48. "Loss of power" or "strength" or general "weakness" are common complaints among those coming to spiritual churches. It is generally suspected that these are the symptoms of bewitchment.

49. Sermon by the founder, Rev. S.A. Okpo, March 6, 1983.

50. E.g. R.C.H. 532.

51. On one occasion the altar table, covered with ritual objects, was sent flying by the disruptive trance behaviour of the prophetesses. It is the men, the church leaders, who try to reestablish order and control the behaviour of the women, although they act in the knowledge that ultimately the Spirit dominates.

52. Cf. also the case of the Brotherhood of the Cross and Star in the previous section.

53. Interview with Rev. Dr. A.O. Akwaowo, Calabar, July 12, 1982.

54. Rev. Akwaowo claims that at least 40 Nigerians were present at the conference in 1981.

55. See the "1980 Presidential Address" by Rev. A.O. Akwaowo, December 4, 1980.

56. The various representatives all met during a Bible conference in the U.S. in 1981.

57. See "Missionary Journey to India" in *The Miracles* (local publication of TLMI), vol. 1, July 1983, pp. 3-4.

58. Cf. A.A. Dubb, *Community of the Saved: An African Revivalist Church in the East Cape* (Johannesburg: Witwatersrand University Press for the African Studies Institute, 1976), which is an account of the African Assembly of East London run by Nicolas Bhengu. The church, which is very similar to those outlined in this section, has a loose association with the Assemblies of God. I am grateful to Professor Bengt Sundkler for drawing my attention to this church.

59. The early issues of the magazine were called *Prayer and News Bulletin*.

60. *Harvest Digest*, 2,1 (January-March 1983):1.

61. See *The Messenger* (Calabar: Fellowship Publishing Centre), [1976], no. 3.

62. A. Peter Akpan, *The Path of Holiness* ([Calabar: the author, 1977]), p. 131.

63. Mr. Akpan claims to have read over 100 "mystical and spiritual books" from organizations such as AMORC, Rosicrucian Fellowship, Lopsong Rampa, White Eagle, the Arcane School and Theosophy. He has been a member of White Eagle, the Arcane School and the Rosicrucian Fellowship. Interview, Calabar, April 20, 1983.

64. See Prof. A. Inyang-Ibom, *Beyond Prejudice* vol. 1 (Calabar: The Brotherhood of the Cross and Star, reprint [of 1971? ed.]).

65. See the *Nigerian Chronicle*, March 5, 1980. Courses at the school include Bible knowledge, Allied Alchemy and Hermetic Mathematics.

66. See the *Nigerian Chronicle*, June 14, 1982.

67. The following account is based on an interview with Cyril
    Owan, Calabar, February 17, 1983.

68. This category could have included or been named neo-
    traditional, however, since the context in question is dominated
    by the healing home variety, we have opted for "healing home"
    as the most suitable term.

69. In fact the most widely used term in Efik-Ibibio to describe
    this type of religious institution is *ufok akam* (house of prayer)
    or sometimes *ufok Abasi nkukut* (church or house of prophecy)
    or *ufok unyanga* (house for help).   These terms are often
    popularly applied to any type of church or religious movement
    which is not *ufok Abasi* (church of God) or "orthodox",
    mainline church (sometimes referred to as *mme ikpo ufok Abasi*
    or the "big churches").   Healing homes may be described as
    ufok ukok udongo (literally house of healing).

70. See F.M. Mbon, "Public Response to New Religious Movements
    in Contemporary Nigeria in *New Religious Movements in
    Nigeria*, ed. R.I.J. Hackett (Lewiston, NY: Edwin Mellen Press, 1987).

71. The most well-known in this respect are the Brotherhood,
    Mount Zion Light House Full Gospel Church and the Divine
    Order of the Cherubim and Seraphim.

Chapter Six

Institutional Distribution

6.1   The religious mapping of Calabar

This chapter is devoted to analyzing the data generated by our mapping survey of religious institutions in Calabar in 1983.[1] The aim of the survey was initially to locate and identify the various religious groups active in Calabar today. The mapping of the area also provided information regarding the distribution of the different types of religious groups. Hence a series of religious maps, based on our operational distinctions between mainline, exogenous and indigenous religious institutions, were drawn up so as to allow more detailed analysis in this regard. To avoid bare statistics, our discussion of general distribution, categories, sub-categories or individual groups has been related to Calabar's demographic and geographical features, as well as to the history and nature of the various religious institutions themselves. Wherever relevant, methodological issues and problems have been treated as part of the discussion, since these often proved to be illuminating for our wider understanding of particular groups or types, as well as for certain theoretical questions.

Our use of the term "institution" needs further qualification as the concept is central to the survey. Since the term "institution" defines something which is established and instituted, whether it be a building, a system of principles or rules or customs, or some object (in this case for religious purposes), this enabled us to employ the following criteria in including or not a religious group in our frequency count:

1. regular worship or other ritual activities
2. regular location (even if property not owned)
3. identifying name

The average religious institution easily fulfills the above criteria, but it is the newer and smaller groups whose status is more debatable. For example, a group of people who meet for informal prayers in one another's homes cannot be considered an institution. If, however, the group decides to meet on a more formal and regular basis, by renting a room (in a school or private building), and eventually adopts a name for itself, thus constituting a religious option or alternative, then such a group has been classed as an institution.[2]

To cite particular examples, the group of Presbyterian women who meet for their own devotions and fellowship on a Sunday afternoon at Edgerley Ballantyne Primary School do not represent a distinct religious body, in contrast to the group of people who have been meeting under the auspices of the Christian Science Society for the last few years at the Barracks Road Primary School. Both the Lutheran Church and the God's Kingdom Society have branches which meet in schools each week, but they place signboards to advertize their presence and attract new members. The Exodus Crusade, a non-denominational revivalist movement, does not feature on the map since it does not meet on a regular basis.

It is obvious that the number of branches of a particular religious organization is not the sole indication of its size and importance. There is the size of the individual branches and membership figures to be taken into consideration. The question of religious affiliation will be examined again in a later chapter; it is an extremely complex and variable phenomenon and virtually impossible to quantify in a satisfactory way. It proved impossible to visit every religious institution to try to assess membership statistics (in any event this has to be a long-term exercise since figures and membership patterns vary); official statistics (of the organization concerned), if there were any, were unreliable since they utilized different criteria to establish membership and/or distorted or exaggerated their figures for obvious reasons. While it would have been preferable to work with two sets of figures (numbers of institutions and numbers of members) in order to gain a more accurate picture of the size and strength of the various religious institutions in Calabar, we have only worked with the first set of figures, for the reasons outlined above. However, wherever feasible, estimates of attendance and membership statistics are given based on information gained in the field.

The numbers of religious institutions acquire greater significance when seen in the light of the historical and contemporary data outlined in previous chapters. For instance, both the Salvation Army and the Apostolic Church arrived in Calabar within a few years of each other (1928 and 1933 respectively); the fact that the former has 2 branches while the latter has 44 is an indication of their relative growth and impact.

In order to preserve visual clarity, the minimum of information was included on the master map of Calabar: main streets and districts, significant landmarks and rivers.[3]   The fact that several religious institutions are situated on small, unpaved roads is not apparent, although from the clusters this might be evident.   It was exceptional to find an institution sited away from some type of thoroughfare (even if during the rainy season access might be limited).   There is an important link between religious growth and expansion and settlement patterns; the former tending to follow the latter rather than vice versa.   No aspiring church or healing home is prepared to gamble on uninhabited territory, even if there is a likelihood of future development.

As will be apparent from the map, there are several areas of (religiously) uninhabited territory.   This is usually government or commercially owned property (such as between Leopards Town and Henshaw Town, an area more commonly referred to as Duke Town; Big Qua Town; east and west of Ishie Town; the military areas at Ikot Ansa and Akim Qua; and the university and college campuses. In some cases the land is uninhabited because of adverse terrain, often due to erosion (areas such as Ekorinim, to the far west of Ishie Town; and south of Henshaw Town) or marshy conditions (the area known as New Airport, to the south of Edibe Edibe).

The scarcity of religious institutions in an area may also be due to other factors, for example, religious or ethnic.   A substantial part of Ikot Ishie (Ishie Town) is strongly Roman Catholic and local landlords have selected or rejected tenants on the basis of their religious affiliations.   In Big Qua Town, the landowners, the Qua, have resisted not only the development of their land, but also the incursion of spiritual churches.   It is only within the last few years that the Brotherhood, Mount Zion and Lutheran churches have gained access to what had been exclusively Presbyterian territory; the Qua, like the Efik, are proud of their Presbyterian heritage.

Our survey revealed a total of 248 religious institutions (see figure 2) of which at least 40% are distinct religious bodies.[4] Many of these are situated in clusters in particular localities such

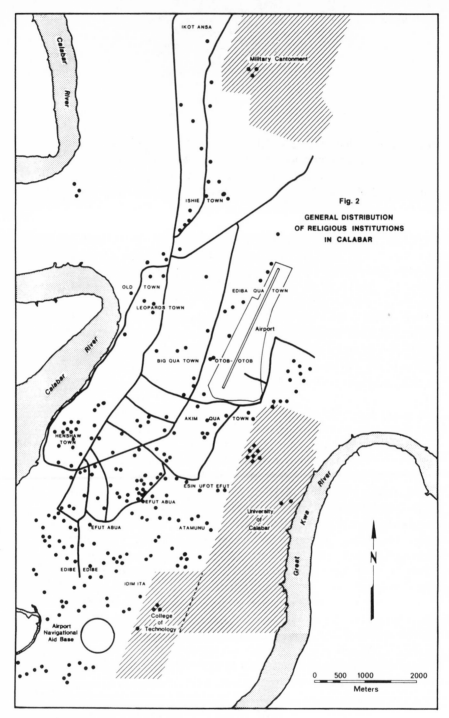

Figure 2: Religious institutions in Calabar

as around Efut Abua, Atamunu, Edibe Edibe, New Airport, Henshaw Town and the area to the east of the airport.[5] It is important to ask whether distribution could be linked to ethnic settlement patterns. The oldest residential districts (Akim Town, Edibe Edibe, Henshaw Town, Efut Town and Duke Town) are predominantly Efik (or minority indigenous groups).[6] There are also Efik settlements at Diamond Hill (between Old Town and Leopards Town) and at Ikot Ishie. There is no marked absence or predominance of particular religious groups in these areas, despite the popular Efik claim that it is the Ibibio who are to blame for turning Calabar into what people commonly refer to as a "city of church industry".[7]

The newer residential areas (Atamunu, Idim Ita, New Airport, Ediba and the eastern airport area) show signs of a bourgeoning of religious institutions. This is undoubtedly linked to the predominantly migrant population who have settled and multiplied there since the civil war.[8] It is also linked to land availability and prices. The earliest religious institutions were able to select prime locations in the town centre and major residential areas; those that came later, often with limited funds and expertise have had to make do with isolated plots of land or, if they are lucky, borrowed or donated land and/or property.

Even though we are talking here in fairly general terms, given the nature of this research and the absence of official demographic data, there are additional considerations concerning the contemporary situation which should be borne in mind when viewing the distribution of religious institutions in terms of ethnic factors. Efik landlords have always constructed and maintained property in a variety of locations all over the town.[9] They themselves have moved out of the older properties into modern dwellings or government quarters. Ibibio landlords, backed by growing Ibibio dominance of Cross River State politics and the economy, have become increasingly involved in property development.[10] All this demonstrates that, together with the recent changes engendered by Calabar's growth as a state capital, it is difficult to identify any correlation between ethnic settlement patterns and institutional religious pattern as in some other Nigerian towns and cities.[11]

Because of the wide range of religious institutions it did not prove practicable to employ symbols to distinguish each separate body. In addition to the main divisions or categories (mainline, exogenous and indigenous) several sub-categories were used (such as healing homes, spiritual churches, etc.) to simplify the analysis of the data. The process of categorization is explained where relevant in the following sections and supplementary information on individual institutions is supplied when this is not evident from the map.

6.1.1   Mainline religious institutions

Our survey revealed a total of 45 mainline institutions which constitutes 18.1% of the total number of religious institutions in the township (see figure 3). Of these, 13 (28.8% of the mainline category) are Presbyterian, 15 are Catholic (33.3%), 12 are Protestant (26.7%), including 2 Methodist, 1 Anglican, 1 Baptist, 1 Qua Iboe, 2 Lutheran and 5 Protestant (multi- or inter-denominational) chaplaincies at the three higher educational institutions (University of Calabar, the College of Technology, and the Teacher Training College at Ikot Ansa) and at the two military barracks at Akim Qua Town and Ikot Ansa. There are 5 mosques or praying grounds (11.1%).

The Presbyterian and Roman Catholic churches are the two most active mainline religious institutions in terms of branch expansion. Reasons of antecedence could be adduced for this development, but it seems to stem also, as far as the Presbyterians are concerned, from their democratically inspired organizational structure. Catholic worship was, on the other hand, up until about ten years ago, focused on the Sacred Heart Cathedral in Egerton Street, just off the main Watt Market, until the current Bishop adopted a policy of decentralization in the hope that it would stimulate the growth and development of the church. This seems to have been the case, for while certain people are attracted to the cathedral for reasons of status, the majority of people (not just Catholics) prefer to attend a church close to their domicile, because of accessibility, cost of transport and even for cultural reasons in that they may be able to worship with those of the same linguistic and ethnic group as themselves.

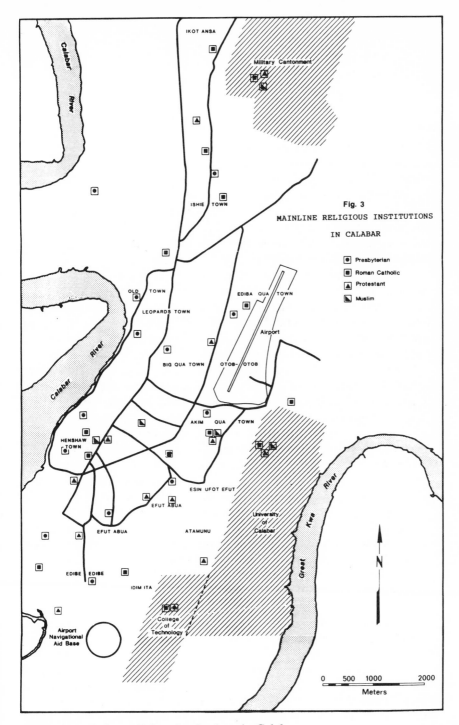

Figure 3: Mainline religious institutions in Calabar

The Methodist Church operates two large churches, one in old Calabar, Henshaw Town, with a large Efik congregation, and the other, a newer building in one of the migrant sectors of the town - Atamunu. The two branches appear to be adequate for their needs at the present time, although the Wesleyan Cathedral congregation in Henshaw Town is frustrated at its inability to expand because of the antiquity of the building and the limited size of the land, and the members are seeking another site.

The Anglican Church is centred around the Holy Trinity Church which occupies a strategic position in the centre of town. All the funds and efforts of this minority religious community have gone into developing the one branch and the situation is unlikely to change, unless, as in the 1930s, the Igbo community in the church moves towards secession.

The older, mainline churches settled first in the more established parts of the town, close to the Marina and old port on Calabar River and near to the central Watt Market. While these may be considered prime historical sites with the attendant prestige of a central location, in some respects they have become disadvantaged because of the urban developments over the last ten years which have fragmented the town's centres of commerce, education and government. For instance, the new Secretariat is now situated on the Murtala Muhammed Highway on the way out of town; the new port complex which began operations in the late seventies is even further up river; the University of Calabar is located to the east of the town, on a site near the Big Kwa River; there have also been attempts to relocate the markets and main post office away from the former centre, which had become congested on account of the presence of the banks and the sprawling Watt Market.

The older churches have also found themselves away from the more densely populated residential areas which are to the south (Esin Ufot Efut, Efut Abua, Atamunu, Edibie Edibe, and the New Airport zone) and to the north (Ikot Ishie and Ikot Ansa), as well as to the east of the airport at Otob-Otob and Ediba.[12] It is in these areas that the Baptist, Qua Iboe and Lutheran churches have taken root, as well as the newer Presbyterian, Lutheran, Methodist and Catholic branches.

Another pattern revealed by the map is that the mainline churches are for the most part situated close to the arterial road system which has both strategic and practical importance, for in the rainy season, many of the smaller, unmade roads are impassable.

The focus of Muslim activity used to be the mosque at Calabar Road in the centre of town, until it became an Ahmadiyya mosque. Many Muslims now worship at the main prayer ground at the Akim Barracks. There is also a mosque close by in the Hausa sector of the town and one to the north in Ikot Ansa, to cater for the diverse migrant population of the Military Cantonment.

6.1.2   Exogenous religious institutions

6.1.2.1   Pentecostal and evangelical movements

Of the 73 exogenous religious institutions in the municipality (29.4% of the total), nearly three-quarters (52 or 71.2%) are of the pentecostal/evangelical variety (see figure 4). The Apostolic Church has the greatest number of branches (43), not just of this category, but in terms of all the religious institutions in Calabar. The Apostolic Church is very much a neighbourhood church and its development in this respect is facilitated by the relatively uncentralized hierarchy and bureaucratic structures which provide the necessary support both in terms of finance and personnel for branch expansion. The absence of a powerful charismatic leader obviously permits a more "democratic" expansion, but it leaves the organization open to fissiparous tendencies as we observed earlier (4.4.1.1).

The Apostolic Faith, in complete contrast, possesses only one branch in Calabar; this rather rigid and centralized structure stems in part from the dominance of the American parent body as a model for organization and demonstrates their belief that uncontrolled expansion presents a serious threat to its tightly sealed world.

The Assemblies of God currently has 7 branches in the municipality which is evidence of the denomination's evangelizing activities after having been virtually depleted after the civil war.

The Pentecostal Assemblies of the World has only one branch, while the Church of Christ maintains four.

6.1.2.2   Jehovah's Witnesses

The JW has 7 Kingdom Halls in Calabar Municipality (9.6%), although this is not an accurate reflection of its institutional strength, since several congregations make use of the same building at different times.   The Kingdom Halls are often difficult to recognize, since their architectural design often resembles a private dwelling rather than a "church", and some of them do not use signboards.   On the whole they are fairly equidistant from one another and tend to be located in the more densely populated sector of the town (around Edibe Edibe and Efut Abua) which is obviously more conducive to door-to-door evangelism.

6.1.2.3   Black American churches

The Black American churches, namely the AME Zion and CME churches, have two branches each and constitute 5.5% of the exogenous religious institutions.

6.1.2.4   Spiritual science movements

Only five spiritual science movements (6.8%) can be located on our map.   These are the Baha'i Centre, AMORC (2), the Institute of Religious Science and Jesus the Superet Church.   Here there is a major discrepancy between the recorded locations and our knowledge of the existence (i.e. a group of people meeting under the aegis of a particular religious organization) of at least 11 spiritual science groups in Calabar itself.   There would seem to be two main reasons here: firstly, in terms of the religious history of the town, most of the groups are fairly recent arrivals (more than half are post-1980), and have not had the chance to acquire land and property and are therefore still meeting in private homes;

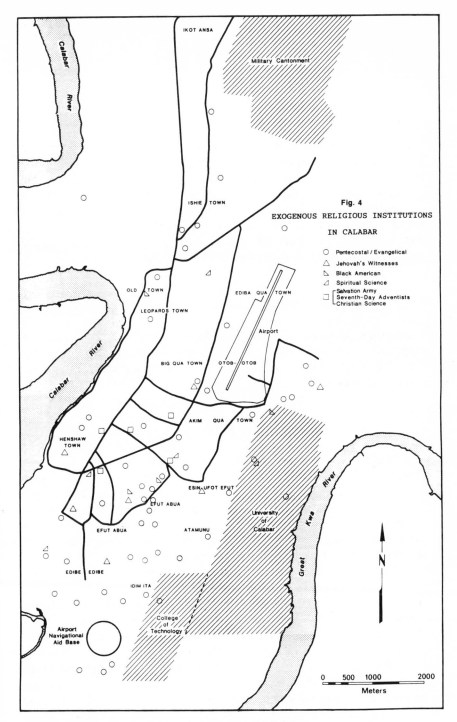

Figure 4: Exogenous religious institutions in Calabar

secondly, the orientation of these religious groups tends to be individualistic encouraging home study, private meditation and individual spiritual development, rather than group fellowship and calendrical worship, and so the need for an institutional location is less strongly felt. It seems fair to surmise, therefore, that the physical or institutional strength of the spiritual science movements does not, and probably will not in the future, reflect their actual influence and impact on the religious life of Calabar.

6.1.2.5   Salvation Army/Seventh-Day Adventists/Christian Science

These three organizations between them represent 5 (6.8%) of the exogenous category. Both the Salvation Army and the Seventh-Day Adventists (including the Church of God [Seventh-Day]) have two branches each.

6.1.3   Indigenous religious institutions

The many and varied religious institutions in this particular category (73 or 29.4%) proved the most difficult of all to locate (see figure 5). The majority are *creatio ex nihilo*: beginning, and indeed often existing for a long time, in private homes, rented property or temporary structures. Many of them do not have permanent buildings or sites; in fact, they are the least institutionalized of all the religious groups we are studying.

There are two main reasons for this: firstly, many are "compound churches" with an ideology which stresses the importance of the small, closely-knit community where pastoral care and fellowship are vital ingredients; secondly, since the majority of these religious groups are independent creations, they lack the support system or infrastructure of a larger organization. Financial difficulties and low membership figures may mean eventual extinction for a small spiritual church. Many of these smaller, independent religious institutions are unable to meet the financial and legal requirements necessary to effect registration with the government. While this does not result in noticeable tax advantages, it does allow the religious institutions in question to function "officially" as it were, without fear of harassment by government and tax officials. Unregistered religious institutions are therefore sometimes reluctant to publicize their presence, refraining from open-air evangelism and erecting noticeboards. This naturally rendered our investigation of the indigenous movements more difficult.

Apart from the problems of trying to locate and identify indigenous religious movements, their classification presents another set of problems. While there are identifiable organizations such as the Brotherhood of the Cross and Star, Mount Zion and the African Churches, many of the movements have had to be classified collectively in two rather expansive categories "spiritual churches" and "healing homes". Both categories include a very diverse range of religious groups. Within the former category, for example, 96.2% are one-branch churches, meaning that no other branches exist or, if they exist, they are situated outside Calabar. The "healing home" category also comprises a wide diversity of groups which draw on a variety of healing techniques. While practical considerations, namely the limitation of symbols and categories to facilitate analysis, were crucial in the ordering of the data, it was felt that there was sufficient homogeneity to justify such categorization.

6.1.3.1   Brotherhood of the Cross and Star

The survey revealed that the Brotherhood (BCS) is the largest spiritual church, in fact the largest of the religious organizations of indigenous creation, in Calabar today. With a total of 30 branches it constitutes 23.1% of the indigenous category and 12.1% of all religious institutions in Calabar.

What is interesting to note from the map is that the branches radiate out from the headquarters at Ambo Street (just above Edibe Edibe on the map); in fact there is a distinct cluster of bethels, twelve within two square kilometers. While these could be considered as overflow groups, their location is more suggestive of a desire to remain in proximity to Leader Obu and his charismatic

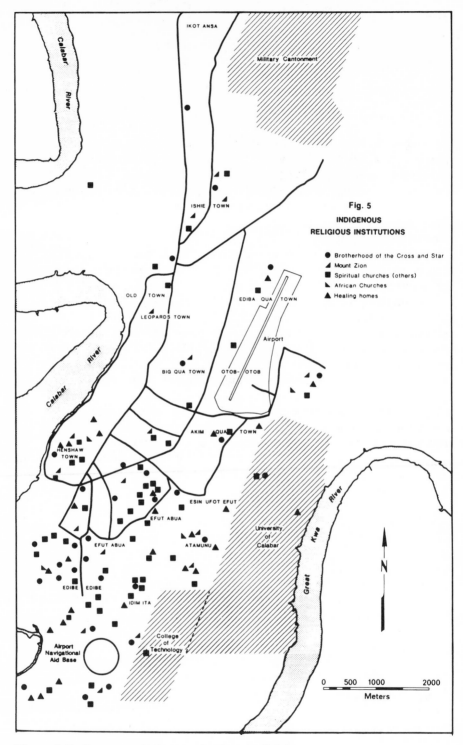

Figure 5: Indigenous religious institutions in Calabar

powers. It may also represent an attempt by the Brotherhood of the Cross and Star to extend its community in the urban context to maximize member interaction and solidarity, also encouraging conformity of behaviour to Brotherhood ideals and strengthening religious commitment.

While some of the newer branches on the periphery of the town may not number more than 50 at their main services, several of the larger branches have a regular attendance of several hundred; the headquarters records over two thousand at a Sunday morning service and over seven thousand at convention time.

6.1.3.2   Mount Zion churches

Within this sub-category we have included not just the larger Mount Zion Light House Full Gospel Church, but also the two smaller schisms: the Mount Zion Mission and the Mount Zion Gospel Church. The Mount Zion group of churches are the second largest indigenous religious group, constituting 13% (17) of the indigenous category and 6.9% of the total count. They are fairly evenly distributed throughout the various sectors of the town.

6.1.3.3   Spiritual churches

As mentioned earlier in section 6.1.3, this sub-category contains a myriad of small one-branch churches. Out of the 52 institutions identified, only two (the Celestial Church of Christ [3] and the Christ Army Church [2]) have more than one branch. The spiritual churches, excluding the Brotherhood and Mount Zion (MZ), represent 40% of the indigenous category and 21% of the total number of religious institutions. If we include BCS and MZ in the total figures, that would represent a percentage of 76.1% for all spiritual churches in this category and 40% for the overall total. If we included the African Churches and created a sub-category "independent churches" this would then constitute 79.2% of all indigenous movements and 41.5% of all religious institutions.

As our earlier discussion of the spiritual churches has shown, the labels "spiritual church" and "independent church" have become increasingly extended as new forms develop. We have nonetheless continued to use the terms to refer to this increasingly heterogeneous sub-category, since the "spiritual church" model still predominates in terms of religious innovation.

The majority of the spiritual churches are located in the southern part of the town, where land is more readily available and the area is more densely settled, particularly with migrants whose religious affiliations tend to be destabilized by their temporary and marginal status.

From the map it is evident that there are clusters of churches such as to the west of Efut Abua (both areas), around Edibe Edibe, Idim Ita and New Airport. There are two streets in particular, Atu Street and Mayne Avenue (just to the west of upper Efut Abua), where at least 10 of the spiritual churches have established themselves. A site next to a main thoroughfare is preferred, but not always possible.

6.1.3.4   African Churches

There are only four churches in this sub-category (3.1%) which is a negligible presence overall (1.6%). This would seem to confirm that the "African Church" is an outdated type, at least in the context under consideration. It represents a bastion of African churchly traditions and traditional customs and values, but eschews any evangelizing or modernizing trends. This type of religious world still has appeal for some, notably older people not involved in the modern sector, which is why the Christ African Church Cathedral located in the heart of old Calabar is still able to fill its pews.

6.1.3.5   Healing homes and traditional shrines

Of all the sub-categories the healing homes and traditional shrines were the most problematic to locate and classify. For this reason they are the most underrepresented in terms of our absolute count. The majority of them operate out of private dwellings and compounds, sometimes adding on small buildings to house the shrine. The Okopedi Healing Home and Enterprises is the only example we encountered of a custom-built healing home. Traditionally the abia-ibok (herbalist or "native doctor") and abia-idiong (diviner) did not publicize their skills and presence; they acquired clients on the basis of a successful reputation. The urban context, however, has generated a new breed of healing home, whose practitioners are aware of the needs of the urban dweller and also of their own needs if they are to survive in a highly competitive religious marketplace. While not engaging in actual proselytization, they have nonetheless taken steps to publicize their activities through the use of signboards (in Efik and/or English) and newspaper advertisements.

Apart from the task of physically locating the healing homes, we were also faced with deciding whether certain healing homes can rightly be classified as religious institutions. While it was not possible to research each healing home and verify its religious content, from our knowledge of selected institutions, we did not encounter any healers or diviners who did not have some recourse to "supernatural powers" either through invocation, prayers, sacrifices or rituals. In addition, one of the main reasons that the healing homes are continuously attacked by the churches is precisely on this score: that their healing techniques depend on the invocation and manipulation of "non-Christian" deities and powers.

Their status as "institutions" is also debatable since many exhibit minimal structures and establishment. They are nonetheless offering on a permanent basis (and for a fee) their skills, in order to solve people's day-to-day problems. Some degree of institutionalization is necessary in order to perform such a role, although it will vary according to the age, experience and orientation of the practitioner in question.

Traditional shrines were the most difficult to locate. Many of the former shrines, in homes and compounds and wards, have fallen into disuse. Traditional priests and priestesses operate out of their private homes or may go to a particular location, such as by the river, to perform either calendrical or critical sacrifices. The most prominent and the oldest of Calabar's traditional shrines is the Efe Asaba (Shrine of the Cobra) which is used for the traditional coronation of Obong of Calabar (Uyara Ntinya). It is situated not far from the main Efe Ekpe (Ekpe lodge) at Eyamba Square. The Efik claim that Efe Asabo was first used as an Ndem shrine in 1660 and that during the reign of Antera Duke in the eighteenth century it was owned by Ekpo Akabom Ene Eyo Ema and was known as Egbo Cobham's cabin.[13]

In front of the Ekpe lodges in the various parts of the town, a hexagonal stone shrine, sometimes with smaller pebbles at the base, is visible. Oblations of food and drink are placed here, and there is occasionally evidence of a blood sacrifice.

In the course of the survey, 27 healing homes and traditional shrines were identified representing 20.8% of the indigenous category and 10.8% of the overall total. All but two are situated in the southern half of the town, and one third of them in the newly inhabited New Airport area, where they are often located in close proximity to one another. All the healing homes in this area have been established since 1978. They are as follows: Eton Nkukim Inuen Isoroke Herbal Healing Home; The Seven Wonders of Acultism and Healing Home; Ibeku Ata Healing Home; Ifa Healing Home; Mbebe Herbal and Spiritual Healing Home; Nkanta Medical Herbalist; Abatim Fraternity Healing Home.

6.2   Concluding remarks

As we mentioned at the beginning of this chapter there is an observable link between general residential patterns and religious expansion. While this is linked to land availability, which we shall return to below, the concept of the "neighbourhood church" and its importance in the religious life of Calabar, sheds some light on these geographical patterns of religious growth. By "neighbourhood church" we understand the church (or healing home, lodge or mosque for that matter) which is physically part of each local community, with resident functionaries and specialists, whether priests or pastors, prophets or diviners, who are active in solving people's problems by being on call twenty-four hours a day. The integration of the religious in people's lives is reminiscent of traditional patterns of worship, with the plurality and accessibility of the family, house and town deities, ancestors and water and nature spirits. It also stems from basic convictions concerning the role of religion in everyday life - that it is not just a once-weekly, "other-worldly" affair, but an ever-present reality and a powerful and transforming force. We would argue that these considerations are important in determining religious growth, not just the emergence of new religious movements, but also the expansion of the mainline and exogenous churches for example.

We have noted that the older parts of Calabar, that is those sections close to the river, house the oldest churches, Presbyterian, Catholic, Methodist. These historically prestigious locations today have their disadvantages, being sited away from the most densely populated areas, and limited by lack of parking and building space. The areas of the greatest religious growth and expansion are to the south of the town centre where there is a substantial migrant population, and increasingly to the north, as the town continues to expand. While land in these areas is still relatively inexpensive and available, people who establish their religious institutions there suffer from poor water and electricity supplies, lack of surfaced roads and isolation from the commercial and administrative centres of the town. And yet the fact that some of the mainline and exogenous institutions have started to open branches in these areas is an indication of a different potential of these areas, that is the human potential.

Despite these trends, we still maintain that land supply is the determining factor with regard to religious distribution, overriding other considerations such as choice of location and ethnicity. We are suggesting that the increasingly random settlement patterns in Calabar have contributed to the pluralism and heterogeneity of its religious institutions. In other words the model of urban development - characterized by heterogeneity, breakdown of divisions, juxtaposition and blending of old and new traditions[14] - has removed the possibility of a particular religious institution or type of institution from dominating the religious scene. We observed earlier that at least 40% or more than a hundred are separate religious bodies. The majority (87%) are one-branch organizations. These latter figures are boosted by the large percentage of indigenous movements overall (52.4%) of which 77 or 59.2% possess only a single branch. These figures may be interpreted differently: either they reflect the inability of many religious institutions to expand, or they point to a powerful spirit of innovation and independency, manifested in perpetual schism and pluralization. The reality seems to lie somewhere between the two. We have argued, in addition, that increasing urban heterogeneity must have contributed to religious pluralization in Calabar.

It is worth noting that of the indigenous movements, at least 25 (almost a quarter of the number of separate organizations and a half of all indigenous bodies) were founded in Calabar itself. Only nine of Calabar's religious institutions have women founders (6 indigenous and 3 exogenous); of these only four (indigenous) churches still have women leaders.

Another interesting fact which emerges from the data is that 85.1% (211) of all the religious institutions could be described as following the "church" model; in other words, they claim to be churches and/or are characterized by a variety of internal and external features (ritual patterns, symbolic forms, organizational structures, doctrinal content, etc.) which distinguish them as such in terms of general opinion. We are not concerned in this study with evaluating the Christian content of each "church". An analysis focusing on doctrinal criteria might divide up the data very differently.

Also worth underlining in these concluding remarks, since it was not anticipated as a finding, is the large proportion, nearly a quarter (58 or 23.4% of the overall total), of pentecostal, evangelical and revivalist movements (both exogenous [and usually of American origin] and indigenous) known to be operating in Calabar today. This points to an interesting trend in the religious life of the town and will receive further discussion in chapter ten.

In conclusion, we wish to emphasize that the figures discussed above and summarized in the tables below may only be considered as a partial indication of the size and strength of the respective religious institutions and of religious activity in Calabar today. They have, at least, helped build up some idea of the religious landscape today as it looks from an institutional perspective. To complete the picture we must next look at the interaction between the various religious groups, before trying to discern the more undifferentiated forms of religion in Calabar at the popular level.

Table 1
Religious institutions in Calabar

	N	%
Mainline religious institutions	45	18.1
Exogenous religious institutions	73	29.4
Indigenous religious institutions	130	52.4
Total (absolute count of places of meeting and/or worship)		248
N.B. Distinct or separate religious bodies (approx.)	110	40.0

Table 2
Mainline religious institutions

	N	%
Presbyterian	13	28.8
Catholic	15	33.3
Protestant	12	26.7
Muslim	5	11.1
Total	45	

Table 3

Exogenous religious institutions

	N	%
Pentecostal/evangelical	52	71.2
Jehovah's Witnesses	7	9.6
Black American	4	5.5
Salvation Army/Seventh-Day Adventist/Christian Science	5	6.8
Spiritual science	5	6.8
Total	73	

Table 4

Indigenous religious institutions

	N	%
Brotherhood of the Cross and Star	30	23.1
Mount Zion	17	6.9
Spiritual churches	52	40.0
African Churches	4	3.1
Healing homes	27	20.8
Total	130	

Notes

1. The actual mapping exercise was conducted in April 1983. However, data on the location of the institutions had been collected since early 1980.

2. We have not entered into doctrinal or hierarchical considerations here, being more concerned with the "visible" signs of organization and establishment such as buildings and signboards, etc. At any rate such observable criteria are a partial reflection of a group's orientation and development.

3. The map was as accurate as it could be - having been established from the most recent map of Calabar (published in 1978) with assistance in updating from staff at the Survey Office in Calabar, together with my own field knowledge of recently developed areas.

4. All percentages have been corrected to the nearest decimal point. See Appendix 3 (Data File on Religious Institutions in Calabar) for name, address and background information on each religious organization.

5. An area so recently developed it has not yet been named or mapped by the authorities (by July 1983).

6. See R.A. Odu Sule, "Housing Problems in Calabar: A Qualitative Assessment" in Inyang, et al., p. 104.

7. There is some truth in this claim for more than one fifth of religious institutions (excluding healing homes) in Calabar are founded by Ibibio people (approximately twenty compared to six by Efik men and women) and well over one third of the various religious bodies currently have Ibibio leaders.

8. Based on a 1975 survey, Ekanem cites 80% as the proportion of migrants (mainly Ibibio, although he does include Efik migrants from the rural areas) in Calabar. See Ekanem, "The Demography of Calabar" in Inyang et al., pp. 30, 39.

9.   See Morrill, *Two Urban Cultures*, p. 209f.

10. This situation may change following the creation of the new Akwa Ibom State with the capital at Uyo in September 1987.

11. See O'Connor, *The African City*, p. 110f, 119, 219f. Port Harcourt is an extreme example of this "melting pot" situation. See H.E. Wolpe, *Urban Politics in Nigeria: a Study of Port Harcourt* (Berkeley: University of California Press, 1974), p. 29 (cited by O'Connor, p. 220).

12. Examples of such disadvantaged branches are the Presbyterian churches at Old Town and Ekorinim - the latter being a rather lifeless fishing community, virtually cut off from the rest of the municipality by severe erosion.

13. See *Souvenir Programme of the Coronation Service*, p. 21.

14. This important point is made by O'Connor in his conclusion to *The African City* (p. 311) when he refers to the "convergence" of urban traditions (indigenous, Islamic, colonial, European) in modern Africa, with most cities shifting towards the "hybrid" category.

Chapter Seven

Institutional Interaction

7.1   Interaction and interdependence

In this chapter we turn our attention to some of the ways in which the religious groups manifest their interdependence through associations, ecumenical activities for example, and interact positively or negatively with each other. Our concern in this chapter is with the more conventional, institutional and "official" forms of interaction, while the next chapter will deal with the less formalized areas of personal and popular religion and cross-fertilization between the two domains. In trying to discern areas of interaction and interdependence we are already starting to move beyond the most observable components of our field of study, that is the religious institutions themselves, to their interrelationships and to the dynamics of the encounter of religious worlds. We shall not be able to do justice here to the theological, ritual and symbolic issues involved, but our brief descriptive analysis will at least reveal the nature and form that such interrelationships and interaction may take, and how these are influenced by internal factors such as inclusivism or exclusivism, and external factors such as a national crisis.

7.2   Conferences, councils and chaplaincies

The initial area of interaction which we considered was the encounter between traditional religion and Christianity. The agreements reached between the Ekpe Society officials and the Christian missionaries, and eventually the colonial authorities, led to the regulation of certain religious practices and institutions. Relations between Christians and traditionalists up until the present day have continued to show signs of strain as will be demonstrated shortly.

As we traced the religious history of Calabar, the consequences of the diversification of the mission field became apparent as the various missionary bodies vied for land and converts. The argument has been made, indeed, that the boundary disputes

actually generated interdenominational cooperation.[1]   For example,
the conferences convened by the Presbyterians in Calabar in 1909
and 1911 (to which the Primitive Methodists, Qua Iboe and Niger
Delta Pastorate churches were invited) demonstrated "a mutual
desire to avoid altercations" and an intent "to discuss, resolve and
minimize competition".[2]   The cooperation and comity generated by
the early encounter of the principal missionary agencies in the
area, led not only to boundary agreements but a greater awareness
of common goals and interests.   The 1911 conference was devoted
to more practical concerns such as the training of ministers,
education, marriage and the attitude to African music and dance.
The agenda of the conference was influenced by the Edinburgh
World Missionary Conference of 1910 and resulted in a call for
"organic unity".[3]   We should not ignore the fact, however, that
there was competition between the missions at this time.

      The church union movement, which was to accelerate at a
national level until its eventual collapse in 1966, was most active in
eastern Nigeria, inspired by Presbyterian missionaries such as A.
Wilkie, J.T. Dean and R.M. Macdonald. It had taken an early form
(1924) as the Evangelical Union of Southern Nigeria.[4] It was also
motivated by a fear of their "common enemy" - the Roman Catholic
Church whose growing influence was of major concern to all
Protestant bodies. It is notable also that African agents were not
instrumental in the early stages of the church union movement.

      The Christian Council of Nigeria (CCN), an association of
Protestant churches, was formed in 1930, with the purpose of
cooperating in various projects - education, pastoral training,
medical and urban ministry and above all, fostering and expressing
the fellowship and unity of the Christian Church in Nigeria.[5]
There was also the necessity for the various missions to be able to
speak with one voice with the government on issues such as
education.[6]   Today the CCN serves to promote international links
with such bodies as the World Council of Churches and the All-
Africa Conference of Churches; however, its influence is barely felt
in Calabar. The Cross River State, together with the Rivers and
Anambra states, make up the Eastern Zone. Meetings are
infrequent, never more than once a year. The state women's wing
of the CCN was active in the launching and fund-raising activities

of the International Year of the Disabled in 1981.

The Christian Community of Nigeria (CCON) by contrast meets on a more regular basis, staging a series of annual activities including inter-denominational worship, a choir competition, a football match and visits to charitable institutions. The origins of this association date back to the civil war, and the response of the Christian community (as a whole) to the devastation of "persons and property, institutions and communication".[7] Many people, refugees, wounded, flocked to the churches for assistance; as a result, some twenty-seven churches agreed in the Christ African Church Cathedral, (c.1969?) to work jointly to relieve suffering and to organize religious services since normal worship had been disrupted by the war. The initiative seems to have come from such church leaders as Leader Obu (Brotherhood of the Cross and Star) and Bishop Ironbar (African Church), while the response was fairly unanimous and even included the Catholic Church, whose representative was Father Dominic Inyang.[8]

The member churches met on a monthly basis to administer resources and aid long after the war had ended in 1970. Eventually the CCON was called on to re-examine its raison d'être, deciding to continue its emphasis on "collective practical Christianity" with the additional task of promoting Christian unity and evangelism in Calabar.[9]

CCON was officially registered with the government in 1977, but by this time the mainline churches had withdrawn their membership and the composition of the organization had taken on the appearance of a rival to the CCN. Today this polarization remains, with most of the older spiritual churches taking part, as well as AME Zion, the Christ African Church and the Pentecostal Assemblies of the World, Inc., who, for one reason or another do not wish to be associated with the mainline churches.[10]

The CCON operates as a federation of churches; they have plans to build a one million Naira "Grace Parliament" which would house the necessary facilities to care for the aged, orphans and religious evangelists and cater for conventions, religious education and book distribution. A supermarket is also part of the project. A plot of land has reportedly been acquired and surveyed at Big Qua Town.[11]

Some of the evangelical churches (both indigenous and exogenous) belong to the Nigerian Evangelical Fellowship, while other evangelists and pastors travel overseas to attend evangelical and pentecostal assemblies and conventions.

Moving to some slightly different examples of religious interaction at the institutional level, we may cite the case of the inter-denominational, Protestant chaplaincies which exist at the University, College of Technology and the military barracks. These chaplaincies, which have traditionally been composed of the mainline Protestant denominations (in addition to the Catholic Chaplaincy), show signs of branching out to include the evangelical and pentecostal churches and indigenous revivalist movements. The University of Calabar Protestant Chapel now invites freelance evangelists on a regular basis from all over Nigeria. There is no attempt to bridge the gap of institutional antagonism between Catholics and Protestants.

7.3   Non-denominational revivals and crusades

The evangelical and pentecostal movements may often provide an ecumenical impetus. For instance, the visit of the American evangelist, T.L. Osborn, in 1976, brought the majority of churches together in Calabar for a evangelistic crusade.[12] The latter was something of an exceptional event and has been remembered as such by anyone in Calabar at that time. The crusade served not only to revive a general sense of spirituality, but also to remind people of the importance of ecumenical cooperation. Following the crusade, several hundred ministers took part in a ministers' conference.

In fact over the last decade, a host of inter-denominational or non-denominational and "evangelistic" associations have sprung up all over Cross River State. They may operate as "churches" in that they hold weekly services, but their chief activity is to organize inter- or non-denominational crusades, rallies, retreats and camp meetings. With their loose organizational structures and common evangelical world-view, there is a resultant pooling of resources and sharing of preachers.

The majority of these groups issue directly from American organizations, or have some indirect affiliation.[13]   Even when it has not been possible to determine their exact provenance, it is safe to assume that the director or evangelist of the group in question has received his training from an American Bible college or seminary (either in residence or through a correspondence course).   American preachers are frequent speakers at these crusades and rallies although they often share the stage with local preachers and evangelists who attend each others' functions.[14]

A sample of some of these associations which have organized rallies and meetings in Calabar during the period of our investigation includes: The Deeper Christian Life Ministry; The Deeper Life Conference of Christ for the World Mission (Nigeria); the Shower of Blessings Crusade; the Christ Kingdom Crusaders led by Evangelist A.E. Henshaw (an Efik man) from Lagos; the Christian Evangelical Association; the UMA Evangelistic Association (from Uyo) and the Good News Evangelistic Association (founded in Abak by a former pastor in the Assemblies of God - Rev. E.A. Mboho).   These organizations are characterized by a conversionist approach and fundamentalist teachings.   Topics treated include "Operation Sweeten Every Marriage", "Spiritual Knowledge and Deliverance", "The Power of Righteousness", "Proclamation of Christ Emancipation", "Whoever is ATHIRST Let Him Come".   There are also specialist seminars and conferences organized for women, businessmen and graduates.   People from all denominations are attracted in their hundreds to these occasions, staged usually at Christmas and Easter and during the long school vacation, not only by the prospect of free food, accommodation and entertainment, but also by such promises as "Come and Expect a Miracle", "Jesus never fails", "God will bless you richly" and so on.

In addition to the healing and problem-solving orientation of these organizations, their lack of structure and institutional demands (i.e. no tithes or membership or attendance obligations), and sporadic activity have an obvious appeal for both regular or lapsed churchgoers.   Their aggressive evangelism and use of the media are factors in their favour.   The greatest impact and significance of these movements seems to lie however in their potential as supplementary or complementary religious sources, and their ability to promote inter-denominational cooperation. For example, the "Greater Uyo for Christ" crusade in April 1983 was publicized as "A gathering of eleven denominations! God must be there!" The following churches were listed as participants: Assemblies of God, Apostolic Church, Anglican, Presbyterian, Methodist and Lutheran Churches, Salvation Army, Christian Fellowship, King of Kings Church, African Church and Christian Assembly. These movements have also served to foster a spirit of revivalism amongst some of the mainline churches in Calabar.

The normal locations in the town for such mass evangelistic events are the Mayne Avenue Primary School grounds and the Christ African Field along White House Street. Also used are schools such as Edgerley Memorial Girls' School and the Hope Waddell Training Institution. A great deal of inter-denominational activity such as we have described above takes place in the higher educational institutions. While some of the evangelistic activity on campus is an extension of the work of the town churches, many organizations are specifically student-oriented, for instance the Christian Union, Student Christian Movement and the Deeper Life Campus Fellowship, A Time of Times - a Mission to UNICAL [University of Calabar]. Students are attracted to meetings and rallies entitled Encounter '82, Solution '83, Jesus'Olution, Deliverance Hour, with promises of "freedom from sin, bondages, failure, ill luck, sickness, nightmare and Satan".[15]

Sometimes the non-denominational intentions (despite their declarations) of these groups are shortlived; for example, the Christian Union and Christ's Ambassadors, had begun meeting on a regular basis with a view to supplanting chaplaincy worship on the university campus. It was even being rumoured in 1983 that one of these organizations, the Evangelistic Church of the Redeemed, run by two university staff, Dr. and Dr. (Mrs.) Eko, had asked for a plot of land on the new campus.

7.4   The Bible and music as common denominators

Despite the varying attitudes to, and divergent interpretations of, the Bible, it has nonetheless proved to be a means of bringing the churches together. Through the agency of the Bible Society of Nigeria,[16] some of the Calabar churches (Roman Catholic, Qua Iboe, Anglican, Methodist, Presbyterian, Brotherhood of the Cross and Star, and occasionally the Assemblies of God) meet with churches from Rivers and Imo states to promote Bible translation and distribution.[17]

Each year "Bible Week" is celebrated in the majority of Calabar's churches; a "flag day" is held and all donations go towards the translation fund. The society (through the Calabar auxiliary) has recently embarked on an Efik (re)translation of the Bible which is intended to provide a more central version which will give greater emphasis to the Ibibio "dialect".[18]

Music is by far the greatest common denominator amongst Calabar's religious groups. This is not just a recent phenomenon but dates back to at least the 1950s when people from other churches openly attended the popular evensong service at Holy Trinity (Anglican) Church. A Roman Catholic, Mr. V. Andorh, shared the organ with the resident organist. Holy Trinity Church claims to have been the first church to hold a choir festival in Calabar and the first to organize an all-Protestant Churches Choir Competition.[19]

Today there are numerous examples of cooperation and interdependency in the musical domain. A non-denominational choir performed carols during Christmas 1981 at the Stadium and the Governor's Lodge. The Cross River State Revival Movement organized a carol competition during Christmas 1983 at which both spiritual and mainline churches participated. For special events and services, churches not only draw on their own branches to supplement their musical forces but may also invite other churches to assist in the proceedings. For example, the popular Salvation Army played at the 7th Anniversary of the Calabar Presbytery Youth Council in July 1982. The Methodist Choir from Atamunu sang at the Hope Waddell valedictory service in 1980. There are also freelance "gospel groups" such as the Trumpets of the Lord

Organisation and the UMA Evangelistic Association Singers whose services may be hired by individuals, churches or the media. The UMA Singers have produced a number of records which are popular with a wide audience.

The musical services of individuals may be engaged by churches of which they are not members. Eric Esin, the Nigerian Television Authority Channel 9 music producer is a Presbyterian, but plays the organ at the Wesleyan Cathedral on a regular basis. Individuals may be choristers in one church, while worshipping in another.

To some extent, the type of cooperation and interdependency outlined above is facilitated by the use of common materials such as the Revised Church Hymnary (in Efik and English), Sankey gospel hymns, anthems and popular gospel songs and native choruses.

7.5   Civic interaction

Another important area of interaction is the civic domain. To celebrate national events like Independence Day, Armed Forces Week, St. John's Ambulance Week or international events such as the International Year of the Disabled or World Prayer Day, selected religious leaders and organizations take part in inter-denominational services. In the past, these services were dominated by the mainline churches (both Protestant and Catholic) with the occasional appearance of the Chief Imam; within the last five years, not only have the exogenous churches joined the ranks of participating churches, but also the indigenous and spiritual churches (usually the more well-known and established ones such as the National Assembly, Truth and Life Ministries, Eternal Sacred Order of the Cherubim and Seraphim). On these occasions a type of civil religion or "national faith" is operative; shared religious and moral values are expressed, including support for the government, and a sense of unity is generated by a common concern for national development and social issues. Such occasions are important not just in ecumenical terms but also in terms of church-state relations: the government derives legitimation from the religious authorities and they in turn enjoy status and recognition from involvement in civic ceremonies.

The Coronation Service of the Obong of Calabar, held at Duke Town Presbyterian Church on November 27, 1982, occasioned an ecumenical gathering in Calabar of hitherto unknown proportions. In the Presbyterian church sat leaders and representatives from the following churches: Roman Catholic, Lutheran, AME Zion, Mount Zion Light House Full Gospel Church, Salvation Army, Apostolic Church, Qua Iboe, Anglican, Christ African, Methodist and Brotherhood.[20]   On a much smaller scale, we may cite the type of religious interaction which occurs at such secular rituals as the opening of new businesses and banks. A church minister is usually present to offer the prayers and the blessing, along with a traditional chief or religious functionary who will make the necessary libations to the ancestors to ensure the success of the business in question. Traditional masqueraders may also be invited to participate in the ceremony. While there is little real interaction to speak of between the religious groups on these occasions, they nonetheless temporarily share the same "stage" and same function.

7.6   Negotiations and affiliations

It is not possible here to discuss all the interrelationships between individual religious institutions. We have referred to many cases of this type of relationship when documenting the history of particular groups. To illustrate further within this context, we might mention the recent negotiations between the Brotherhood of the Cross and Star (BCS) and both the Rosicrucian Fraternity (AMORC),[21] and the Unification Church. The relationship between the BCS and AMORC is not surprising given the association of the BCS with a local spiritual science movement, the Esom Fraternity.[22]   There are also informal connections between BCS and certain Indian mystics. The contact with the UC is initially for economic purposes: the UC is considering financing a fishing project of the BCS.[23]   Usually such relationships are generated by like-minded religious institutions who have a vested interest in each other's potential. The Nigerian institution is interested in overseas connections because of potential financial and training assistance and an input of spirituality; the overseas organization views the Nigerian partner as offering new prospects for evangelism and additional prestige. A host of examples could be adduced to illustrate this new type of interdependence: the forthcoming "merger" or "link-up" of the Crystal Cathedral with a black Baptist church in Boston; the loose affiliation of the Truth and Life Ministries International with the Faith Pool Prayer groups in Ghana and Florida; the Presbyteries Partnership between Calabar and Dundee; the visit of Rev. Gary Rowner of the Liberty Chapel, Kansas City, to preach in the Christ Apostolic Church and to stage a ten-day evangelistic crusade (Exodus Crusade) at the Mayne Avenue Primary School, organized by the Rock Foundation Ministry from Eket.

Alternatively, some religious organizations see themselves as a forum for religious interaction and cooperation and a source of spiritual revitalization for others. The Subud Brotherhood, on the occasion of its planned launching in 1981, wrote to the Governor, the African Church and Catholic bishops and the Methodist archbishop, declaring itself a non-denominational spiritual brotherhood with a mission to "restore power to the Church", "to unite all worshippers into one fold as prophesied in the Gospels", "to awaken the soul of man" and "to restore spiritual worship of God".[24]

7.7   Negative interaction

An ongoing area of conflict and tension exists between several Christian groups and traditional religion. It must be emphasized here that we are speaking of the "official" standpoint, as expressed and mediated by the church authorities, since, at the popular level, tensions and distinctions are blurred, if not non-existent. A typical example is the act of libation. This customary mark of respect to the ancestors before a meal or ceremony has been condemned by the Catholic authorities, for example, as "non-Christian".[25]

The majority of church leaders in Calabar can be heard on occasion imploring their members to refrain from visits to traditional diviners and herbalists. It is argued that such people deal with evil, or at least unknown, spirits, and that recourse to their skills and powers constitutes a compromise or departure from the Christian faith, as well as a risk to their "individual souls". While it may be acknowledged that herbalists possess useful knowledge in the domain of traditional medicine, it is generally believed that they do not operate on an "objective", non-ritual basis. The spiritual churches and revivalist movements are especially vehement in their attacks on "herbalism" and do not hesitate to discipline their members if they are discovered to be violating this code.

Bitter battles have also been fought over membership of Christians in secret societies. Under this rubric are classifed both traditional secret societies such as Ekpe as well as more modern equivalents (in terms of popular understanding) such as freemasonry and AMORC. It is argued that secret society membership constitutes at least a tacit acceptance of polytheism, if not direct involvement in "un-Christian" practices. Churches have been known to send out vigilantes to identify those "dare-devil Christians" who attend the mid-weekly meetings at the various lodges and "cult-houses". At burial time there are sometimes clashes as rival groups seek to bury the deceased according to their own rites and customs. Some churches will refuse to perform the funerary rites if they discover that the dead person had maintained an allegiance with proscribed groups.

While there is an important distinction to be made between the activities of Ekpe or other traditional secret societies, and the cultural groups which perform traditional dances on public occasions, some of the churches (particularly spiritual and evangelical/pentecostal/revivalist) have placed an overall ban on their members' participating in any such activities. Other churches such as the Presbyterian, are not so rigid in this respect and may even have their ecclesiastical occasions graced by traditional masqueraders.

Many of the churches are upset that their sacred festivals of Christmas and Easter have become a time for masquerade activities.   After a spate of violence by masqueraders, many (*Ekpe, Nnabo, Ekpo, Okpo, Ekpe Obong, Ebonko*) were banned from "playing" at Christmas by the Traditional Rulers' Council of Calabar Municipality and public notices were issued to that effect. Occasionally there are reports, although usually from the rural areas, of masqueraders destroying church property or of Christians defying Ekpe taboos.

There are also cases of discord, even hostility, between churches.   The mainline churches have long resisted the exodus of their members into the spiritual churches and have sought to prevent this in a variety of ways - usually through preaching and counselling and sometimes through disciplinary action against "wayward" members.   Their stand in this respect is based on their perceived role as defenders of the "true" Christian faith, while the Christianity of the spiritual churches is judged to be a blend of "superstition", "occultism" and economic exploitation.   The mainline churches have also employed a subtle discrimination to undermine the growth of their rivals.   For several years, through the agency of the Christian Council of Nigeria, they succeeded in monopolizing the religious broadcasting in the state.   Protest from the spiritual churches has led to a modification of this exclusivist policy, and the latter are beginning to enjoy broadcasting privileges and air-time.   The exogenous churches, whose world-views are generally conservative and fundamentalist, are critical of the liberalism of the mainline churches and wary of ecumenical moves.

The Brotherhood of the Cross and Star, as the most successful and perhaps the most controversial of the spiritual churches, has been particularly subject to both criticism and attack.   It is not uncommon to hear preachers in many churches (mainline, exogenous or spiritual) condemning the "Obu Cult" or "Obuism", on account of the divine claims of Obu.   Such anti-Brotherhood feelings came to a head in 1977 precipitating a religious crisis in the area.   Pastor Paul Louis Eyo, a disaffected Brotherhood member, on return from the United States, mobilized an anti-Brotherhood faction in the Apostolic Church.[26]   A series of rallies were organized to condemn publicly the activities of Obu and the Brotherhood; feelings ran high, BCS bethels and members were attacked and several protesters arrested, until the police issued a temporary ban on all religious demonstrations in town.

There is also an area of latent antagonism between the exogenous churches, notably of the fundamentalist type, and the mainline churches, with the former tending to criticize the latter for their weighty historical traditions and liberal moral compromises. The mainline churches, for their part, are critical of the exclusivism and fundamentalism of the exogenous churches.

7.8   Concluding remarks

The absence of any established religion and the constitutional guarantee of religious freedom have in part contributed to the remarkable religious growth and diversity that characterizes Calabar today.   This religious heterogeneity has generated a complex network of relationships and interaction between the various religious institutions.   In this chapter we have limited our analysis to the institutional level where interesting patterns and trends have emerged.

It is obvious that such a religiously pluralistic situation generates competition between groups, as they vie for converts and status.   Even the most inclusive of religious institutions is at times obliged to protect its identity and resist compromise and subordination.   However, religious pluralism is capable of fostering tolerance between the various groups as they recognize their shared objectives and need for cooperation.   We have seen how external factors could promote this type of interdependence: the civil war generated the formation of an indigenous council of churches, which is still in existence, and even before that, during World War II, "state services" were held at the Anglican Church and continued for many years after.

None of the examples outlined above demonstrates any real attempt to reach ecumenical agreement, let alone union.   If there is dialogue between the religious institutions it is generally over secondary issues such as education and morality.

While we have detected areas of borrowing and inter-dependence between the various groups, for the most part institutional interaction is limited by tradition, prejudice and instincts of self-preservation. It is at the popular level, described in the following chapter, that the processes of interaction and interdependency are more active, exerting in turn an influence on the institutional domain.

Notes

1. Kalu, *Divided People of God*, pp. 2-3; Taylor, "Missionary Education", pp. 202-3.

2. Ibid.

3. Ibid., pp. 4-5

4. See Groves, vol. 4, pp. 232-33.

5. Kalu, p. 11; see also McFarlan, p. 175.

6. See Groves, vol. 4, p. 226.

7. Brief of the Christian Community of Nigeria sent to the Cross River State Governor's Office [in 1978?].

8. Ibid.

9. The use of the term "practical Christianity" is indicative of the influence of the BCS in the CCON. See Christian Community of Nigeria, *13th Anniversary Programme*, October 28 - November 1, 1981, p. 2. The programme also contains the order of service for the joint anniversary service and it is significant to note that all the hymns are taken from the Revised Church Hymnary (see below, 7.4).

10. It is interesting to note that one spiritual church, the Eternal Sacred Order of the Cherubim and Seraphim, belongs to the CCN, while a "relative", the Divine Order of the Cherubim and Seraphim, belongs to the CCON.

11. See the Brief of the CCON. From conversations with some of the member churches, it seems unlikely that this ambitious project will materialize.

12. The crusade was organized from Lagos and through a well-known Nigerian evangelist, Reverend Benson Idahosa, of the Church of God Mission in Benin City. The local organizing officer was the then secretary of the CCN, Mr. Noel.

13. See for example the Christian Evangelical Association based at Uyo, whose "evangelist" belongs to the Unmovable Mover Foundation in California. See *The Nigerian Chronicle*, April 20, 1981.

14. See for example, "Easter Retreat '83" organized by the Nigeria Council of Gospel Ministers at Oron which brought together over 20 ministries during Easter 1983.

15. From the poster advertizing the "Deliverance Hour" organized by the Deeper Life Campus Fellowship, April 15-17, 1983.

16. Founded in 1965 and affiliated to the United Bible Societies. The Bible Society of Nigeria held its first ever conference at the Apostolic Field in Calabar in 1972.

17. In December 1982 they met in Calabar and the conference was preceded by a joint service at the Roman Catholic Sacred Heart Cathedral.

18. Two translators, one Catholic and one Protestant, were (in 1982) engaged on the project at Uyo. Information obtained from the auxiliaries general secretary (eastern zone), Rt. Rev. Msgr. J.P Ekarika. Msgr. Ekarika believes that the indigenous churches should play a greater role in the society since all make use of the Bible. To this end the CCON was petitioned for its support in 1980 but without response.

19. See Asuquo, *Patronal Festival Sermon*, p. 7.

20. Each church leader or representative had a specific function to perform, whether reading a lesson or introducing a hymn. See "Order of Service" in *Souvenir Programme of the Coronation Service*, pp. 7-9.

21. A BCS delegation visited the AMORC headquarters in California in 1982. There have also been background moves to persuade Obu to become a full member of AMORC. Information from an anonymous informant on January 23, 1983.

22. See 5.4; the BCS have published works by the founder, Professor Assassu Inyang-Ibom.

23. Information obtained from a UC representative and Bishop Roland Obu of the BCS in July 1983.

24. Letter from Subud Nigeria Zonal Co-ordinator, Peter Nta Odusip to the Governor of Cross River State, October 6, 1981.

25. See Rev. Fr. M. Offiong, "Christians and Libation", *The Nigerian Call*, November 15-21, 1981; "The Pouring of Libation is Pagan", *The Nigerian Chronicle*, March 6, 1982.

26. See Offiong, "Schism and Religious Independency", p. 40f.

Chapter Eight

Popular Religion

8.1   Introduction

A growing number of scholars argue that the study of religion in a society should not be limited to its most institutionalized and "churchly" manifestations.[1]   Beneath the "official" and normative dimension, that is to say the religious ideologies propagated and regulated by formally organized religious bodies, there lies a rich substratum of informal and unorganized religious beliefs and practices. This form of religion, which is commonly referred to as "folk" or "popular" religion, is characteristically more diffuse and heterogeneous than the more specific religious institutions, and yet by virtue of its intimate connections with people's beliefs, fears, and needs, it provides an underlying unity in a religiously pluralistic milieu.

A series of studies in recent years on the subject of popular religion has promoted the official/popular religion model as an important interpretive framework. Several of these studies have been written from a Western sociological perspective, although P.H. Vrijhof and J. Waardenburg's important edited volume *Official and Popular Religion* is subtitled *Analysis of a Theme for Religious Studies*.[2]   Robert Towler has been instrumental in highlighting and analyzing the phenomenon of what he calls "common religion": "those beliefs and practices of an overtly religious nature which are not under the domination of a prevailing religious institution".[3] From 1979-83, he directed a project on "Conventional Religion and Common Religion in Leeds" (hereafter referred to as the Leeds Project) - a major empirical survey which aims at quantifying and analyzing religious beliefs, practices and attitudes in the city of Leeds.[4]

In areas where there has been an anthropological tradition and where there is greater integration of the religious and the social, aspects of the popular religious culture have received greater recognition, particularly with regard to Hinduism and Buddhism.[5] Robert Redfield introduced the concepts of "great tradition" and "little tradition" in order to distinguish between the religion of institutions, specialists and tradition, and that of the ordinary people which is characterized by direct religious experience, spontaneity, and lack of organizational control.[6]

While focusing on a particular form of religion, the studies on popular religion, outlined briefly above,[7] have contributed to the wider understanding of the role and function of religion in a variety of contexts. In Britain, for instance, the Leeds Project revealed, even before more concrete results were available, that private beliefs and practices such as fate, astrology and luck show "a remarkable degree of persistence", with obvious implications for theories of secularization and rationalization.[8]   The studies on village Hinduism, for example, have served to demonstrate not only the extremely rich and varied complexity of religion at the individual and family levels, but also its complementarity with more classical and cultic forms.   In Japan, H. Byron Earhart describes the various aspects of "folk religion" as "the living fabric of the everyday practice of religion in traditional Japan".[9]

The theme of popular religion does not appear to have been widely discussed in the African context.   One reason for this is the division of academic labour between the anthropological and historical traditions.   The former has provided valuable accounts and analyses of traditional cults and world-views, as well as of the newer indigenous religious movements, but has shown less interest in the more heterogeneous and syncretistic religious phenomena which are a feature of modern urban life in Africa.   Historians of religion and missiologists have tended to concentrate on religious institutions and traditions, and observable phenomena.

This places a severe limitation on our understanding of the modern religious situation in Africa if we ignore the fertile substratum of popular religious beliefs and practices which complements the more manifest and authoritative stratum of institutionalized religion.   J.G. Platvoet, in an article entitled "The Akan Believer and his Religions" displays his reluctance to employ the official/popular religion model in the Akan situation, because of the religious pluriformity of present-day southern Ghana and the mobility of the participants between Christianity and traditional religion.[10]   He also emphasizes that there is no "official" religion or denomination as such in the area he studied which in his opinion invalidates the model.   He does, however, consider that

Christianity in general assumes the role of official religion because of its exclusivistic attitudes towards traditional religion.[11] P. Radin, in the 1930s, advocated a distinction between "formulated religion" and a "magical substratum", suggesting that the two strata differed not so much in kind as in authority.[12]

In this chapter we aim to show that the concept of popular religion is both useful and relevant for the analysis of contemporary Nigerian religion; this is particularly the case for the urban contexts which have been shaped by years of Christianization, Islamicization and Westernization. In previous chapters we have concentrated on the institutional forms of religion, we now turn to the non-institutionalized, unconventional and unorganized forms.

The concept of popular religion has no constant universal definition; it has a range of meanings both positive and negative. It may be used to connote all that is "pagan" as opposed to "Christian"; it may refer to a vulgarized version of of the dominant religion; it may designate the source of popular revolt in the form of millennial movements.[13] There is a tendency by Western scholars to include magical and paranormal phenomena and superstitious beliefs and fears in the category. Clearly there is a need to examine carefully our criteria when employing this interpretive framework in the African context. For instance, it would not make sense to classify all aspects of traditional religion as popular religion, nor would it be appropriate to consider new religious movements as such, despite their "anti-institutional" and "anti-traditional" traits at times.[14] Certain aspects of traditional religion and the new religious movements may be included in the popular religion category because they are informal, spontaneous and available to a wider clientèle than the membership normally defined by the institution. In this respect, we would cite special prayers, healing, burial, exorcism, divination and prophetism.

We also have reservations about distinguishing all forms of individual religious experience, as "popular". As R. Toon rightly emphasizes: "A person's pattern of religiosity may well include elements from both conventional and non-conventional sources".[15] We are not therefore trying to establish a dichotomy on the basis of public religious organizations and private religiosity,[16] even though a good deal of popular religion, by virtue of its informal and critical orientation, is directed towards the individual. Likewise we should be wary of classifying popular religion on the basis of emotional and experiential aspects.[17] The existence of the Nigerian spiritual churches, which are religious institutions characterized by their emotion-filled worship and emphasis on direct contact with the sacred, means that these criteria may not be usefully employed to distinguish popular religion in the African context.

While popular religion is intimately related to everyday concerns and therefore considered by some observers to be the religion of the masses, we are reluctant to suggest in the present study that it is exclusively the domain of the ordinary people, and that institutional religion is the preserve of the élite. The extreme fluidity, mobility and interaction which characterize religious behaviour in Calabar, would invalidate such a correlation. Many of the time-honoured areas of popular religion - tracts, devotional literature, music, radio and television programmes, newspaper and magazine articles are oriented towards mass circulation. However, it is a phenomenon which cuts across, in terms of appeal and relevance, the social and cultural spectrum.

Problems of definition and identification naturally occur when trying to describe such a heterogeneous phenomenon. We are not including in our definition "implicit religion"[18] or "surrogate religion",[19] because these include non-religious categories and we shall not attempt to discuss them in the present study, although the relevance of both concepts to the African context should provide an interesting topic for future research. In any case, the conditions in a Western context (greater differentiation, secularism etc.) are obviously more conducive to the development of these types of religion. In Calabar the religious factor is still sufficiently predominant and integrated in people's lives to preclude to a large extent the secularizing trends of the West.[20] We are therefore insisting on the *religious* nature of popular religion, in other words, some form of reference to supernatural agency.[21]

We wish to show that the absence of an "established" religious institution in Calabar and the general situation of religious heterogeneity do not preclude the existence of popular religion. As we have suggested above, popular religion is a different *type* of religion, characterized chiefly by its lack of regulation by specialist organizations as well as by its eclecticism and informality.[22]   How then is it to be located for the purposes of analysis?   Popular religion traditionally operates in boundary situations where human needs are unmet by society and spiritual needs are unmet by organized religion.[23]   It consists of those "beliefs and practices which impart a sense of security in those natural situations of life which are characterized by doubt and uncertainty".[24]

We may therefore examine the areas and stages of life which are critical to the people of Calabar: conception, birth, adolescence, marriage, sickness, misfortune and death.   This could be done, as in comparative studies by Deniel and the Leeds Project, through the use of systematic interviewing and questionnaire techniques.[25]   The data on popular religion in Calabar were, however, not systematically collected as in the above surveys, they gradually emerged and took shape during the course of the research, from informal interviews, the mass media, popular literature and observation of popular festivals and life-cycle rituals.   We have sub-divided the material according to the main themes and channels of popular religion, although overlapping inevitably occurs between the various sections.

8.2   The human condition

In this section it is proposed to treat the beliefs and practices which surround the human condition: birth, growing up, marriage and death.   The next section will deal more specifically with the themes of healing and suffering.

Calabar is not any different from other parts of Africa in that human fertility and reproduction are primary concerns.   It is through the perpetuation of the lineage that the vital continuity of past, present and future life is maintained.   Children also represent a source of potential economic security: successful, educated offspring may provide the necessary protection for a whole (extended) family.

It is women who bear the burden of reproduction and child-rearing. It is they who are blamed in cases of infertility and failure to rear a healthy family. While this reflects inadequate medical knowledge and male-dominated ideologies, it also points to the persistence of traditional beliefs in this domain. Infertility and difficult pregnancies were regarded as a symptom of divine punishment for sexual immorality on the part of the woman or attributed to the maleficent activities of others. Even today, despite increased medical knowledge, family gossip may include such traditional "diagnoses" and cases of lengthy and "mysterious" pregnancies make newspaper headlines.[26]

Given the hazardous nature of childbirth and the fact that medical facilities, particularly for the poor, are extremely inadequate, even in the urban situation, it is not surprising that women seek alternative and supplementary forms of support. It is significant that they frequently turn to religious sources, since children are seen as a divine blessing, affording the woman recognition and status, while infertility is perceived as a curse, leading to possible rejection and ostracism, and must be treated by mystical means.[27]

The spiritual churches attract many women, both members and non-members, since they operate ante-natal prayer groups and special prayer sessions for those wanting children. While most of the churches and healing homes offer little real medical help, apart from basic hygiene and, in some cases, strict instructions to attend hospital regularly, what they do provide for desperate women is psychological reassurance through ritual activity, communal solidarity and pastoral care. In many cases the relief of anxiety may be the necessary catalyst and would account for the continuing success rate claimed by the spiritual churches and their advocates.

There is a range of beliefs and practices of an overtly religious nature that women may turn to for help with fertility, childbirth and childrearing. What they choose, in what order and in what combination, will depend upon individual choice, the gravity of the problem, family pressures and decisions and the advice of peers. The majority of these beliefs and practices may be classed as "popular religion" since they are of a critical nature and often conducted outside the formal patterns of worship offered by the various religious institutions and are not usually linked to the regular religious affiliation of the supplicant.

For example, a woman may consult a diviner or herbalist and be instructed to perform certain sacrifices to a particular ndem, some of whom (Anansa for example) are renowned for their ability to cure infertility. Alternatively she may purchase traditional charms and medicines from the "juju lady" in the market. She may make libations and address prayers to her ancestors on a private basis and observe traditional taboos such as avoiding certain foods and contact with a corpse. A very popular course of action, as already mentioned above, is to consult a prophet or prophetess in a spiritual church for special prayers. The Mount Zion Light House Full Gospel Church has built up a considerable reputation in this respect. Many women, including educated professionals, attend these prayer sessions with no intention of becoming regular affiliates. Some may change their minds after receiving a cure.

The greatest concerns of today's Nigerian youth, apart from basic survival, are education and employment. The uncertainties surrounding education - payment of fees, lost or failed exam results, inadequate schools - generate and stimulate fears of evil influences in the lives of unsuccessful individuals and result in counteractive practices, such as the use of charms and the consultation of diviners and sorcerers. Sometimes it is not the youth themselves who engage in such practices, but their parents who may be desperate for their children to succeed.

The extent of unemployment is unknown in Nigeria, yet many young people end up at the churches and healing homes praying and searching for jobs.[28] They may also write to the various organizations which advertize their prayer request lists in the local newspapers. It is generally a time when religious traditions are questioned and new ideas are experimented with; evangelistic tracts in particular tend to be very popular amongst young people.

The successful marriage bond - in terms of harmony and numerous, healthy offspring - is the ambition of almost every Nigerian. And yet the institution of marriage has undergone a series of transformations in the urban context. Because of economic, social and religious pressures, polygamy is on the decline and monogamy has become the modern marital institution. In practice, the transition is uneven, since cultural conceptions of a wealthy man include a retinue of wives and children. Concubinage is common and marriage often occurs late in life, when sufficient bride-wealth has been accumulated. For many people in Calabar today, the marital situation is a potentially difficult and unstable situation, since they are uprooted from their family and village contexts and the possibility of invoking traditional sanctions on wayward or defaulting spouses.

In the face of such insecurity, many, particularly the women (since they are more at risk and have more to lose), turn to popular "remedies" such as love-potions, dispensed by traditional specialists or the more modernized, "mail-order sorcerer" to maintain or recreate the status quo. Women in polygamous households are popularly renowned for resorting to such tactics to try to win the favour of the husband over the other wives. The unexpected death of such husbands is still readily attributed to the administration of love-potions by their wives. So too is male impotency (although this may also be accounted for in terms of witchcraft), a predominant fear amongst men in Calabar, judging from the some of the drawings on the signboards of local healing practitioners.

The wedding ceremony itself has been influenced by Western Christianity. Many families and young couples aspire to a "white wedding". This may take place in the church of their affiliation or in a popular church location such as the Hope Waddell Chapel or the Sacred Heart Cathedral. A recent trend has been noted at this type of wedding - that is, to invite a local evangelist to deliver the wedding sermon. It is believed that the evangelistic message is an important "additive" which may safeguard the success of the marriage.

The beliefs and practices surrounding death must be seen in the light of general cultural conceptions regarding the human person and spiritual and earthly dimensions of existence. Under normal conditions, at death the soul of the dead person passes to the next life to become an ancestor and may eventually reincarnate in some way (beliefs on this vary and have been weakened by contact with Christianity). This desired pattern of events may be disturbed on two accounts: bad death and bad burial.

In short, bad death is an untimely and unexpected death and hence considered "unnatural" - evil forces having intervened to upset the natural course of life. Despite rational explanations for early death (e.g. car accidents, malaria, cholera, etc.), there is still an overwhelming desire to attribute such misfortune and human tragedy to mystical causes. Relatives of the victim of a car accident may visit several diviners to identify the "spiritual enemies" of the deceased. While witchcraft accusations are less overt and indeed illegal, it is not uncommon for family members to accuse one another indirectly of having "engineered" the death of a loved one.

"Bad burial" is a fate dreaded by all in Calabar. To protect against one's descendants and family being unable or unwilling to perform the "correct" burial and wake-keeping ceremonies, several people take out "funeral insurance policies" with a variety of organizations, religious and non-religious. By contributing financially and/or as active members, they are guaranteed a respectable burial.[29] Questions of status and prestige intervene here, as well as beliefs about death and the after-life. Eminent chiefs expect an elaborate burial, not only as a reflection of their social and economic status on this earth, but as an anticipation of the status they will enjoy in the next life. For traditional chiefs a mourning house or shrine (*ufok ikpo*), containing the deceased's clothes and personal effects, may be erected by the family and traditional plays and masquerades may be performed at the traditional wake-keeping. It is rare, in Calabar at least, for some type of Christian service to be absent. It usually takes the form of a memorial and thanksgiving service on the Sunday after the wake-keeping on the Friday and burial (if it has not occurred before) on the Saturday. It has also become customary for a Christian priest or pastor to "dismantle" the ufok ikpo to mark the end of the mourning period.

Fine coffins, glass wreaths and obituary announcements in the press are essential features of every funeral, and so too is the social aspect. While the mourning period has been considerably reduced, because of the financial burden it placed on the berereaved family, death is still a major occasion for social interaction. Raffia mats are traditionally laid throughout the home of the deceased to accommodate relatives and friends, although many attend only for the weekend activities, beginning with the wake-keeping on the Friday evening. Chairs are rented and outdoor shelters are erected; food and drink must be in endless supply. It is a time when the many groups and societies with which the deceased was associated rally round the family and contribute in various ways. They may be old boys' or old girls' associations, church groups, devotional associations, traditional and masonic fraternities, professional associations and political chapters. Members of these associations may attend at least one funeral a month, not just in Calabar but in other parts of the state as well as further afield. Also popular are the (second) memorial services which may take place at least a year later and which have replaced the the traditional second burial ceremony.

Funerals are also a time of significant religious interaction, not just between traditional and Christian as described above, but between different Christian groups, freemasons and other religious movements. There are occasional clashes as rival groups attempt to bury the dead according to their particular rites.

In general, however, the funeral is an occasion of great religious significance, and very much a popular event with many of the rituals being conducted outside the confines of a religious building. The importance of the ceremonies is linked not just to the fate of the deceased, but also to that of the bereaved, for a "badly buried" relative becomes a wandering ghost who may come back to trouble those on this earth for their neglect of his or her spiritual welfare.

People fear the dead and anything connected with death. This is evident in a number of taboos and practices which still persist. For example, corpses are feared and avoided wherever possible. Some churches refuse to allow the coffin to be taken on to the church premises before being taken to the cemetery. Any vehicle transporting a corpse ties young palm fronds at the front to ward off evil spirits. The children of the deceased are supposed to show the maximum of honour and respect for their late parent, by weeping and wailing at the graveside and dancing around the town; failure to do so is not only considered disrespectful but may lead to rumours of involvement (through witchcraft or sorcery) in the death of their family member. People attending the actual burial ceremony go back to the deceased's compound before returning to their own homes; otherwise it is considered that they will carry back the bad luck from the cemetery to their own house. Black is avoided by many even in mourning. Children rarely receive a full burial.

The death of someone important, particularly a traditional leader, is not announced until the commencement of the funerary rites so as not to disrupt the normal course of events. For instance, the former Obong of Calabar died in January 1981 but it was not officially announced until September 1981 when the new obong had been named. The funerary rites did not begin until November 1981.

In short, death represents the most critical of the life-cycle rituals; it constitutes the greatest threat to communal well-being. While many claim that life and death are ultimately "in God's hands", more often than not explanations are sought as to the reasons for the death. Diviners and prophets continue to meet this need for explanation.

The churches, particularly the mainline churches with their dignified funeral services, provide the equally important ceremonial legitimation. To some extent they have exploited this popular need by refusing burial rites to non-Christians and sometimes non-members and non-paid-up members. Christian burials and memorial services have gradually become more prestigious, although some of the festivity and rejoicing characteristic of traditional ceremonies seems to have found continuity in present-day practices.

8.3   "Why die in silence?"

The herbalists', sorcerers' and diviners' motto - "Why die in silence? - is seen on noticeboards all around Calabar. It constitutes a clarion call to all those who are suffering from whatever ailment or problem, to come and seek help from those whose profession is problem-solving. In recent times the function of problem-solving has been extended to a wider range of religious specialists, such as prophets in the spiritual churches and itinerant "mystics".

People most frequently consult a "problem-solver" for healing purposes. Healing is conceived in holistic terms - it involves body, mind and soul and their interrelationships. It is also founded on a dualistic theory of sickness - "natural" illnesses and accidents such as malaria, broken limbs and arthritis may be treated by modern medicine alone, but "unnatural" illnesses, caused by mystical means, such as infertility, epilepsy, madness, must be treated by religious specialists.

In practice, however, both categories are fluid and reference to either or both will vary according to individual beliefs. So while a supplicant may consult a herbalist for a lingering sore, both he/she and the herbalist suspect that the physical ailment is a symptom of bewitchment and therefore herbal remedies may be accompanied by sacrificial and ritual requirements. Even when directed to take antibiotics, many people supplement such modern medical techniques with charms, sacrifices and/or special prayers. They may openly consider modern medicine to be theoretically more effective and powerful, but in practice, everyone knows that there are many factors which militate against its efficacy: drug shortages, badly run and ill-equipped hospitals, poorly trained and unmotivated staff and unhygienic conditions caused by lack of water and electricity.

So it is not surprising that in the case of sickness, particularly prolonged sickness, people resort to a variety of means to restore health. That choice, as we are at pains to emphasize, will depend on the beliefs, religious asssociations and affiliations of the person in question. For example, some Christian organizations indoctrinate their members to avoid traditional specialists, while others place a total ban on all forms of medicine. The choice will depend as well on people's perception of the problem and awareness of alternatives and the means at their disposal. Some traditional specialists and modern clinics may charges fees beyond the pocket of the average worker). In this respect the pastoral care system available to casual clients in the spiritual churches is gaining in popularity over the traditional or neo-traditional network, because people feel the former to be less commercialized. Indeed the majority of the spiritual churches make no financial demands on occasional customers; sometimes they may request that a thanksoffering be made in church at one of the services. Some churches try to make membership a condition for treatment (Brotherhood of the Cross and Star and the Celestial Church of Christ), but prophets and prophetesses from these and other churches may be consulted on an "off-duty" or "unofficial" basis for diagnosis, exorcism and special prayers.[30]

The quest for healing is the greatest cause of religious mobility in Calabar today. Not only does it stimulate mobility between the various religious institutions, but also recourse to protective and curative mechanisms which are more attuned to critical needs. Sickness causes confusion, insecurity and anxiety in individuals, families and communities; the sick person is on the potential road to death, if the right "action" or "solution" is not found. It is not uncommon for people to experiment with the maximum number of options, either concurrently or successively. Behaviour and attitudes to suffering, sickness and misfortune are ultimately connected with notions of power as we shall see in the following section.

8.4   Power and protection

Power and protection are two concepts which are particularly appropriate for understanding the mass of beliefs and practices which may be characterized as "popular religion". The two go hand in hand. The acquisition of spiritual power entails protection against evil forces and enables the individual to progress in life, unimpeded by "spiritual obstacles". Both concepts must be understood in the context of beliefs concerning the activity and intervention of the supernatural in human affairs. It is generally held that in addition to the actions of deities and spirits, human beings may actively influence, if not manipulate, supernatural forces to achieve desired ends, whether good or evil. This they may do directly (if they have spiritual knowledge or power) or through intermediaries such as diviners, "native doctors" and prophets.

In this section we are concerned with those beliefs and practices which serve as "additives" to the type of spiritual power and knowledge people normally hope to acquire from their regular major affiliations. These supplementary sources of spiritual power and protection are more irregular, individualistic, and eclectic in nature. They range from objects sold as direct sources of power and protection, such as charms, concoctions, and magical rings, to more indirect sources such as books on faith-healing, yoga, hypnotism, powerful prayers, the "Astrology of Accidents", etc.[31]

We must also include the use people make of sacred objects which they extract from their "regular" contexts and employ in their personal worlds. For instance, holy oil, water and incense become agents of personal protection. The objects take on a manipulative power in addition to their symbolic value. The Christian cross or images of Christ may be used in this way. Those who have had association with the spiritual churches tend to use their white soutanes as garments of protection - sleeping, working or travelling in them at times of "spiritual need". It is also possible to see people sitting in their offices on "sanctified handkerchiefs". For members of the Brotherhood of the Cross and Star the letters of their leader's name - O.O.O. - are believed to have a sacred, protective quality and are seen painted on houses, car doors, lapel badges, etc. Rosicrucian paraphernalia have become popular for creating domestic altars and their Egyptian symbols are believed to be a source of special power.

It will be seen from the above that the symbols and artefacts of popular religion are obtained from both local and international sources. An organization such as Okopedi Enterprises (Mystic Division), which advertizes itself as "Merchants, Mystic Adepts and Master Occultists", is able to obtain a wide variety of items and literature - herbal products, Indian amulets and talismans, "lucky jewelry", "love-potions", lodge accessories and books on Kabbalism, astrology, Egyptian religion, yoga and "secret" biblical texts.[32] As in so many other areas of Nigerian life, overseas products seem to hold a greater attraction.

The appeal of this supplementary religiosity is its versatility. Power and protection can be obtained through a variety of sources: personal consultations with specialists - the majority are locally based, although some may be peripatetic, for example, two "great divine masters, mystical consultants and professors in Metaphysics" - one a Nigerian, one a Sierra Leonean, both claiming a variety of Indian qualifications in astrology, spiritualism, homeopathy, psychotherapy and metaphysics - arrived in Calabar in February 1981 for an "international healing crusade";[33] objects and books may be ordered by mail; through prayer sheets, "orations" and chain letters received from organizations such as St. Anthony of Padua Mission in America and the "Sociedad de Jesus, Maria y Jose" in Caracas, Venezuela; through a chance meeting in the street with an itinerant Hausa diviner, who will offer his blessing to anyone with the promise that their money will be doubled if his palm is crossed with silver;[34] and through personal practices such as fasting, prayer and libations.

It is interesting to note that the "protective" aspects of popular religion reflect the Christianization of the area - Christian symbols and methods are frequently incorporated, partly because they are readily available and partly because many would consider the power of Christian symbols to be greater than traditional or occult ones. For example, the exorcism of evil spirits and "medicines" from homes and places of work, formerly undertaken by traditional specialists, is becoming more and more the responsibility of the spiritual churches, notably the Brotherhood of the Cross and Star. When a series of misfortunes befalls a household, the landlord may be requested by the tenants to "call for the Brotherhood" to come and exorcize the compound. It is popularly believed that witches fear the name of Jesus, particularly when it is shouted.[35] Fasting has also become popular as a result of the influence of the spiritual churches.

In contrast, it is believed that destructive power appears to draw more readily on traditional sources. Witchcraft (ifot) is held to be a mystical force acquired from diviners usually of Ekoi (Ejagham) origin situated in Cameroon or just close to the border in the northern part of the Cross River State. There are believed to be many different types of witchcraft, mainly destructive, but generally it is held that the greater the power acquired the greater the sacrifices demanded.[36] It is for this reason that a series of mysterious deaths in a family is usually attributed to a successful survivor.[37]

The means by which witchcraft is transmitted are believed to vary: it can be passed to unsuspecting victims through food and drink, but is not considered to be a form of direct poisoning.[38] It is a form of mystical destruction, which is known more by its symptoms and effects - prolonged illness and misfortune, mysterious and premature deaths, pregnancy complications (such as the "locked womb" syndrome). It may even be passed from parents to their children, the latter only becoming aware of their "power" in later life. It is also believed that children may suffer for the sins of their parents; a well-known family in Calabar, beset by tragic accidents, mental illness and alcoholism, is a case in point. Secondary school students fear *umen*, when witches engage in mystical sexual intercourse with their victims at night, leaving scratch marks on their faces.

Many of the traditional channels of redress against witchcraft - accusations, poison ordeals, oath-taking (mbiam), confessions - have been eradicated. And yet the conditions which generate witchcraft beliefs still exist - economic and political tensions, family and ethnic disputes.[39] Most people would affirm that education and Christianity have not succeeded in weakening the witchcraft beliefs. The insecurities of a modern, urban existence have served to aggravate beliefs and fears. In some respects, the law courts provide a forum for the working out of social conflicts as manifested in the number of litigation cases in recent times, particularly during the period of civilian rule (1979-83). The media carry public information announcements warning that "character assassination" is a "double-edged sword", which would seem to be a modern euphemism for witchcraft accusations.

Occasionally there are public confessions by witches within the township. They cause a great deal of excitement. People leave their places of work to catch a glimpse of the self-confessed witch and traffic usually comes to a halt in the vicinity. The police inevitably have to intervene to prevent the witch being lynched by the incensed crowd.[40]

The repercussions of the 1978 witch-hunt in Ibibioland led by Edet Edem Akpan, alias "Akpan Ekwong" from Ibiaku Issiet, Southern Uruan in Uyo Local Government Area, were felt in Calabar. Akpan Ekwong initiated a campaign in 1978 aimed at eradicating witchcraft from the Cross River State.[41] At least twenty people died and many were tortured. The police moved in finally to stamp out the movement and Akpan Ekwong and his team were arrested.[42]

Calabar has always been renowned as a centre of witchcraft activity[43] - some people from other parts of the country are afraid to visit the town for the first time; many of the town's indigenes, particularly the educated, prefer to live away from home; Calabar's relative lack of development has been attributed to witchcraft. Many therefore hoped that the anti-witchcraft crusader would come to Calabar to purify the town. No-one dared to speak out for fear of being accused. While Akpan Ekwong never did come to Calabar, the witch-hunt and its consequences were heavily reported in the newspapers.[44]

8.5   Festivals

In Calabar, there are no great traditional festivals, so it is the Christian holy days - Christmas and Easter - which have become the popular festivals. New Year's Eve has also developed into a time for the manifestation of popular beliefs and practices.

Christmas is an important time for family reunions - relatives return from abroad or other parts of Nigeria. The dry season has just begun and favours outdoor festivities and celebrations. It is not only a time for church-going but also for traditional plays and masquerades; the various troupes move around the streets of Calabar with their colourful and dramatic costumes.[45] The children join in the merriment by donning their own masks and performing for passers-by and friends in the hope of financial reward.

Easter is greeted with great joy, particularly after the period of Lenten fasting which several churches observe. On Good Friday, life-size effigies of Judas Iscariot are paraded around the town and then publicly flogged and denounced for the betrayal of Jesus Christ. The continuity between this popular ritual known as *mbre Judas* and the traditional ceremony for purifying the town of evil spirits (ndok) has been noted by Simmons.[46] This annual ritual catharsis not only serves to reinforce Christian values and mythology but also functions as a form of social criticism for dramatizing and mocking disloyalty, dishonesty and the quest for personal gain.[47]

New Year celebrations also demonstrate an observable continuity with traditional rites of ndok.[48] The rite of purification and renewal has been readily adapted to the practice of seeing out the old (calendar) year and welcoming in the new. Rowdy, disorderly behaviour, the breaking of bottles at crossroads (believed to be a meeting-place for spirits) and the use of guns and firecrackers and any noisy object represent an attempt to scare away evil spirits in preparation for the order and harmony of the incoming year. Such behaviour is generally limited to groups of men and young boys, with others preferring to attend New Year's Eve services in their respective churches. The midnight services are very popular and churches are packed as people offer thanks for having survived the year and pray for blessings in the next.

New Year's Day itself, a public holiday, is a time of festivity and rejoicing - traditional masquerades appear on the streets together with a series of improvised masquerades by people dressed in all manner of costumes (crash helmets, raincoats, leaves, painted faces, bowler hats, etc.) The Biblical theme is growing more popular and in 1983 a troupe of dancers and players known as "Religious Group" were witnessed performing on the streets of Calabar.

The Christmas period is also a busy time for a variety of religious gatherings such as conventions, crusades and retreats. While the majority of these evangelistic gatherings are staged by specific religious organizations, they may be considered as a forum for popular religion since they are organized in such a way (open air, "neutral" territory, over several days) as to allow non-members to participate. For some, these occasions represent a form of supplementary devotionalism, for others they may be a potential channel of conversion. In addition, there is the attraction of free food and accommodation, entertainment and social interaction with like-minded people.

Pilgrimages to holy places are virtually non-existent in Calabar. Members of the Brotherhood of the Cross and Star occasionally visit the founder's birthplace at Biakpan and bathe in the waters of the holy stream there; members of the National Assembly Church go for special prayers to a sacred hill just outside Calabar near Ikot Omin. Members of the Muslim community in Calabar perform the Hajj and a handful of Christians may make the journey to the Holy Land.

The more typical "pilgrimage" is by individuals and families to the various conventions, camp meetings and festivals of their respective religious organizations. People frequently travel to other parts of the state and the country in order to attend such gatherings.

8.6   Freelance evangelism

By "freelance evangelism" is understood any type of religious activity, of an informal, often spontaneous nature, which seeks to promote and revitalize the Christian faith. For example, "early morning evangelism" has become a common feature of Calabar's religious life. Around 5 a.m. individuals or groups, using locally-made loud-hailers, start preaching around the residential districts. Some proclaim the end of the world and the need for moral repentance and redemption, others engage in such evangelism as a means to an end, in other words, seeking followers with a view to establishing an independent religious organization.[49]   On the university campus also, such "early morning evangelism" is common; students complain that they are being exploited as they have no choice but to listen at that time of the day! Some students also practice "room-to-room evangelism", distributing tracts and trying to convert "lost sheep" into "born-again Christians". This type of religious activity is carried out by inspired or aspiring individuals or by groups operating under the auspices of established bodies such as the Christian Union, Scripture Union or the Assemblies of God (Christ's Ambassadors).

The hospital is an important source of popular religious activity. Special prayers are offered informally and spontaneously for the sick by freelance evangelists and also by patients themselves and even the hospital staff. It is not uncommon to witness a group of out-patients being led in song (usually popular gospel songs and "native choruses") by one of the nursing sisters. In addition, the majority of the religious institutions in Calabar send representatives on a regular basis to the hospitals and clinics in the town to pray for the sick and sometimes distribute devotional literature, as this is considered to be an important aspect of their social welfare and outreach activities.[50]

The Calabar prison is an important location for the type of religious activity described above. Many local preachers and groups view the prison as a testing ground for their ability to convert and save "sinners". The Calabar-Oron ferry, as well as the large buses which ply the Calabar-Lagos-Calabar route, are amenable locations for popular religious activity, with many evangelists taking advantage of the ready-made audiences and the fear and anxiety or travelling by water or by road.

Informal prayer groups are another interesting development in the religious life of Calabar. These are groups of people who congregate on an informal basis in one another's homes or in a rented school-room for the purpose of prayer, Bible study, faith-healing and singing of popular songs. Their intention is to supplement and revitalize their conventional worship. Some of these groups may go on to become religious institutions in their own right.

The work place is a location of considerable religious interaction. In offices, one frequently sees posters, calendars, notices and mottoes expressing quasi-religious "nice thoughts" as well as devotional objects such as crosses, pictures of Christ, Obu, the Pope and the Virgin Mary. Tracts are to be found lying around most offices and there is a good deal of sharing of the former as well as religious texts and biblical verses. Employees regularly discuss religious issues and problems and will recommend to fellow workers the name of a good herbalist, prophet or church.

8.7 Music

In the course of the research, particularly worshipping in the various churches, it became apparent that music was an important channel of religious expression which cuts across the institutional spectrum. We are not referring here to the official, conventional music such as hymns and anthems, but to the popular songs and choruses which are sung in and outside the churches, usually at the time of thanksoffering or spontaneously during the course of the service or in some other location such as described above. These songs and choruses may be black American spirituals, gospel music or local "native airs": "Rock My Soul in the Bosom of Abraham", "Jesus is Alive"; "I Will Make You Fishers of Men"; "Walk, Walk in the Light, Walk in the Light of God"; "Today, Today, Tomorrow No More, If I Die Today, Tomorrow I Shall Live". All have simple, catchy tunes, rarely more than two or three lines long, in both English and Efik, which are usually accompanied by dancing and clapping. They are christocentric in orientation and have simple devotional and evangelical themes such as the assurance of salvation, redemption, resurrection, goodness, power of God, defeat of evil and Satan, belief, faith, thanksgiving and praise.[51]

The importance of this type of music is that it is played and enjoyed in nearly every religious institution in Calabar whether mainline, exogenous or indigenous, as well as in non-religious locations where some sort of musical and spiritual revitalization is required. It therefore has a unifying function, as well as serving to transmit the basic tenets of the Christian faith.

Gospel music recorded by local evangelistic groups (such as the UMA Evangelistic Association Singers and the Brotherhood of the Cross and Star) is popular with a wide audience. So too are some of the religious classics such as Handel's *Messiah* and Bach's *Jesu,*

Joy of Man's Desiring. At Christmas, carols are to be heard in every shop and petrol station, as well as on the radio and in people's homes. The inspirational and devotional qualities of music are manifested in the fact that the majority of religious programmes broadcast on Sunday on Calabar radio are musical in orientation - "Lift Up Your Hearts"; "Music for Meditation"; "Golden Voice Gospel Singers".

8.8   Spiritual experience

While much spiritual experience is shaped and fashioned by the religious institutions themselves, a good deal occurs outside such formal structures. Spiritual experiences such as visions, auditions, dreams, answered prayers, miraculous healings and glossolalia are readily claimed and indeed sought after. Where these experiences occur in isolation, the advice and interpretation of religious specialists may be solicited (not necessarily from the individual's own religious organization since some disapprove of certain varieties of spiritual experience). The predilection for this type of experience varies according to individuals; some are encouraged to seek proofs of their "nearness to God" and spiritual power through their association with a spiritual church. Others regard their spiritual experience as a manifestation of God's grace in their lives. It is not uncommon for people to attribute their "escape from death" (i.e. serious accidents, attacks by armed robbers, illnesses etc.) to God's intervention on their behalf. This is illustrated in the many testimonies and thanksofferings heard and performed informally and in the churches. The converse may also apply, as we saw earlier, in that bad dreams, serious misfortune and mysterious and inexplicable events are frequently attributed to malevolent forces. Fasting has become a popular means of stimulating spiritual power and experience. While this is formally prescribed by some religious organizations, an increasing number of people resort to ad hoc periods of fasting in times of personal need.

In some cases, as we observed in chapter three, a spiritual experience (or series of experiences) in the life of an individual may prove decisive in stimulating religious initiative and innovation.

8.9   Names and mottoes

Names are an indicator of popular religious beliefs. Many children are named after the circumstances of their birth (e.g. Akpan - first-born son, or Essien Akpan Essien - "the grandfather has been born", indicating that the soul of the grandfather has been reincarnated in the new child); some are still named according to the tutelary deity of the family in question even though the child is later baptized as a Christian.[52]

Vehicle mottoes provide another medium of expression for popular religiosity. Below is listed a sample of the numerous mottoes that may be seen painted on Calabar's buses, taxis and lorries:

    Grant Me Peace O God
    Jesus Saves
    Jesus is Coming
    When God Say Yes, Who Will Say No?
    Christians Escort
    Hallelujah Hallelujah
    With God I Stand
    God's Time
    God First
    Live and Let Live
    If Men Were God
    Life is a Journey
    One With God is a Majority
    Psalm 91,   Psalm 106, Psalm 121

Apart from the general "philosophy of life" mottoes, the majority seem to have God as their key component, reflecting popular awareness and conviction that God is the ultimate life-giver, judge and ruler of the universe.

8.10   A kaleidoscope of religious activity

As stated at the outset, our aim in this chapter has been to
describe and account for the myriad beliefs, attitudes and practices
which complement and supplement the more formal and conventional
religious structures offered by institutional religion. We would
argue that popular religion and religiosity constitute a vital and
determining factor in people's religious worlds and hence to ignore
this dimension would be seriously detrimental to our task of
understanding the religious life of the town of Calabar.

Initially the beliefs and practices designated as popular religion
appeared as a mass of unrelated data, of little use or value. On
further   investigation,   this   kaleidoscopic   array   of   religious
phenomena revealed a series of unifying themes, all of them firmly
grounded in human needs and realities and cutting across
artificially imposed denominational structures, as well as ethnic and
cultural differences.

Unbounded by dogma and tradition and unregulated by "official"
religious institutions, popular religion is therefore important in that
it constitutes a type of basic religious and cultural medium on
which people draw according to their needs, experience, means,
background, etc. We have emphasized that this fund of beliefs and
practices   is   basically   complementary   to   the   activities   of
institutional religion and is useful in that it highlights what people
consider to be the "weaknesses" or shortcomings of organized
religion. While we have insisted on the distinction between popular
and institutional religion, it would be mistaken to assume that
there is a clear-cut boundary between the two. In fact some of
the examples of popular beliefs and practices that we have cited
occur within the context of organized religion, although not always
officially sanctioned by the institution in question. Popular religion
also reflects patterns of thinking about divine intervention, issues
of ultimate significance, as well as about the institutions and
specialists which are responsible for promoting religious knowledge
and traditions.[53]

We also need to consider the ways in which popular religion
may influence and even modify institutional religion.   Popular

religious beliefs and practices are characterized by their pragmatic orientation and this serves to counteract the tendency of institutional religion to deemphasize individual needs and problems. Popular religion is ecumenical. It serves to reduce the divisive and exclusivistic aspects of organized, institutionalized religion since it is linked to everyday human and religious needs, beliefs and fears.

Many of the churches, particularly of the mainline variety, discourage their members from indulging in supplementary religious practices and holding popular or "superstitious" beliefs. There is little they can do to prevent this except through indoctrination and occasional disciplinary measures. Some churches have tried to accommodate popular religious needs in a variety of ways - through music, special healing services, increased prayer and devotionalism, the incorporation of evangelistic teachings and techniques,[54] increased use of the media, greater lay participation, greater emphasis on festivals and conventions, and greater recognition of witchcraft problems.[55]

The study of popular religion in the African context is not without methodological problems. Given the diffuse, critical and informal nature of popular religious beliefs and practices, we are faced with the task of locating and identifying the areas and channels of this type of religious expression in each cultural context. Overlapping inevitably occurs, for instance, the various neo-traditional healers which abound in Calabar may be classified as both traditional religious specialists or purveyors of popular religion. Similarly, the attribution of the erosion of the main road out of Calabar to the displeasure of the goddess Anansa (who is opposed to modern development) is an example of traditional or popular religious belief. Such cases are only answerable on an individual basis, by taking account of a participant's religious background, affiliations and motivations. The popular religious dimension is characterized by flux and mobility, lacking the parameters of institutional religion, but it allows us a more accurate insight into people's religious worlds, which are being continually shaped and modified by processes of selection, rejection, adaptation and experimentation.

Popular religion is the bedrock of the religious life of Calabar. We have noted that many of the beliefs, fears and practices stem from traditional sources; even the "foreign input" is selected on the basis of its cultural affinity with prevailing world-views. It is therefore an important, if not the most important, expression and manifestation of the "Calabar-ness" of religious beliefs and behaviour, providing historical continuity for common cultural forms and identity.

In this respect, we are emphasizing that popular religion is not just an affair of the "masses" or lower classes in Calabar today. The incorporation of Christian symbols has meant that a wider spectrum of people make use of popular religious techniques, in other words those that would normally reject anything with "pagan" connections as dangerous or superstitious. Eastern- or Western-style magic provides a legitimate veneer for otherwise outlawed traditional beliefs and practices. Additional research needs to be done on the significance of gender, social status and education in relation to the phenomenon of popular religion. Some of these questions will receive further treatment in connection with religious conversion and mobility in chapter ten.

Notes

1. The foundations of this approach were laid by such scholars as G. Lenski, *The Religious Factor* (New York: Doubleday, 1961); T. Luckmann, *The Invisible Religion* (New York: Macmillan, 1967); and to some extent by David Martin in his ongoing critique of the theory of secularization, *A General Theory of Secularization* (Oxford: Basil Blackwell, 1978). See also S. Acquaviva, *The Decline of the Sacred in Industrial Society* (Oxford: Basil Blackwell, 1979) which is an account of religiosity in Western Europe during the Middle Ages.

2. The Hague: Mouton, 1976. Cf. also the work of the historian, K. Thomas, *Religion and the Decline of Magic* (London: Weidenfeld, 1971).

3. *Homo Religiosus* (London: Constable, 1974), p. 148.

4. The preliminary results of the project are discussed in "End of Year Report January 1982 - January 1983", Research Paper no. 10 (Leeds: Department of Sociology, University of Leeds, [1983]). A number of religious research papers have also been issued during the course of the project. Some of these discuss methodological issues, e.g. R. Toon, "Methodological Problems in the Study of Implicit Religion", no. 3, 1981; R. Towler, "Conventional Religion and Common Religion in Great Britain", no. 11, [1983]; others treat more specific issues such as media portrayals of religion (nos. 5 and 9), Asian religions (nos. 4 and 6).

5. See for example the important work done by sociologists, anthropologists and historians of religion on "Village Hinduism", e.g. U. Sharma, "The Problem of Village Hinduism: 'Fragmentation' and Integration" in *Man's Religious Quest*, ed. W. Foy (London: Croom Helm in association with The Open University Press, 1978), pp. 51-74 and the type of beliefs and rites - religious, magical and superstitious, which constitute this oft-neglected dimension of Indian religious life. See also S. Kakar, *Shamans, Mystics and Doctors* (New York: Knopf, 1982). Two articles on Buddhism in the village context are John Brohm's study of "Buddhism and Animism in a Burmese Village", *Journal of Asian Studies* 12,2 (February 1963):155-67 and A.W. Sadler, "Pagoda and Monastery: Reflections of the Social Morphology of Burmese Buddhism", *Journal of Asian and African Studies* (Leiden) 5,1 (October 1970):282-92. More recently M. Southwold has written on "True Buddhism and Village Buddhism in Sri Lanka" in *Religious Organization and Religious Experience*, ed. by J. Davis. (London: Academic Press, 1982), pp. 137-152. See also D. L. Overmyer, *Folk Buddhist Religion: Dissenting Sects in Late Traditional China*, (Cambridge, MA: Harvard University Press, 1976). There are several works dealing with Islamic popular beliefs and practices: D.B. MacDonald, *The Religious Attitude and Life in Islam* (Chicago: Chicago University Press, 1909); R. Kriss and H. Kriss-Heinrich, *Volksglaube im Bereich des Islams, 2 vols.* (Wiesbaden: Otto Harrassowitz, 1960 and 1962) is a study by folklorists of pilgrimage, saint worship, oaths, magical formulae and the use of amulets, especially in the Arab region. See also J. Kennedy, *Nubian Ceremonial Life* (Berkeley: University of California Press, 1978) and H. Barclay, *Burri al-Lammab: A Suburban Village in Sudan* (Ithaca, N.Y.: Cornell University Press, 1964).

6. *Peasant Society and Cultures* (Chicago: The University of Chicago Press, 1956), p. 70.

7. For a fuller discussion see Towler, "Conventional Religion and Common Religion in Great Britain" (see footnote 4).

8. Ibid., p. 12.

9. *Japanese Religion: Unity and Diversity*, 3rd. ed., The Religious Life of Man series (Encino, CA.: Dickenson Publishing Co., 1974), p. 39. He treats popular religion as made up of "the popular expressions of organized religion" and as one aspect of the heterogeneous, unorganized category of "folk religion" (p. 38).

10. In *Official and Popular Religion*, eds. Vrijhof and Waardenburg, p. 585f.

11. Ibid., pp. 583-4.

12. *Primitive Religion: Its Nature and Its Origin* (London: Hamish Hamilton, 1938), pp. 15-39 and 59-65, cited in Towler, *Homo Religiosus*, p. 150.

13. See J. Rémy, "La 'religion populaire', réinventée et la mise en question de la rationalité formelle", paper presented at the 17th Conference of the International Conference of the Sociology of Religion, London, August 1983, p. 4.

14. Cf. P. Williams, who, in his book on *Popular Religion in America: Symbolic Change and the Modernization Process in Historical Perspective* (Englewood Cliffs, N.J.: Prentice-Hall, 1980), includes sects and cults in the category of popular religion.

15. Toon, "Methodological Problems", p. 6.

16. Ibid.

17. See Vrijhof and Waardenburg, eds., *Official and Popular Religion*, p. 638.

18. See E. Bailey, "The Implicit Religion of Contemporary Society: An Orientation and Plea for its Study", *Religion: A Journal of Religion and Religions* 13 (1983):69-83.

19. See Toon, "Methodological Problems", p. 7.

20. There will be more discussion on the theme of secularization in chapter 10.

21. See Toon, "Methodological Problems", p. 6.

22. This is a more debatable characteristic of popular religion. Arguably many forms of popular religion are not without organization and conventionality. They rather exhibit "diffusive institutionalization" which is a feature of pre-industrial, pre-urban societies. Personal communication from J.G. Platvoet, March 2, 1986.

23. Comments by N. Kokosalakis during the presentation of his paper on "Popular Religion and the Public Domain in Greece" at the 17th Conference of the International Conference of the Sociology of Religion, London, August 1983.

24. Towler, *Homo Religiosus*, p. 155.

25. See R. Deniel, *Croyances religieuses et vie quotidienne.* See also R. Toon and R. Towler, comps., "Religious Research Project Interview Schedule" (Leeds: Department of Sociology, University of Leeds under SSRC Grant no. HR 7720, Sept./Oct. 1982).

26. See "Agony of 18-Month Pregnancy Ends", *The Sunday Chronicle*, April 5, 1981. Mrs. Agnes Michael of Mbarakom village near Akamkpa just north of Calabar was delivered of a baby girl at the Brotherhood of the Cross and Star Healing Centre at Akim Road, Calabar, after modern medicine reportedly failed to help her with her abnormally long pregnancy. The "doctor/spiritualist", Dr./Prophet Innocent Essien, had successfully located and removed, through a "spiritual X-ray", an "object" in the woman's womb, allowing the eventual birth of the child.

27. This point is confirmed by J. Uyanga, "The Medical Role of Spiritual Healing Churches in Southeastern Nigeria", *Nigerian Behavioral Sciences Journal* 2,1/2 (1979), who cites the popular sayings that "Only God gives children" and "Children come from God" (p. 50) and argues that these beliefs account for the fact that many women, in the rural areas especially, go straight to "spiritual healing churches" to solve problems of childlessness (p. 51).

28. Some churches may offer direct employment of one form or another (for instance the True Church of God runs a bed factory and a fleet of ice-cream vans and the Brotherhood of the Cross and Star has a printing press, hostel, tailoring business, and catering and transport concerns). Sometimes the church may provide the necessary contacts to find a job in the town.

29. Some people continue to pay tithes and dues to churches that they no longer attend.

30. The fact that this is a common practice is proved by the different steps taken by churches to ban the practice and to discipline offending prophets.

31. A visit to the Ubeh Bookshop in Calabar in March 1983 revealed a religion section stocked with books on Zen, meditation, "Self-Control, Will and Word-Power", astrology, as well as a full range of Rosicrucian and Lobsang Rampa books. Cf. Harold Turner's article on "Searching and Syncretism: A West African Documentation", *International Review of Mission* 49 (1960):189-94.

32. See their *Okopedi Healing Home Catalogue*, 1978/79 edition, where over 100 items are listed; one of the major sources appears to be De Lawrence of Chicago.

33. *The Nigerian Chronicle*, February 5, 1981.

34. These wandering Muslim diviners became more numerous during the dry season, many of them having migrated down from northern Nigeria or Niger to avoid the drought.

35. Information from Rev. E. Ayankop, Aberdeen, December 19, 1983.

36. Toon, "Methodological Problems", p. 8, makes the point that witchcraft may be assigned to either conventional or common religion depending on "whether or not involvement is regulated by a specialist organization such as a local covern." This is an important consideration, but as soon as we try to apply it to the Calabar context we encounter difficulties. Witches are popularly believed to belong to "secret societies" or "witchcraft fraternities", but actual empirical knowledge of these organizations and their meetings is lacking. We have therefore decided to treat witchcraft as popular religion, in the absence of proof of the activities of specialist organizations.

37. See G.I. Jones, "A Boundary to Accusations", in *Witchcraft Confessions and Accusations*, ed. M. Douglas (London: Tavistock, 1970), pp. 323-25.

38. Jones argues that witchcraft and sorcery in the Cross River area are mutually supportive, ibid., p. 324.

39. See A.J.H. Latham, "Witchcraft Accusations and Economic Tension in Pre-Colonial Calabar", *Journal of African History* 13,2 (1972):249-60.

40. See *The Nigerian Gong*, July 26 - August 1, 1982, "I Killed My Nine Kids" for the account of a forty-year old woman who confessed in Calabar to "eating the flesh" of nine of her thirteen children, as well as being responsible for the death of a popular Calabar footballer and being involved in nocturnal sexual orgies. She eventually took refuge in St. Mary's Convent School, badly injured by stones and missiles thrown by the angry crowd.

41. See D. Offiong, "Witchcraft among the Ibibio of Nigeria", *African Studies Review*, 26,1 (March 1983):107f.

42. The exact fate of Akpan Ekwong is unknown. He was condemned to death in late 1978, but appears to have been acquitted after some months; he retired to an isolated rural area to prepare anti-witchcraft medicines, but was later re-arrested on another charge - the murder of his driver.

43. See Jones "A Boundary to Accusations", p. 322, for a map of eastern Nigeria showing "differential concern with witchcraft". Calabar and the surrounding area are the most heavily shaded.

44. O.O. Obu, Sole Spiritual Leader of the Brotherhood of the Cross and Star, issued a statement on December 23, 1979 in *The Nigerian Chronicle* on the witchcraft scare, denying any belief or association with witchcraft. He took the opportunity to denounce those who had accused him of having acquired *ekpenoi* (a form of witchcraft that one may purchase).

45. In recent years, selected masquerades have been banned on account of their harassment of members of the public.

46. See Simmons "An Efik Judas Play" and 1.2.5.

47. The plays are always well publicized by the media, particularly the government-owned newspaper - *The Nigerian Chronicle*.

48. Amongst the Efik this traditional rite for the purgation of the community took place on a biennial basis, while for the Ibibio it is an annual rite and still performed in the rural areas.

49. Paul Louis Eyo's spiritual church - Christ the Shepherd's New Kingdom Flock - began in this way.

50. A sick colleague in the University of Calabar Medical Centre reported that he had been prayed for by at least fifteen different religious organizations or individuals in the course of one Sunday afternoon.

51. See for example, Rev. O.B. Ekpenyong, comp., *PYPAN Songs* ([Calabar]: The Presbyterian Young People's Association of Nigeria, 1981) which is a collection of popular choruses in English and the major Nigerian languages. In the Presbyterian Church, as well as elsewhere, it is the youth who are responsible for leading the congregation in this type of music.

52. For example, Andem, Ekanem, Nsa and Ansa are all names associated with ndem.

53. These points are particularly well illustrated in the following chapter (especially 9.2.3 and 9.2.4) where media portrayals of religion are examined.

54. The Presbyterian Church, for example, has started staging "revival weeks". A large banner which now hangs permanently in the Efut Ekondo church reads - WHERE WILL YOU SPEND ETERNITY?

55. In 1975 the Presbyterian Church introduced two rituals on
    popular demand - the churching of women and the presentation
    of children (in addition to infant baptism).

Chapter Nine

Religion in the Media

9.1   Introduction

This chapter is a continuation of the previous one, except that it focuses on one particular channel of religious expression, namely the media.   The references to, selections and treatment of religion in the media provide a primary source of religious beliefs and attitudes, mainly of the popular variety, although there are some official statements from time to time by church leaders.   We shall focus chiefly on the press, since this is the most versatile medium of expression, allowing a fairly comprehensive coverage of religious events and issues as well as lively debate on the subject.[1]   Many people listen to the radio, but religious programmes are mainly of a musical orientation, or are directly informative (i.e., public service announcements regarding forthcoming events of particular religious institutions).   Television is a restricted medium since many people do not own or have access to a television set, and there is the additional problem of electricity cuts.

While the actual circulation figures for the town's newspapers are low, there is in effect a large readership.   The reason for this being that most government offices, commercial enterprises and educational institutions receive the daily newspapers which are read by numerous employees and visitors.   All four newspapers which appeared on the streets of Calabar during the period of investigation (*The Nigerian Chronicle/The Sunday Chronicle, The Nigerian Call, The Nigerian People, The Nigerian Gong*) were produced in

English.[2]   Newspapers are also freely shared amongst friends and family. Given the higher degree of literacy (in English) in the urban context, we may assume that the majority of people read a newspaper fairly regularly.

As will be argued in more detail later, there is a significant interrelationship between the mass media in Calabar and popular religious beliefs and practices. This stems from the degree of public participation (individuals and organizations) in all forms of the media and the importance attached to a dynamic and virulent press as a forum for popular opinion.

9.2   Newspaper religion

9.2.1   Headline news

News items with a religious content are less numerous than feature articles.[3]   Headline news is usually of a sensational nature, often concerning mysterious and inexplicable phenomena, such as "Man Finds Strange Spear on Bed", "How Did Boy, 18 Disapppear?", "Police Wade in to Save Bewitched Child", "Unusual Pineapple Discovered" and "Agony of 18-Month Pregnancy Ends". Items with a more Christian content tend to focus on the scandalous such as - "Ex-Pastor Sentenced to Death", "Student Leader in Oath Drama" and "Church Loses All-Quarter Offerings".[4]

Many of the news items concern traditional fears and beliefs such as ritual murders, witchcraft and "juju". Coverage was provided of the World Conference of Witches in Benin City in 1983. The sports pages are not without reports of the occasional discovery of charms.[5]

The case of the anti-witchcraft crusader, Edet Edem Akpan (alias Akpan Ekwong), who was sentenced to death in 1978/79 for his part in the ritual murders of "witches", has made the news headlines at every turn. He was acquitted of the original charge and later rearrested for the murder of one of his employees.[6]

The Pope's visit to Nigeria in early 1982 was a major news item for the local press, even though the Pope did not visit

Calabar itself. The Maitatsine riots in 1980 and 1982, caused by a Muslim movement in the north of Nigeria, generated concern in the press for the dangers of religious fanaticism and its potential spread to all parts of Nigeria.[7]

Small news items appear regularly about the launching of new religious institutions, opening of new branches, fund-raising activities and events, major sermons or pronouncements of well-known religious figures, Christian and Islamic holidays, welfare activities, donations by or to religious institutions and visits by government officials to churches. The majority of news items are of local origin, some concern other parts of Nigeria, very few treat international issues.

9.2.2   Prophecies and predictions

A popular newspaper feature, albeit infrequent, is the prophecies and predictions of religious leaders and parapsychologists. A regular contributor is G.O. Okunzua, who terms himself a High Parapsychologist. He publishes lengthy predictions at the beginning of each year for the *Nigerian Chronicle*. His forecasts are, for the most part, optimistic and oriented towards the Nigerian public as a whole. He predicts which months are going to generate the most financial success, the greatest political instability, as well as times of student unrest and the imminent defeat of armed robbers. His language is infused with spiritual science concepts, as well as modern astrology.[8]   Potential disaster and chaos are the messages of spiritual church leaders such as Reverend E.T. Etokidem (Mount Zion Light House Full Gospel Church) and Bishop J. Ema Udok (Divine Order of the Cherubim and Seraphim).[9]   Others predict continuing economic gloom caused by "demonic operations".[10]

9.2.3   Features and opinion columns

Traditional religious beliefs and practices receive varying treatment in the feature articles and opinion columns of Calabar's newspapers. There is an ongoing debate over the value of traditional medicine; the majority of the articles are in favour of encouraging traditional healers and advocate increased government support and research,[11] although some writers are concerned to make the distinction between herbalism and the more "questionable" spiritualism, magic and metaphysics.[12]

The questions of cultural revival and development touch on religious issues. Some supporters of cultural revival (in its external form) have reservations about reviving those aspects which they believe to compromise their Christian faith. For example, libation has come under attack by the Catholic Bishop of Calabar and some of his clergy.[13] The banning of several traditional masquerades from the streets during the Christmas and Easter periods (1981 and 1982) generated mixed public reaction, with readers writing in to criticize the state police decision as a "violation of freedom of worship".[14] Others welcomed the move because the terrorizing activities of some masqueraders were a denial of the spirit of Christmas.

Occasionally journalists make allusions to the power of traditional religious specialists such as rain doctors and diviners, particularly in a time of crisis (for example during the 1983 drought)[15] or to the power of traditional religious objects and places such as the famous *Udara* tree which stands at the middle of the road in Ikot Ekpene (Nto Udo Ntia) and which defies any attempt to fell it, whether by Europeans or Africans, because it was planted on the direction of an oracle over a century ago.[16]

A limited number of articles are purely confessional and devotional in orientation such as "Christians Why Do We Tarry?"; "Born Again: Is It Foolish Talk or Sober Fact?"; "Vote for Christ".[17] By far the majority of features set out to debate a particular aspect of Christianity such as "Is There Hell?"; "Eve, Daughter of Devil"; "There's Pope in the Bible"; "Why Christians Worship on Sunday instead of Saturday"; "Of Sin and Punishment" and "Does Bible Say Mary is Holy?".[18]

Articles are quite frequently written on the merits of Christianity in general, or particular types of Christianity. A symposium organized by the Hope Waddell Old Students' Association in Calabar in May 1982 entitled "The Impact of Missionary Education in the Development of Nigerian Society" sparked off a series of reports and discussions, such as: "Missionaries Killed Our Culture"; "The Challenge of Mission Education to its Products"; "Missionaries Did Not Kill Our Culture".[19]   In an earlier piece, Reverend Edemikpong argues that "Christ of the Bible was not a 'White'".[20]

Some journalists are unashamedly critical of the impact of the Christian church: Ebieme Ebieme, in a feature entitled: "The Church Has Failed" contends that church leaders have failed to set a good example for their flocks by parading as "pompous prelates and executive ecclesiastics" who are "politically ambitious and materialistic",[21] and have succeeded in widening the gap between their sacred institutions and the spiritual needs of the people. He criticizes the Roman Catholic Church for its inherent capitalism and quest for temporal power, while the Protestant churches are attacked for their ceaseless controversies and intolerance. A similar tone is noted in the contribution of Livina Essien who uses the medium of the *Nigerian Gong* to condemn "Moral Pollution in Our Churches".[22] She voices the opinion of many when referring to today's churches as "thriving business enterprises", whose leaders are more concerned with financial and material achievements than "the real spread of the Gospel". Church members are also attacked for their hypocrisy, many of them are "profound and unrepentant abortionists, wife-beaters, cheats, fornicators and hemp-peddlers." The "self-righteousness" of the Scripture Union and the fanatical shouting of Jesus' name by "S.U. Girls" come in for ridicule by a regular satirical columnist - Sam the Sham.[23]

In an article with an intriguing title - "Is Churchianity a Better Way of Life?" Emman Anso asks whether church-going is worth the effort. He begins on a negative note suggesting that:

> to attend church regularly is to invite criticism
> and ridicule; to many church going has become
> synoymous with social climbing and snobbery.[24]

He goes on to outline the numerous reasons why people attend church in Nigeria - dissatisfaction with materialism; escapism; dependency; comfort and solace; fear and ignorance of life after death; civic and social reasons; ceremonial reasons (weddings and funerals). Despite his observation that many find the churches to be lacking in one way or another, he ends with the comment that Christian beliefs "still seem valid to many in the world today", in other words, Christianity is preferable to "Churchianity".

Notwithstanding the desire of some journalists to highlight the shortcomings of Christianity, there is a general underlying conviction that churches are a positive force in Calabar and Nigerian society as a whole. Given the foundations that they laid in terms of health and education, the churches are still looked to as a source of welfare, as well as moral direction. The present climate of corruption and moral dislocation in Nigeria has revived calls for the churches to reorder their "strategies for the realisation of a morally re-armed society".[25] There are also occasional calls for the schools to be returned to the churches.

As a result of their growth since the civil war, the spiritual churches have moved increasingly into the public eye. In a feature entitled "Focus on the Spiritual Churches" Udoma Inyang enumerates the points for and against the spiritual churches. According to him, they have succeeded in being the number one tourist attraction in the state; they provide employment for the jobless as tailors, or as fruit, bread and biscuit sellers; regular attendance offers relief from psychological and emotional disturbances. On the debit side, the author does not consider that they may make any claims regarding effective and lasting cures from sickness; their prophesyings and spirit possession are nothing more than "gibberish... and tantrum"; "everyone tries to out-dance and out-give so as to be out-rewarded"; they exhibit lack of forgiveness of enemies; women members neglect their domestic duties; men use the churches "to gratify their sensuality"; dropouts, tramps and those who refuse to learn a trade "now carry Bibles about claiming to be led by the spirit. They too want a spiritual church, the shortest avenue to wealth." Despite the author's apparent bias against the spiritual churches, the article provides a useful indicator of public opinion and attitudes towards the spiritual churches.[26]

In September 1981, the *Nigerian Chronicle* published a series of reports on faith-healing - "The Matter of Faith"; "Why Some Christians Prefer to Die 'In Faith'"; and "Prayer Houses Delay the

Right Treatment".[27]   The survey revealed public concern for the way some churches, particularly the spiritual churches, encourage their members to avoid modern medicine, with often harmful consequences.   The reporters do attempt, however, to investigate the reasons that the churches themselves give for the emphasis on spiritual healing and the type of cures claimed by members.

A particularly stimulating area of debate in Calabar's newspapers is the application of Christianity to everyday life, in other words the social and moral issues which affect Christians as a whole.   One of these issues, abortion, became a subject for discussion at the end of 1982 after a government report revealed alarming statistics about the number of deaths from illegal abortions (45% or 230,000 annually).   Marriage continues to raise a variety of questions: "Should Christians Marry Non-Christians?" and the merits of a church wedding as opposed to native law and custom.   Gambling, including the ever-popular football pools, generated discussion about its incompatibility with Christian ethics. B.I. Otu-Udofa asks "Christianity and Business: How Compatible?" and insists on the importance of "clean business" for the Christian which brings about blessings and prosperity.   A fiery debate arose in the newspapers in the early months of 1982 over whether the churches should pay taxes.   A popular backlash revealed strong support for the churches and for a policy of non-interference (by the government) in religious affairs.[28]

Surprisingly the most lengthy and heated of the debates in Calabar's newspapers during the period of investigation was over the issue of oath-taking.   In March 1982, the *Nigerian Chronicle* issued a front-page report concerning the refusal of a student union official at the University of Calabar to swear by the Bible, because "God said let your yes be yes and your no be no".[29]   The majority of students objected to his extremist position and refused to recognize his oath-taking.   As a result of the incident at least eight articles and letters to the editor appeared in the *Nigerian Chronicle* over the next eight weeks.   A statement by the Catholic and Methodist bishops of Calabar, in defence of swearing by the Bible, provoked sharp criticism from readers - "Bible Forbids Swearing"; "Oath-Taking is Wrong"; "That Bishop's Claim on Oath-Taking"; "Oath-Taking and Bible Interpretation".[30]   The incident is both interesting and important in that it reveals a strong current of Biblical fundamentalism amongst readers (they all quoted Matthew 5:33-37 and James 5:12) and a greater liberalism amongst (mainline) church leaders. It also emphasizes the importance of the Bible in many people's lives, as a source of all laws governing human behaviour and as a sacred object, with a power of legitimation and even punishment.

There are relatively few articles addressing the relationship between religion and politics. Apart from regular coverage of the Governor's visits to the various churches in the town for Sunday worship or special anniversary celebrations, there is little political comment by clergy or laity. Occasionally the clergy, at launching or installation ceremonies, warn traditional and government leaders about the dangers of corruption and material gain and this is reported by the daily newspapers; prophets from the spiritual churches tend to be more outspoken, but often in a disguised way through their prophecies and predictions which are sometimes reported in the press. The apparent reluctance by Calabar's religious institutions to comment publicly on political affairs is linked not only to the constitutional separation of church and state, but also to the fairly widespread dislike and distrust of politics and politicians by the majority of churches, particularly since the civil war. It does not work both ways, however, as the government considers religion to be an important source of legitimation for its activities as well as providing supplementation in the medical, welfare and educational spheres.

Features on magic, occultism and metaphysics are published from time to time,[31] but, in general, despite a growing interest in such phenomena, the spiritual sciences have not received the exposure and publicity that they have enjoyed on television.

9.2.4   Christmas and Easter

By far the greatest volume of religious comment and articles occurs at Christmas and Easter time.[32] The texts of the Governor's goodwill messages for Christmas and New Year and Easter are reprinted, together with reports on the different festivities and celebrations throughout the township - church services, choir festivals, traditional masquerades, etc.

Most of the features discuss the meaning and value of the festival, whether it is truly Christian, what merit it has for Africans, etc. [33]   There is usually a popular debate about the actual date of Jesus's birth; the God's Kingdom Society contributes a number of advertisements on this point. Newspapers editorials emphasize the importance of the Christmas message - love, peace, goodwill, brotherhood - for all.

Easter is a time to emulate the Christian values of love, sacrifice, selflessness according to Calabar's local press. It is also a time for journalists and local contributors to debate the resurrection, to ask "What is Good about Good Friday?" and to show their skills concerning the computation of the date of Easter.[34]

9.2.5   Horoscopes, obituaries and advertisements

The horoscope, "Your Stars Today" or "Stargazing", has become an increasingly regular feature of the *Nigerian Chronicle* during the 1980-83 period.[35]   The format and content resemble those in any Western newspaper and it is likely that they are composed, if not directly copied from an American source.[36]   The horoscope is not yet widely used for the majority of people are not even familiar with their birth-date (due to the virtual absence of public records, notably in the rural areas), let alone its astrological significance. There is, however, a category of people, notably those who have travelled and studied abroad, who take astrology extremely seriously.   Some have their own collection of astrological texts; they are attracted by this modern, "scientific" form of divination. Given the general fascination with, and importance of, "knowing the future", the horoscope seems destined to stay, even if it has yet to be adapted to this new cultural medium.

It seems impossible to conceive of opening a Calabar newspaper without encountering some form of obituary and remembrance announcement.[37]   We have earlier described the importance of funerary rites in Calabar (8.2) and this is to some extent reflected in the amount of space devoted to the subject.[38]   The death of traditional rulers and chiefs entails elaborate announcements with the biography of the deceased, his numerous wives and children and funeral arrangements.   The sudden death of a prominent local figure is also an occasion· for numerous public messages of condolence.   For example, a local barrister and politician, Hon. Chief Ita Ekong Ita, M.H.A. aged 41, died in confusing circumstances following an altercation one night in June 1980.   For many days the newspapers were dominated by announcements of his death and messages of sympathy.

The obituary announcements and *In Memoriam* notices (sometimes up to thirty years after the death) are therefore social acts with religious significance; they provide an important channel for the display of status and wealth, as well as being part of the funerary rites which are believed to ensure the successful transition of the deceased person to ancestorhood.   The expressions of sympathy through the newspaper medium by family members, friends and associates also provide an indirect means of expression of their "non-involvement" in the death of the person.

Religious advertisements are an important indicator of both religious needs and influences.   A fairly wide range was observable: leather-bound family Bibles advertised for sale at the Christian Witness Book Centre; a "Guide to Mortuary Services" available from an Uyo bookstore; literature available from various evangelical ministries; the "Wonderful Spiritual Healing Catalogue" from Okopedi Enterprises (Mystic Division); news of latest Indian occult and mystical imports from an Aba merchant; Bible correspondence courses, advice on Christian birth control and sex selection of offspring; Christian pen friends in America; pilgrimage to the Holy Land; invitations to send name and address to get on a "prayer list"; oils, incense, charms, lucky rings, candelabra, jewels, lodge paraphernalia, church bells from a local supplier/diviner; Rosicrucian, Zen and Christian literature from the Ubeh Bookstore in Calabar.

As may be seen from the above selection, the source of these advertisements is not limited to Calabar alone; there are frequently advertisements from Aba, Lagos, Port Harcourt and overseas.   This and the frequency of this type of advertisement, (usually one every few days) suggest that Calabar is a fruitful market in terms of "religious consumerism". The content of the advertisements is also an indicator of the wide range of choices available to the Calabar public - traditional, Christian, occult, etc. It is also a reflection of "spiritual needs" - i.e., protection, enhanced spiritual power, healing, fertility, increased Biblical knowledge, as well as a desire for "religious internationalization" - to be part of an international religious network (if only, in most cases, through the agency of literature and objects).

9.2.6   "Philosophy of Life"

The title for this section comes from a regular feature column in the *Sunday Chronicle*, but the content of which may be found in other newspapers as well as in certain television programmes. We shall begin by listing a selection of the topics which have been treated by the compiler and author - B.I. Otu-Udofa from March 1981 - January 1983:

> Satisfaction in Life
> The Principle of Reward
> Divine Justice
> Christ is Power
> Why Christians Fail
> Lodges and Re-Incarnation
> Practical Benefits of Christianity
> Nigerians and Ritual Killings
> Sermon of the Devil
> Spiritual Healing versus Medical Therapy
> Generation of Hypocrites
> Fortune Telling and Soothsaying
> The Future is Determinable
> Of Stars, Fate and Man
> Karma and Success in Business
> Sex and Godliness
> Proliferation of Secret Societies
> Need for Discipline[39]

Otu-Udofa, who is a lecturer in General Studies at the University of Calabar, is described by his readers as a "Christian mystic". He epitomizes the new breed of "religious consumer" and thinker in Calabar today. He claims that he began his search for "Truth" via lodges and philosophical schools, but abandoned this when "called by the Master Jesus".[40] His language and ideas indeed reflect a variety of influences as he himself emphasizes:

> So you see, my dear readers, the Truth as revealed in articles published or to be published in the column "Philosophy of Life" cannot be taught or found in any one school, lodge or church. These are *sifted materials gathered from here and there.* They are designed to shed light in a world full of darkness, obscurity and deceit, since there is no school, lodge or church on this earth plane in possession of the whole Truth (italics added).[41]

Despite his eclecticism, he does not hide his pro-Christian stance - "I can only recommend the Master Jesus - the Greatest Teacher - to anybody whose goal is excellence" and "Christ is the only real energy that can subsist to eternity. Christ is power".[42]

He is readily critical of exploitative and hypocritical "holy men" and seems to include traditional religious specialists in this category:

> Learn from native or witch doctors and lies-peddling spiritualists and dishonest mystics.... Even if they dupe their victims of hundreds of naira, they can never prosper. This is because they offend natural laws,[sic] they can never be permitted to rise.[43]

He is obviously concerned with moral issues (in this respect he is heavily influenced by Christian ideals), particularly in Nigerian society, and is fond of quoting sayings of popular wisdom, for example - "This world is only wicked to the wicked". The concept of karma or retribution is central to his thinking and he refers often to the "laws of life" and "natural laws".

His writings are also interesting because they convey popular beliefs and practices, such as the:

> ... mad rush to join secret societies, to be decorated with Satan's insignias, and to be forearmed with amulets, talismans, and what-have-you so called "Protection".... The society is terrorized into believing that unless you belong to one of those odd groups, you cannot be safe, nor can you live in peace.[44]

They also reflect a concern for different types of "power" (i.e., spiritual power).

In short, Mr. Otu-Udofa's popular "Philosophy of Life" column contains patterns of thought, sources and attitudes to religion which are familiar to a growing number of people, particularly educated men, who are generally more religiously mobile than their female counterparts (the latter being excluded from lodges and restricted in spiritual science organizations).

9.2.7   Statistical analysis

In this section, we analyze the frequency of religious articles in the most widely read newspaper in Calabar - the *Nigerian Chronicle*. From January 10, 1980 - August 9, 1982 (a period of 30 months), any type of article or feature with an overtly religious content was recorded and classified. For instance, some articles or news items concerned a particular religious institution, such as the Catholic or Presbyterian churches, while others addressed more general topics such as described above (9.2.3). Advertisements of a religious nature were included, while obituary notices were not.

During the thirty-month period of investigation, a total of 577 newspapers was possible, but due to newspaper shortages or machinery breakdowns, this figure was reduced by approximately 10% to 527. A total of 558 references was collected which gives an average of 1.06 per day. There were 323 editions, out of the 527 surveyed, which contained at least one reference (61.3% of the total). The maximum number of references was six (Easter 1982).

The references were classified in the same way as the religious institutions themselves and we may therefore make some comparison between the size and importance of the institution (or group of institutions) and press coverage.[45]

Table 5

Press coverage: mainline religious institutions

			$\underline{N}$	
Presbyterian			29	
Catholic			85	
Protestant	Methodist	13		
	Lutheran	13		
	Anglican	12	50	
	Qua Iboe	11		
	Baptist	1		
Islam			29	
Total			193 (34.6%)	

Table 6

Press coverage: exogenous religious institutions

	N
Pentecostal/evangelical	23
Jehovah's Witnesses	2
Salvation Army	5
Seventh-Day Adventists	8
Christian Science	0
Spiritual science	17
Total	55 (9.9%)

Table 7

Press coverage: indigenous religious institutions

	N
Brotherhood of the Cross and Star	27
Mount Zion	8
Spiritual churches	16
African churches	6
Independent revivalist[46]	33
Traditional[47]	52
Total	142 (25.4%)

Table 8

Press coverage: religion, general

	N
The state and religion[48]	56
Joint religious organizations[49]	6
General religious features	106
Total	168 (30.1%)

Table 9

Press coverage: summary

	N	%
Mainline religious institutions	193	34.6
Exogenous religious institutions	55	9.9
Indigenous religious institutions	142	25.4
General	168	30.1
Total	558	100.0

As is clear from table 9, the mainline religious institutions receive the greatest coverage in the *Nigerian Chronicle*, when in fact they represent the smallest of the categories (see table 1, chapter 6) in terms of numbers of religious institutions. This is partly linked to the fact that the *Nigerian Chronicle* is a government newspaper and therefore shows greater support for its traditional "allies" - in other words, those churches such as the Presbyterian, Catholic, Methodist, and Lutheran which share the government's social and moral aims. It is also due to the fact that a larger percentage of their members occupy government jobs. The Catholic Church (see table 5) receives the most exposure in the press; this is partly attributable to the Pope's visit to Nigeria in March 1982, but it must also be due to the church's own well-developed information network and preparedness of its clergy to speak out on all manner of social and moral issues. Islam was found to have a relatively large number of references considering its marginal position in Calabar. This would appear to be due to newspaper policy to "balance" coverage of Christian and Muslim festivals, as well as a concerted attempt by local Muslims to publicize their religion (see 4.3).

The exogenous religious institutions received a minimal amount of press coverage; this is linked in part to their "sectarian" position and lack of concern with wider social issues. The spiritual science movements are something of an exception here (see table 6) which would indicate public interest in this growing phenomenon. The pentecostal and evangelical groups also appear fairly frequently in newsprint, although several churches are included in this sub-category. The Jehovah's Witnesses receive virtually no coverage, because of their rejection of allegiance to nation-states, even though they are a considerably larger and more active group than, for example, the Seventh-day Adventists.

The Brotherhood of the Cross and Star is the second most publicized religious institution in Calabar (after the Catholic Church) (see table 7). The group is aware of the importance of the media in promoting their cause and a favourable public image. The large proportion of articles and features on traditional religious issues (10% of the overall total) is an indication of continuing public interest in this domain, despite the decline experienced in traditional cultic activity in modern times.

A sizeable number of articles are devoted to church-state issues, such as religious education, which again is a reflection of the ownership of the newspaper, as well as the interest of the general populace. 18.9% of religious articles are of a general, non-denominational nature.

The frequency of references to a particular religious institution is in part a reflection of its importance and status, and public interest in its activities, but there is another factor which should be emphasized here: the action taken by religious organizations themselves to involve the press, or the broadcasting media for that matter, in their undertakings. Access to the press and utilization of the medium are more characteristic of the well-established churches, although some of the newer spiritual churches and revivalist movements, whose leaders have been trained in the U.S., show a distinct propensity for media coverage.

9.3   Television religion

Up until 1982, religious programmes on Calabar's NTA (Nigerian Television Authority) Channel 9 had a very musical bias.[50] This was due to the fact that the producer of religious programmes was also reponsible for music broadcasts. "Sing-a-long" on a Sunday evening was a half-hour programme for church choirs and "Watch and Pray" was a recording of a church service, showing primarily the hymns and sermon. Prayers and religious discussions were avoided as they were felt to be most representative of denominational differences. "Choral Voices" on a Monday often included religious music, although it was not a specifically religious broadcast.

NTA policy was not to discriminate in favour of a particular religious organization, so that services were recorded in different churches each week.[51] However, spiritual churches, in fact any non-mainline church, were excluded from selection. The argument given by the Programme Controller was that "they had to draw the line somewhere" and the spiritual churches were "too numerous to mention". So in reality, while there was an obvious attempt to maintain a balance between the mainline churches, the lack of official coverage of the services or activities of any other type of religious institution served to promote an image of the mainline churches as guardians of conventional worship, morality and orthodoxy. This form of discrimination has increasingly come under attack by the spiritual churches, and the Brotherhood of the Cross and Star has been particularly active in this regard.

Change has occurred, however, in a roundabout way. A number of spiritual churches (the wealthier ones) have gained access to the air waves by taking advantage of the fact that anyone may purchase air-time if they are able to pay for it (30 minutes of air time cost N 600 in 1981). This opening (usually scheduled under "Social Diary") was originally intended for anyone wishing to broadcast their funerals, marriages and chieftaincy celebrations or launching of business companies. The Brotherhood of the Cross and Star was one of the first religious organizations to take advantage of this. They now run an hourly programme (6-7 p.m.) each Sunday called "Brotherhood Pulpit".[52] Since then a number of spiritual churches have come forward, but it is interesting to note that they almost always choose to broadcast gospel music sung by their choirs. Not only is music felt to be a shared medium, but it is also considered to be an important way of advertizing and promoting a particular religious institution.

An important distinction is made between religious and spiritual programmes. While the former are a potential source of denominational controversy, the programme "Contemplation", had, by 1982, become a regular and popular Sunday evening feature. Billed as "our spiritual and metaphysical programme for mature minds", the programme consisted of talks by local "spiritual leaders" (i.e., prominent members of spiritual science organizations as well as independent "spiritualists"). The usual pattern of the programme was for the speaker to be questioned by a moderator and approximately three selected participants. The latter were positioned at the feet of the speaker, who sat in a throne-like chair surrounded by what one might only describe as a "celestial" set. Strains of classical music were played in the background throughout the programme. The programme credits were viewed against scenes of snowy-topped mountain peaks.

The programme was generally dominated by two local organizations - the Rosicrucians (AMORC) and Eckankar. The Grand Master of the Apollonius Lodge, Calabar, defended the non-religious and non-sectarian activities of AMORC and Benjamin Anyaeji, the Area Mahdi for Eckankar, was a frequent contributor, advocating the need for spiritual development, through meditation, spiritual and mental discipline and training, in order to reach the higher planes of existence and knowledge. He would readily declare that the churches were unable to offer such spiritual development and higher forms of power.

Other contibutors included the British representative of the Aetherius Society Sir [sic?] Richard Lawrence, a speaker on the Grail Movement, as well as A. Peter Akpan, author of *The Path to Holiness* and Chief K.O.K Onyioha, founder of Godianism (from Umuahia). The programme's producer and moderator (a woman) also seemed concerned to counteract the impression that the programme relied on external spiritual sources and on several occasions went out into villages in different parts of the state to interview traditional healers and "witch-doctors" about their techniques and powers. Some local spiritual healers were interviewed in the studio. For example, Mr. Umoren spoke on March 6, 1983, about how he extracted a snake from a living human body.

The emphasis of this series of programmes was most obviously on metaphysical, occult and mystical themes (such as karma, meditation, hidden knowledge, spiritual power and awareness), with a good measure of the "philosophy of life". They were broadcast at a strategic time, late on a Sunday evening, when many people were at home, in preparation for the week's work ahead. Their popularity serves to confirm the remarks made in chapter four about the growing influence of this type of religious, or, as they prefer to be called, spiritual organization.

The appearance of a rather different type of religious programme, that of the American televangelist tradition, also points to trends described earlier in the study. For one hour on a Sunday evening, usually around 8 p.m., viewers were treated to one hour of religious showmanship and evangelistic devotions - prayers, music, interviews and testimonies, by the very debonair and eloquent Jim and Tammy Bakker on the PTL Club. Their message was unequivocal - do as we do (i.e., become born-again Christians) and yours will become a success story like ours. Those interviewed (by the present researcher) about the programmes admitted to being highly impressed by the style of preaching and air of assurance and well-being of the two evangelists, as well as finding the conversion and "miracle" stories very convincing.

9.4   Radio religion

As mentioned earlier (8.7), religious programmes on the radio had a mainly musical orientation. Church services were broadcast live, often for the complete duration, particularly if it was an important service, such as at Christmas or Easter or the anniversary celebrations of a particular church in the town. Similar attitudes existed towards the spiritual churches, although there seemed to be greater possibilities for this type of religious organization, if it had a good choir, to feature on the music programmes.

One advantage of the radio is that it charged far less than the television authority for air-time, enabling aspiring groups to purchase a weekly slot (approximately N 150 for 30 minutes) to evangelize. One such group which has developed this aspect of their ministry is the Truth and Life Ministries International. As part of a carefully coordinated "Radio-Literature Ministry" known as "Deliverance Hour", Reverend Akwaowo's objective, in incorporating the broadcasting medium, is to reach a wider audience and enrich the spiritual experience of those in other churches. He claims to have "reaped many souls" from this exercise and is now planning a similar style of programme (introductory gospel songs followed by preaching) for the television.[53]

9.5   Concluding remarks

As far as the press in Calabar is concerned, religion is far from being a marginal element.[54]   Religious news is regularly reported as well as the views and opinions of religious leaders and experts. Calabar's journalists exhibit a range of attitudes to religion - from the satirical and humorous, to the critical, the serious and the committed.   While there is a tendency, as in any popular daily newspaper, to highlight the sensational, the mysterious and the deviant aspects of religion, there is also a concern to expose fraud, hypocrisy and exploitation by religious specialists and to evaluate critically the role and practicality of religion.   The question is frequently asked whether religion is succeeding in improving the spiritual and material well-being of the people.   The theme of morality constantly recurs and is closely linked to religious beliefs.[55]

One of the most important functions of the press is the way in which it provides a forum for public debate of religious issues.   We have seen how lively and varied this discussion may be, with a sizeable input from local (non-professional) contributors (which ensures feedback and prevents journalistic manipulation of events and ideas).

The press is a far more accurate indicator of religion and religiosity in Calabar than any of the other media.   Popular beliefs and practices are well recorded in addition to those of the more conventional religious channels.   It could be argued that all of the media reflect popular attitudes to religion to some extent since none of them is regulated by formal religious institutions or by government censorship.   The press does not exhibit the same conservatism manifested by the radio and television authorities. While there are distinct signs of political and ethnic bias in things religious, tolerance and heterogeneity are the order of the day. This stems in part from newspaper policy, but it must also reflect the diversity of religious affiliations amongst newspaper personnel. The chances of an editor being a member of the Brotherhood of the Cross and Star are just as high as his or her being a Catholic or a Lutheran.

The media in general could be said to portray the predominance of Christian religious institutions in the area, even if some of the sub-types are denied (or do not know how to seek) public exposure in relation to their growth and status in the wider society. The growing influence of evangelical forms of Christianity is beginning to affect media output, as is the popularity of the spiritual sciences. The press in particular is prepared to express from time to time a certain dissatisfaction with church-going and the multiplicity of Christian churches, and allow proponents of magic, the occult, metaphysics and mysticism to argue their respective positions.

In conclusion we may say that media portrayals of religion in Calabar are generally positive and to some degree constitute a representative microcosm of religious trends and developments in the town today. The frequency of religious news and features, which far exceeds that of an average Western daily newspaper, conveys the importance of, and interest in, religion in the lives of the people of Calabar. What is also worthy of emphasis is the way the press is prepared to tackle and debate theological questions. The nature of these debates provides us with an indication of issues of "ultimate concern", as well as highlighting the ways in which people come to terms with religious changes in their lives.

It remains to be asked whether the media influence religion and religiosity in any way. This is difficult to determine since we are unable to take account of individual response, but there seems little doubt that the media serve to inform a sizeable percentage of the public of new religious ideas, viewpoints and institutions and that this must have some effect on religious choice and behaviour. In addition, the media serve as a means of indirect communication for like-minded people - thereby fertilizing and reinforcing world-views. We have also seen how the different religious groups have developed media strategies to convey their respective messages. To be more specific about the role of the media in this respect would require a more detailed study than is possible within the present survey. The findings revealed in our analysis, as well as the general trend towards the development of the mass media in Africa as a whole, point to a potentially fruitful and interesting area of investigation for those concerned with patterns of contemporary religious change and expression in Africa today.

Notes

1. Cf. A.F. Walls, "Religion and the Press in the *Enclave* in the Nigerian Civil War" in *Christianity in Independent Africa*, ed. Fasholé-Luke et al., pp. 206-15, which provides an interesting comparative example of the religious orientation and content of the Biafran press during the civil war.

2. The newspapers listed here are all published in Calabar and appeared with varying degrees of regularity. The *Nigerian Chronicle* (and the *Sunday Chronicle*), is a (state) government-owned concern and appeared with the greatest frequency-- approximately 95% despite frequent staff problems (for an explanation of the calculation of the percentages, see 9.2.7); the *Nigerian Call* (and the *Sunday Call*) is a private newspaper heavily influenced by its owner, a local (Ibibio from Eket) politician and businessman (regularity approx. 80%); the *Nigerian People*, owned and run by a radical Efik journalist, Chief Ernest Etim-Bassey, beset by financial problems and limited circulation, it disappeared from the streets completely during 1982 (regularity approx. 15%); the *Nigerian Gong*, also privately owned, was the most irregular (5%) due to financial restraints. We have not included in our consideration national dailies such as the *Daily Times* or the *New Nigerian*, for example, which were also available in Calabar (one day after publication). A local news magazine (monthly, in English) *Inside Out*, commenced publication in 1982 but appeared irregularly. It was a business venture of the Brotherhood Press (run by O.O. Obu jr.), but its content remained primarily oriented towards news comment and political and economic affairs (local, national and international).

3. In this section the emphasis is on articles and features of a general religious nature rather than on those which refer to specific religious institutions. The latter have, in many cases, already been mentioned in earlier sections pertaining to the religious institution in question.

4. *The Sunday Chronicle*, May 15, 1983; ibid., January 16, 1983 (this was a story which contained implications of ritual murder); The Sunday Chronicle, May 3, 1981; ibid., January 3, 1983; The Sunday Chronicle, April 5, 1981; ibid., December 7, 1980; The Nigerian Chronicle, March 1, 1982; The Sunday Chronicle, November 16, 1980.

5. See "Juju Doctors for Football?" *The Nigerian Chronicle*, April 30, 1980 and "The Juju in Football", *The Nigerian Call*, May 30 - June 1, 1982.

6. See *The Nigerian Chronicle*, August 28, 1980 and *The Sunday Chronicle*, August 30, 1980. Numerous reports and features appeared in the press in late 1978 concerned with the anti-witchcraft crusade in Ibibioland and witchcraft in general, but these precede the period of research.

7. "An End to Fanaticism", *The Nigerian Chronicle*, November 23, 1982 and "Maitatsine Riot: Don't Blame Shagari", *The Nigerian Chronicle*, December 30, 1982. Press coverage of the riots seemed to be restricted until after the situation had been brought under control by the government, and consisted of comments on the proscription of the movement and sentencing of its participants. See "Federal Axe Falls on Maitatsine Bigots", *The Nigerian Call*, November 24 - 25, 1982 and "Maitatsine Bigots Jailed", *The Nigerian Call*, February 2-3, 1983. A local news magazine carried articles entitled "The Maitatsine Riots: The Story as Told", *Inside Out* December 1982, pp. 128-29 and "Islamic Fanaticism", p. 130. Cf. also R. Hickey, "The 1982 Maitatsine Uprisings in Nigeria: a Note", *African Affairs* 83,331 (April 1984):251-56.

8. For a critique of Okunzua's predictions by a local journalist, see E. Anim, "The Fortune Tellers", *The Sunday Chronicle*, January 4, 1981.

9. "Nigeria Heads For Disaster?" *The Nigerian Gong*, May 3-9, 1982; "Let's Pray", *The Sunday Chronicle*, December 20, 1981.

10. "Nigeria's Economic Gloom Blamed on Witches", *The Sunday Chronicle*, April 23, 1983.

11. See for example, "Making Humanity Well Through Traditional Medicine", *The Nigerian Call*, June 12-15, 1982 and S. Bassey, "Traditional Medicine in Health Care Delivery", *The Nigerian Chronicle*, June 9, 1982.

12. See Reverend E. Eket, "Nature's Medicine and Nigerians", *The Sunday Chronicle*, August 10, 1980.

13. "The Pouring of Libation is Pagan", *The Nigerian Chronicle*, March 6, 1982 and Father M. Offiong, "Christians and Libation", *The Nigerian Call*, November 15-21, 1981.

14. E.E. Okon, *The Sunday Call*, January 9, 1983 and "Don't Ban the Masqueraders", *The Nigerian People*, January 11-16, 1982.

15. E. Ettah, "Where Have All the Rain Doctors Gone?" *The Nigerian Chronicle*, February 24, 1983.

16. See U. Etim, "'Mystery' Tree That Has Defied Civilization", *The Nigerian Gong*, January 31 - February 6, 1983.

17. S. Ninedays, *The Nigerian Gong*, July 5-11, 1982; E. Eko, *The Sunday Chronicle*, April 25, 1982; P.O. Okoi, *The Nigerian Call*, August 4-7, 1982.

18. E. Ebieme, *The Sunday Chronicle*, October 19, 1980; E. Boyeze, *The Sunday Chronicle*, April 19, 1981; Prophet Umoh Faithmann, *The Sunday Chronicle*, May 16, 1982; Brother A. Akpabio, *The Nigerian Chronicle*, April 15, 1982; A. Effiong, *The Sunday Chronicle*, February 13, 1983; B.B. Edet, *The Nigerian Chronicle*, September 1, 1980.

19. *The Sunday Chronicle*, May 16, 1982; O.E. Uya, *The Nigerian Chronicle*, June 12, 13, 14, 1982; U. Ekon, *The Nigerian Gong*, June 14-20, 1982.

20. *The Nigerian Chronicle*, December 21, 1980.

21. *The Sunday Chronicle*, July 20, 1980.

22. May 23-30, 1982.

23. See *The Sunday Chronicle*, March 14, 1982 and March 21, 1982.

24. *The Nigerian Call*, July 14-17, 1982.

25. "Comment" in *The Sunday Chronicle*, May 2, 1982.

26. A spirited defence, "Personality and Ministry of the Holy Spirit", was published on August 8, 1982 in *The Sunday Chronicle* by Etim Udo.

27. September 24, 1981.

28. See E. Iniodu, "Abortion: A Nation's Scourge", *The Nigerian Chronicle*, December 15, 1982; Rev. I. Umoren, "No It's a Sin Against God", *The Sunday Chronicle*, March 8, 1981; S.D. Hezekiah, *The Sunday Chronicle*, May 10, 1981; T.A. Udoerte, "Christians May Marry Non-Christians!" *The Sunday Chronicle*, May 17, 1981."NLC or Church Wedding", *The Nigerian Chronicle*, November 5, 1980; E.U. Ekong, "Gambling: Incompatible with Christian Ethics", *The Sunday Chronicle*, September 21, 1980; The Sunday Chronicle, February 15, 1981; "Churches Should Pay Tax", *The Nigerian Chronicle*, January 14, 1982 and "That Rejoinder on Taxing Churches", *The Nigerian Chronicle*, February 25, 1982; S. Okorukpong, "Churches and Taxes: Misplaced Patriotism", *The Nigerian Chronicle*, March 12, 1982.

29. Incidentally the student in question, Benjamin Essien, was a member of the Apostolic Church and the Scripture Union.

30. "Oath by the Bible is Right", *The Nigerian Chronicle*, March 10, 1982; E. Udofia, *The Nigerian Chronicle*, March 27, 1982; *The Nigerian Chronicle*, April 30, 1982; E. Eko, *The Sunday Chronicle*, March 28, 1982; G. Ikpe, *The Sunday Chronicle*, April 18, 1982.

31. "Mystery of the Psychic Phenomenon", *The Sunday Chronicle*, August 17, 1980; C. Offiong, "Christians and Magic", *The Sunday Chronicle*, May 1, 1983 and "God, Satan and Spiritual Powers", *The Sunday Chronicle*, May 22, 1983; V.E. Ekpenyong, "Apostle Comments on Christians and Magic", ibid.; E. Iniodu, "Beware! Aquarian Age", *The Nigerian Chronicle*, August 4, 1982.

32. A total of 24 Christmas articles and 15 Easter articles were collected during the research period (January 1980 - July 1983).

33. For example, "The Meaning of Xmas", *The Nigerian Chronicle*, December 25, 1982; A. Effiong snr., "Christmas: Pagan or Christian?" *The Nigerian Chronicle*, December 11, 1982; N. Imoibom Akpan Umoh, "African Religion Vs. Christmas", *The Nigerian Chronicle*, December 27, 1980; I. Inyang, "Must We Celebrate Christmas?", *The Nigerian Chronicle*, December 25, 1982.

34. F. Ajoku, "Resurrection: Is It Fact or Fiction?", *The Sunday Chronicle*, April 19, 1981; Ajoku, *The Nigerian Chronicle*, April 17, 1981; E. Akang, "The Calendar of Easter", *The Nigerian Chronicle*, April 16, 1981; U.S. Umoren, "Was the Crucifixion on Good Friday?" *The Nigerian Chronicle*, April 23, 1981.

35. Although it is still somewhat erratic, appearing chiefly in the *Sunday Chronicle*.

36. Because of phrases such as "Not a good day to enter into negotiations in connection with real estate" and "Cancers can improve their standing in the community by becoming involved in a local community drive".

37. In many instances obituary announcements are not "announcements" as such, since everyone already knows about the death or, as in the case of a traditional ruler, it is published many months, sometimes years, after the actual death, once the funerary rites are about to commence.

38. At least one page of a newspaper averaging 14-16 pages.

39. N.B. All references in this section are from *The Sunday Chronicle*: March 29, 1981; April 5, 1981; April 12, 1981; April 26, 1981; August 2, 1981; March 14, 1982; March 21, 1982; March 28, 1982; April 25, 1982; May 16, 1982; August 8, 1982; September 19, 1982; October 10, 1982; November 21, 1982; December 5, 1982; December 12, 1982; January 16, 1983; January 23, 1983.

40. March 14, 1982.

41. August 2, 1981 (italics added).

42. March 14, 1982 and August 2, 1981.

43. December 5, 1982.

44. January 16, 1983.

45. It should be noted that the scope of the *Nigerian Chronicle* extends beyond Calabar alone and includes references to religious organizations in other parts of the state. This therefore limits our comparison.

46. Because of the size of this group we have listed it separately.

47. References in this sub-category concerned anything related to traditional religious beliefs and practices (e.g. witchcraft, sacrifices, healing).

48. This sub-category included articles on the church-state relationship i.e., governor's visits to churches, governor's Christmas and Easter messages, government support for or condemnation of aspects of religion, the debate over religious education and returning the schools and the hospitals to the churches.

49. E.g., the Christian Council of Nigeria.

50. This was the only television channel operating out of Calabar. It was government-owned. The Aba and Port Harcourt stations could also be received (with a powerful aerial), along with certain broadcasts from Fernando Po.

51. Interview with Programme Controller, Okokon Ndem, Calabar, January 20, 1981.

52. In 1984 an individual Brotherhood member paid for the programme to be aired daily for four months. Personal communication from Essien A. Offiong, July 1985.

53. See the "President's Letter - January 1984", published by the Deliverance Hour Ministry, Calabar. They began their radio broadcasts in October 1982.

54. My analysis of the relationship between religion and the media has been aided by discussions with Dr. K. Knott of the University of Leeds and a transcript of her talk, "Conventional Religion and Common Religion in the Media", given at the IBA Religious Broadcasting Consultation, April 1983 (University of Leeds Religious Research Papers no. 9).

55. Williams, in his account of "Religion and Mass Media", describes this type of morality as "ecumenical moralism", p. 202.

Chapter Ten

Unity in Diversity: Themes and Developments in Calabar Religion

10.1 Introduction

An important question which has been with us throughout the study is whether there is an identifiable entity known as "Calabar religion". As we traced Calabar's expansion and increasing heterogeneity as a town and the pluralization of religious groups from the end of the nineteenth century onwards, it seemed impossible that there existed sufficient unity to employ such a concept. It was only in the later stages of the research that a common core of beliefs, attitudes, patterns and structures emerged which seemed to justify the use of a collective and singular term. The unity and continuity are provided by the common cultural context rather than by any central overriding belief system (as in the case of "Christian religion" or "Buddhist religion"). The concept of "Calabar religion" is not that of an "ethnic" religion such as "Efik religion", "Yoruba religion" or "Iroquois religion". At one time Calabar religion was identifiable with Efik religion, but gradually the concept has become much broader, encompassing a wide variety of peoples and their religious worlds. It is a concept which possesses an inherent dynamism - its former characteristic features, viz. Ndem, Ekpe and Presbyterian being gradually superseded by Brotherhood, Apostolic and Rosicrucian.

In the present chapter, we identify those overall, common themes and developments which provide the unity behind the diversity of Calabar religion in general. It is these recurrent patterns which form the basis on which the particular expressions of institutional religion are built and which give Calabar religion its special character. It is important to state that the themes and developments which are the subject of this chapter have emerged from the data; in other words, as recurrent ideas and patterns they presented themselves for further analysis. This chapter is, therefore, a culmination of the previous ones in that it seeks to draw together the overriding characteristics and underlying themes of Calabar religion which cut across popular and institutional and personal and communal categories. Our main interest is, as stated at the outset, in religious themes and issues but not to the point of isolating them completely from their cultural and social context. In this chapter especially, as our discussion proceeds in more comprehensive terms, the boundaries between religious and moral values on the one hand, and social and cultural trends on the other, may be indistinguishable. Our choice of categorization reflects the attempt to convey the "embeddedness" and "interrelatedness" of religious patterns and ideas.

Several of the themes and developments described do not differ radically from the role and function of religion described in other contexts; the uniqueness stems from the interplay of historical, social, cultural and religious forces resulting in a configuration of religious institutions and forms of expression which are unique to the Calabar context. As will become apparent, the various patterns and trends as we have characterized them are interdependent. The process of homogenization, for example, is, in part, a consequence of religious mobility; secularization and privatization are closely linked themes. The concept of power is central to an understanding of "conversion". Some of the developments exist in tension or opposition to one another: for example, the forces of spiritualization seek to counteract institutionalization.

10.2   Religion as transformative power

The theme of religion as "power" is central to an understanding of the religious life of Calabar.[1] In this section we examine how religion is held to be and exploited as a power for transforming people's lives. It is believed to be more than a symbolic transformation; there is a tendency to view religion instrumentally. This instrumentality derives from beliefs that God (or other spiritual beings) is (are) actively concerned and involved in human problems and everyday lives. The divine and the human, the supernatural and the natural, are seen as interdependent. These fundamental beliefs explain why people readily resort to religious means as solutions to the disorders and misfortunes of everyday life.

10.2.1   The counteraction of evil and sickness

Misfortune is frequently perceived in religious terms, that is as the effect of malevolent forces (referred to as "spiritual enemies", witches and evil spirits). Religious means (prayers, purificatory rituals, use of protective charms etc.) are therefore sought both as a way of neutralizing the evil forces and also as a preventive measure. The role of religion in this respect is not limited to the spiritual churches and the myriad traditional healers; the invocation of divine protection against evil forces is expressed in every religious context, whether formal services or informal prayers. It is interesting to note some cultural continuities concerning spiritual protection. Traditionally it was believed that one's animal familiar or "double" (particularly the "leopard spirit") could provide the power to enable one to become invisible, fly, go under water, perform superhuman feats, travel great distances and demonstrate great knowledge. Nowadays it is such organizations as the Rosicrucians or Eckankar which claim to offer these powers to their initiates. The power of invisibility is especially valued since it is believed that it allows one to escape unharmed from road accidents.

The fear of witchcraft continues unabated, despite earlier predictions that it would disappear with education and social development. The belief in witchcraft as an existential reality, is nurtured by social, economic and political instability. The witchcraft scare of 1978 in Ibibioland served as a confirmation of the latency of witchcraft beliefs. The Roman Catholic Church in Calabar, for example, decided to review its attitude to and treatment of witchcraft as a result of the 1978 events; greater pastoral emphasis was to be given to this persistent cultural phenomenon. Several of the younger, local clergy are very aware of the witchcraft problem and have chosen to study it at seminary and university level.[2]

Sickness also, particularly certain types of illness such as barrenness, impotency, incurable diseases, pregnancy complications and persistent sores, is readily attributed to spiritual causes and must be treated accordingly. The majority of people may begin their course of action by consulting a medical doctor, but if a cure is not forthcoming they will then try a "native doctor" (herbalist/diviner) either in Calabar or in their home town (if they are from another part of the Cross River State). They may subsequently visit any number of spiritual churches until definitive results are obtained.

The search for healing is the main reason why people experiment with a variety of religious alternatives.[3] Faith-healing is now a major and popular feature of many churches. Special prayer and healing sessions have been introduced into some of the mainline religious organizations in an attempt to stem the exodus of members. The Presbyter of the Methodist Church, the Very Reverend E. Eshiet, regularly holds prayers for the sick and troubled. The Presbyterian Church in Calabar sponsored a young minister, Rev. U. Utuk, for training in clinical theology in Kentucky, U.S.A. from 1979-84. He plans to revitalize the healing and pastoral functions of the church in response to the success of the spiritual churches in this regard.[4] The latter have promoted a holistic approach to healing and problem-solving, which as we have stated earlier, is one of the explanations for their successful growth in Calabar. The attraction of faith-healing as promoted initially by the American pentecostal movements is important in the light of popular theories concerning the aetiology of sickness, as well as the inadequate medical facilities and poor standards of health care which persist in Calabar as in other parts of the country.

10.2.2   Religion as source of explanation and control

In the event of misfortune, either personal or family, it is common for people in Calabar to seek an explanation of some type. This is to secure an answer as to "why" rather than "how" something occurred. In other words, a child may die of malaria, but this is insufficient explanation for many parents. They will consult diviners and prophets to know who, amongst their neighbours and relations, plotted the destruction of their child. Traditional diviners and the spiritual churches with their prophetic orientation are well equipped to deal with this particular religious need. Some offer ritual means of redress; but for many clients the explanation or interpretation provided by the religious specialist may offer sufficient cognitive satisfaction to allow them to cope emotionally with the suffering.

In modern-day Calabar, direct witchcraft accusations are extremely rare (they are in fact illegal), even though bewitchment as an explanation for social disorder or individual problems is still extremely prevalent. The mainline churches are less concerned with satisfying individual needs for explanation than with providing over-arching systems of meaning based on tradition. Church teachings reflect the belief that deviations from the norm and lack of personal faith entail sin and suffering for the individual. This therefore represents a more internalized explanation than the more externalized orientation of many of the indigenous groups.

10.2.3   Religion as source of blessings

The recurring theme of blessings is a useful indicator of attitudes to religion amongst the people of Calabar. Blessings are frequently referred to as *mbunwum Spirit* (fruits of the Spirit) and conceived of in the form of health, wealth, success and numerous offspring. The appeal to God, the ancestors, deities, angels, etc. through prayers, rituals, revivals (such as the Shower of Blessings Crusade), for blessings reflects beliefs in divine providence and the contingency of the human world on the supernatural world for survival and enrichment. Failure to achieve or receive these expected blessings is a major cause of religious mobility. The spiritual churches in particular advertize themselves as possessing the necessary formulae to facilitate communication with the supernatural world and, therefore, access to divine blessings.

10.3   Religion as sustaining force

Religion has the potential to be a revolutionary force in the life of an individual; the adoption of a new religious world can result in changes in ideology, behaviour, morality, and familial and social relationships. On the whole, however, religion is an expression of an individual's conception of his/her place in the world and the surrounding network of divine and human relationships. It is the sacralized values which sustain these beliefs and relationships which are expressed through regular worship.

Most people in Calabar would affirm that religion is a "good thing". This popularly held view stems from the close links believed to exist between religion and morality. This is why religious education (both by religious institutions and state schools) is still strongly supported by government, clergy and laity. It is also why those that assume public office, notably politicians, are expected to declare that they are "church-goers" and make some show, usually through religious language, of their faith. Some would even argue that without some church affiliation, one is by default a secret society member (although as will be shown later these are not exclusive categories). Morality without religion, i.e., some form of divine guarantee or sanction, is held to be worthless.

The concern for discipline is a persistent theme not just of religious groups but of life in general in Calabar. This stems from the moral and social dislocation generated by the rapid growth of the town (unemployment, robbery, corruption) and the moral climate of Nigeria in general.[5] Sermons in the churches are full of moral exhortations; biblical verses with an ethical orientation are popular as sermon themes. Newspapers frequently discuss the problem of corruption and look to the religious institutions to uphold the moral order and set an example for the rest of society.

Religion in general is seen as a conservative force, and this is borne out by the evidence. If the churches speak of change it is in terms of moral reform; there is little attempt to disturb the social fabric. In this way they maintain favour with the government and protect their own interests.

Religion was traditionally a family affair and a unifying force in a politically segmented community; it retains this function in (extended) family situations in Calabar today. At times of family crisis, or family rites of passage such as births, deaths and marriages, people draw on a common core of beliefs, values and practices regardless of the denominational differences which exist today in most families. This basic religious repertoire, which Mbiti terms "transfused religion", is composed of both traditional beliefs ("the way of our forefathers") and Christian ideals and practices.[6] One may recognize in the latter the influence of the earlier mission churches since many of the older generation were at some stage reared, educated or initiated into this type of religious institution. For public religious occasions or family rituals, therefore, people turn more readily to the mainline churches as the least controversial common denominators. They are also better oriented towards these types of religious needs.

10.4   Spiritualization

As we noted in previous chapters, there has been a steady increase in the number of religious institutions which are popularly classified as "spiritual". These include the "spiritual churches" themselves - a term we have used to describe the independent churches with a prophet-healing and/or pentecostal/evangelical orientation. But many people also tend to include the non-indigenous organizations such as the Apostolic Church and Assemblies of God. In other words any religious organization which in popular estimation lays emphasis upon healing, prayer, visions, dreams and prophecy and accords a central role to the Holy Spirit may be referred to as a "spiritual" organization.

The trend towards a more "spiritual way of worship" has been most noticeable since the end of the civil war in 1970. This traumatic period caused many people to examine their religious allegiances and turn to religious groups whose activities they felt to be more relevant and effective in times of need. Many would argue that the reason the spiritual mode of worship is ultimately more "effective" (i.e. in terms of answered prayers, spiritual

satisfaction, tangible results) is because it is more attuned to the
African world-view. There is an important continuity in terms of
spirit possession, spiritual development, dreams, visions, prophecy,
healing and conceptions of evil.

Receiving the Holy Spirit and spiritual gifts provides direct,
visible and sometimes immediate evidence of the interaction and
communication between the spiritual and human worlds. "Spirit-
filled" worship, characterized by spontaneity, movement, lively
music, is believed by many to be a more conducive environment for
spiritual and moral renewal, and material blessings. The Holy Spirit
is seen as devoid of restrictive cultural attributes and therefore
more relevant, more meaningful, more accessible and, consequently,
more powerful than the other members of the Trinity. Jesus Christ
is a historical figure subject to Western representation while God is
a transcendent and distant figure. A pneumatological emphasis is
therefore common and, in fact, increasingly apparent. For example,
Leader Obu of the Brotherhood of the Cross and Star is referred to
as the Holy Spirit Personified. The names of indigenous movements
also reflect this trend - Holy Face Spiritual Church, Spiritual
Fellowship, Spiritual Kingdom Church of Christ, etc.

Not everyone's conception of spiritual power and its
manifestations follow pentecostal lines. For instance it is possible
to discern - amongst those who reject more "churchly" forms of
worship and who espouse more occult and mystical forms - a
predilection for "spiritual development". By this is understood a
nurturing of one's (hidden) spiritual forces through the study of
esoteric texts by spiritual masters, meditation techniques and self-
discipline. The acquisition of spiritual power, which is a
counteractive, as well as a positive force, is believed by such
devotees to be the product of years of study and training, in
contrast to the more immediate and spontaneous manifestations of
spiritual power witnessed in many of the spiritual and pentecostal
churches.

10.5   Institutionalization

By institutionalization we understand the process whereby religious groups seek to establish more permanent, institutional structures such as buildings, hierarchies, evangelizing techniques, branches, codified policies and liturgies.   There is little evidence amongst Calabar's religious groups and institutions of any anti-institutionalism.   Even those marginal and informal groups such as house prayer meetings ultimately aspire towards the formation of an autonomous institution with its own rules and regulations, name, property, etc.   For instance, the Evangelistic Church of the Redeemed began life in the late 1970s as an interdenominational revivalist campaign on the University of Calabar campus.   By 1983 the "church" was seeking to establish a more autonomous identity and had requested a plot of land from the university authorities.

This desire to institutionalize reflects in part the influence of the social sector where "development" and conspicuous consumption are the order of the day.   For a religious group, therefore, to have legitimacy and credibility in a modernizing Nigeria, it must display the accoutrements of successful expansion: fleets of evangelism buses, church magazines and other propaganda, concrete buildings, electricity generators, electronic musical instruments, printing presses, schools, commercial enterprises, bookstores, hospitals, media appearances, etc.   The True Church of God, a medium-sized spiritual church with one branch in Calabar, runs a bed factory and a fleet of ice-cream vans ("True Faith Ice Cream").   Even long-established religious institutions such as the Presbyterian Church have been forced to develop new institutions of a more commercial nature in order to maintain the church's financial stability and fund its more conventional projects and activities.   In July 1983 the elders of Duke Town Church declared that a Presbyterian Bookshop Committee had been formed to reactivate the Hope Waddell Bookshop and Press.   Shares were offered (to both individual Presbyterians and parishes) in what was hailed as the first company in the history of the Presbyterian Church of Nigeria.

The trend towards institutionalization must be outlined against the background of religious competition generated by a religiously pluralistic situation. Some degree of institutionalization is necessary for a group to survive, even to commence, for followers need to be attracted and then converted into permanent members or "affiliates". While it might be expected that the process of institutionalization might function to suppress or stifle the forces of spiritualization, this is not always the case. The routinization of charisma is regarded as a necessary means to stability, survival and success, and several movements, such as the Brotherhood and the Celestial Church of Christ, have developed elaborate methods of disseminating spiritual power. Examples of this include holy oil, holy water, holy cloths and candles, devotional literature, records and cassettes, which are seen as ways of "storing" and "sharing" spiritual power.

10.6   Secularization

While it is not proposed here to enter into an elaborate discussion of the secularization theory and its applicability in non-Western contexts, we shall venture some remarks regarding secularizing trends in Calabar.[7]

In the pre-missionary period, there was little or no differentiation between religious and political authority. The Obong Efik was both spiritual and secular ruler until his political functions were taken over by the burgeoning Ekpe Society. The arrival of the Presbyterian missionaries heralded a new era in the relationship between religion and politics. Motivated by a religious ideology, they constituted a pressure group which attempted to effect changes of a social, cultural and religious nature. The missionaries sought to recreate a ruler who combined both political and religious roles, only his authority was considerably weakened by the presence of external power sources - colonialism and Christianity. King Archibong III represented the first "Christian King" of this nascent African Christian "kingdom".

The pluralization of mission bodies served to interfere with the development of the Presbyterian microcosm, even if these bodies served to reinforce the model established by the Presbyterians of close interaction and interdependence of religious and secular institutions - notably schools, hospitals and to some extent the law courts, where oath-taking by the Bible was encouraged.

As colonial structures expanded and the number of religious bodies multiplied, there was a gradual drifting apart of the two domains. This pattern continued until after political independence in 1960. It was only during the period of military rule following the civil war that a divestment of authority occurred and the government gradually took over the control of schools and medical institutions in an attempt to promote indigenization and greater self-sufficiency.

This move to secularize areas formerly controlled by religious institutions was welcomed at first as a necessary path to development. However, as the government (both military and later civilian) increasingly failed to live up to expectations in fulfilling the educational and medical needs of the people, there was a call for the schools and hospitals to be returned to the churches. The churches themselves had mixed feelings about the issue: many wished to regain control of their educational institutions but were unwilling because of the considerable financial burden. The outcome was undecided as far as the Cross River State was concerned at the time of the 1983/84 military coup d'état.[8]

The development of secular societies and associations in the urban context arguably represents a secularizing trend. The relationship between the growing number of ethnic unions, political associations and cultural and philosophical fraternities and religious organizations needs to be researched in a more systematic way.[9] There are obvious functional similarities and there may be a tendency for the secular associations to supplant or undermine the work of religious institutions.[10] From the limited investigation that was possible within the present study, it would seem that many people do not see any opposition, even if they do perceive a distinction, between secular and religious associations.[11] It is considered to be rational behaviour to belong to as many associations as is financially possible in order to secure optimum protection for oneself and one's family.

Some form of secularization is inevitable in a developing

society; it is not necessarily unilinear, as the above evidence suggests. While religion is not such an organic element in the overall social structure as in the traditional context, because of the increasing scale of society, it has nonetheless retained many of its original legitimizing functions, such as for the rites of passage and the installation of the new ruler, as well as adapting to new ones such as the sanctification of motor vehicles (rather than canoes) and the blessing of public buildings (banks and schools) and ceremonies (Independence Day and Childrens' Day as opposed to Ndem festivals). In terms of individual belief and behaviour, there is far less evidence of the declining role of religion.

10.7   Privatization

In former times, religion was predominantly a communal affair. Even up to the 1960s it was not uncommon for religious affiliations to be determined by one's family. For instance, if the first convert in a family was a Catholic, then for the next generation at least everyone else would be a Catholic. Within most families now it is not uncommon for each individual member to belong to a different church or religious organization. Husbands no longer request their wives to renounce their religious allegiance(s) at the time of marriage. Religious choice has become increasingly an affair of the individual.

Also included within the concept of privatization is the development of more "private" and "individualized" forms of religion which do not require communal membership or participation, or the presence of intermediaries, or attendance at a cultic location. Instead the individual, through the aid of sacred texts, literature, visual materials and religious objects, often acquired from a variety of local and overseas sources, constructs his or her own private religious milieu. This may be in the form of a personal shrine in the privacy of the home where ritual devotions are performed or simply a conducive location for meditation and reading (either in the home or office).

For some educated men, this has become their sole religious

activity. Disillusioned by conventional religious institutions, they have sought to determine their own religious experience and the freedom to experiment with a variety of religious forms. Some professional men with busy schedules are unable to attend church regularly and find the flexibility of privatized religion an attractive alternative. For others it may represent a form of supplementary religiosity - a series of religious "additives" which are believed to complement and enhance more "conventional" religious behaviour such as church attendance. Women feature more readily in this category even though their choice of devotional literature is more likely to be of a Christian and evangelical variety rather than the more mystical and occult materials preferred by men. Private Bible study is also extremely popular amongst a wide spectrum of people regardless of religious affiliation.

There is a third category of person who may adopt a more private mode of religious activity and that is the person who finds him or herself "between religious institutions". In other words he/she has ceased to attend a particular group or institution but has not yet discovered a suitable alternative. In such cases, it is not uncommon for an individual to fall back on his or her own spiritual resources during the interim period.

There are a number of reasons that may be put forward to account for the development of more privatized forms of religion. First the increase in levels of literacy and education has stimulated a greater religious self-sufficiency; there is less need for individuals to be dependent on religious intermediaries. Even for those only literate in Efik-Ibibio, there is an Efik Bible and a host of pamphlets, booklets and tracts disseminated by several religious institutions. There is also a growing number of audio-cassettes ("cassette ministries") available in the local languages. The possibilities for independent study and development are continually on the increase. Second, the social dislocation occasioned by an urban existence may contribute to individuals seeking or resorting to (on a temporary or permanent basis) individual religious means. For instance, the move from rural to urban areas may entail a forced break with previous religious traditions and affiliations; sometimes rural churches do not have a branch in Calabar.[12] Some people decide to worship privately while in Calabar and attend church services whenever they return to their home town or village.[13]

Third, the desire to opt for a more privatized form of religion is a manifestation of the growing trend of tailoring one's religious beliefs and practices to meet one's spiritual needs. This reflects the belief that direct experience and manipulation of the sacred at the individual level is not only possible but indeed preferable if one is to achieve results.

Our observation that privatization in the religious sector is on the increase does not mean that religion is still not a major source of community in the town today. Nor does it imply that a form of "utilitarian individualism" is becoming the dominant ideology.[14] The development of private religious practices undermines to a limited extent institutional religion but not in any radical way, since for the most part these are supplementary practices. People may consider their religious institutions inadequate at times but there is no general desire to deinstitutionalize religion on a wide scale. Nor does the evidence of privatization necessarily entail an interiorization process, i.e., a general shift in the locus of religion from groups and organizations to individual minds.

10.8   Religious self-determination

Religious self-determination constitutes one of the most important themes of Calabar religion. By religious self-determination we understand the process whereby an individual/group/institution assumes increasing control of his/her/its religious affairs and destiny. The concept is broader than that of religious innovation, independency or indigenization: it includes the freedom to select one's religious associations and affiliations (indigenous and non-indigenous). To facilitate our discussion we have made use of three sub-themes namely: indigenization, democratization and internationalization.

10.8.1   Indigenization

Indigenization has been an important theme in African affairs not just in connection with political structures and the transfer of power at the time of independence, but also in terms of economic dependency. In the religious domain, the call for indigenization, i.e., the creation of an African ecclesiastical leadership and the adaptation of Western religious forms and institutions to African traditions has also proved to be a central issue. In the case of some Christian denominations, which is what primarily concerns us here, the development of an African Christianity did not proceed fast or far enough and caused an exodus of disenchanted members some of whom created their own independent churches and movements or who joined pre-existing ones.

In Calabar, right from the early days of the Presbyterian Mission, there were moves to train local clergy and mission teachers. This did not stifle the criticism in some quarters that the mission remained a white patriarchy for too long. The question of delegation of ecclesiastical authority to local leaders has been treated in varying ways by the respective missionary institutions depending upon ideology, policy, resources and local pressure. Even if links with overseas mother institutions are maintained, at the local level indigenization has effectively occurred in the majority of Calabar's religious institutions. A white presence may be ˊfelt on an occasional basis - at conventions and anniversaries, for example. The Roman Catholic Church retains the largest non-Nigerian contingent, but most of these are engaged in teaching, welfare or medical work. Full-time white clergy are an increasingly rare breed.

In terms of beliefs and practices, external manifestations of the indigenization process abound with African hymns, music and dancing in evidence in most of the churches in Calabar today. The Roman Catholic Church, especially, makes use of local crafts and architectural styles. There are those who would argue that such changes only represent a superficial form of indigenization and that liturgical patterns and doctrinal content remain virtually unchanged from the Western models. We are unable to give these issues the theological treatment they deserve here, but suffice it to say that in the mainline churches especially, areas such as healing, witchcraft and polygamy have remained virtually untouched theologically and pastorally speaking. Church officials have often ignored these sensitive areas which has resulted in many of their members seeking alternative help from traditional religious specialists or spiritual church prophets. There are, of course, individual clergy who have taken concrete steps to meet local needs. For example, the Very Reverend Eshiet, Presbyter of the Methodist Church in Calabar conducts midweek healing and prayer sessions. The more spiritually oriented religious organizations, particularly the indigenous ones, have shown themselves more prepared to tackle the existential problems of the African cultural milieu.

The question of language is an important factor in the indigenization process; the majority of Calabar's churches now use Efik-Ibibio as their medium of communication. Only a few may use English because of their non-Efik-Ibibio origins or because of their linguistic heterogeneity.

Support for the indigenization of imported religious structures and world-views is by no means unanimous. There is a strong contingent of older members in the mainline churches for example who prefer Western ecclesiastical music and have tried to preserve Western traditions at all costs. The Qua Iboe Church in Calabar, for example, has resisted the introduction of African rhythms. The Anglican Church allows "native airs" only from time to time.

10.8.2   Democratization

One way of describing the process of democratization would be "popularization" or the growth of "grass-roots religion". It signifies the trend whereby the laity assumes increasing involvement in and control over religious affairs. Specific examples of this in the Calabar context include the growing numbers of devotional associations, youth groups, men's and women's associations, prayer bands, house prayer groups, etc. Implied here is a shift in the locus of religious activity from formal services to more informal and peripheral events such as open-air evangelism, revivals and prayer meetings.

The processes of decentralization and fragmentation are significant here. The move away from dependence on conventional religious authorities and hierarchies to small, virtually autonomous groups serves to weaken the forces of centralization. It also functions to break down the large, impersonal religious organization into more personal and manageable units. The Jehovah's Witnesses are a good example of this type of "democratic" religious activity with its tendency to greater spontaneity and freedom of expression (see 4.4.2).

The democratizing process leads to a reshaping of religious experience and structures. For instance, the involvement of youth groups in evangelizing activities has generated a dynamic, sometimes aggressive, goal-oriented type of religious behaviour. The various women's associations allow women to organize their own worship and to give vent to their own form of spirituality. It is the informality of this type of grassroots religion which lends itself to greater adaptability, particularly for marginal groups.

What are the implications of the democratization process for Calabar religion in general? Greater participation at the popular level may lead to the fullest expressions of religious self-determination, that is the formation of new, independent religious groups. But it may also have the opposite effect - as in the case of the Methodist Church - an improved "prayer life" with informal prayer and healing sessions, has helped stem the flow of worshippers to the spiritual churches. An interesting feature in this respect is the activity of the prayer-women (*iban okok udono* - "women that heal") in the Methodist Church today.[15] Situated in Calabar (the most well-known is Ma Jekova) and other parts of the state, these prayer-women engage in preaching, praying and healing (usually with the aid of *edidiong* - blessed "salvation" water) in their own compounds. In the Roman Catholic Church also, the various devotional associations which have spread rapidly since the 1960s have played an important role in meeting the spiritual needs of the ordinary worshipper and providing a channel for increased lay participation and influence. One of these groups is the Blue

Army Crusade founded by Dominic U. Jack in 1966 in Calabar after his escape from a near fatal road accident.

We would also include within the category of democratization the preference for neighbourhood and compound churches instead of the larger impersonal branches established by some of the churches. The Catholic Church underwent a process of decentralization following Vatican II; the Apostolic Church, the Brotherhood and Mount Zion are particularly good examples of "neighbourhood churches". The smaller church is more accessible not just for frequent attendance, greater participation and impromptu prayers, but is also a more conducive location for socializing in the evenings, an aspect which should not be overlooked.

10.8.3   Internationalization

The concept of religious "internationalization" is used to describe the tendency whereby individuals or groups seek to (re)establish links with international or overseas religious organizations. It is generally the independent and indigenous groups which are the keenest to establish institutional links in the hope that they will receive moral, religious and sometimes financial support from like-minded overseas religious organizations.

At the individual level, the desire to be part of an international religious network is frequently manifested not just by well-read, well-travelled people but also by those with little education. The latter's interest may stem from fascination with "exotic" forms of religion as well as with the prospect of overseas visits for training or further education.

In some respects religious internationalization represents an unexpected dimension of religious self-determination. There is a tendency to think of the latter as a process which involves schism, innovation and independency - in other words religious groups seeking to discover and establish an identity in contradistinction to Western religious traditions, customs and institutions.[16] This avid desire for "external" religious input and support does not necessarily reflect a sense of inadequacy or inferiority. Rather it demonstrates the stage of maturity that many groups have reached in that they now feel the need to branch out and link up with overseas religious bodies on an equal footing. There is, for example, the case of the Presbyterian Church and the recent setting up of the Presbyteries Partnership between Calabar and Dundee (4.2). Some groups have even embarked on missionary work in other countries. For example, the Truth and Life Ministries International has conducted crusades in India, the Revival Valley Ministries in Cameroon and Gabon and the Brotherhood of the Cross and Star in Britain and the U.S.

The phenomenon of religious internationalization serves to question the concept of religious independency. Is a spiritual church which becomes affiliated with an American evangelical body still correctly termed an "independent church"? Perhaps the answer lies in the nature of the affiliation, in other words to what extent the Nigerian body becomes dependent on the overseas organization. For instance, in its early stages the Truth and Life Church was largely a satellite of the Faith Pool Prayer Groups based in Tampa, Florida. Today it has broadened its range of contacts and developed its own identity and evangelistic ministry and is arguably a successful "independent" church. Nevertheless, one is left with the impression that "independent" will become increasingly invalidated as an appropriate term to describe many of Nigeria's religious movements.

An important manifestation of the internationalization process is the preponderance of religious literature (both imported and indigenous) in English (see bibliography of primary sources). This cannot be attributed to inadequacy of local resources, for local printing presses abound and it would be just as easy to publish in Efik-Ibibio as in English.[17] The Brotherhood of the Cross and Star, for example, the most prolific of all the religious institutions in the area in terms of literature output, publishes almost everything in English. Local worship may be in the local language, but propaganda must be transmitted through the medium of an international language. The concern for outreach, not just to a multi-ethnic but also a global community, is paramount here.

One needs to ask whether the internationally oriented religious movement is peculiar to Nigeria or even Calabar alone. Adrian

Hastings in his *A History of African Christianity*, observed of
Ghana in the late 1960s "the tendency of independent churches to
re-acquire American or European links" (p. 179). The Kimbanguist
Church in Zaïre has a wide range of international connections,
some directly religious (Moravian and Mennonite), some
development-oriented (OXFAM).[18]   A number of independent
African churches have established links with Mennonite churches to
help with their clergy-training programmes.[19]   Nigeria is perhaps
one of the best examples of the growth of religious
internationalization since generally speaking Nigerians have
demonstrated a predilection for international interaction in the
commercial, political and cultural spheres. This has certainly had
some influence on the religious domain.

Calabar's status as a port has undoubtedly broadened its range
of religious contacts. The desire for European religious links began
in the late seventeenth century with requests from Calabar nobles
for Portuguese Catholic missionaries. Similar requests were made in
the nineteenth century to Britain and increasingly since then to
America. These early religious contacts were pursued by the Efik-
Ibibio in the hope that they would obtain schools, hospitals, and
commercial, technical and agricultural training. For the most part
it was the missionary bodies who were the primary motivators,
although in some cases (Salvation Army, Apostolic Church)
"branches" were set up before the missionaries arrived (due to
literature and information filtering through in advance).

In more recent times the pattern has changed somewhat with
many Nigerians studying and working abroad and returning to
Nigeria bearing the seeds of some overseas religious organization,
such as in the case of the Unification Church in Calabar and the
Aetherius Society. In a number of cases, Nigerians have written
directly to the organizations concerned. The emphasis is less on
education as the primary value of the relationship (since the
government takeover of educational institutions), but rather as
stated earlier, on moral and spiritual support, staff training and the
supply of literature.

10.9   Homogenization

One of the most significant trends that we have noted in the course of our study of religion in Calabar is that of homogenization. This refers to the process whereby the differences between religious groups are reduced and a "common religious milieu" is generated.[20]   This process has been referred to as one whereby distinctions between types of institutions become meaningless, such as between the mainline and the independent churches.[21]   For example in terms of worship, there are fairly standardized patterns observable in most churches: prayers, hymns and sermon, followed by the more spontaneous thanksoffering section with dancing to gospel songs and native choruses.

There are a variety of reasons why homogenization in the religious domain is a growing phenomenon. First, the pluralization of religious groups and increasing fragmentation (through schisms and innovation), which we have described in previous chapters, has the net result of creating greater uniformity. In other words the smaller the units the less differentiation that is likely to exist between them. Distinctions come to be based on leaders and personalities rather than on ideological differences. Second, the mobility which characterizes patterns of religious behaviour in Calabar also serves to weaken religious differentiation. As people move between groups or are associated with a number of religious institutions concurrently, there is an interaction and diffusion of ideas and practices, as well as a breaking down of institutional barriers. A third contributory factor in the homogenization process is the prevailing atmosphere of religious tolerance both amongst individuals and groups. Nigerians in general tend to view this tolerance as an integral part of their social fabric and something that should be respected and protected at all costs. This ideal is given the force of law in section 35 of the Nigerian Constitution (1979).

We may see the homogenization process occurring in two ways. First there is a "filtering up" and "filtering down" of beliefs, practices and attitudes between the formal and informal or institutional and popular levels of religion.[22]   We have already referred to this type of interaction in chapter eight. Second, there is the interaction between religious institutions such as described in chapter seven. There may be even more informal and unconscious forms of interaction which are more significant in promoting unity. Our focus here, however, is on the agents of homogenization, the most important of which we consider to be music, literature, evangelicalism, the spiritual sciences and institutionalization.

Music cuts across both the institutional and popular religious expressions. There are examples of popular refrains being taken up by particular churches and then being transmitted from church to church by itinerant organists and choristers or by mobile worshippers referred to earlier. Not only does this serve to homogenize music styles, but the hymns and choruses are vehicles of religious teachings and attitudes. Religious literature in the form of pamphlets, booklets and tracts travels freely between individuals and groups. For example, the Blessed Spiritual Mother of the Holy Chapel of Miracles uses a Jehovah's Witnesses' Bible (because it is in simple English and attractively illustrated) for her Bible study talks. She also uses Adventist leaflets to provide material for the same purpose. The Truth and Life Ministries International makes considerable use of the publications of the American evangelist - T.L. Osborn. Tracts from the Deeper Christian Life Ministry (based in Gbagada, Lagos) are commonly found in offices and on the university campus.

It is the teachings of evangelicalism in particular which have such a unifying influence. Despite their diversity of sources, there is considerable unity in such evangelical themes as repentance, conversion, sanctification, new life, miracles, salvation, the power of the living Jesus and the Holy Spirit. Thanks to forceful evangelistic methods and the use of modern media techniques, the impact of evangelicalism (and pentecostalism) on the religious life of Calabar has been considerable. Spiritual churches and mainline churches alike stage revivals, hold prayer sessions, advocate fasting and faith-healing and proclaim the importance of receiving the Holy Spirit and being "born again". This is very much in line with the trend towards spiritualization described in 10.4.

Albeit less overt, the spiritual sciences provide unifying

influences behind the diversity of Calabar religion. The emphasis upon contemplation and meditation, esotericism, graduated spiritual development and karmic concepts is starting to pervade a variety of religious contexts. As in the case of evangelicalism, literature is freely available on the subject and there is considerable media coverage.

We may also point to the role of institutionalization in the overall homogenization of Calabar religion. The widespread desire for buildings, names, hierarchies, vehicles, printed literature and recorded music serves to standardize the various religious manifestations and expressions.

As homogenization continues, facilitated by the processes of assimilation and religious self-determination, the differences between old and new, and African and Western, will diminish and the origins of traditions, forms and beliefs will become more obscure. This will render it all the more important to study a range of religious expressions in a particular area as an ensemble, rather than as separate strata.[23]

It is clear that homogenization is the result of both internal and external factors. We need to appreciate the influence of a common cultural context in reducing differentiation and determining form and orientation. In this respect we may talk of a "Nigerianization" process whereby religious institutions adapt or are adapted to their cultural landscape. There is also the influence of the external factors described above, such as imported religious ideas, music, literature, which are contributory factors in the generation of a common religious milieu.

10.10   Religious conversion and mobility

If, despite the pluralization of religious groups in Calabar, they increasingly resemble one another and display functional similarities,[24] then this raises important questions about "conversion" and the perception of religious alternatives and mobility between religious worlds. In this section we propose to treat these central themes of religious behaviour in Calabar. This is, of course, a topic which merits a study in itself[25]; however, our treatment of it here is limited to observations regarding patterns of religious behaviour which emerged from the survey.

From an early stage in the research it became evident that the concepts of conversion and membership would have to undergo a serious reappraisal if they were to be applied in any meaningful way in the Calabar context. This was primarily due to the phenomena of mobility - passing from one religious organization to another, and "multi-membership" - association with more than one religious organization at any one time.[26]   This causes us to question seriously the validity of the term "conversion" in the sense of a radical change in religious convictions accompanied by emotional and intellectual, as well as moral and spiritual, renewal. The only way that "conversion" may be used in the present context is in the sense of changing from one religious group to another. This should not be viewed in exclusivist terms, in other words the adoption of a particular religious allegiance excluding another, for as mentioned above it is common for people to be associated with a range of religious groups concurrently. So if the term conversion is to be used (and we feel it should be avoided wherever possible) it needs to be understood in a weaker sense - the adoption of a new (additional) religious orientation. In the majority of cases, the process of selecting a new religious institution occurs over a length of time,[27] with the potential member often opting for a probationary period before undertaking the necessary initiatory procedures.[28]

Dramatic, personal conversions do occur particularly in the evangelical and pentecostal churches (where they are distinctly encouraged) or for example following a miraculous healing in a spiritual church. Given that an individual opts to join another religious organization (and not just engage in a temporary or casual association), we need to consider what is involved in such a changeover. It is of course difficult to generalize, since there are different levels of membership which we shall discuss below; but it is possible to identify it as both a personal and a social experience. At the internal level, an emotional reaction may occur as the individual experiences a sense of liberation and renewal, and anticipation at the prospects of his/her new religious affiliation. Cognitive changes may also be involved as the "convert" accommodates him/herself to another world-view; these will of course vary according to the convert's former and new affiliations (the move from mainline to spiritual church being less radical than from mainline to spiritual science organization for example). Allegiance to a new religious community may entail moral changes also: many of the spiritual and evangelical/pentecostal churches advocate radical, personal restructuring and the convert may rationalize his/her "conversion" on the basis of a sinful past and hope for moral renewal.

Many converts tend to interpret their religious reorientation in spiritual terms. Since many reject religious institutions on the basis of their spiritual inadequacies (lack of spiritual power, neglect of spiritual needs), they, as one might expect, give spiritual regeneration and increased spiritual power prominent places in their explanations of changes of allegiance.

At the external level, the new member is called upon to make a social commitment through outward symbols of conversion such as baptism and adoption of the church uniform. These means of social reinforcement and identification are not only an attempt by the institution to consolidate its membership gains but also a means of communicating its identity.

As we have already indicated, the concept of membership is complex, with different levels of allegiance and participation. We have been able to classify these as follows:

1. active affiliation
2. nominal affiliation
3. active association
4. occasional association[29]

There are two main ways in which people identify with and participate in a religious organization - either through affiliation or association. An active affiliation implies active and regular participation and identification with a particular institution. Nominal affiliation suggests irregular participation (usually at festival times and family rituals) but continuing identification with the organization in question. For example, many people, particularly men of higher social standing, may be lapsed church-goers but still consider themselves as Presbyterian or Catholic and attend such services on ceremonial occasions. They will also plan to be buried according to the rites of those particular religious institutions. Alternatively, they may be active members of another religious organization (such as a spiritual church) but still wish to retain links with the church of their family and/or education. The concept of association implies a weaker or looser commitment than that of affiliation. Active association refers to the active links that people maintain with a religious organization but which they consider to be as secondary or supplementary to their primary religious affiliation. For instance, it is not uncommon for mainline church members to attend the mid-week services of a spiritual church or they may subscribe to Rosicrucian literature and training programmes, but without claiming this as their primary religious activity. In some cases their associations may be clandestine. Occasional association occurs in a very irregular fashion, usually in response to a critical situation. Examples include visits to diviners, herbalists, prophets and healers, as well as the occasional visits that a husband may make to his wife's church (or vice versa) or the casual visit made by an interested person to the launching of a new religious organization.

It must be emphasized that each individual constructs his or her religious universe or configuration of affiliations and associations in accordance with his/her religious beliefs, attitudes, education, social status and needs. Patterns of affiliation and association vary considerably not just from person to person, but also within an individual's lifespan. What may be a occasional association one day may become an active affiliation the next. We should not underestimate the dynamism and fluidity of religious behaviour in this respect. This is popularly known as "decamping" - a phenomenon which is well known in the political sphere. For instance, during an Eckankar seminar in February 1982 a number of "Eckists" recounted "How I came into Eckankar" and their accounts are illustrative of the facility with which people move from group to group until they obtain what they consider to be satisfaction:

Member A. A young male student recounted how for many years he had been "questioning" as part of his search for truth. Reared in an environment of traditional worship, he had converted to Catholicism. However his mother discouraged him as she did not want him to become a priest and not marry. He later joined AMORC (the Rosicrucians) in order "to enable me to conquer witches". Disillusioned, he moved on to join an Aladura church - "I tried always to see visions". He concluded that the methods of this group were simply "native ways in disguise". He returned to "juju" and soon his home was "littered with shrines", but "something was missing - I had no peace". In April 1979 he saw an advertisement in a newspaper concerning Eckankar and wrote immediately to California and "has never felt the same again".

Member B. A young man explained how he had never been a convinced Christian and had started reading books on philsophy, occultism, psychology and Lopsong Rampa. But he "was still not satisfied" so he joined a "mystic school" while at university but felt the pressure of having to submit a monthly report was too much. He then joined AMORC for six years but "was not getting results". During all this time he still continued attending church. In 1978 he learnt of Obu and left home in Ugep to come to Calabar to be baptized in a river as "Brotherhood". A year later he was obliged to go on National Service to Oyo State where he began reading Christian Science literature until he finally joined in 1980. But he concluded that "it was the same thing as before". He had maintained his contacts with the Rosicrucians

> during this time. He learnt of Eckankar - "the
> path to total God awareness" - through the *Daily
> Times* and realized that it was different from all
> the other "holy sciences". He felt happy as soon
> as he had sent off his joining fee to the Area
> Mahdi in Lagos - so he felt that "he must have
> been initiated somewhere". From then on he
> started experiencing good luck wherever he went.

In general, there appears to be greater associational than affiliational mobility:[30] people tend to maintain a primary religious affiliation and experiment more in terms of their secondary associations. The latter may in time subvert and replace the former.

To what should we attribute these behavioural patterns? While the social changes which have occurred within one generation have obviously played a role in establishing models of social mobility, these are not sufficient explanations. Nor is it realistic to suggest that increased religious mobility is a reflection of greater social, economic and political powerlessness. Such factors may be influential, but they are not determinants. We must rather look to religious attitudes for a more satisfying explanation. As long as people consider the religious variable to be an integral part of their lives and a force or power for transformation, they will continue to express their ultimate experiences in religious terms and resort to religious means to solve their problems. They will continue to search for more effective and efficient means of "tapping" supernatural power.[31] This pragmatic approach to religion which derives from traditional religio-cultural conceptions is the motivating force behind the dynamism and mobility that we have described above. It accounts for the pluralization and eclecticism and lack of absolutism and exclusivity.

We have emphasized the incidence of misfortune or the "accidents of life",[32] notably sickness (in its fullest sense), as the major cause of religious mobility. Geographical mobility may also be significant in that migrants (those coming to Calabar and those living away from Calabar) may be forced into making alternate religious choices because of their new circumstances. An Efik expatriate, established for many years in Lagos but who returns frequently to Calabar, reported that those of his friends and family who had stayed in Calabar had tended to remain faithful to the two main Efik Christian traditions - Presbyterianism and Catholicism. Those who were now resident in other parts of the country had more readily renounced these allegiances and converted to alternative religious institutions. Some form of insecurity, therefore, is likely to generate a religious search. We believe also, however, that the general interest in things religious and the importance of religious knowledge and spirituality play a role in stimulating religious experimentation and hence mobility. A less well known factor is the issue of disciplinary sanctions - a number of people are forced to leave churches because they have violated the moral code of the institution. The Apostolic Church is renowned for its action in this regard. One of the most frequent offences is adultery. Sometimes a temporary suspension may be sufficient to trigger feelings of dissatisfaction and resentment which in many cases may lead to a search for new religious affiliations.

We would argue that no one group or class of people is likely to be more religiously mobile than another. The educated and wealthier classes are more mobile in general and have more access to and awareness of religious alternatives, but they may reject certain alternatives because of social and cultural attitudes. They are more likely to make religious choices on an intellectual basis alone. They may find it harder to break with their religious traditions because of having acquired positions of prestige in their respective institutions. The semi-educated classes have less to lose and more to gain from finding the most suitable religious institution(s) to meet their needs and aspirations. The poorer classes are less aware of, and have reduced access to, the full range of alternatives and yet display the most pragmatic approach to their religion as they move from group to group in search of cures to their problems. They are also more likely to become attached to a particular community which provides them with identity, security and support.

In terms of gender, men would seem to show greater religious mobility than women because of their increased social and educational opportunities and economic means. Because of their culturally dominant position they are able to be more critical and act freely and independently. Many clergy would point to the female members of their congregations as the most loyal and stable elements. And yet women bear greater responsibility for family problems and are thus obliged to seek out the most beneficial and effective religious options. They have less access to secular alternatives (e.g., modern medicine) and therefore turn more readily to religious means. They also tend to have fewer commitments (i.e., leadership positions) in the religious institutions they become affiliated with and can therefore break ties more easily.

As a final consideration in this section, we should examine the attitudes of the religious institutions themselves to religious conversion and mobility. The mainline churches whose entry procedures are far less rigorous than they used to be seem to suffer most from membership loss and members with supplementary commitments. The general response has been to condemn such "Nicodemus-like" religious behaviour (i.e. secret visits to herbalists and prophets and membership of lodges and secret societies) as "superstition" and "paganism". For the most part, however, the churches are powerless to control such "deviationism"; in some cases there has been a more aggressive response such as in the case of Methodist youth groups spying on "offenders" during their mid-week trips to the Rosicrucian Temple or the Brotherhood Bethel. Some priests and ministers may threaten their members with denial of burial rites in such circumstances. Other non-indigenous institutions such as the pentecostal and evangelical churches are generally more tightly structured and comprehensive in their hold over members.

The spiritual churches exhibit a mixed response to the phenomenon of fluidity and mobility amongst their members - some emphasize exclusivism through a variety of ritual and symbolic mechanisms (such as the Brotherhood and the Celestial Church of Christ), others exhibit a remarkable flexibility such as the Friends of Jesus Church which invites potential members to indicate on a card whether they will be 1) sustaining member 2) associate member or 3) visiting member. Several of the smaller indigenous movements, many of which start out as prayer groups, hold their meetings on a Sunday afternoon to allow members to attend their "regular" churches in the morning period.

Traditional cults and healing homes maintain the least restrictive structures in terms of affiliation which is why they continue to be exploited on an occasional and critical basis by a large cross-section of the Calabar population.

Notes

1. See Peel's remarks about the significance of power in understanding religious change in "Conversion and Tradition in Two African Societies: Ijebu and Buganda", *Past and Present* 77 (November 1977):126-7.

2. Interview with Rev. Fr. F. Akpan, Sacred Heart Cathedral, Calabar, July 13, 1983.

3. See M.F.C. Bourdillon, "Religion, Health and Healing in Odukpani Local Government Area" (mimeo) - report of a research project funded by the University of Calabar Senate Research Grant Committee and conducted for the Mother Child/Family Planning Project (Calabar) in 1978. The author explores the relationship between religious beliefs and practices on the one hand, and physical health and the treatment of disease on the other in three rural communities on the outskirts of Calabar (approx. 8 miles from the centre).

4. Interview with Rev. U. Utuk, Calabar, January 12, 1980.

5. See E. Amadi, *Ethics in Nigerian Culture* (Ibadan: Heinemann, 1982).

6. J.S. Mbiti, *African Religions and Philosophy* (London: Heinemann, 1969), pp. 275-6.

7. For a discussion of this complex phenomenon see B. R. Wilson, *A General Theory of Secularization* (Oxford: Basil Blackwell, 1978). We are using the term "secularization" to refer to the gradual differentiation of religious and secular institutions and the weakening of the social influence of religion.

8. By January 1983 Anambra, Imo and Bendel states had already handed over some of the schools to the church authorities.

9. E.g. the Great Alpha Fraternity, the Cee Club and the Scottish Freemasons. The role and influence of the latter in particular would provide material for a fascinating, if difficult to research, study. Many of these secular associations were banned when the military government seized power in January 1984.

10. This point is made by V. Neckebrouck in his work on the African Independent Pentecostal Church in Kenya, *Le Onzième Commandement: Etiologie d'une Eglise Indépendante au pied du Mont Kenya* (Immensee, Switzerland: Neue Zeitschrift für Missionswissenschaft, 1978), p. 533.

11. Secret societies and lodges are borderline cases - secular but with a considerable religious content.

12. One example would be the Samuel Spiritual Church at Ikot Abasi.

13. This is the case for members of the Church of Jesus Christ at Atai Otoro, near Abak. See chap. 4 n.60.

14. See R.N. Bellah, "New Religious Consciousness and the Crisis in Modernity" in *The New Religious Consciousness*, eds. C.Y. Glock and R.N. Bellah (Berkeley, CA: University of California Press, 1976), p. 349.

15. There are reported cases of men and women (usually women) operating in the same way under the auspices of other churches such as the Lutheran and Anglican.

16. The present writer was petitioned on numerous occasions by indigenous religious groups, mainly spiritual churches, to put them in contact with British or American churches and to bring back religious literature from overseas.

17. The Efik Bible is still widely used and is readily available not only through bookstores, but also through roadside newspaper vendors.

18. See S. Asch, *L'Eglise du Prophète Kimbangu* (Paris: Karthala, 1983), chap. 9.

19. See Turner, *Religious Innovation in Africa*, p. 175.

20. This is not equivalent to a situation of full-blown syncretism such as described by Geertz in his account of Javanese religion (*The Religion of Java*).

21. See A.F. Walls, "The Anabaptists of Africa? The Challenge of African Independent Churches", *Occasional Bulletin of Missionary Research* 3,2 (April 1979):51.

22. Cf. Earhart, *Japanese Religion*, pp. 38-39.

23. This point is made also by Earhart, ibid., p. 2.

24. To recall a few examples, the Brotherhood of the Cross and Star has assumed an exorcizing role akin to that of the traditional diviner. Spiritual church prophets are the modern diviners; mainline churches hold special prayer sessions, stage revival weeks and pray to the ancestors. Nka Ekpenyong Nnuk is a traditional age group society centred around a traditional deity but which attends church services and supports church activities. Many traditional healers have a Christian background and employ Christian (as well as occult) symbols in their ritual systems.

25. There exist a number of articles relating to the theme of conversion in Africa - R. Horton, "African Conversion", *Africa* 41,2 (1971):85-108; idem, "On the Rationality of Conversion," *Africa* 45 (1975):219-35, 373-99; H.J. Fisher, "Conversion Reconsidered: Some Historical Aspects of Religious Conversion in Black Africa", *Africa* 43,1 (1973):27-40; C. Ifeka-Moller, "White Power: Social Structural Factors in Conversion to Christianity in Eastern Nigeria", *Canadian Journal of African Studies* 8,1 (1974):55-72; R. Horton and J.D.Y. Peel, "Conversion and Confusion: a Rejoinder on Christianity in Eastern Nigeria",

Candadian Journal of African Studies 10,3 (1976):481-498; B. Jules-Rosette, "The Conversion Experience", *Journal of Religion in Africa* 7 (1976):132-64; J.D.Y. Peel, "Conversion and Tradition in Two African Societies" (1977); idem, "The Christianization of African Society" (1978); F. Salomone, "Competitive Conversion and its Implications for Modernization (Nigeria)," *Anthropos* 75,3/4 (1980):383-404.

26. Morrill in his study of the Efik remarks upon their readiness to change church allegiance and the fact that they "consider all religious activity in Calabar good" (*Two Urban Cultures*, pp. 220-1, 243, 254-5). The phenomenon of "religious mobility" or "fluidity" of membership has been noted in other African contexts: cf. Hastings, *A History of African Christianity*, pp. 271-2; Murphree, "Religious Interdependence", p. 176f.; Porter, "Religious Affiliation in Freetown"; Peel, *Aladura*, p. 208 and "The Christianization of African Society", p. 453; Middleton, "One Hundred and Fifty Years of Christianity in a Ghanaian Town", p. 7.

27. See S. Bruce, "Born Again: Conversion, Crusades and Brainwashing", *The Scottish Journal of Religious Studies* 3,2 (Autumn 1982):107-23. Cf. also Peel, *Aladura*, with regard to processes of conversion to the Christ Apostolic and Cherubim and Seraphim churches.

28. In some religious organizations, such as the Brotherhood of the Cross and Star, a baptismal commitment has to be made on entering the church before any of the services or benefits may be enjoyed.

29. "Temporary" and "casual" are also appropriate terms but not in all cases.

30. Murphree uses the terms "affiliational and temporary mobility", "Religious Interdependence", p. 177.

31. See Horton and Peel, "Conversion and Confusion", p. 491.

32. Ibid. p. 493.

Conclusion

The religious history of Calabar might appropriately have been labelled "the Christianization of a Nigerian town". To all intents and purposes this would prove initially correct, for a modern census would most likely reveal more than 95% of the population as "Christian" in that they claim allegiance to a Christian-related institution, undergo the Christian rites of baptism, marriage and burial and send their children to Sunday school.

In addition, visitors to the town discover that Sunday has replaced the traditional *akwa ederi* as the weekly day of rest and worship, and the day when markets are closed; Christmas and Easter are now the major festivals of the town. Christian symbolism is omnipresent through architecture, dress, music, even in the shops and markets where one may purchase Christian devotional posters, calendars, Bibles and holy objects. Several streets and schools are named after well-known missionaries. The new religious education syllabus adopted by the Cross River State has a predominantly Christian emphasis. It is rare to encounter someone of working age in Calabar today who has not had some form of church, Bible college or seminary education. Christian clergy dominate at civic ceremonies and Christian values permeate political addresses and the mass media. Traditional rulers are professed Christians and may be seen worshipping in churches with their entourages. Many of the newer movements are Christian-related. In general terms, therefore, Calabar is ostensibly a Christian town after a nearly a century and a half of activity by the missions and the churches. But having spent four years living and researching in the town, this writer finds that this pale, two-dimensional description ignores the complex and colourful religious scene in Calabar.

The theme of religious change, notably the conversion from traditional religious world-views to the universal religions of Christianity and Islam, has continued to fascinate scholars from a variety of disciplines. Fortunately the tendency to account for this type of religious change in terms of a single explanation (intellectual, theological, materialistic, political) has declined in recognition of the complexity of the process and a greater awareness of the role of the participants themselves. Our main interest in the present work has been not so much with the Christianization of Calabar, but rather in the resultant pluralization and diversification of religious groups, particularly in the last twenty-five years. A large proportion of the study has been devoted to documenting the religious pluralism of Calabar today as extensively as possible and tracing its genesis. We have tried to highlight the various religious and socio-economic factors, and their interaction, which have contributed to the present-day situation. We have seen, however, that Calabar's religious pluralism is not based on social or cultural groupings.[1]

Throughout the study we have treated religious pluralism as a fact rather than as a value. And yet it implies something more than just religious heterogeneity.[2] So we have been especially concerned with the areas of interaction and interdependence between the various groups. There is a good deal of competition between them as they vie for clients and members and a distinctive identity in this "religious marketplace". No longer able to compete in terms of schools and hospitals, they have shifted their emphases to issues of tradition, power, spirituality, blessings and evangelism. However some form of secular consensus and inter-group action is necessary, such as humanitarian welfare and social development, in order to develop mutual respect and tolerance.[3]

At the individual level, we have emphasized the theme of religious self-determination. People are not passive consumers of institutional religion; they critically select and construct their own religious configurations or world-views from, as we have shown, a variety of sources. Sometimes this may lead to affiliational and associational mobility or even religious innovation, unless the individual finds a religious organization whose world-view provides a system and structure which may provide in toto for his/her continuous needs. We have stressed the disordering effect of crisis and misfortune. The readiness to experiment with a variety of religious institutions or groups reveals the tolerance with which people view religious diversity (e.g., "everyone is entitled to his or her own religion" and "we all worship the same God"). This type of tolerance, which is more marked at the individual level, ensures the smooth functioning of a religiously plural system. It is also indicative of basic religious attitudes concerning the purpose of religion, which we would characterize as world-affirming and pragmatic spirituality.

Is Calabar's religious pluralism characteristic of other Nigerian towns and cities? In the absence of recent, extensive studies, we can only comment on the basis of personal observations. The southern urban centres display far greater diversity and heterogeneity than the northern towns and cities which are subject to the unifying forces of Islam. Ibadan, Onitsha, Benin City and Lagos, as important centres of commerce and government and cultural and ethnic interaction, are most certainly treasure troves of religion, if not daunting prospects for the intending researcher. Our impression is, however, that for its size, Calabar enjoys a remarkable number and range of religious institutions and types of religious expression. There is, of course, no single explanation for this although a number of factors have been referred to such as early literacy among the Efik élite, the early translation of the Bible into Efik, Calabar's status as a port and its international contacts, the role of the Efik diaspora, the relative isolation of Calabar from the rest of Nigeria, the early pluralization of missions, the virtual absence of Islam and the influence of Ibibio migrants coming from a fragmentary, decentralized social structure with a tradition of "atomistic" religious activity.

What are the effects of religious pluralism on a town like Calabar? We could find little evidence that religion loses its plausibility for individuals under such circumstances. The people of Calabar show a remarkable capacity for operating in, and manipulating, a confusing, if not aggressive, religious environment. People enjoy their religion, but they also take it very seriously. There is a general conviction that religion is good and that some form of it is necessary to sustain life and the community. Religion is not an option, as in Western society; the choice lies in which elements (leaders, literature, institutions, etc.) are chosen to construct one's religious world-view.

The churches, in particular, have emerged as social institutions in their own right, as foci of social relationships, transcending kinship and family ties, as organizations independent of the state and, in some cases, substantial entities in the economic domain. And yet pluralism has weakened organized, institutional religion. The formerly powerful traditional cults and societies have declined, and the Presbyterian Church, while sentimentally known as the "state church", wields no effective power or authority by virtue of this status. While religion is still an element in the overall legitimating system, there is no single source of religious authority, i.e. no dominant denomination which could constitute a viable political force. Although, as we have argued, the political instability since independence has caused the churches, at least, to construct their religious worlds on the periphery of, if not in isolation from, the mainstream of political activity.

There are other areas, however, where religion has made its mark on the life of the town. It has redrawn the boundaries of association and identity; where religion formerly reinforced family and kinship structures, it has now transcended these divisions and created broader, inter-ethnic groupings. And yet with the continuing processes of fragmentation and reintegration and creation of new divisions ("saved", "born-again", "Brotherhood", "Celestial", etc.), the overall role of religion in Calabar as a force for social and cultural unity is an ambiguous one.

From an economic point of view, Calabar's church industry keeps numerous bricklayers, carpenters, tailors, seamstresses, musicians and printers in business. The majority of the churches make either direct or indirect contributions to the humanitarian needs of the wider community. But they are also renowned for the financial demands they place upon members through tithes and numerous building and evangelism funds. Founding a church or a healing home is generally considered to be a good business proposition and an appropriate and respectable occupation for early retirement.

The world-creating tendency of religion has manifested itself in Calabar through the emergence of a number of sub-cultures (such as Ndem, Brotherhood, Presbyterian, Mount Zion, Rosicrucian, etc.). Neither individually nor collectively do these religious worlds represent a counter-cultural force. Generally speaking they are world-affirming and serve to legitimate the over-arching cultural values of Calabar society - the importance of family, elders, morality, law and order, community and increasingly, with the influence of modernization, the significance of the individual. In addition, religion provides a strong sense of continuity between past, present and future (particularly in terms of kinship relations) which is sustained and expressed through ritual beliefs and practices.

Ultimately, however, religion in Calabar, as in any other context, is about salvation. While differences exist between the conceptions of and paths to salvation disseminated by the various religious institutions (this-worldly/other-worldly, direct/mediated, short-term/long-term), at the popular level a cultural consensus prevails. Salvation is protection and liberation from evil; it is the realization of human potential and divine blessings in this world. It is redemption from suffering and the transformation of evil and misfortune into peace and well-being. It is the visible and tangible evidence that one has a right relationship with God both here and now and in the hereafter.

At the concluding stage of such a study, one is led to speculate as to future trends in Calabar religion. It is hard to foresee any decline or major changes in basic religious beliefs and attitudes and reliance on religion in times of need. Based on our findings, we are suggesting that the following changes and developments will occur: first, there will be a greater recourse to individual means and more privatized forms of religion; second, pentecostalism and evangelicalism will become the most dominant and widespread types of religious expression; third, the range of religious ideas, symbols, practices and rituals being appropriated by Calabar's religious leaders or the ordinary worshipper will become more diversified, with increasing use of "spiritual science" resources (occultism, mysticism and magic). In this regard religious internationalization will continue to flourish with an ever-widening religious network - Europe, Africa, the United States, Latin America, India, outer space... Lastly, names and labels will lose value as tools of identification; Calabar's religious groups and institutions will grow increasingly to resemble one another.

Looking back over our attempt to describe and analyze the breadth and depth and unity and diversity of Calabar religion there is the inevitable feeling that we have merely scratched the surface of a phenomenon of untold depth and ramifications. The written word alone does not do justice to the subject matter. Ideally such a study should employ all possible audio-visual methods (e.g., the field of visual anthropology) to capture and document the religious life in all its dynamism, depth and diversity.[4] We believe, nonetheless, that our macro-analysis, while sacrificing detail on specific religious strata and institutions, has provided some much-needed insights into modern religious behaviour and trends in black Africa's most populous nation. It is hoped that our study will stimulate further research in this direction so that eventually the full mosaic of Nigerian religion may be known more accurately and appreciated more fully by insiders and outsiders alike.

And finally, in a continent where the concepts of change and development are now being radically questioned by both African intellectuals and Western international institutions alike, there is an urgent need to gain a better understanding of cognitive and affective processes and behavioural patterns. Studies, such as the present one, which focus on relatively well defined areas of thought and action, using both historical and contemporary perspectives, may help provide solutions to this *vasta questio*.

Notes

1. Cf. J.M. Yinger, "Pluralism, Religion and Secularism", *Journal of the Scientific Study of Religion* 6,1 (Spring 1967):18.

2. Ibid., p. 22.

3. Ibid., p. 27.

4. Three video productions were in fact made during the course of the survey. They were entitled as follows: "Tradition and Change - the Presbyterian Church of Nigeria, Calabar" (1980); "Abia-Edim - an Ibibio Rain Expert" (1981) and "The Brotherhood of the Cross and Star" (unedited). The programmes were produced for educational television with the assistance of Mr. Frank Speed, cinematographer and head of the Department of Theatre Arts, University of Calabar, and Mr. Alan Grimley, Director of the University Television Service, University of Aberdeen.

Appendix 1

Methods

In this section I wish to make some remarks and observations concerning methods of data collection and problems encountered during the field work.

As mentioned briefly elsewhere in the introduction, plans for commencing the survey in a systematic fashion, i.e. establishing an inventory of all religious institutions and working through them in a pre-determined order, had to be shelved for two reasons. Firstly, in 1979/80 the government imposed stricter regulations concerning the research activities of non-Nigerians and clearance had to be sought. In the interim, we were forbidden to undertake any form of research which involved field work, especially interviewing or surveying. Secondly, the University of Calabar withheld our research grants pending approval by the government.

In any event it was a year before the final clearance was received (April 1981 - April 1982). During that time, I confined myself to visiting a number of churches informally as an interested worshipper. I also used this time to collect data on religion in the media, which I could do in the privacy of my own home. In addition, I made use of my Nigerian students who were able to go out and collect data for term papers without too much problem. I was also able to conduct informal discussions on religious topics with interested people. The advantages of this less structured, piecemeal approach became apparent at a later stage. Instead of being dominated by the desire for statistical information, I had been gaining an insight into more popular, informal types of religious expression. This level might easily have been under-emphasized or ignored.

By the time formal permission came, my research assistant and myself had got used to operating on a more ad hoc basis, i.e., visiting and collecting data on individual institutions as we heard about them. In fact, it was often more appropriate and convenient that way for we were able to gain initial access to organizations by responding to their public invitations for special services, festivals, etc.

With regard to the identification and location of the various religious institutions, there were basically three methods at our disposal: visual sighting, direct and indirect reports and newspaper reports and announcements. The first method was suitable for someone like myself who was living and working in the town and was able to discover churches, etc. while out on other assignments. Direct and indirect reports came from people (colleagues, friends, office staff and students) who either belonged to particular religious groups or knew of people who did, or had sighted an interesting new movement in their neighbourhood. The newspapers (which fortunately were still being printed on a fairly regular basis) were an extremely valuable source of information on the existence of religious institutions. They either contained announcements by the organizations themselves (regarding their registration, planned expansion or activities) or reports and features by newspaper journalists on the above.

Obviously our task would have been aided by government records on the religious institutions in the area. Such data did exist at the Federal Ministry of Internal Affairs in Lagos but we were unable to gain access to this. There were no records in Calabar. At any rate such records would have only provided information on those religious institutions registered with the government (perhaps just over half). In April 1983, the process of identifying and locating religious institutions in Calabar was completed through the religious mapping of the town which is described in chapter six.

Since we were interested in the different types of religious institutions in Calabar, we were obliged to visit as many as we could in person, given the absence of secondary sources. It was difficult at times to judge the nature of a religious institution from its name, for instance, the problem of distinguishing between indigenous spiritual churches (Redeemed International Calvary Mission, Christ Salvation Church) and exogenous pentecostal churches (Church of God of Prophecy, Calvary Baptist Church). As a rule we tried to make at least three or four visits to each religious institution: a preliminary visit was often made by my research assistant, then arrangements were made for us both to attend a major service, after which (usually the following day) we would make an appointment for a more formal interview with the founder/church leader(s)/official, etc. At a later stage, we would try to attend another type of service, this time in order to talk with ordinary members as well as to demonstrate to the authorities our sustained interest in their organization. We collected literature produced by the various religious institutions wherever possible. In some cases church leaders were kind enough to lend us documents, which we took away for photocopying.

In order to transcend the limited insights that this method generated, I associated myself with three key groups (Presbyterian Church, Brotherhood of the Cross and the Star and the Truth and Life Ministries International) on a long-term basis. I attended their services fairly regularly over the four-year period and maintained close contacts with leaders and individual members. This enabled me to appreciate their growth and development as well as the different structures and means employed by each group to construct its own religious world. I also spent much time with several Efik elders discussing Efik traditional religion and witnessing a number of traditional festivals.

My limited knowledge of the Efik-Ibibio language presented far less of a barrier than anticipated. It is rare in Calabar to encounter people who do not speak even a small amount of English. While many of the churches did employ Efik as the medium of communication, it was very common (particularly in the larger churches) for the main components of a service (i.e., sermon, announcements and sometimes prayers) to be interpreted simultaneously into English for the benefit of non-Efik speakers (a good example of this was the coronation of the Ntoe of Big Qua Town, a traditional Qua ruler, which was narrated from start to finish in English over a public address system). It was also easy to find someone to discuss with afterwards if I did not have my assistant with me. Most of our interviews with leaders and founders were conducted in English. It was only some of the traditional priests and diviners who spoke no English, but there was usually someone around to assist me.

As for any field worker, my status and identity were important considerations. Most of the churches that I visited sought to retain me as a "member". Some argued that the only way I would learn about their church or movement was by being "initiated" or "baptized". In many respects, of course, they were right, but given the nature of the present study this would have been practically impossible. It was therefore necessary to make clear to them, particularly as for the most part I worshipped with them only once or twice, my express intentions and "real" identity. I explained that I and my students were engaged on a research project in the Department of Religious Studies and Philosophy to collect data on Calabar's various religious institutions. This explanation was readily understood and appreciated for the following reasons: first, the terms "university" and "research" are familiar enough to most people in Calabar today. Second, many of the smaller groups and movements were enthusiastic about "being studied" for they realized that it would give them publicity by "putting them on the map".

In general, therefore, the participants manifested a favourable response to my work and cooperated in numerous ways. As mentioned above, this stems from a desire to expand and be socially accepted as well as a genuine interest in discussing religious and theological matters. The area where I encountered difficulty in collecting data was the traditional sector; until recently many of the masquerades were not allowed to be seen in public by non-initiates and women and children. Women are still not allowed to know the ritual secrets of Ekpe and other (male-dominated) secret societies. Several informants were helpful in partially overcoming these barriers, but it was not easy to find people who were well versed in Efik traditional religious beliefs and practices. On some occasions my research assistant visited healing homes and other locations under the guise of a supplicant, in order to collect information which he could not have otherwise obtained.

There seems little doubt that in a survey of this nature, a variety of methods must be employed - participant observation (arguably the most important), formal and informal interviewing techniques, literature and media surveys and mapping. By combining the maximum number of sources, one may reduce data errors or omissions as well as bias. Based on my earlier experience in Ibadan, I decided that the use of formal questionnaires should be avoided, since this would have limited success and would require greater financial and personnel support than we had at our disposal. Many of the smaller, unregistered religious institutions would have been reluctant to cooperate in such a scheme, for they fear that any sort of "official" visitors may be a guise for government tax inspectors.

During the second semester of 1982, as part of the course I was teaching on "New Religious Movements in Africa", fourteen undergraduate students were assigned to various spiritual churches throughout the town. They were required to interview the founder or leader, an official close to the latter, at least two ordinary members, and attend a minimum of two services (one major, one mid-week). They were supplied with an interview schedule in order to offer guidance on the main points to be covered during their interviews. In some cases I accompanied the students to their respective churches on the first visit. They all carried an official letter explaining the nature of the project, that it had received government clearance and that they were bona fide students. The whole exercise was remarkably successful and the students produced excellent reports on their respective movements, considering their inexperience in field research. One student conducted most of his interviews at the local hospital, where he had tracked down the church leader in his hospital bed! Another underwent full baptismal rites in order to gain the full cooperation of the church authorities and members.

The use of long-term informants proved especially valuable throughout the course of the study. An attempt was made to select as wide a range as possible: old and young, male and female, rich and poor, indigenes and migrants.

In the course of the fieldwork the theme of reciprocity grew in importance. In order to get good results one needed a good relationship which in turn was built on confidence and a sense of sharing. For providing information on their movements and churches people expected something in return; this materialized in a number of ways: through copies of photographs, filming, help with editing transcripts of sermons and tracts, help with getting members of their congregation admission to the University of Calabar, preaching or some other form of participation in a special service, acquisition of books or Bibles from overseas, and transmitting parcels and letters to parent churches or affiliated bodies abroad. Most importantly, I was asked to find "sister churches" overseas who would be prepared to twin up with the Nigerian church and offer spiritual, moral and perhaps even financial assistance. For some, the mere fact that I was teaching "religion" to students in their country, having temporarily renounced my own, was sufficient stimulation.

In conclusion, I would say that our greatest problem lay in treating such a diverse range of data: the problem of classification and categorization, the confusion over names of churches and movements (for example, there were three Holy Face churches, three Spiritual Christ Army churches, four Mount Zions and one Hill of Salvation Mission and one Light of Salvation Mission) and the need to be alert to manifestations of religion at all times and in all places. It was also extremely frustrating to discover that in several cases people did not know about the origins or history of their churches (particularly those that originated outside of Calabar).

Appendix 2

Chronology

pre-1650?	Efik settlement at Creek Town
1668	First recorded contact of European trade with Old Calabar
1692	Calabar chiefs write to Portuguese Catholic Mission requesting missionaries
c.1750?	Ekpe Society founded
c.1780?	Two German Methodist missionaries arrive, but die shortly after
1834	Great Duke Ephraim dies
1841	Baptist missionaries visit Calabar from England Slave trade ends in Calabar
1842	Letters from Kings Eyamba and Eyo Honesty requesting missionaries
1846	Arrival of Presbyterian missionaries and establishment of first Christian mission
1847	Eyamba V dies Rev. Hugh Goldie arrives from Scotland
1848	Rev. and Mrs. William Anderson arrive from Jamaica Presbytery
1849	Calabar becomes first headquarters of the British Consul on the Bights of Benin and Biafra
1850	Society for the Abolition of Inhuman and Superstitious Customs and for promoting Civilization in Calabar formed First Christian marriage performed in Creek Town Sunday markets banned by Ekpe law

	Women attend church for the first time First extracts of Bible published in Efik
1851	"Blood Companions" (Nka Iyip) formed by plantation slaves to curb human sacrifice Eyo Honesty II forbids movement of missionaries into interior without consent
1853	First Christian baptism
1855	Bombardment of Old Town First Presbyterian chapel opened
1856	Mission House established
1857	Death of Samuel Edgerley, pioneer Presbyterian missionary and printer
1858	Presbytery of Biafra formed Rev. Hope Masterton Waddell leaves Eyo Honesty II dies
1859	First collection of hymns in Efik
1862	New Testament translated into Efik
1868	Full Bible translation in Efik Bunyan's "Pilgrim's Progress" translated into Efik
1870	Bishop Samuel Crowther visits Calabar
1872	Ordination of first Efik Presbyterian minister
1873	Goldie publishes Efik Grammar
1876	Mary Slessor arrives

1878	Hopkins Treaty
1879	King Archibong III crowned in Duke Town Presbyterian Church
1881	Ross secession from Presbyterian Church Alexander Cruickshank stationed at Ikorofiong
1885	Oil Rivers Protectorate created
1888	Expansion of Presbyterian mission field to Okoyong
1891	Islam brought to Calabar by Hausa soldiers Calabar becomes capital of Protectorate
1894	Primitive Methodist Mission established at Jamestown
1895	Hope Waddell Training Institution created Goldie dies
1897	St. Margaret's Hospital founded
1902	Proclamation concerning Obong of Calabar and Obong of Creek Town
1903	Roman Catholics begin work in Calabar Salvation Army representative visits Calabar
1904	Old Calabar renamed Calabar Duke Town Presbyterian Church opened
1905	"Nka Erinyana no Christ" formed
1908	Father Shanahan arrives
1909	Conference convened in Calabar to discuss mission fields

1911	Foreign and Native Pastorate Church formed
	Missionary conference in Calabar
1914	Wesleyan Methodist congregation formed
	World War I begins
1915	Mary Slessor dies at Use
1918	Christ African Church arrives
	First mosque built
	World War I ends
	First publication of hymns composed by Efik
1921	Presbyterian Synod of Biafra formed
1923	Sister Mary Charles Walker arrives
1926	Primitive Methodist Mission takes over
	Wesleyan Methodist Church in Calabar
1927	Spirit Movement in Uyo begins
1928	Salvation Army arrives
	Watchtower representatives visit Calabar
1930	Christian Council of Nigeria formed
	Holy Child Sisters arrive
1931	Handmaids of the Holy Child Jesus formed
1933	Apostolic Church begins work in Calabar
	Witchcraft scare
1936	Rev. Dr. A. Cruickshank dies
1938	Hill of Salvation Mission created (first independent church)

1939	World War II begins
1940	Electricity installed in Calabar
1943	St. Patrick's College opens at Ikot Ansa
1945	Presbyterian Church of Biafra formed World War II ends
1946	Presbyterian centenary celebrations Church of Christ the Good Shepherd arrives Mount Zion Church formed
1947	Maternity Hospital and Calabar Library established
1948	First Lutheran pastor moves to Calabar
1950	Calabar Diocese (Catholic) formed Church of Christ begins work in Calabar
1952	Presbyterian Church of Eastern Nigeria formed National Assembly Church created
1953	Apostolic Faith Mission formed
1954	Holy Child Secondary School for Girls established
1955	Baha'i missionary visits Calabar
1956	First Baha'i Spiritual Assembly established in Calabar Holy Chapel of Miracles arrives AMORC begins officially Eternal Sacred Order of the Cherubim and Seraphim arrives O.O. Obu founds healing home Queen Elizabeth II visits Calabar

1957	Calabar opts for Action Group Party
1960	Nigeria achieves political independence Presbyterian Church of Nigeria formed
1961	Christ Apostolic Church arrives Southern Cameroon leaves Nigeria
1962	Pentecostal Assemblies of the World, Inc. begins work in Calabar
1964	Brotherhood of the Cross and Star registered Spiritual Christ Army Church opens branch in Calabar Christ Apostolic Freedom Church begins work Enquiry into Obongship dispute led by Hart Obong of Calabar becomes sole paramount ruler of Efik
1965	Qua Iboe Mission established in Calabar Divine Order of the Cherubim and Seraphim establishes a branch
1966	Christian Methodist Episcopal Church opens branch Edgerley Memorial Modern School for Girls upgraded to Secondary Grammar School
1967	Calabar becomes capital of South-Eastern State Nigerian Civil War begins Christ Salvation Church founded Assemblies of God brought to Calabar The Church, the Body of Christ founded
1968?	God's Kingdom Society establishes a branch
1969?	Christian Community of Nigeria founded in Calabar

1970	Nigerian Civil War ends
	Spiritual Kingdom Church of Christ opens branch
	Christian Science brought to Calabar
	Okopedi Healing Home officially established
	Missionary Fellowship commences activities

1971   Holy Face Church created
        Jesus the Superet Church commences activities

1972   First Efik Catholic priest ordained
        Church of God Congregation arrives
        Crystal Cathedral Church opens branch
        Bible Society of Nigeria holds first conference in
        Calabar

1974   Calvary Baptist Church opens branch

1975   Redeemed International Calvary Mission arrives
        Institute of Religious Science established
        University of Calabar created

1976   Christ Faith Evangelical Church arrives
        Friends of Jesus founded
        Christ the Shepherd's New Kingdom Flock created
        Church of God Lamentation of Jehovah founded
        American evangelist, T.L. Osborn, visits Calabar
        Cross River State created

1977   Truth and Life Church founded

1978   Church of God of Prophecy arrives
        Mount Olive Church of Christ founded
        Celestial Church of Christ officially established
        Clashes between Brotherhood and Apostolic
        Church members
        Anti-witchcraft crusade in Ibibioland

1979   Civilian government takes office
                Christ Holy Church of Nigeria arrives
                Spiritual Fellowship formed
                Unification Church begins activities

1981   Apostolic Church celebrates Golden Jubilee
                Church of Jesus Christ of Latter-Day Saints stages
                conference in Calabar
                Eckankar introduced
                International Society of Krishna Consciousness begins
                activities
                Unification Church closes branch in Calabar
                Subud Brotherhood planned launching
                The Grail Movement begins public lectures
                Revival Valley Ministries created in Calabar
                Christ Healing and Evangelical Movement brought to
                Calabar

1982   Calabar/Dundee Presbyteries Partnership launched
                First Presbyterian woman minister ordained in Aba
                Pope visits Nigeria
                Aetherius Society introduced
                Edidem Bassey Eyo Ephraim Adam III installed as
                new Obong of Calabar
                Holy Face Spiritual Church founded

1983   Calabar Baha'i Centre inaugurated
                Presbyterian Church launches first limited liability
                company in Calabar
                Military government takes over

Appendix 3

Data File on the Religious Institutions of Calabar

Key

1. Name of institution
2. Abbreviation used
3. Place of origin (country, town/area); headquarters (overseas and/or Nigeria)
4. Date of origin (if applicable or known)
5. Date of entry into Nigeria (if applicable or known)
6. Date of entry into Calabar
   OR Date of founding in Calabar
7. Address in Calabar (headquarters)
8. Schism from previous church or body; present schism(s)
9. Name of founder(s); nationality; ethnic group
10. Sex of founder; date of birth; date of death (if applicable); occupation
11. Current leader in Calabar; sex; ethnic group
12. Number of branches in Calabar; in Nigeria; overseas branches
13. Links with local or international religious organizations
14. Language used
15. Literature: origins; language

*	No longer active
-	Information unavailable
n.a.	Not applicable
CCN	Christian Council of Nigeria
CCON	Christian Community of Nigeria
CRS	Cross River State
WCC	World Council of Churches

1.   1.   **AETHERIUS SOCIETY**
     2.   AS
     3.   UK; Los Angeles; Port Harcourt?
     4.   1955
     6.   1982
     7.   c/o Dr. Gabriel Ukott
          Ministry of Health
     9.   George King; British
     10. m; -; -; -
     12. 1; -; US and UK
     14. English
     15. Los Angeles; English

2.   1.   **AFRICAN METHODIST EPISCOPAL CHURCH (ZION)**
     2.   AMEZ
     3.   US (New York); -; -
     4.   1821
     6.   1950s? (from Uyo)
     7.   7 Diamond Hill
     8.   Methodist Church
     11. Dr. Young E.O. Eta; m; Ibibio
     12. 2; -; US
     13. CCON, World Methodist Council
     14. Efik-Ibibio

3.   1.   **ANGLICAN CHURCH**
     3.   UK; England; Lagos
     4.   17th century
     5.   1843
     6.   1911
     7.   81 Calabar Road
     11. Canon W.G. Ekprikpo; m; Igbo
     12. 1; -; worldwide
     13. CCN, WCC
     14. English, Yoruba, Igbo
     15. Local and international; English, Yoruba, Igbo

4.   1.   **APOSTOLIC CHURCH**
      2.   AC
      3.   UK; Wales; Lagos
      4.   1904-5
      5.   1931
      6.   1933
      7.   Field Headquarters
           101 Marian Road
     11.   Superintendent E.E. Okon; m; Ibibio
     12.   43; -; Europe
     14.   Efik-Ibibio
     15.   Calabar, Lagos, Bradford; English and Efik-Ibibio

5.   1.   **APOSTOLIC FAITH**
      2.   AF
      3.   US (Portland, Oregon); Portland; Ikot Enwang, CRS
      4.   Early 20th century
      5.   1950?
      6.   1952 (from Ikot Enwang)
      7.   Ekpo Abasi Street
      8.   Methodist Church?
      9.   Florence L. Crawford; American
    10.   f; -; -; -
    11.   Pastor A.F. Ufford; m; Ibibio
    12.   1; -; US
    14.   English
    15.   US; English

6.   1.   **ASSEMBLIES OF GOD**
      2.   AG
      3.   US (Arkansas); Aba
      4.   1914
      5.   1940
      6.   1965/6
      7.   98 Fosbery Road
      9.   -; American
     11.   Pastor Isangidigh; m;
     12.   7;- ; worldwide

13. Federated Assemblies of World Pentecostal Organizations?;
     Nigerian Evangelical Fellowship
14. Efik-Ibibio and English
15. Accra and Aba; English

7.   1.   **BAHA'I FAITH**
     2.   BF
     3.   Persia (Iran); Haifa, Israel; Lagos
     4.   Mid-nineteenth century
     5.   1950s?
     6.   1956 (from the Cameroons)
     7.   19B Idang Street
     8.   Islam
     9.   Baha'u'llah; Persian
     10. m; 1817; 1892; -
     11. Friday Ekpe; m; Ibibio
     12. 1; -; worldwide
     14. English
     15. Lagos, Calabar and international headquarters; English
     (Efik-Ibibio trans. in progress)

8.   1.   **BAPTIST CHURCH**
     3.   US ; US; Ogbomosho, W. Nigeria
     7.   28 Uwanse Street
     11. -; -; Yoruba
     12. 1; -; worldwide
     13. CCN

9.   1.   **BELIEVERS' ASSEMBLY OF NIGERIA**
     7.   10 Ewa Henshaw Street
          off Eyo Ita Street

10. 1.   **BROTHERHOOD OF THE CROSS AND STAR**
     2.   BCS
     3.   Nigeria (Calabar); Calabar
     4.   1956
     6.   1956
     7.   34 Ambo Street

9.   Olumba Olumba Obu; Nigerian; Biakpan
10.   m; 1918; n.a.; trader
11.   As above; Biakpan
12.   30; 1000+; UK, US, Ghana, Cameroun, Gabon
13.   CCON; (Unification Church, AMORC)
14.   Efik-Ibibio
15.   Calabar; English with some Efik-Ibibio

11.   1.   **CALVARY BAPTIST CHURCH**
      3.   US (Kentucky); Uyo?
      5.   1960s
      6.   1974
      7.   11 Obufa Obutong
     11.   John Imeh; Nigerian; Ibibio
     12.   1; -; US

12.   1.   **CELESTIAL CHURCH OF CHRIST**
      2.   CCC
      3.   Republic of Benin/Dahomey (Porto-Novo); Ketu, Lagos
      4.   1947
      5.   1950
      6.   1978
      7.   Ikot Ansa
      8.   n.a.; e.g. Cross of Christ World Mission (Ibadan)
      9.   S.B.J. Oschoffa; Beninois/Nigerian; Gun/Yoruba
     10.   m; 1909; n.a.; timber trader
     11.   Superior Senior Leader E.A.A. Averechi; m; Igbo?
     12.   3; several hundred; UK, US, West Germany, West Africa
     13.   Aladura Fellowship
     14.   English, Yoruba, some Efik-Ibibio
     15.   Lagos; English

13.   1.   **CHRIST AFRICAN CHURCH**
      3.   Nigeria; Lagos
      4.   1901
      6.   1918
      7.   36 Macdonald Street
      8.   Anglican Church

9.   J.K. Coker; Nigerian; Yoruba
10. M; -
11. Bishop E.E. Ironbar; m; Efik
12. 4; 1000+; none
13. CCN
14. Efik-Ibibio
15. Local and Lagos (many trans. Anglican texts and hymns); English and Efik-Ibibio

14. 1. **CHRIST APOSTOLIC CHURCH**
     2. CAC
     3. Nigeria (Lagos); Lagos
     4. 1930s
     6. 1961
     7. 80 Mbukpa Road
     8. Apostolic Church; Christ Apostolic Freedom Church
     9. Nigerian; Yoruba
     11. Rev. E. G. Essien; m; Ibibio
     12. 2; -; -
     13. Aladura Alliance

15. 1. **CHRIST APOSTOLIC FREEDOM CHURCH**
     2. CAFC
     3. Nigeria (Ukpon, Eket); Ukpon, Eket
     4. 1950
     6. 1964
     7. 19 Atuambon Street
     8. Christ Apostolic Church
     9. Bishop N.N. Ukoro; Nigerian; Ibibio
     10. m; -; c1975; -
     11. Pastor A.A. Udonwa; m; Ibibio
     12. 10 (in Calabar district); -; -
     14. Efik-Ibibio

16. 1. **CHRIST FAITH EVANGELICAL CHURCH**
     2. CFEC
     3. US: Eket
     6. 1976

7.   Nyong Edem Street

12. 1; 3; -

17. 1.   **CHRIST FOLLOWERS' CHURCH**

     7.   2 Okon Edak Street
          off Oyo Efam, off Atamunu

18. 1.   **CHRIST FOR THE WORLD MISSION**

     2.   US ?; -

     7.   8 Adam Duke Street

19. 1.   **CHRIST HOLY CHURCH OF NIGERIA**

     2.   CHCN

     3.   Nigeria (Onitsha); Onitsha

     6.   1978

     7.   Edibe Edibe Road, off Eyo Ita

     9.   Prophetess Odozi Obodo (The Holy Prophetess of God);

    10. Nigerian; Igbo

    11. f; -; n.a.; -

    12. As above; Igbo

    13. 1; -; -

    15. Igbo

20. 1.   **CHRIST LIFE EVANGELISTIC MINISTRY**

     2.   CLEF

     3.   Nigeria (Calabar); Calabar

     4.   1980s

     5.   n.a.

     6.   1980s

     7.   St. Mary Primary School
          Howell Street

     9.   Brother A. E. Oroh; Nigerian; Ibibio

    10. m; -; n.a.; -

    11. As above; Ibibio

    12. 1; 6; none

    15. Local; English

21. 1. **CHRIST SALVATION CHURCH**
     2. Nigeria (Calabar): Ikot Ishie, Calabar
     3. 1967
     7. 10 Ishie Drive
         off Odukpani Road
         Ikot Ishie
     8. Brotherhood of the Cross and Star
     9. Effiong Etim ("Itu"); Nigerian; Ibibio
     10. m; -; n.a.; -
     11. As above; Ibibio
     12. 1; -; none
     14. Efik-Ibibio

22. 1. **CHRIST THE SHEPHERD'S NEW KINGDOM FLOCK**
     2. CSNKF
     3. US; Calabar
     4. 1976/77
     6. 1977
     7. 40 Target Road
     8. Brotherhood of the Cross and Star
     9. Paul Louis Eyo; Nigerian; Efik
     10. m; 1930; n.a.; Brotherhood pastor
     11. As above; Efik
     12. 1; none; none
     13. none
     14. Efik-Ibibio
     15. Local; Efik-Ibibio and English

23. 1. **CHRIST'S CHOSEN CHURCH OF GOD**
     7. 46 Ebito Street

24. 1. **CHRISTIAN METHODIST EPISCOPAL CHURCH**
     2. CME
     3. US ; -
     4. 1870
     6. 1966
     7. Edim Otop Lane
         Akim Qua Town

8.   Methodist Church
12. 2; -; US
13. World Methodist Council

25. 1. **CHRISTIAN REFORMED CHURCH**
     3. Nigeria (Calabar); Calabar
     7. Opposite Army Cantonment
         Ikot Ansa

26. 1. **CHRISTIAN SCIENCE**
     2. CS
     3. US (New England); -
     4. 1860S and 1870s
     5. 1950s
     6. 1970
     7. Barracks Road Primary School
     9. Mary Baker Eddy; American
     10. f; 1821; 1910; -
     11. Essien Okon; m; Ibibio
     12. 2; -; worldwide
     14. English
     15. Boston; English

27. 1. **CHURCH OF CHRIST**
     3. US (Nashville, Tennessee); Calabar?
     4. 19th century
     5. 1946
     6. 1946
     7. Hawkins Road
     11. Evangelist Effiong Ekpe; m; Ibibio
     12. 4; -; US
     14. Efik-Ibibio
     15. US; English

28. 1. **CHURCH OF CHRIST, THE GOOD SHEPHERD**
     3. Nigeria (Lagos); Calabar
     4. 1940
     6. 1946

7.   52 Egerton Street
9.   Lucy Harriet Harrison (Big Mmama Prayer); Efik
10. f; 1900; 1981; -
12. 1; 3?; -
13. CCON
14. Efik-Ibibio

29. 1.   **CHURCH OF GOD (7th Day)**
     3.   US ?; -; -
     6.   1980s?
     7.   50 Webber Street

30. 1.   **CHURCH OF GOD CONGREGATION**
     3.   Nigeria (Etinan)?; Calabar?
     6.   1972
     7.   11 Uwanse Street
     8.   Presbyterian Church
     9.   L.E. Etukudo; Nigerian; Ibibio
     10. m; -; -; -
     11. -; m; Ibibio?
     12. -; 4; -

31. 1.   **CHURCH OF GOD OF LAMENTATION OF JEHOVAH**
     2.   CGLJ
     3.   Nigeria (Calabar); Calabar
     4.   1976
     6.   1976
     7.   21 Atakpa Lane
     9.   Theresa Sunday U. Inyang; Nigerian; Ibibio
     10. f; -; n.a.; trader
     11. As above; Ibibio
     12. 1; -; none
     13. None
     14. Efik-Ibibio

32. 1.   **CHURCH OF GOD OF PROPHECY***
     2.   CGP
     3.   US ; Cleveland, Tennessee; Etinan

4. 1903
6. 1978 (from Etinan)
7. Neta Land
   Ikot Ansa
11. Bishop Ekpene; m; Ibibio
12. 1; 3; -

33. 1. **CHURCH OF JESUS CHRIST OF LATTER-DAY SAINTS**
     2. CJCLDS
     3. US (New York State); Utah; Uyo?
     4. 1820s (late)
     5. 1970s?
     6. 1981
     9. Joseph Smith; American
    10. m; 1805; 1844; farmer
    12. (1); 32?; worldwide
    14. English
    15. English; Utah

34. 1. **CHURCH OF THE NEW JERUSALEM***
     2. CNJ
     3. Sweden; London; -
     4. 18th century
     5. 1930?
     6. 1980? (from Etinan)
     9. Emmanuel Swedenborg; Swedish
    10. m; 1668; 1772
    11. None
    12. -; -; US and UK
    15. London; English

35. 1. **CRYSTAL CATHEDRAL CHURCH**
     2. CC
     3. Nigeria (Lagos); Oku-Iboku, Cross River State
     4. 1967
     6. 1972
     7. 6 Bassey Edim Street
        Ediba

9.   Leader Brother E.A. Inyang; Nigerian; Ibibio
10.   M; 20/8/1928; n.a.; Nigerian Ports Authority
11.   As above; Ibibio
12.   1; 3; none
13.   None
14.   English and Efik-Ibibio
15.   Local (Presbyterian hymns); English

36.   1.   **DEEPER CHRISTIAN LIFE MINISTRY**
      2.   DCLM
      3.   Nigeria (Lagos); Lagos
      7.   Primary School
            Howell Street
            Efut Abua
      9.   W.F. Kumuyi; Nigerian; Yoruba?
      10.   m; -; n.a.; university lecturer in mathematics
      14.   English
      15.   Lagos; English

37.   1.   **DIVINE ORDER OF THE CHERUBIM AND SERAPHIM**
      2.   DOCS
      3.   Nigeria (Port Harcourt); Port Harcourt
      4.   1965
      6.   1965
      7.   50 Ebito Street
      8.   Eternal Sacred Order of the Cherubim and Seraphim
      9.   -; Nigerian; -
      11.   Bishop John Ema Udok; m; Ibibio
      12.   3; -; -
      13.   CCON
      14.   Efik-Ibibio
      15.   Local; Efik-Ibibio

38.   1.   **ECKANKAR**
      2.   ECK
      3.   US (California); California; Lagos
      4.   1965
      6.   1981

7.   14A Foster Street
9.   Paul Twitchell; American
10. m; -; -; -
11. Okokon Ndem; m; Efik
12. 1; -; US
14. English
15. US; English

39. 1.   **ETERNAL SACRED ORDER OF THE CHERUBIM AND SERAPHIM**
     2.   ESOCS
     3.   Nigeria (Lagos); Lagos
     4.   1925
     5.   n.a.
     6.   1956; Enugu
     7.   3/5 Awka Street
     9.   Moses Orimolade Tunolashe; Nigerian; Yoruba
     11. Senior Apostle N.E. Ekpo; m; Ibibio
     12. 1; 496; -
     13. CCN
     14. English and Efik-Ibibio
     15. Lagos; English

40. 1.   **FAITH TABERNACLE CONGREGATION**
     3.   US (Philadelphia); Philadelphia; Lagos?
     5.   1917
     7.   57 Ekondo Lane/5 Atu Street
     12. 1; -; US

41. 1.   **FRIENDS OF JESUS**
     2.   FOJ
     3.   Nigeria (Calabar); Calabar
     4.   1976
     6.   1976
     7.   8B Odukpani Road
     8.   Church of Christ Unity (Los Angeles)
     9.   Efiota Efiom; Nigerian; Efik
     10. m; -; n.a.; electrical engineer

11.   As above; Efik
12.   1; -; -
14.   English
15.   Local and international; English

42.   1.   **FULL GOSPEL CHURCH OF GOD**
      3.   Nigeria (Ikot Ukpong); Ikot Ukpong, CRS
      7.   9 Adam Duke Street
      9.   Rt. Rev. Donald Etim Asuquo; Nigerian; Ibibio
      10. m; 1930?; n.a.; palm oil trader
      11. -; m; Ibibio

43.   1.   **GOD THE HOST PRAYER TEMPLE**
      3.   Nigeria (Calabar); Calabar
      4.   1956
      6.   1956
      7.   38 Egerton Street
      8.   National Assembly Church?
      9.   Ekpenyong Ekeng (with Effanga Odiong Effanga); Nigerian;
           Ibibio
      10. m; -; 1970; pharmacy superintendent
      12. 1; -; none
      13. CCON
      14. Efik-Ibibio

44.   1.   **GOD'S KINGDOM SOCIETY**
      2.   GKS
      3.   Nigeria (Warri); Warri
      4.   1934
      6.   1969 (from Lagos)
      7.   Old Primary School/ Commercial School
           Old Ikang Road
      8.   Jehovah's Witnesses
      9.   Gideon M. Urhobo; Nigerian; Urhobo
      10. m; 1903; 1952; postal clerk and telegraphist
      11. Brother Ekpo; m; Ibibio
      12. 1; -;-

14. English
15. Warri; English

45. 1. **HILL OF SALVATION MISSION**
     3. Nigeria (Calabar); Calabar
     4. 1938
     6. 1938
     7. 38 Inyang Street
     8. Apostolic Church

46. 1. **HOLY CHAPEL OF MIRACLES**
     2. HCM
     3. Nigeria (Oshogbo); Calabar
     4. 1947
     6. 1956
     7. Itu Street
     8. Roman Catholic
     9. Theresa A. Effiong (Blessed Spiritual Mother); Nigeria; Efik
     10. f; c1918?; n.a.; midwife
     11. As above; Efik
     12. 1; 2; none
     13. CCON
     14. English and Efik-Ibibio
     15. Local (+ sabbatarian and adventist literature from international sources); English

47. 1. **HOLY CHRIST CHURCH**
     7. 45 Edibe Edibe Street

48. 1. **HOLY FACE (SPIRITUAL) CHURCH**
     2. HFSC
     3. Nigeria (Calabar); Calabar
     4. 1982
     6. 1982
     7. 3 Murtala Muhammed Highway
     8. AME Zion and Holy Face Church
     9. Rev. S.A. Okpo; Nigerian; Ibibio

10. m; 1940s; n.a.; building contractor
11. As above; Ibibio
12. 1; none; none
13. None
14. Efik-Ibibio
15. None

49. 1. **HOLY FACE CHURCH**
2. HFC
3. Nigeria (Calabar); Calabar
4. 1971
5. n.a.
6. 1971
7. No. 2 Ndon Edet Street
   Off Atakpa Street
8. Roman Catholic Church (Holy Face Society); Holy Face
   Spiritual Church
9. Rev. Dominic Essien Edet; Nigerian; Ibibio
11. As above; Ibibio
12. 1; 3; -

50. 1. **HOLY FACE CHURCH***
3. Nigeria (Oron); Oron
7. Atamunu Street
8. Roman Catholic Church
9. -; Nigerian; Ibibio
12. 1; -

51. 1. **INSTITUTE OF RELIGIOUS SCIENCE (renamed in 1984 -
    CHRIST HOPE SALVATION CHURCH: FIRST CHURCH OF
    RELIGIOUS SCIENCE)**
3. US (Los Angeles); Los Angeles; -
6. 1975
7. 7C Eta Agbo Road
   Akim
9. -; American
11. Rev. Mike M. Obionwa; m; Ibibio
12. 1; -; -

13. International New Thought Alliance/ New Thought Movement
14. English
15. Los Angeles; English

52. 1. **INTERNATIONAL SOCIETY OF KRISHNA CONSCIOUSNESS**
2. ISKCON
3. US ; Los Angeles; Lagos
4. 1965
6. 1981
7. c/0 Mr. K. Ramchandani
   Eta Agbo Road
9. A.C. Bhakti-vedanta Swami Prabhubada; Indian
10. m; 1896; 1977; -
12. (1); -; worldwide
14. English
15. US; English

53. 1. **ISLAM**
6. 1918
7. Bogobiri Mosque
11. Chief Imam; m; Hausa?
12. 4; worldwide
13. None
14. Arabic
15. Arabic

54. 1. **JEHOVAH'S WITNESSES**
2. JW
3. US (Pennsylvania); Pennsyvania
4. 1881
5. 1920s
6. 1928
7. 22 Atu Street
9. Charles Taze Russell; American
10. m; -; 1916; -
12. 7;-; worldwide

13. None
14. English and Efik-Ibibio
15. Lagos, London and New York; English

55. 1. **JENEFA EVANGELISTIC FELLOWSHIP**
    3. Nigeria (Calabar); Calabar
    4. 1980s?
    6. 1980s?
    7. 57 Ibesikpo Street
    9. -; Nigerian; Ibibio
    11. Ibibio

56. 1. **JESUS CHRIST HEALING AND EVANGELICAL MOVEMENT**
    3. Nigeria (Lagos); Calabar
    4. 1960s (mid)
    6. 1981
    7. 51 Akim Road
    8. Apostolic Church
    9. Apostle Samuel Adam Ephraim Bassey Adam; Nigerian; Efik
    10. m; 1911; n.a.; painter and carver then pastor
    11. As above; Efik
    12. 1; 1; none
    13. Apostolic Church; World Healing Crusade (Blackwood, NJ)
    14. English
    15. Local and international; English

57. 1. **JESUS THE SUPERET CHURCH (SUPERET LIGHT MISSION)**
    2. JSC
    3. US (Los Angeles); -
    4. 1925
    5. 1953 (to Ibeno)
    6. 1971
    7. 77 Mbukpa Street
    9. Dr. Josephine Trust (Mother Trust); American
    10. f; -; 1958; aura scientist
    11. Rev. Francis U. Akpan; m; Ibibio

12. 1; -; US
14. English and Efik-Ibibio
15. Los Angeles; English

58. 1. **LIGHT OF SALVATION MISSION**
3. Nigeria (Calabar); Calabar
4. 1974
6. 1974
7. 28A Yellow Duke Street
9. Rev. Sunday Udo Obot; Nigerian; Ibibio
10. m; 1920s?; n.a.; -
11. As above; Ibibio
12. 1; 9; none

59. 1. **LUTHERAN CHURCH**
3. Germany; -; Obot Idim, Ibesikpo, CRS
4. 16th century
5. 1936
6. 1940s
7. 115 Fosbery Road
11. -; m; Ibibio
12. 2; -; worldwide
13. CCN, WCC
14. Efik-Ibibio
15. Local and international; English and Efik-Ibibio

60. 1. **METHODIST CHURCH**
2. WMM/PMM
3. UK ; London; Lagos
4. 18th century
5. 1842
6. 1916
7. Beecroft Street
8. Anglican Church; Spiritual Fellowship
11. Archbishop F. U. Ekanem; Nigerian; Ibibio
12. 2; -; worldwide
13. CCN; WCC, World Methodist Council

14.   English and Efik-Ibibio
15.   Lagos; English and Efik-Ibibio

61.   1.   **MISSIONARY FELLOWSHIP**
      2.   MF
      3.   Nigeria (Calabar and Oron); Calabar
      4.   1970
      6.   1976
      7.   1 White House Street
      9.   -; Nigerian; Ibibio
      11. As above; Ibibio
      12. 1; 2?; none
      13. Baptist Church (US), Scripture Union
      14. English
      15. Local and international; English

62.   1.   **MOUNT OLIVE CHURCH OF CHRIST**
      2.   MOCC
      3.   Nigeria (Calabar); Calabar
      4.   1978
      6.   1978
      7.   8 Ekpenyong Ekpe Street
      8.   Maddie Raymond; Nigerian; Ibibio
      9.   f; 1950s; n.a.; government clerk
      10. As above; Ibibio
      11. 1; none; none
      12. None
      13. Efik-Ibibio
      14. None

63.   1.   **MOUNT ZION GOSPEL CHURCH INCORPORATED**
      3.   Nigeria (Calabar); Calabar
      7.   23 William Genge Street
      8.   Mount Zion Light House Full Gospel Church
      12. 2?; -

64. 1. **MOUNT ZION LIGHT HOUSE FULL GOSPEL CHURCH**
    2. MZLH
    3. Nigeria (Calabar); Calabar
    4. 1946
    6. 1946
    7. 9 Inyang Street
    8. Apostolic Church; Mount Zion Mission, Mount Zion Gospel
    9. Church
    10. John Eshiet Etefia, John Ubok Udom, J.B. Ettefiah, Robert Prince Akpabio; Nigerian; Ibibio
    11. m; -; all deceased except Etefia; -
        John Eshiet Etefia; m; Ibibio
    12. 17; -; -
    13. Mount Zion Light House Full Gospel Church, Oakland, California; Federated Assemblies of World Pentecostal Organizations
    14. Efik-Ibibio
    15. Local; English and Efik-Ibibio

65. 1. **MOUNT ZION MISSION**
    3. Nigeria
    7. 1 Eket Street
    8. Mount Zion Light House Full Gospel Church
    9. -; Nigerian; Ibibio
    11. As above; Ibibio

66. 1. **NATIONAL ASSEMBLY OF NIGERIA**
    3. Nigeria (Ikot Omin, Calabar); Calabar
    4. 1952
    6. 1952
    7. 9 Azikiwe Street
    8. A.M.E.; God the Host Prayer Temple
    9. Etim Akpan Otong; Nigerian; Ibibio
    10. m; 1943, n.a.; cook/steward
    11. As above; Ibibio
    12. 4?; 7; London and Madrid
    13. CCON (founded by Otong)

67. 1. **OKOPEDI HEALING HOME AND HEALING ENTERPRISES**
    2. OHH
    3. Nigeria (Calabar); Calabar
    4. 1970
    6. 1970
    7. 57B Atamunu Street
    9. O. Okopedi; Nigerian; -
    10. m; -; n.a.; herbalist
    11. As above
    12. 1; none; none
    14. Efik-Ibibio
    15. Local; English

68. 1. **ORDER OF THE BLOOD OF JESUS FULL GOSPEL ASSEMBLY**
    3. Nigeria (Calabar); Calabar?
    7. 13 Ekorinim Road
    8. Full Gospel Assembly of Nigeria?

69. 1. **PENTECOSTAL ASSEMBLIES OF THE WORLD, INC.**
    2. PAW
    3. US (Indianapolis, Indiana); Uyo?
    4. Beginning of 20th century
    5. 1944-47
    6. 1962 (by Bishop E. Ironbar from Ikot Abasi)
    7. 39 Mayne Avenue
    8. (AME Zion)
    11. Pastor E.E. Ephraim; m; Ibibio;
    12. 1; several in Ibibioland; US
    13. CCON
    14. English and Efik-Ibibio
    15. US; English

70. 1. **PRESBYTERIAN CHURCH**
    2. UFCS (United Free Church), USC (United Secession Church), UPC, (United Presbyterian Church) CSM (Church of Scotland Mission)
    3. UK (Scotland); Edinburgh; Lagos

4. 16th century
5. 1846
6. 1846
7. Duke Town Presbyterian Church
8. 13 Eyamba Street
11. Rev. O. Ogbonnaya; Nigerian; Igbo
12. 13; -; worldwide
13. CCN, WCC
14. Efik-Ibibio
15. Local and Scotland; Efik-Ibibio

71. 1. **PSYCHOLOGY SCHOOL OF THOUGHT**
3. US ?; Lagos
7. Ekpo Abasi Street

72. 1. **QUA IBOE CHURCH**
2. QIM
3. Nigeria (Ibeno); Belfast (Northern Ireland); Etinan
4. 1887
5. 1887
6. 1965
7. 15 Mbukpa Road
9. Samuel Alexander Bill; Northern Irish
10. m; 1864; 1942
11. Rev. I.F. Umoren; m; Ibibio
12. 1; -
13. CCN
14. Efik-Ibibio
15. Local and international; English and Efik-Ibibio

73. 1. **REDEEMED INTERNATIONAL CALVARY MISSION**
3. Nigeria (Ikot Abasi); Ikot Abasi
6. 1975
7. Iman Street, off Mbukpa Road

74. 1. **REVIVAL VALLEY MINISTRIES**
2. RVM
3. Nigeria (Calabar); Calabar

4. 1981
6. 1981
7. West African People's Institute
P.O. Box 1067
9. Rev. Idem Ikon; Nigerian; Ibibio
10. m; 1940s?; n.a.; -
11. As above; Ibibio
12. 1; -; -
13. Nigerian Council of Gospel Ministers
15. Local; English

75. 1. **ROMAN CATHOLIC CHURCH**
2. RCM
3. Rome; Vatican; Lagos
5. 1515
6. 1903
7. Sacred Heart Cathedral
Egerton Street
11. Rt. Rev. Dr. B. Usanga; Nigerian; Ibibio
12. 15; -; worldwide
14. English, Efik-Ibibio
15. Local and international; English and Efik-Ibibio

76. 1. **ROSICRUCIANISM**
2. AMORC
3. US (New York City); San Jose, CA; Calabar
4. 1915
5. c1925
6. 1956
7. Apollonius Lodge Nigeria Administration Hqtrs.
111 Marian Road Corporation Crescent
9. H. Spencer Lewis; m; American
10. m; -; -; -
11. Alphonsus Akpan Akpabio, Master of the Rosicrucian
Apollonius Lodge; m; Ibibio
12. 1; -; worldwide
15. US; English

77.   1.   **ROYAL FAMILY OF GOD'S MISSION**
       3.   Nigeria (Calabar); Calabar
       4.   1982?
       6.   1982?
       9.   -; Nigerian; Ibibio
     11.   As above; Ibibio

78.   1.   **SACRED ORDER OF THE MORNING STAR AND ST. MICHAEL STAR**
       3.   Nigeria (Lagos); Lagos
       7.   80 Okukpani Road
            Essien Town
       8.   Cherubim and Seraphim movement
       9.   -; Nigerian; Yoruba?

79.   1.   **SALVATION ARMY**
       2.   SA
       3.   UK ; London; Lagos
       4.   c1878
       5.   1903?
       6.   1928
       7.   32 Goldie Street
       9.   William Booth; English;
     10.   m; -;-; former Methodist minister
     11.   Captain M.U. Ekpo; m; Ibibio
     12.   2; worldwide
     13.   CCN
     14.   Efik-Ibibio
     15.   Local and UK; /Efik-Ibibio and English

80.   1.   **SEVENTH-DAY ADVENTIST CHURCH**
       2.   SDA
       3.   US ; Washington, D.C.; Ikeja
       4.   c1860
       5.   1920s
       6.   1940s?
       7.   Goldie Street
       9.   James and Ellen White; American

10.   m & f; -; Ellen (1915); -
11.   Pastor H. Lukko; m; Finnish
12.   2; -; worldwide
14.   English and Efik-Ibibio (Bible classes)
15.   Lagos; English

81.   1.   **SPIRITUAL CHRIST ARMY CHURCH**
      2.   SCAC
      3.   Nigeria (Bakana, Port Harcourt); Abak?
      4.   1916
      6.   1964
      7.   21 Atakpa Street
      8.   Christ Army Church; St. John Christ Army Spiritual Church, St. Paul Christ Army Spiritual Church
      9.   Garrick Braid; Ijaw
      10. m; -; 1918; -
      11. -; Ibibio
      12. 3; -; -;

82.   1.   **SPIRITUAL CHURCH OF GOD**
      7.   Ekpenyong Abasi Street
           off Anantigha

83.   1.   **SPIRITUAL FELLOWSHIP**
      2.   SF
      3.   Nigeria (Calabar); Calabar
      4.   1979
      6.   1979
      7.   Effiong Nwan Street, off Ekpo Abasi Street
      8.   Methodist Church
      9.   A. Peter Akpan; Nigerian; Ibibio
      10. m; 1940s; n.a.; head, Federal Ministry of Commerce (Calabar branch)
      11. As above; Ibibio
      12. 1; none; none
      14. English
      15. Local and international; English

84. 1. **SPIRITUAL KINGDOM CHURCH OF CHRIST**
    2. SKCC
    3. Nigeria (Ikot Ekpene); Ikot Ekpene
    4. 1946-48
    6. 1970
    7. 7 Adam Duke Street
    8. Apostolic Church
    9. John Akpan Bassey (Edidem "Spiritual King" Bassey; Nigerian; Ibibio
    10. m; -; -; -
    11. Apostle Joshua; m; Ibibio
    12. 1; -; -
    14. Efik-Ibibio
    15. Aba; English

85. 1. **SUBUD BROTHERHOOD**
    2. SB
    3. Indonesia; -; Calabar
    4. 1933
    6. 1981
    7. 9 Chalmers Lane
        P.O. Box 424
    9. Bapak; Indonesian
    10. M; 1901; government official
    11. Peter Nta Odusip; m ; Ibibio
    12. 1; UK, US
    14. English
    15. International (UK) and local reprints; English

86. 1. **THE BODY OF GOD CHURCH**
    3. Nigeria; -
    7. 4 Iboku Lane

87. 1. **THE CHURCH, THE BODY OF CHRIST**
    2. CBC
    3. Nigeria (Calabar); Calabar
    4. 1967
    6. 1967

7.   31 Hart Street
8.   Apostolic Church; United Body of Christ (Etinan), The
     Church, the Body of Christ (6 Nkwa Street)
9.   Eyo I. Ita; Nigerian; Efik
10. m; -; 1972; radiographer
11. E.O. Eyo; m; Efik
12. 2; -; none
14. Efik-Ibibio

88. 1.   **THE FATHER, SON AND HOLY GHOST MISSION**
     3.   Nigeria
     7.   92 Fosbery Road
     11. Pastor Otu Mboho; Nigerian; Ibibio?

89. 1.   **THE GRAIL MOVEMENT**
     3.   Austria; Vomperberg, Austria
     4.   1920s
     6.   1981
     7.   36 Chamley Street
     9.   Oscar Ernst Bernhard; Federal Republic of Germany
     10. m; -; -; -
     15. -; English

90. 1.   **THE TEMPLE OF GOD CHURCH**
     3.   Nigeria (Calabar); Calabar
     4.   1982
     6.   1982
     7.   55 Webber Street/31 Atu Street
     9.   -; Nigerian; Efik-Ibibio
     10. f; -; n.a.; -
     11. As above; Efik-Ibibio
     12. 1; none; none

91. 1.   **THE TRUE GOD'S CHURCH**
     3.   Nigeria; -
     7.   10 Edebom Street

92. 1.   **TRUE CHURCH OF GOD**
     3.   Nigeria (Lagos); Mkpat Enin, CRS
     4.   1930s
     7.   7 Abasi Do Street
     8.   First Century Pentecostal Church
     9.   Apostle C.E. Umoh and Apostle J. King; Nigerian; Ibibio/
          Igbo
     11. -; -; London and Cameroun
     13. Efik-Ibibio
     14. Local; Efik-Ibibio

93. 1.   **TRUTH AND LIFE CHURCH MINISTRIES
          INTERNATIONAL**
     2.   TLMI
     3.   Nigeria (Calabar); Calabar
     4.   1977
     6.   1976
     7.   5B St. Mary Street
     8.   Apostolic Church
     9.   Rev. Dr. A. O. Akwaowo; Nigerian; Ibibio
     10. m; 1940s?; n.a.; personal secretary in government
     11. As above; Ibibio
     12. 1; 1; none
     13. Church of God Mission (Benin City); Faith Pool Prayer
          Groups (Tampa, Florida and Ghana); Osborn Foundation
          International (Tulsa, Oklahoma); Oral Roberts Evangelistic
          Foundation (Tulsa, Oklahoma); Christ for the Nations
          Inc. (US); evangelistic contacts in England and India.
     14. English and Efik-Ibibio
     15. Local and international; English

94. 1.   **UNIFICATION CHURCH***
     2.   UC
     3.   Korea; US; Lagos
     4.   1958
     5.   1960s (late)
     6.   1979
     9.   Sun Myung Moon; Korean

10. m; 1920; n.a.; -
11. Mr. Kijima; m; Japanese
12. 1; -; worldwide
13. Brotherhood of the Cross and Star
14. English
15. US; English

LIST OF HEALING HOMES

1. **ABATIM FRATERNITY HEALING HOME**
    Okon Eyo Street

2. **ABIA-UMAN HEALING HOME**
    96 Kono Street

3. **AFRICAN TRADITIONAL HEALING HOME**
    1B Abua Street

4. **ASUQUO EFFIOM HERBALIST HOME**
    Asuk Atu

5. **DR. BASSEY NWAN: MEDICAL HERBALIST**
    261 Goldie Street

6. **DR. OFFIONG MEDICAL HERBALIST HOME**
    6 Ekpo Nkpo Street

7. **EDIM UDO MEDICAL HERBALIST CENTRE**
    2 Etim Effiom Street, off Atamunu by Uqua Ibom Street

8. **EKPE BONE HEALING HOME**
    6 Adam Duke Street

9. **ETO NKUKIM INUEN ISOROKE HERBAL HEALING HOME**
    9 Edebom/ Anantigha Street

10. **GENERAL WORLD PRAYER HEALING HOME**
    5 Ekong Bassey Street by Otu Ansa Street and Atimbo
    Road

11. **HOMEOPATHIC   AND   BOTANIC   MEDICAL
    CLINIC: OCCULTIST,
    ASTROLOGER, PHYSICIAN**
    59 Ebito Street

12. **IBEKU ATA HEALING HOME**
26 Megembe Street (off Ekpenyong Abasi St.)

13. **IBOK ETE: HERBALIST HEALING HOME**
23 Mount Zion Street

14. **IFA HEALING HOME**
13 Megembe Street

15. **MBEBE HERBAL AND SPIRITUAL HEALING HOME**
4 Ekpo Edem Street

16. **MKPARAFOM HEALING HOME**
21 Bassey Erim Street

17. **MOTHER JAH SHRINE***
Efio Okoho Street

18. **NKANTA MEDICAL HERBALIST**
22B Jebs Road/105 Afokang Street

19. **OKON AKPANYANG (alias OFUM OSON AWAK NKOK-ETO)**
39 Akpanika Lane

20. **OWO'S WELFARE SERVICE CLINIC**
Atamunu Street, by Mount Zion

21. **THE SEVEN WONDERS OF ACULTISM AND HEALING HOME**
6 Fitzgibon Street

22. **(Healing home - no name)**
95 Uwanse Street

Religious groups heard about in Calabar but not traced

"I HAVE FOUND IT"
University of Calabar evangelistic association

CHRIST HOLY SANCTIFIED CHURCH
Mainland church with one small branch in Calabar?

HERITAGE PENTECOSTAL ASSEMBLIES MISSION

JESUS SAVES
c/o Oju A. Wariboko
PMB 1089
Calabar

THE DISCIPLES OF THE CROSS AND THE NAIL

Religious groups which attempted to settle in Calabar but failed

CROSS OF CHRIST WORLD MINISTRY (Aladura church which came from Ibadan in 1979/80)

Bibliography

Primary Sources

The following materials collected by my research assistants and myself have been classified by institution. They constitute a representative sample of the literature being used by the various religious groups at the time of the research (1979-83) and which was available for consultation, distribution or purchase. Additional references to literature not cited here may be found in preceding sections relating to particular institutions.

Cross-references have also been made to works in the next bibliographic section which treat a particular church or movement, but at the same time contain material which is of wider significance.

Anglican Church

Asuquo, Orok O. 1979. *Patronal Festival Sermon.* Calabar: Holy Trinity (Anglican) Church.

History of the Holy Trinity Anglican Church 1911-1961. 1961. Calabar: Jubilee Committee, July 1-9.

Magazine of the Church of the Province of Nigeria. 1981. 1,1.

Apostolic Faith

A Historical Account of the Apostolic Faith: A Trinitarian Fundamental Evangelistic Organisation. 1965. Portland, Oregon: Apostolic Faith Publishing House, 315 p. [Africa pp. 252-8].

Apostolic Church

The Apostolic Church Nigeria Golden Jublilee Souvenir Brochure. 1981. [Lagos]: the Church.

Clyne, J.B. 1970. *Asked and Answered: A Cathechism of Apostolic Principles.* Bradford: the Church, 28 p.

Fundamentals of the Apostolic Church. n.d.   Bradford: the Church, 30 p.

Ita, I.B.I. Rev. n.d. Early History of the Apostolic Church in Great Britain and Calabar Province. Uyo: Inter-Church Study Group Paper. Mimeo.

Things Most Surely Believed. n.d. Calabar: the Church. (Pamphlet).

See also: Turnbull, 1959.

Apostolic Faith

The Light of Hope (Portland, Oregon). 1980. 73,2 (March-April), 8 p. [Official bi-monthly newspaper].

Purity of the Bride; The Bible on Healing; Sanctification for Born-again Christians; Divine Healing Included in the Plan of Redemption; How Were You Baptized?; Power for Service. n.d. Portland, Oregon: Apostolic Faith Church. [Tracts].

Assemblies of God

Ayorinde, Mrs. J.T. n.d. *A Sin That Destroys.* Accra: Assemblies of God Literature Centre.

Good News God Loves You. n.d. Accra: Assemblies of God Literature Centre, 11 p. (Pamphlet).

Smoking: Good or Bad?; A Glass of Wine. n.d. Accra: Assemblies of God Literature Centre. [Tracts].

Standards of Christian Doctrine and Practice. n.d. Accra: Assemblies of God Literature Centre.

Study Guide (John). 1969. Missouri and Accra: Assemblies of God Literature Centre.

Sunday School Lessons. Accra: Assemblies of God (January-June 1980; January-June 1981).

The Nigerian Evangel (Aba). [Bi-monthly official publication].

Baha'i Faith

The Baha'i Faith: An Introduction. n.d.   Calabar: Local Spiritual Assembly of the Baha'is of Calabar, 7 p.

Baha'i Faith: the Universal Religion. n.d. Lagos: the National Spiritual Assembly of the Baha'is of Nigeria. [Tract].

Holley, H. 1956. *Religion for Mankind.* London: George Ronald, 248 p.

An Outline of Baha'i History, Laws, Administration. 1957. Lagos: National Spiritual Assembly of the Baha'is of Nigeria, 76 p.

The Spiritual Destiny of Africa. 1982. Lagos: the National Spiritual Assembly of the Baha'is of Nigeria, 26 p.

Brotherhood of the Cross and Star

I am Not God But Olumba Olumba Obu. n.d. Calabar: Brotherhood Press, 48 p. [A classic, but early text written by Obu in response to his critics].

Brotherhood of the Cross and Star Journal. 1982. 1,1 (JAN.), 84p. [One issue published].

Christmas Message from the Sole Spiritual Head Leader O.O. Obu to the Entire World. n.d. Calabar: Brotherhood Press, 19 p. Mimeo.

The Crucifixion of Our Lord Jesus Christ. n.d. Calabar: Universal Spiritual School of Practical Christianity for the Brotherhood of the Cross and Star. 12 p. Mimeo.

Events of the Holy Week in Pictures: April Pentecostal Assembly 1981. 1981. Calabar: Brotherhood Press, [56 p.], illus.

Events of the Holy Week and Programme for the April Pentecostal Assembly. 1981. Calabar: Brotherhood Press, 8 p. [Programme for the Pentecostal Assembly, April 3 - May 3, 1981].

The Everlasting Gospel. (Pentecostal Special Release by the Holy Father). 1979. Calabar: Brotherhood Press. Mimeo.

The Everlasting Gospel: Pentecostal Special Message to the Entire World. Vol. 1. n.d. Calabar: Brotherhood Press, 105 p. [Sermons delivered by Leader O.O. Obu]. Mimeo.

The Everlasting Gospel: the Transcendent Teachings of the Holy Spirit. Vol. 2. n.d. Calabar: Brotherhood   Press,   101   p. Mimeo. [Sermons delivered by Leader O.O. Obu].

Everla\ting Gospel Centre. 1979. *Christ Universal Spiritual School of Practical   Christianity: the   Students' Handbook.* 2d. ed. Calabar: Brotherhood Press, 46 p. [Contains duties of Students, their testimonies and background to the School].

----- n.d. *The Supreme Leader of the Universe in 2001 Years; a Man Who Could be a Living God in Disguise; the World's End is Near.* Calabar: Brotherhood Press. [Tracts printed in London].

Extra-ordinary   Meeting   of   Leader's   Representatives.   1976. Calabar: Brotherhood Press, 24p. [Minutes of a meeting held on June 26, 1976].

Eyo, Apostle E.B. n.d. *The Truth Has Come*. Calabar: Brotherhood Press, 38 p.

Eyo, Pastor E.B. 1981. *The Truth About Olumba Olumba Obu and Brotherhood of the Cross and Star*. Calabar: Brotherhood Press, 62 p. [Useful source of members' attitudes to and beliefs about Obu].

Father's Prediction for 1981 (Farewell Address at End of December Pentecostal Assembly). 1981. Calabar: Brotherhood Press, 107 p. Mimeo.

The Handbook of the Brotherhood of the Cross and Star. n.d. Calabar: Brotherhood Press, 12 p. [Contains orders of service, prayers, details of meetings (some Efik translation)].

Herald of the New Kingdom (Official Organ of the Brotherhood of the Cross and Star). 1984- VOL. 1, No. 1 (April? -).

His Deity is Revealed. n.d. *Your Word is Truth*. Special ed. Calabar: Brotherhood Press, 32 p.

Interview with O.O. Obu. 1979. *Drum* (Lagos) (March).

The Light of the World. n.d. Calabar: Brotherhood Press, 51p. Mimeo. [Sermons and testimonies].

Living Testimonies, Dreams and Revelations. 2d. ed. n.d. Calabar: Brotherhood Press, 44 p. Mimeo.

Marts, Sister Beverley. n.d. *Testimony*. [Calabar: Brotherhood Press], 13 p. [Much-circulated testimony of a European (Irish?) member].

The Memorandum of the Brotherhood of the Cross and Star. n.d. Calabar: Brotherhood Press. Mimeo. [Information on the movement].

Minutes of the Spiritual Council of Churches Meeting. (Held on January 7, 1983 in Calabar). 1983. Calabar: Brotherhood Press, 12 p.

Mkpanam, Rev. O. n.d. *Come and See: Can Anything Good Come Out of the Continent of Africa?* Calabar: Brotherhood Press, 18 p.

Nwed Ikwo (Hymn Book). 4th ed. 1980. Calabar: Brotherhood Press.

The Spiritual Council of Churches Held During December Pentecostal Assembly. n.d. [1980?]. Calabar: Brotherhood Press, 59 p.

The Supernatural Teacher: Book One. n.d. Calabar: Brotherhood Press, 41 p. Mimeo.

The Supernatural Teacher: Book Two. n.d. [1981]. Calabar: Brotherhood Press, 146 p. Mimeo. [Sermons and testimonies].

The Supreme Being: Holy Father Olumba Olumba Obu. [1983]. Calabar: Brotherhood Press, 131 p. Mimeo.

Sure Foundation Hymnary. 1977. Calabar: Brotherhood Press, 128 p.

The Spiritual Council of Churches Held During 1978 August Pentecostal Assembly. n.d. [1978?]. Calabar: Brotherhood Press, 34 p.

The Supernatural Teacher: Bible Class Lectures Book One. "Crusaders' Edition". n.d. Calabar: Brotherhood Press, 50 p. Mimeo.

Umoh, Pastor James Umoh and Ekanem, Pastor Asuquo. 1979. *Olumba Olumba Obu: the Mystery Man of Biakpan. Vol. 1 of Brotherhood of the Cross and Star: Facts You Must Know.* Calabar: Brotherhood Press, 179 p. [Extremely valuable source for the Brotherhood in general - history, biography of the leader, doctrines, worship, membership, testimonies etc.].

Weekly Gospels (December Pentecostal Assembly 1980). Nos. 1-4.
    Calabar: Brotherhood Press, 60-100p. Mimeo. [Collections of
    sermons and testimonies].

Weekly Review. 1981. 1,18 (May 4 - May 10), 8 p. [Irregularly
    published newspaper].

What is Brotherhood? What is Cross? What is Star? Rev. ed. [1983]
    Calabar: Brotherhood Press, 56 p.

*What is Cross?; What is Star?; What is Brotherhood?; Biakpan
    Paradise Regained and Epistle to All Elects of God; More Than
    Bread: Simple Rules of Health and Happiness; Pathway to
    Godliness; the First Step to God; the Second Step to God;
    Those Who Will Go to Heaven; Those Who Will Go to Hell; the
    Comforter Has Come; Faithful Ambassadors of the New Kingdom
    (1978); My Father Worketh Hitherto and I Work*. n.d.
    Calabar: Brotherhood Press. [Booklets, mainly sermon texts and
    biblical commentaries, ranging from 10-80 p.].

Your Word is Truth. n.d. Vol 1- Calabar: Brotherhood Press.
    [Irregular mimeographed series of sermons delivered by the
    Father, Leader O.O. Obu].

See also: E.A. Offiong, 1983; Amadi, 1982.

Brotherhood of the Cross and Star/ Esom Fraternity

Inyangibom, Professor Assassu. 1971. *Beyond Prejudice*. Vol. 1. and
    Vol. 2. Calabar: Brotherhood Press, 36 p. and 59 p. [A local
    "metaphysician" and member of the Brotherhood writes
    favourably of Obu's power and status].

----- n.d. *Events Around the World: Revelation*. Calabar:
    Brotherhood Press, 20 p.

Celestial Church of Christ

1982 Order of Service. Lagos: the Church, 88 p. [In French, English and Yoruba].

Christ African Church

The Constitution of the African Church. [1979?]. Ibadan: Aowa Press and Publishers, 49 p.

Christ the Shepherd's New Kingdom Flock

Entrance Song, Closing Song. n.d. Calabar: the Church. Mimeo.

The Temple of Eternal Blessings of God for Prayer Healing, Devotion and Charity. Calabar: the Church. [Pamphlet].

Christian Community of Nigeria

Christian Community of Nigeria. [1978?]. Brief of the Christian Community of Nigeria sent to the Cross River State Governor's Office. Calabar: CCON, 4 p. Mimeo.

----- 1981. *Thirteenth Anniversary Programme* (October 28-November 1). Calabar: CCON.

Church of Jesus Christ of Latter-Day Saints

The Book of Mormon. 1978. Solihull, U.K.: the Church, 560 p.

Family Home Evening. 1979. Salt Lake City, Utah: the Church, 164p.

The Prophet Joseph Smith's Testimony. n.d. Salt Lake City, Utah: the Church, 27 p.

Richards, L. 1978. *A Marvelous Work and a Wonder.* Salt Lake City,
Utah: Deseret Book Co., 424 p.

What the Mormons Think of Christ. 1976. Salt Lake City, Utah: the
Church, 32 p.

Church of the New Jerusalem

Lazer, B., comp. 1965. *A Great Revelation.* Canberra, Austalia: the
author, 26 p.

----- 1965. *This is our God.* Canberra, Australia: the author, 77 p.;
2d. ed. enl., 1978.

Swedenborg, Emmanuel. 1949. *Angelic Wisdom Concerning the Divine
Providence.* London: the Swedenborg Society.

----- 1953. *Conjugal Love.* London: the Swedenborg Society.

----- n.d. *The New Jerusalem and its Heavenly Doctrine.* London:
the Swedenborg Society.

----- 1969. *The Divine Love and Wisdom.* London: the Swedenborg
Society.

----- 1975. *The True Christian Religion.* London: the Swedenborg
Society.

Crystal Cathedral Church

Short History of the Crystal Cathedral Church. 1976. Lagos: the
Church, 40 p., illus. [Contains biography of leader, doctrinal
and ritual aspects, spiritual messages.]

Divine Order of the Cherubim and Seraphim

The Order and Services and the Rules and Bye-laws of the Church.
    1966. Calabar: the Church (Eastern Nigeria), 85 p.

Udok, Rt. Rev. J.E. (inspired by) n.d. *The Facts about Cherubim and
    Seraphim Church.* Rev. ed. n.p.

See also: Akpabio, 1983.

Eckankar

Newsletter (Benin City). 1981. 1,2 (July-December). [Published
    biannually by the Benin Eckankar Satsang].

Twitchell, P. 1980. *The Dangers of the Psychic World for Truth
    Seekers.* Menlo Park, CA: Eckankar.

Eternal Sacred Order of Cherubim and Seraphim

Daily Bible Reading 1981 Pamphlet. 30th ed. 1981. Lagos: the Mount
    Zion (Religious) Enterprises. 120 p. [Contains church data].

*The "Order": Rules and Regulations, Duties of workers and Forty
    Days Lenten Programme for "Cherubim and Seraphim".* n.d.
    Lagos: the Church, 76 p.

See also: Nweneka, 1982.

General Revivalist

Eko, Ewa and Ebele. n.d. *The Parable of the Egg; the Urgent
    Reminder; the Times Are Upon Us.* Calabar: the authors.
    [Tracts].

Osborn, T.L. 1963. *The Purpose of Pentecost.* Tulsa, Oklahoma:
    Osborn Foundation, 121 p.

----- 1977. *Faith's Testimony*. Tulsa, Oklahoma: Osborn Foundation, 84 p.

God the Hosts Prayer Temple

Constitution. n.d. Calabar: the Church, 28 p.

Institute of Religious Science

Holmes, E. 1964. *Your Mind is Creative*. Los Angeles: Science of Mind Publications. [Tract].

Kinnear, W., ed. 1973. *Spiritual Healing: the Art and Science of Meditation*. Los Angeles: Science of Mind Publications, 110 p.

Science of Mind (Los Angeles). (Monthly publication of the United Church of Religious Science, Los Angeles, California).

Tornay, S. n.d. *Philosophy and Science of Mind*. Los Angeles: Science of Mind Publications. [Tract].

Jehovah's Witnesses

Awake and the Watchtower (London and New York: Watch Tower Bible and Tract Society). [Monthly magazines].

Life Does Have a Purpose. 1977. New York: Watch Tower Bible and Tract Society, 191 p.

Our Incoming World Government: God's Kingdom. 1977. New York: Watch Tower Bible and Tract Society.

Our Kingdom Ministry (Lagos). [Monthly Nigerian newsletter].

Theocratic Ministry School: Guidebook. 1971. New York: Watch Tower Bible and Tract Society, 192 p.

Umoh, Udoh G. 1980. *The Rise of New Heaven: the Battle of Armageddon and the Expulsion of the Rosicrucians.* Uyo: New Heaven, 58 p. [This is apparently a private publication by an individual JW member against the Rosicrucians].

Jesus the Superet Church/ Superet Light Mission Nigeria

Trust, Dr. Josephine. 1928. *The Little Miracle Superet Church.* Los Angeles: the Superet Press; 1978 ed., 16 p.

----- 1948. *Key to Success: Revealed by Parchments.* Los Angeles: the Superet Press, 160 p.

----- 1954. *Superet Everlasting Peace: Prince of Peace Movement.* Los Angeles: the Superet Press, 104 p.

Lutheran Church

See Volz, 1961; H. Nair, 1945.

Methodist Church of Nigeria

Esin, Mr. Justice O.A. 1980. *Government Policy on Education Has Left a Lot to be Desired.* Lagos: Methodist Literature Department, 11 p. (Text of a toast at the Dinner marking the Diamond Jubilee of the Methodist Boys' High School, Oron, September 18, 1980).

Remembrancer (Official Organ of the Methodist Church Nigeria). 1980. 8,24 (July-September).

Miscellaneous

Information Concerning the Bible Society of Nigeria. n.d. Apapa,
Nig.: the Society, 8 p.

Missionary Fellowship

The Messenger (Calabar). [1976]. NO. 3 (Published quarterly
[irregular] by Fellowship Publishing Centre), 48 p.

Paschall, E.L. n.d. *Study Guide for Doctrines of the Faith.* McKenzie,
TN: Southside Missionary Baptist Church and distributed by the
Fellowship Publishing Centre, Calabar, 16 p.

Mount Zion Light House Full Gospel Church

An Important Revelation for the Children of Zion. Testimony
delivered to Obot Uboho, Ikot Eka Idem branch, Calabar,
January 1982, 2 p. Mimeo.

Okopedi Healing Home

Okopedi Healing Home Catalogue. 1978/79. Calabar: Okopedi
Enterprises, 52 p. [Contains letters/testimonies from clients.]
Mimeo.

Proclamation of the Okopedi Healing Society. n.d. Calabar: Okopedi
Enterprises (Mystic Division), 3 p. Mimeo.

Pentecostal Assemblies of the World, Inc.

Almanac 1982. n.p. [Includes "We Believe" - statement of beliefs].

Presbyterian Church

Ogarekpe, Rev. M.O., comp. [1976] *Mary Slessor Centenary
    Celebration, Calabar - Nigeria*, 1876-1976. Calabar: the Church,
    12 p. [A short biography compiled for the centenary
    celebrations.]

Otu, the Very Rev. Akanu A. 1982. *The Ordination of the Reverend
    Mgbeke G. Okore: First Woman Minister of the Presbyterian
    Church of Nigeria.* n.p., 104 p. Mimeo.

*Programme of Inaugural Service of Calabar/Dundee Presbyteries
    Partnership.* (July 11). 1982. Calabar: the Church.

See also: Aye, 1967; Buchan, 1980; Christian and Plummer, 1970;
Goldie, 1890; Latham, 1980; Livingstone, 1916; Luke, 1929; Marwick,
1897; McEvoy; McFarlan, 1946, 1955; Missions of the UPC, 1894;
O'Brien, 1958; Okon, 1973; Taylor, 1980, 1984; Waddell, 1863; Wilkie
and Macgregor, 1914.

Qua Iboe Church

The Church and Culture. 1974? Etinan: the Church, 13 p. [Booklet
    prepared by a three-man committee set up by the Qua Iboe
    Conference in Dec. 1974 to examine the church's attitude to
    the Revival of Culture].

The Constitution of the Qua Iboe Church (December 1972). 1978.
    Etinan: the Church, 10 p.

Ekong, Pastor David. n.d. *The Christian Attitude to Strong Drink: a
    Small Conversation with the Children of God's House
    Concerning Drink.* Etinan: the Church, 6 p.

Manual of Doctrine and Practice - Qua Iboe Church. n.d. Etinan: the
    Church.

Qua Iboe Mission. 1965. *Joseph Ekandem.* Belfast: the Mission, 95 p.

A Short History of the Qua Iboe Church 1887-1978. 1978. Port Harcourt: the Church. (Presented at the Qua Iboe Church 91st Anniversary, October 15-28, 1978), 7 p.

See also: Corbett, 1977; M'Keown, 1902; Wall, 1951.

Revival Valley Ministries

Victory Tabernacle. 1982. *Prayer and News Bulletin* (Calabar). January-February 1982; March-April 1982; May-July 1982.

----- 1983. *Harvest Digest* 2,1 (August-September). [Replaces *Prayer and News Bulletin*].

Roman Catholic Church

Golden Jubliee Magazine of the Holy Child Federated Alumnae - Cross River State Zone. 1980. Calabar.

See also: Cooke, 1977, 1978; Edet, [1979?]; Jordan. 1949.

Salvation Army

Allott, Major W. 1970. *Pioneering in Nigeria.* Lagos: Salvation Army Territorial Headquarters. Mimeo.

Salvation Army Songbook, 5th ed. (Efik). n.d. Lagos: the Church.

The Salvation Army Handbook of Doctrine. n.d. London: International Headquarters. [For officers only.]

Spiritual Kingdom Church of Christ

Bassey, Edidem (the Spiritual King). 1957. *Declaration by Edidem the Spiritual King*. Aba: the Church. [Pamphlet].

Spiritual Fellowship

Akpan, A. Peter. 1977. *The Path of Holiness*. Calabar: the author, 197 p.
----- 1977b. The Ultimate Home (Supplementary Reading). Calabar: the author, 2 p. Mimeo.

----- 1981a. Spiritual Fellowship, Spiritual Development. Calabar: the author, 3 p. Mimeo.

----- 1981b. The Human Mind. Calabar: the author, 2 p. Mimeo.

----- n.d. The Constitution: the Spiritual Fellowship. Calabar: the author, 2 p. Mimeo.

Subud Brotherhood

Bapaks Mission by Almighty God. n.d. [1970?]. Calabar: National Spiritual Centre for the International Subud Congress Committee, 11 p. [Extracts (in translation) from Bapak's Talk at Skymont, U.S.A. on August 11, 1970].

Constitution for Subud Nigeria. n.d. [1981]. Calabar: Subud Nigeria, 21 p.

For Applicants to Membership of the Subud Brotherhood: a Selection of Appropriate Extracts from Bapak's Writings and Talks, Followed by an Outline of the Organization of Subud. 4th. ed. 1980. n.p.: Subud U.K., 15 p.

Inaugural Address by the National Chairman of Subud Nigeria
Presented at the Formal Launching of Subud World Association
in Nigeria. n.d. [1981]. Calabar: Subud Nigeria, 28 p. [Text of
inaugural address at planned launching on December 11, 1981;
includes a discussion on "What is Subud"].

Sumohadiwidjojo, Muhammad-Subuh. 1975. *Bapak and the Coming of
the Latihan.* n.p.: Subud Publications International, 24 p.

----- 1981. *Bapak's Message to the World.* Transcript of Sharif
Horthy's Oral Translation. Calabar: National Spiritual Centre for
the International Subud Committee, 34 p. [Text of a talk by
Bapak given in London on March 28, 1981].

Truth and Life Ministries International

Akwaowo, Rev. A.O. n.d. [1981?]. Church Ministries and Ministers.
Calabar: the author, 19 p. Mimeo.

----- *Deliverance Hour.* Calabar: Deliverance Hour Ministry. [Monthly
transcript of sermons in booklets of 15-35 p. containing titles
such as *Deliverance* (no. 01, 1981); *The Rapture and Second
Coming of Christ* (No. 02, 1981); *The God of Miracles* (no. 03,
1981); *Have Faith in God* (no. 04, n.d.); *He Loves You* (no. 05,
1982); *Deliverance from Secret Societies* (no. 06, 1982); *Why
Jesus Came* (07, 1982); *The New Birth* (no. 08, 1982)].

The Miracles. Monthly newsletter (Vol. 1 July 1983 -). Calabar:
T.L.M. International, 6 p.

Unification Church

Divine Principle. 5th ed. 1977. New York: the Holy Spirit Association
for the Unification of World Christianity, 536 p.

Calabar Newspapers

The Nigerian Chronicle; The Sunday Chronicle; The Nigerian Call; The Sunday Call; The Nigerian People; The Nigerian Gong

Books and Articles Relating to Calabar

Adams, R.F.G., Akaduh, Etim and Abia-Bassey, Okon. 1981.
  English-Efik Dictionary. Oron: Manson Bookshop (Publishers).

Affiong, J.S. 1981. The Efik Traditional Marriage System.
  University of Calabar long essay (Theatre Arts).

Afigbo, A.E. 1965. Efik Origins and Migrations Reconsidered.
  Nigeria Magazine 87 (December):267-80.

----- 1973. The Calabar Mission and the Aro Expedition of
  1901-1902. *Journal of Religion in Africa* 5,2:94-106.

Africanus, Ami Ndi. 1882. Letter to Editor. *African Times* 1 June.

Ajayi, J.F.A. 1965. *Christian Missions in Nigeria,
  1841-1891: the Making of a New Elite*. London: Longman.

Akak, E.O. 1981a. *A Critique of Old Calabar History*.
  Calabar: Ikot Offiong Welfare Association.

----- 1981b. *Efiks of Old Calabar*. Vol. 1, *Origin and History*.
  Calabar: Akak and Sons.

----- 1982a. *Efiks of Old Calabar*. Vol. 2, *Language Origin and
  Grammar*. Calabar: Akak and Sons.

----- 1982b. *Efiks of Old Calabar*. Vol. 3, *Culture and
  Superstitions*. Calabar: Akak and Sons.

Akan, Mina Uwe. 1982. Changes in Some Christian Churches in
  Calabar since 1960. University of Calabar undergraduate
  project (History).

Akpabio, A. 1982. *Ibibio Language and Customs*. Uyo: Marshall Press.

Akpabio, G.U. 1983. The Religious and Social Impact of Three
  Independent Religious Movements in Calabar Municipality.
  University of Calabar long essay (Religious Studies).

Akpan, Monday B. 1984. Ibibio Traditional Religion and Cosmology. Paper presented at the Pan-Ibibio Language and Culture Association, (PILCA) University of Calabar, April.

Akpan, Chief N.U. n.d. The Christian Attitude Towards Current Cultural Revival. *Heritage* 2:32-37.

Amadi, G.I.S. 1982. *Power and Purity: a Comparative Study of Two Prophetic Churches in Southeastern Nigeria.* Ph.D. dissertation, University of Manchester.

Andreski, I. 1970. *Old Wives' Tales: Life-stories from Ibibioland.* New York: Shocken Books.

Asuquo, Chief Ukorebi U. 1978. The Diary of Antera Duke of Old Calabar (1785-1788). *The Calabar Historical Journal* 2,1 (June):32-54.

Ayandele, E.A. 1966. *The Missionary Impact on Modern Nigeria,* 1842-1914. London: Longman.

Aye, E.U. 1967. *Old Calabar through the Centuries.* Calabar: Hope Waddell Press.

Bassey, E.O. n.d. Ekpe Society. *Heritage* 1:36-37.

Blier, S. Preston. 1980. *Africa's Cross River: Art of the Nigerian Cameroon Border Redefined.* New York: L. Kahan Gallery.

Bordoh, A.M. 1977. Traditional Funeral Rites among the Efiks. University of Calabar undergraduate project (Social Sciences).

Buchan, J. 1980. *The Expendable Mary Slessor.* Edinburgh: the Saint Andrew Press.

Calabar. 1956. *Nigeria Magazine* 52:70-98.

Christian, C. and Plummer, G. 1970. *God and One Redhead: Mary Slessor of Calabar*. London: Hodder and Stoughton.

Clinton, J.V. 1961. King Eyo Honesty of Creek Town. *Nigeria Magazine* 69 (August):182-8.

Commission of Enquiry. 1930. *Report of the Commission of Enquiry Appointed to Inquire into the Disturbances in the Calabar and Owerri Provinces*. December 1929. Lagos: Government Printer.

Cooke, C.M. 1977. *The Roman Catholic Mission in Calabar: 1903-1960*. Ph.D. dissertation, University of London.

----- 1978. Church, State and Education: the Eastern Nigerian Experience, 1950-67. In *Christianity in Independent Africa*, edited by E. Fasholé-Luke et al., 193-206.

Corbett, J.S. 1977. *According to Plan: the Story of Samuel Alexander Bill Founder of the Qua Iboe Mission Nigeria*. Worthing, Sussex: Henry E. Walter, 160 p.

Cotton, J.C. 1905a. The People of Old Calabar. *Journal of the African Society* 4,15:302-306.

----- 1905b. The Calabar Marriage Law and Custom. *Journal of the Royal Anthropological Society* 4,15/16:302-6.

Cross River State of Nigeria. 1980. *Christian Religious Education Syllabus for Secondary Classes I-III*. Calabar: Cross River State Ministry of Education in association with the Christian Religious Bodies and Organisations.

Daniell, W.F. 1848. On the Natives of Old Callebar, West Coast of Africa. *Journal of the Ethnographical Society of London* 1:210-24.

Dayrell, E. 1910. Some "Nsibidi" Signs. *Man* 10:113-114.

----- 1911. Further Notes on "Nsibidi Signs with their Meanings from the Ikom District, Southern Nigeria". *Journal of the Royal Anthropological Institute* 41:521-40.

Dike, K.O. 1956. *Trade and Politics in the Niger Delta: 1830-1885.* Oxford: Clarendon Press.

Dodds, Rev. F.W. 1939. Memorandum on Boundaries. (Report on 1909 Conference in Calabar). Typescript.

Ekarika, J.P. 1975. *The Social Mission of Christianity as a Basis for Community Organization in the Context of Efik/Ibibio Ethnic Cultures.* M.A. thesis, Pontificia Studiorum Universitas, Rome.

Ebong, D.D. 1980. The Belief and Worship of Ndem in Efik and Ibibio Societies. University of Calabar term paper (Theatre Arts).

Ebot, W.A. 1978. *Witchcraft and Sorcery among the Ejagham.* Ph.D. dissertation, University of Leeds.

Edet, Sister R.N. n.d. [1979?]. *History of the Catholic Church in Calabar (1903-50).* Calabar: the author, 34p. Mimeo.

----- 1983. *The Resilience of Religious Tradition in the Dramas of Wole Soyinka and James Ene Henshaw.* Ph.D. dissertation, Catholic University of America.

Efik Dances. 1957. *Nigeria Magazine* 53:150-169.

Ekanem, E.U. 1980. Consumer Religion in Ididep, in Itu Local Government Area. University of Calabar long essay (Sociology).

Ekpe Systems in South Eastern State. 1975. Calabar: Information Division. Mimeo.

Ekpiken, A.N. 1970. *A Bibliography of the Efik-Ibibio-Speaking Peoples of the Old Calabar Province of Nigeria 1668-1964.* Ibadan: Ibadan University Press.

Ema, A.J. Udo. 1938. The Ekpe Society. *Nigeria Magazine* 16 (4th quarter).

Enang, K. 1979. *Salvation in a Nigerian Background: its Concept and Articulation in the Annang Independent Churches.* Marburger Studien zur Afrika- und Asienkunde, Serie A: Afrika, Band 19. Berlin: Verlag von Dietrich Reimer.

Essien, I.C. 1980. Witchcraft Accusations in an Ibibio Community. University of Calabar long essay (Sociology).

Forde, D. ed. 1956. *Efik Traders of Old Calabar.* London: Oxford University Press for the International African Institute.

Forde, D. and Jones, G.I. 1950. *The Ibo and Ibibio Speaking Peoples of South Eastern Nigeria.* Ethnographic Survey of Africa. Part 3: Western Africa. London: Oxford University Press for the International African Institute.

Gammie, A. [1938]. *Cruickshank of Calabar.* London: Pickering and Inglis.

Goldie, H. 1868. *Principles of Efik Grammar, with Specimen of the Language.* Edinburgh: Muir and Patterson.

----- 1874. *Dictionary of the Efik Language.* Glasgow: Dunn and Wright. Reprint. Ridgewood, NJ: Gregg Press, 1964.

----- 1890. *Calabar and its Mission.* Edinburgh and London: Oli phant Anderson and E. Ferrier. Rev. ed. with additional chapters by Rev. J.T. Dean, Edinburgh and London, 1901.

Grimley, J.B. and Robinson, G.E. 1966. *Church Growth in Central and Southern Nigeria.* Grand Rapids, Michigan: William B. Eerdmans.

Groves, C.P. 1954. *The Planting of Christianity in Africa.* 4 vols. London: Lutterworth Press.

Hair, P.E.H. 1967. Beating Judas in Freetown. *The Sierra Leone Bulletin of Religion* 9,1(June):16-18.

Harris, R. 1976. Efik History Reconsidered. Africa *46,3:285-90*. *[Review of Latham, Old Calabar and Nair, Politics and Society]*.

Hart, A.K. 1964. *Report of the Enquiry into the Dispute over the Obongship of Calabar*. Official Document 17. Enugu: Government Printer.

Henderson, R.H. 1966. Generalised Cultures and Evolutionary Adaptability: a Comparison of Urban Efik and Ibibio in Nigeria. *Ethnology* 5,4:363-91.

Henshaw, Ewa Ekeng. [1981]. Old Calabar: the City States and [the] Europeans, 1800-1835 [*sic*] by Sunday [*sic*] Efiong Noah. Typescript.

Heritage (Cultural Magazine of Nigeria's Cross River State), vols. 1-3. n.d. Calabar: Ministry of Information and Social Development.

Inyang, P.E.B. et al. 1980. *Calabar and Environs: Geographic Studies*. Calabar: Department of Geography, University of Calabar for the 23rd Nigerian Geographical Association Conference, Calabar March 16-21, 1980.

Jeffreys, M.D.W. 1935. *Old Calabar, and Notes on the Ibibio Language*. Calabar: Hope Waddell Training Institute Press.

----- 1966. Witchcraft in the Calabar Province.
African Studies (Johannesburg) 25,2:95-100.

----- 1966. Efik Origin. *Nigeria Magazine* 91 (December):297-99.

John, D.O. 1980. Witchcraft in an Annang Community.
University of Calabar long essay (Sociology).

Jones, G.I. 1956. The Political Organization of Old Calabar.
In *Efik Traders*, ed. D. Forde, 116-160.

----- 1963. *The Trading States of the Oil Rivers.* London: Oxford
University Press for the International African Institute.

----- 1970. A Boundary to Accusations. In *Witchcraft, Confessions
and Accusations,* edited by M. Douglas, 321-32. London:
Tavistock.

Jordan, J.P. 1949. *Bishop Shanahan of Southern Nigeria.* Dublin: Elio
Press.

Kalu, O.U. 1978a. *Christianity in West Africa: the Nigerian Story.*
Ibadan: Daystar Press.

----- 1978b. *Divided People of God: Church Union Movement in
Nigeria, 1875-1966.* New York: Nok Publishers.

----- ed. 1980. *The History of Christianity in West Africa.*
London: Longman.

Kingsley, Mary H. 1901. *West African Studies.* 2d ed. with additional
chapters. London: Macmillan.

----- 1965. *Travels in West Africa.* 3rd ed. with a new introduction
by John E. Flint. New York: Barnes and Noble.

Kirk-Greene, A. and Rimmer, D. 1981. *Nigeria Since 1970: a Political
and Economic Outline.* London: Hodder and Stoughton.

Knight, C.W. 1951. *A History of the Expansion of Evangelical
Christianity in Nigeria.* D.Th. dissertation, Southern Baptist
Theological Seminary, Louisville, Kentucky.

Latham, A.J.H. 1972. Witchcraft Accusations and Economic Tensions
in Pre-Colonial Old Calabar. *Journal of African History*
13,2:249-60.

----- 1973. *Old Calabar 1600-1891: the Impact of the International Economy upon a Traditional Society.* Oxford: Clarendon Press.

----- 1980. Scottish Missionaries and Imperialism at Calabar. *Nigeria Magazine* nos. 132-133:47-55.

Leib, E. and Romano, R. 1984. Reign of the Leopard: Ngbe Ritual. *African Arts* 18,1 (November):48-57.

Lieber, J.W. 1971. *Efik and Ibibio Villages.* Human Ecology and Education Series, Vol. 2 South East State, Occasional Publication No. 13. Ibadan: Institute of Education, University of Ibadan.

Livingstone, W.P. 1916. *Mary Slessor of Calabar: Pioneer Missionary.* 6th ed. London: Hodder and Stoughton.

Luke, J. 1929. *Pioneering in Mary Slessor's Country.* London: Epworth.

M'Keown, R.L. 1902. *In the Land of the Oil Rivers: the Story of the Qua Iboe Mission.* London: Marshall.

Marwick, W. 1897. *William and Louisa Anderson: a Record of Their Life in Jamaica and Old Calabar.* Edinburgh: Andrew Elliot.

McEvoy, C. n.d. *Mary Slessor.* 6th ed. London: the Carey Press.

McFarlan, D.M. 1946. *Calabar: the Church of Scotland Mission, 1846-1946.* London: Thomas Nelson.

----- 1955. *The White Queen: the Story of Mary Slessor.* London: Lutterworth.

Messenger, J.C. 1959. Religious Acculturation Among the Anang Ibibio. In *Continuity and Change in African Culture,* edited by W.R. Bascom and M.J. Herskovits, 279-99. Chicago: University of Chicago Press.

----- 1960. Reinterpretation of Christian and Indigenous Belief in a Nigerian Nativist Church. *American Anthropologist* 62,2:268-78.

----- 1982. Ancestor Belief among the Anang: Belief System and Cult Institution. In *African Religious Groups and Beliefs,* edited by S. Ottenberg, 63-75, Meernt, India: Archana Publications for Folklore Institute.

Missions of the United Presbyterian Church. 1894. *Story of the Mission in Old Calabar.* Edinburgh: the Church (by Rev. W. Dickie).

Morrill, W.T. 1961. *Two Urban Cultures of Calabar, Nigeria.* Ph.D. dissertation, University of Chicago.

----- 1963. Immigrants and Associations: the Ibo in Twentieth Century Calabar. *Comparative Studies in Society and History* 5,4:425-48.

N'Idu, A. 1959. Ekpe, Cross River Cult. *West African Review* 30,384 (November).

Nair, H. 1945. *We Move into Africa: the Story of Planting of the Lutheran Church in Southeastern Nigeria.* St. Louis: Concordia Publishing House.

Nair, K.K. 1972. *Politics and Society in South Eastern Nigeria 1841-1906: a Study of Power, Diplomacy and Commerce in Old Calabar.* London: Frank Cass.

----- 1975. *The Origins and Development of Efik Settlements in Southeastern Nigeria.* Papers in International Studies: Africa Series, no. 26. Athens, OH: Ohio Center for International Studies, Africa Program.

----- 1977. King and Missionary in Efik Politics: 1846-1858. *Journal of African Studies* 4,3 (Fall):243-80.

Nicklin, K. 1977. *Guide to the National Museum Oron*. Lagos: National Museum.

----- 1984. Cross River Studies. *African Arts* 18,1 (November): 24-27.

Nigeria Year Book 1983. 1983. Apapa: Daily Times.

Noah, M.E. 1978. African Religion in Old Calabar. *Journal of African Studies* 5,1:3-8.

----- 1980. *Old Calabar: the City States and the Europeans 1800-1885*. Uyo: Scholars Press (Nig).

Nwaka, G.I. 1978. Secret Societies and Colonial Change: a Nigerian example. *Cahiers d'Etudes Africaines* 18,1-2:187-200.

Nweneka, W. 1982. A Study of Religious Acculturation and Rejection in an Independent Church in Nigeria: a Case Study of Eternal Sacred Order of Cherubim and Seraphim. University of Calabar long essay (Religious Studies).

O'Brien, B. 1958. *She had a Magic: the Story of Mary Mitchell Slessor*. London: Jonathan Cape.

Offiong, D. 1983. The Social Context of Ibibio Witchcraft Beliefs. *Africa* 53,3:73-82.

Offiong, E.A. 1983. Schism and Religious Independency in Nigeria: a Case Study of Calabar. University of Calabar long essay (Religious Studies).

Offiong, Sister Maria Immaculata. 1979. A Closer Look at African Spiritual Churches. *World Mission* 30,1:25-31.

Okon, E.E. 1973. *The Church of Scotland and the Development of British Influence in Southern Nigeria*. Ph.D. dissertation, University of London.

Ottenberg, S. and Knudsen, L. 1985. Leopard Society Masquerades: Symbolism and Diffusion. *African Arts* 18,2 (February):37-44.

Parkinson, J. 1906. Notes on the Efik Belief in "Bush Soul". *Man* 6:121-22.

----- 1907. A Note on the Efik and Ekoi tribes of the Eastern Province of Southern Nigeria, West Central Africa. *Journal of the Royal Anthropological Institute* 37:261-67.

Partridge, C. 1905. *Cross River Natives*. London: Hutchinson. Reprint, Nendeln, W. Germany: Klaus Reprint, 1973.

Payne, P. 1954. Calabar Coronation. *The Nigerian Field* 19,2:85-96.

Public Lectures on Religion '77. 1978. Calabar: Information Division of the Research Unit of the Ministry of Information and Social Development. (Being the papers read at a seminar on "Culture and Religion" held at Calabar, April 22-23, 1975. Lectures by Ufot and Akpan are published in HERITAGE 2).

Ruel, M. 1965. Witchcraft, Morality and Doubt. *Odu* (Ife) 2,1 (July):3-27.

----- 1969. *Leopards and Leaders: Constitutional Politics among a Cross River People*. London: Tavistock.

Salmons, J. 1977. Mammy Wata. *African Arts* 10,3 (April):8-15.

Shepherd, A.I. 1980. *The Origins and Development of Literacy in English in Old Calabar to c.1860*. M.Litt. thesis, University of Aberdeen.

Simmons, D.C. 1955. Specimens of Efik Folklore. *Folklore* 66,4:417-24.

----- 1956a. Efik Divination, Ordeals and Omens. *Southwestern Journal of Anthropology*. 12,2:223-38.

----- 1956b. An Ethnographic Sketch of the Efik People. In
       Efik Traders. ed. D. Forde, 1-26.

----- 1959. *An Analysis of the Reflection of Culture in Efik
       Folktales*. Ph.D. dissertation, Yale University.

----- 1960. Sexual Life, Marriage and Childhood among the Efik.
       Africa 30,2:153-65.

----- 1961a. Analysis of Cultural Reflection in Efik Folklore. *Journal
       of American Folklore* 74,292:126-41.

 ----- 1961b. An Efik Judas Play. *The Nigerian Field* 26,3:100-110.

*Souvenir Programme of the Coronation Service of his Royal Highness
       Edidem Bassey Eyo Ephraim Adam III Obong of Calabar*. 1982.
       Calabar: Coronation Service Committee.

The Spirit Movement in Ibibio Land. n.d. Uyo: Uyo Inter-Church
       Study Group. Mimeo.

Talbot, D.A. 1915. *Woman's Mysteries of a Primitive People*.
       London: Cassell. Reprint, London: Frank Cass, 1968.

Talbot, P.A. 1912. *In the Shadow of the Bush*. London: Heinemann.

----- 1914. Some Ibibio Customs and Beliefs.
       Journal of the African Society 13,51:223-28.

----- 1923. *Life in Southern Nigeria*. London: Macmillan.

----- 1926. *The Peoples of Southern Nigeria*. 4 vols. London: Oxford
       University Press. New ed. London: Frank Cass, 1969.

Tasie, G.O.M. 1978. *Christian Missionary Enterprise in the Niger
       Delta: 1864-1918*. Leiden: E.J. Brill.

Taylor, W.H. 1980. *Calabar: an Educational Experiment.* Ph.D. dissertation, University of Exeter.

----- 1984. Missionary Education in Africa Reconsidered. *African Affairs* 33,331 (April):189-206.

Thompson, R.F. 1974. *African Art in Motion: Icon and Act.* Los Angeles and Berkeley: University of California Press.

----- 1983. *Flash of the Spirit: African and Afro-American Art and Philosophy.* New York: Random House.

Turnbull, T.N. 1959. *What God Hath Wrought: a Short History of the Apostolic Church.* Bradford: the Puritan Press.

Udo, R.K. 1967. The Growth and Decline of Calabar. *Nigerian Geographical Journal* 10:91-106.

Ufot, O.A. n.d. To What Extent is Nigerian Culture Basically Anti Christian? *Heritage* 2:24-31.

Ukpong, J.S. 1982. Sacrificial Worship in Ibibio Traditional Religion. *Journal of Religion in Africa* 13,3:161-88.

Uyanga, J. 1979. The Medical Role of Spiritual Healing Churches in Southeastern Nigeria. *Nigerian Behavioral Sciences Journal* 2,1/2:48-52.

Volz, P. M. 1961. *The Evangelical Lutheran Church of Nigeria: 1936-61.* Calabar: Hope Waddell Press, 80 p.

Waddell, H.M. 1849. *A Vocabulary of the Efik or Old Calabar Language with Prayers and Lessons.* 2d ed. rev. and enl. Edinburgh: Grant and Taylor. Reprint of 2d ed. Leipzig: Zentralantiquariat der Deutschen Demokratisches Republik, 1972.

----- 1863. *Twenty-nine Years in West Indies and Central Africa: a Review of Missionary Work and Adventure, 1829-1858.* London: Nelson. New ed. London: Frank Cass, 1970.

Walker, J.B. 1877. Notes on the politics, religion and commerce of Old Calabar. *Journal of the Royal Anthropological Institute* 6,2:119-24.

Wall, E.S. 1951. *The Quest of Souls in Qua Iboe.* London: Marshall Morgan and Scott, 158 p.

Wanabo, F.C.T. 1882. Letter to Editor. *African Times* 2 January.

Weaver, E.I. and Weaver I. 1970. *The Uyo Story.* Elkhart, Indiana: Mennonite Board of Missions.

Webster, D. 1963. "A 'Spiritual Church'" *Frontier* 6,2:116-20; also in *Practical Anthropology* 11,5 (1964):229-32, 240. [Account of a visit to the Holy Chapel of the Miracle (Holy Chapel of Miracles) in its early stages in Lagos].

Weiss, E. and Udo, A.A. 1979. The Calabar Rural MCH/FR Project, 1975-1979: What We Have Learned About Family Planning. Paper presented at the National Workshop on Population and Economic Development in Nigerian in the 80s, University of Lagos, 12-14 September, 1979, 24 p., appendices. Mimeo. [Contains information on attitudes towards medicine and contraception by women who belong to spiritual churches.]

Westermann, D. 1928. Gottesvorstellungen in Oberguinea. *Africa* 1,2 (April):189-209.

Westgarth, J.W. 1946. *The Holy Spirit and the Primitve Mind.* London: Victory Press.

Wilkie, A.W. and Macgregor, J. 1914. Industrial Training in Africa III: In the Calabar Mission of the United Free Church of Scotland. *International Review of Missions* 3:742-47.

Comparative and Theoretical Works

Acquaviva, S. 1980. *The Decline of the Sacred in Industrial Society.* Oxford: Basil Blackwell.

Acts of the 17th International Conference for the Sociology of Religion: Religion and the Public Domain. 1983. Paris: CISR.

Ada, Sister M.J. and Isichei, E. 1975. Perceptions of God and the Churches in Obudu. *Journal of Religion in Africa* 7,3:165-173.

Ahlstrom, S.E. 1975. *A Religious History of the American People.* 2 vols. Garden City, NY: Image Books.

Akama, E.S. 1981. *A Religious History of the Isoko People of the Bendel State of Nigeria.* Ph.D. dissertation, University of Aberdeen.

Amadi, E. 1982. *Ethics in Nigerian Culture.* Ibadan: Heinemann.

Baer, H.A. 1984. *The Black Spiritual Movement: a Religious Response to Racism.* Knoxville, TN: University of Tennessee Press.

Bailey, E. 1982. The Implicit Religion of Contemporary Society: an Orientation and Plea for its Study. *Religion* 13:69-83.

Barker, E. ed. 1982. *New Religious Movements: a Perspective for Understanding Society.* Studies in Religion and Society, 3. New York: Edwin Mellen Press.

Barrett, D.B. 1968. *Schism and Renewal in Africa.* Nairobi: Oxford University Press.

----- ed. 1982. *World Christian Encyclopaedia: a Comparative Survey of Churches and Religions in the Modern World, A.D. 1900-2000.* Nairobi and New York: Oxford University Press.

Beidelman, T.O. 1982. *Colonial Evangelism: a Socio-Historical Study of an East African Mission at the Grassroots.* Bloomington, Indiana: Indiana University Press.

Berger, P.L. 1969. *The Sacred Canopy: Elements of a Sociological Theory of Religion.* Garden City, NY: Anchor.

Bond, G., Johnson, W. and Walker. S. eds. 1979. *African Christianity: Patterns of Religious Continuity.* Studies in Anthropology Series. New York: Academic Press.

Curley, R. 1983. Dreams of Power: Social Process in a West African Religious Movement. *Africa* 53,3:20-38.

Deniel, R. 1970. *Croyances Religieuses et Vie Quotidienne: Islam et Christianisme à Ougadougou.* Recherches Voltaïques 14. Paris/Ougadougou: CNRS/CVRS.

Douglas, M. and Tipton, S.M. eds. 1982. *Religion and America: Spirituality in a Secular Age.* Boston: Beacon Press.

Dubb, A. 1976. *Community of the Sacred: an African Revivalist Church in the East Cape.* Johannesburg: Witwatersrand University Press for the African Studies Institute.

Earhart, H.B. 1974. *Japanese Religion: Unity and Diversity.* 2d ed. Encino, CA: Dickenson.

Ellwood, R.S. Jr. 1973. *Religious and Spiritual Groups in Modern America.* Englewood Cliffs, NJ: Prentice-Hall.

----- 1979. *Alternative Altars: Unconventional and Eastern Spirituality in America.* Chicago History of American Religion Series. Chicago: University of Chicago Press.

End of Year Report January 1982-January 1983: Conventional and Common Religion in Leeds. Research Paper No. 10. 1983 Leeds: Department of Sociology, University of Leeds. Mimeo.

Epelle, E.M.T. 1972. The Sects. *West African Religion* 13/14 (December):41-50.

Fasholé-Luke,   E. et   al. eds. 1978. *Christianity   in   Independent Africa*. London: Rex Collings.

Fernandez, J.W. 1978. African Religious Movements. *Annual Review of Anthropology* 7 (Winter):195-234.

Geertz,   C. 1960. *The   Religion   of   Java*. Chicago: the   University of Chicago Press.

Glazier,   S.D. ed. 1980. *Perspectives   on   Pentecostalism: Case   Studies from   the   Caribbean   and   Latin   America*. Washington,   DC: University Press of America.

Glock,   C. and   Bellah,   R.N. eds. 1976. *The   New   Religious Consciousness.*   Berkeley   and   Los   Angeles: University   of California Press.

Hastings, A. 1967. *Church and Mission in Modern Africa*. London: Burns and Oates.

----- 1979. *A History of African Christianity: 1960-1975.* Cambridge: Cambridge University Press.

Hollenweger,   W.J. 1972. *The   Pentecostals*. Minneapolis: Augsburg Publishing.

Holt, B.P. 1977. Healing in the Charismatic Movement: the Catholics in Nigeria. *Religions: a Journal of the Nigerian Association for the Study of Religions* 2,2:38-58.

Isichei,   E. ed. *1982,   Varieties   of   Christian   Experience   in Nigeria*. London: Macmillan.

----- 1983. *A History of Nigeria*. London: Longman.

Iwuagwu, A.O. 1971. *The "Spiritual" Churches in the Eastern States of Nigeria*. Ph.D. dissertation, University of Ibadan.

Janzen, J.M. and MacGaffey, W. 1974. *An Anthology of Kongo Religion: Primary Texts from Lower Zaïre.* University of Kansas Publications in Anthropology, no. 5. Lawrence, Kansas: University of Kansas Press.

Jules-Rosette, B. 1975. The Conversion Experience: the Apostles of John Maranke. *Journal of Religion in Africa* 7,2:132-164.

----- 1975. *African Apostles: Ritual and Conversion in the Church of John Maranke.* Ithaca, NY: Cornell University Press.

----- ed. 1979. *The New Religions of Africa.* Norwood, NJ: Ablex Publishing Corporation.

Kiernan, J.P. 1982. Authority and Enthusiasm: the Organization of Religious Experience in Zulu Zionist Churches. In *Religious Organization and Religious Experience.* A.S.A. Monograph 21, edited by J. Davis, 169-180. London: Academic Press.

Knott, K. 1983. Conventional and Common Religion in the Media. Religious Research Paper no. 9. Leeds: Department of Sociology, University of Leeds. Mimeo.

Kokosalakis, N. 1983. Popular Religion and the Public Domain in Greece. Paper read at 17th CISR congress, London, August 1983.

Lloyd, P.C., Mabogunje, A.L. and Awe, B. eds. 1967. *The City of Ibadan.* Ibadan: Cambridge University Press in association with the Institute of African Studies, University of Ibadan.

Luckmann, T. 1967. *The Invisible Religion.* New York: Macmillan.

MacGaffey, W. 1976. The Diversity of Churches in Matadi, Zaïre, 1970. *Cahiers des Religions Africaines* 10,19 (janvier):31-49.

----- 1983. *Modern Kongo Prophets: Religion in a Plural Society.* Bloomington, Indiana: Indiana University Press.

Martin, D.A. 1978. *A General Theory of Secularization.* Oxford: Basil Blackwell.

Mbiti, J.S. 1969. *African Religions and Philosophy.* London: Heinemann.

Melton, J. Gordon. 1978. *The Encyclopedia of American Religions.* 2 vols. Wilmington, NC: McGrath.

Melton, J. Gordon with Geisendorfer, J.V. 1977. *A Directory of Religious Bodies in the United States.* New York: Garland.

Middleton, J. 1983. One Hundred and Fifty Years of Christianity in a Ghanaian Town. *Africa* 53,3:2-19.

Murphree, M.W. 1969. *Christianity and the Shona.* London: the Athlone Press.

----- 1971. Religious Interdependence among the Budjga Vapostori. In *African Initiatives in Religion,* edited by D.B. Barrett, 171-180. Nairobi: East African Publishing House.

Needleman, J. 1970. *The New Religions.* New York: E.P. Dutton.

Nwanunobi, C.O. 1976. *The Significance of Separatist Movements (Indigenous Sects) in Contemporary Nigeria.* Ph.D. dissertation, University of Toronto.

O'Connor, A. 1983. *The African City.* London: Hutchinson.

Olupona, J.O.K. 1983. *A Phenomenological/Anthropological Analysis of the Religion of the Ondo-Yoruba of Nigeria.* Ph.D. dissertation, Boston University.

Parrinder, E.G. 1953. *Religion in an African City.* London: Oxford University Press. Reprint, Westport, Conn.: Negro Universities Press, 1972.

Pauw, B.A. 1960. *Religion in a Tswana Chiefdom.* London: Oxford University Press for the International African Institute.

Peel, J.D.Y. 1968. *Aladura: a Religious Movement among the Yoruba.* London: Oxford University Press for the International African Institute.

----- 1977. Conversion and Tradition in Two African Societies: Ijebu and Buganda. *Past and Present* 77:108-141.

----- 1978. The Christianization of African Society: Some Possible Models. In *Christianity in Independent Africa,* edited by Fasholé-Luke et al., 443-54.

----- ed. 1983. Christianity and the Local Community. *Africa* 53,3:2-72.

Pobee, J. ed. 1976. *Religion in a Pluralistic Society.* Leiden: E.J. Brill.

Rounds, J.C. 1982. Curing What Ails Them: Individual Circumstances and Religious Choice among Zulu-Speakers in Durban, South Africa. *Africa* 52,2:77-89.

Sanneh, L. 1983. *West African Christianity: the Religious Impact.* Maryknoll, NY: Orbis Books.

Shulman, A.M. 1981. *The Religious Heritage of America.* San Diego: A.S. Barnes.

Simpson, G.E. 1970. Religious Changes in Southwestern Nigeria. *Anthropological Quarterly* 43,2:79-92.

Toon, R. [1981]. Methodological Problems in Study of Implicit Religion. Research Paper No. 3. Leeds: Department of Sociology, University of Leeds. Mimeo.

Toon, R. and Towler, R. comps. 1982. Religious Research Project Interview Schedule. Leeds: Department of Sociology, University of Leeds. Mimeo.

Towler, R. 1974. *Homo Religiosus: Sociological Problems in the Study of Religion.* London: Constable.

----- n.d. Conventional Religion and Common Religion in Great Britain. Religious Research Paper, no. 11. Leeds: Department of Sociology, University of Leeds. Mimeo.

Turner, H.W. 1972. Pentecostal Movements in Nigeria. ORITA 6,1 (June):39-47. Reprinted in his *Religious Innovation in Africa*, 121-128.

----- 1977. *Bibliography of New Religious Movements in Primal Societies.* Vol. 1, *Black Africa.* Boston: G.K. Hall.

----- 1979. *Religious Innovation in Africa: Collected Essays on New Rreligious Movements.* Boston: G.K. Hall.

Vrijhof, P.H. and Waardenburg, J. eds. 1979. *Official and Popular Religion: Analysis of a Theme for Religious Studies.* Religion and Society, 19. The Hague: Mouton.

Wallis, R. ed. 1975. *Sectarianism: Analyses of Religious and Non-Religious Sects.* London: Peter Owen.

----- 1975. The Aetherius Society: a Case Study in the Formation of a Mystagogic Congregation. In *Sectarianism*, edited by R. Wallis, 17-34.

Walls, A.F.W. 1976. Towards Understanding Africa's Place in Christian History. In *Religion in a Pluralistic Society*, edited by J. Pobee, 180-189.

----- 1979. The Anabaptists of Africa? The Challenge of African Independent Churches. *Occasional Bulletin of Missionary Research* 3,2 (April).

Webster, J.B. 1964. *The African Churches among the Yoruba: 1888-1922.* Oxford: Clarendon Press.

Williams, P.W. 1980. *Popular Religion in America: Symbolic Change and the Modernization Process in Historical Perspective.* Englewood Cliffs, NJ: Prentice-Hall.

Wilson, B. 1970. *Religious Sects.* London: World University Library.

Wylie, D. 1969. *Religion in an African Municipal Township.* Ph.D. dissertation, University of Wisconsin.

Wyllie, R.W. 1980. *Spiritism in Ghana: a Study of New Religious Movements.* AAR Studies in Religion, 21. Chico, CA: Scholars Press.

Yinger, J.M. 1967. Pluralism, Religion and Secularism. *Journal for the Scientific Study of Religion* 6,1 (Spring):17-28. Followed by a comment by C.Y. Glock, 28-30.

Zaretskty, I.I. and Leone, M.P. eds. 1981. *Religious Movements in Contemporary America.* Princeton, NJ: Princeton University Press.

Index

N.B. This is a computer-generated index. As such, it contains no page references followed by an "f." or "ff." designating the continuation of the discussion of an index item over one or more succeeding pages.